FABRIC
of FAITH

Ardis Dick Stenbakken, Editor
Iris Stovall, Administrative Assistant

REVIEW AND HERALD® PUBLISHING ASSOCIATION
HAGERSTOWN, MD 21740

The authors assume full responsibility for the accuracy of all facts and
quotations as cited in this book.

This book was
Edited by Jeannette R. Johnson
Copyedited by Jocelyn Fay and James Cavil
Designed by Emily Harding
Electronic makeup by Tina M. Ivany
Cover illustration by Michael-Che Swisher
Typeset: Minion 11/13.5

PRINTED IN U.S.A.
04 03 02 01 00   5 4 3 2 1

R&H Cataloging Service
Stenbakken, Ardis Dick, 1939-   ed.
    Fabric of faith, edited by Ardis Dick Stenbakken.

    1. Devotional calendars—SDA.   2. Devotional calendars—women.
3. Women—religious life.   4. Devotional literature—SDA.   I. Title.

242.643

ISBN 0-8280-1514-7

The Women's Devotional Series

To order, call 1-800-765-6955.

Visit us at **www.reviewandherald.com** for more information on other Review and Herald products.

GOD IS SO GOOD

Now you've got my feet on the life path, all radiant from the shining of your face. Ever since you took my hand, I'm on the right way. Ps. 16:11, Message.

A new year, a new beginning. You, me, the commentator on TV—we all seem to pause and reflect on the time gone by and the chance for better things to come, or at least different things to come. The inauguration of the president, inventory, long-range work objectives—people are tuned to taking stock and looking forward at this time of year. We all sense we haven't lived up to our best, either individually or collectively, and we need to do better. New Year's resolutions . . . Need I say more?

As Christians we can all give testimonies to the willingness of God to forgive and His eagerness to help us achieve the life to which we aspire. Thank God, we don't have to wait for a new year in order to start over. God is so good! As we consecrate ourselves to Christ and His body on earth, every Communion service becomes a Rosh Hashanah and Yom Kippur, a time of reflection and acceptance of atonement. A time for seeing ourselves through God's eyes—weak and miserable, but as precious as that naked, struggling newborn as it is swaddled and placed in its mother's hungry arms. God is so good! Every week He calls us to Himself so He can put His arms around us as we recall who we are and who He is and why we're here, and start over. The gift of Sabbath means we can taste heaven, the joy of conquered sin, the glory of life as it was meant to be, the future resplendent with loving friends and fulfilling vocation.

Ah, God is so good! Every night as we go to bed we cease our frenzied pursuits. In the morning we rouse to new life, blinking at the unaccustomed brightness, momentarily disoriented. Then we recognize ourselves and, looking up, greet our God. Morning, the time for being reborn, a time when the hand of God erases the past and gives us a brand-new slate, if we permit it. A new beginning, the chance to start over and get it right this time. Every day. What a miracle!

Lord, as we face this new year we thank You for Your goodness. We ask for Your support and guidance to face each coming day with joy and hope. With You I know we can get it right.
HELENE RABENA HUBBARD

THE GIFT

The gift of God is eternal life through Jesus Christ our Lord. Rom. 6:23.

In nurse's training we seemed to have an eternity of classroom lectures before we were allowed to get some hands-on experience. I was nervous at first, but Mrs. Allen, one of my first patients, was a sweet little woman. As I changed her linen, she told me she was being discharged the next day. And since she was leaving, she wanted me to have her beautiful gloxinia plant.

"Oh, I couldn't," I replied.

"Please," she insisted. "I want you to have it. You have taken such good care of me."

I told her it was my job to take good care of her. But the only words she wanted to hear were Thank you! So I accepted the gorgeous plant as a reward for my efforts.

When my instructor came in, I proudly showed her my new gift. "You can't take it! If she wants to give it away we will place it up at the nurses' station for all her caretakers to enjoy. You have to remember you've been here only a few hours. What about all the others who cared for her the rest of the time?"

I knew she was right, but I really would have loved to have had that plant. Later I complained to a couple coworkers about how unfair the instructor had been not to have let Mrs. Allen fulfill her wishes by giving me that plant. They started to laugh.

"Mrs. Allen tried to give me her plant on Monday," Karen said.

Donna confessed, "Mrs. Allen insisted I take the plant on Wednesday."

Come to find out, Mrs. Allen had given the plant to every nurse—and even to the janitor.

So the beautiful gloxinia was placed at the nurses' station when Mrs. Allen was discharged. It became a living reminder of her wonderful gratitude to all. It reminded me also of the gift Jesus has offered to us all—the gift of eternal life. That's the one I really do not want to miss out on. It is the best gift ever and, just like Mrs. Allen's plant, it is offered to you and me, everyone alike. And none of us should take it solely for ourselves; we should be willing to share it with the entire world.   JO ANN HILTON

THE BLESSINGS OF A FROZEN SHOULDER

"For I know the plans I have for you," says the Lord. "They are plans for good and not for disaster, to give you a future and a hope." Jer. 29:11, NLT.

A few years ago I developed a frozen right shoulder, and the range of motion in that arm was severely restricted. I am right-handed, so fortunately I could still write and use the computer. But zipping my skirts or stocking top shelves was awkward. The pain was becoming more intense each day. I needed help. Four weeks of physical therapy brought no reprieve. I prayed for relief, as did my parents and scores of family members scattered across the globe. Nothing seemed to happen.

Eventually my physician suggested that I see a therapist in a neighboring state, even though my medical insurance would not cover the cost. She told me that she had worked with the therapist during the years of her residency and was amazed at the progress of patients in his care. Traveling the 40 miles to his clinic at sunrise twice a week, I had more time to commune with my Father. One golden morning I wondered aloud if my lack of progress correlated with my wavering faith. I received no immediate answer. But during the agonizing process of that morning's therapy, I was stunned when the therapist suggested, "During the half hour it takes to come down here for therapy, why don't you spend the time praying or saying the shepherd's psalm? That should relax you. It definitely will make the session easier on us both."

I knew that my not-so-muffled screams as he tried to reeducate my muscles distressed him, but I could not resist asking why he thought that he could risk talking about religious matters to me.

"I don't usually," he admitted. "But I saw the name of your university on your T-shirt. I know what that university stands for, and I can see that you represent its mission. You never swear. You rarely complain. And by the time the session is over, your ubiquitous smile is back in place." His smile mirrored my own.

Silently I telegraphed a message to my heavenly Physician. *Thank You, beloved God, for providing the context for wordless witness, even if it brings pain for a moment. Thank You for giving me the faith to accept "not yet" as I move forward in my spiritual journey. Thank You for reminding me that You have a plan for me that is bigger, better, and brighter than my own.*

GLENDA-MAE GREENE

THE WOODS

That they might be called trees of righteousness, the planting of the Lord, that he might be glorified. Isa. 61:3.

My dad always called me a "woodsy girl," referring to my love for the beautiful trees and for walking in the woods. This description of me confirmed my future husband's opinion that he had indeed chosen the right gal to wed!

In the spring, no matter how carefully I watch the buds on the trees, it seems that one day, *pop!* The leaves are just there. I marvel at God's timing. A very humbling experience in the summer is to lie on the ground beneath a tree, looking up to see the very top of the giant towering over me. Shuffling through the bushels of leaves shed by the trees in the fall can raise an aroma that makes one feel shivers of anticipation for the winter.

And then it's here—winter! The tree branches are bare and black and look lonely without their lovely coverings. That is, until the snowflakes begin to fall—then something miraculous happens. Every tree, especially the firs, appears to be wearing ermine or, if you prefer, marshmallow fluff.

Recently my husband and I snowshoed through a lovely woods in Michigan's Upper Peninsula. A fine misty snow was falling; the branches were piled high from previous snowfalls. The deeper we went into the woods, the more silent Mother Nature became. Suddenly a quail flew from her hiding place; then the chickadees began to bob to and fro above our heads. I observed rabbit tracks from one spruce tree to another, and by bending low I could see that the little hare had spent some time secluded there.

Brushing snow from a fallen tree, we sat quietly to observe. It was so quiet I could actually hear the tiny snowflakes falling on my jacket. The whiteness of the snow always reminds me of the hymn "Cover With His Life": "My life of scarlet, my sin and woe, cover with His life, whiter than snow." Sitting in that quiet cathedral, I asked God to grant me the blessing of the words of this hymn. Later, backtracking on our trail, I could hear the little hum of the snowshoes on the snow as we walked. It was a wonderful experience to be in God's woods that day, a very special moment in time.

BETTY R. BURNETT

BEYOND ALL EXPECTATION

With men it is impossible, but not with God: for with God all things are possible. Mark 10:27.

O ur family had just spent the first few days of the new year at Durban's North Coast, Ballito Bay, South Africa. On our last morning we packed up the cars before walking down to the beach so the children could enjoy their last dip in the boisterous sea. My 19-year-old daughter and I were the last to go down. As we walked, I gave her the car keys to hold. She promptly put them into the pocket of the shorts she wore over her swimsuit

We both forgot about the keys as she joined those who were already swimming. Two hours later we were ready to leave, and I asked her for the keys. After much searching, we realized that she had gone into the sea with them, and they were gone!

We all prayed the impossible prayer: *Lord, You know where those keys are. Please wash them up onto the beach.*

My husband and his brother-in-law waded in to see if they could feel the keys. The sand was loose and granular, and the sea was very wild. The lifeguards told me it was very unlikely that the keys would wash up; they were too heavy. Just in case they did, we left a message at the tower for swimmers to watch out for them.

Because it was already past noon, we decided we had to do something or we would never get home. A locksmith tried until almost 3:00 to open the car but could not short-circuit the alarm system. The car just kept switching off.

Just then we heard an announcement over the loudspeakers: "Would those who lost the Volkswagen Jetta keys please come claim them!"

God had done the impossible! We had asked and believed that He would do it. We had faith, but what about our works? If we believed, why didn't we sit on the beach and wait for Him to answer? Don't we often ask our heavenly Father for something, and then snatch it out of His hands because it takes too long to wait? We are impatient!

Andrew Murray said of today's text, "Faith expects from God what is beyond all expectation." God truly specializes in the impossible.

DENISE NEWTON

"RACHEL NEEDS ME"

Am I a God at hand, saith the Lord, and not a God afar off? . . . Do not I fill heaven and earth? Jer. 23:23, 24.

On a recent visit I took my two granddaughters to church. Usually 5-year-old Rachel sits in the cradle roll division with her sister, 3-year-old Bethany. But that morning Rachel decided to go to her kindergarten class. Bethany and I followed to make sure she got in the right room.

"No, Grandma; please don't leave Rachel there all alone!" Bethany protested.

"She will be quite all right alone," I insisted. "She's a big girl now."

In her own class, Bethany began to sob. She took no interest in songs or stories. "I want to go with Rachel," she whispered. "Please, Grandma, she needs me. She'll get lost down there all by herself. She really needs me." Several times during the program she implored me to take her to find Rachel, who needed her help.

When the program ended we went to Rachel's room to wait outside the door for the children to be dismissed. Nothing doing! Bethany barged right in and gave her sister a hug, a look of triumph on her face. She was there to look after her big sister!

We chuckled about it later. It tickled us all to think that a 3-year-old thought she needed to take care of her 5-year-old sister.

Not so long ago I was worrying about my children who were half a world away. My grandson might have to have another operation, and I knew my daughter and son-in-law had a lot of decisions to make. They were in Maryland, and I was in India. I needed to be there, where I could do something! They needed me!

At the same time, I was in Pune, 600 miles from Hosur, where my husband was at that moment. I worried about being away from him. *He needs me, Lord. He must be lost without me. How will he ever manage alone?*

After writing out my prayer of concern, I opened my Bible to Jeremiah 23 and read: "Am I a God at hand . . . and not a God afar off? . . . Do not I fill heaven and earth?"

I knew the Lord had put it there for me. *Yes, Lord, it is true. You are there, even though I am not. You can supply all their need. Thank You, Lord.*

DOROTHY EATON WATTS

PROVIDENCE AND PROOF

Who is like the Lord our God, who dwells on high, who humbles Himself to behold the things that are in . . . the earth? Praise the Lord! Ps. 113:5-9, NKJV.

God's done it again! Our exerciser snapped in half last week. My husband and I depended on it! Since winter had just begun, we needed a replacement. Finding one wouldn't be easy. I had bought it on clearance several years before for $17 and hadn't seen another since. I checked a local store and found a variety of exercise equipment, but none so compact and versatile. The toll-free number on the accompanying exercise booklet was no longer valid. Directory assistance turned up no phone number for either the manufacturer or the distributor. It seemed that we were out of possibilities.

Traveling 50 miles to the city for a meeting one evening, we decided to check a few stores. At the second one, there it was! But now it came only as part of a set—*two* exercisers, a video, and an exercise book—for $30. In spite of our tight budget, we chose to buy it. At the checkout counter the price registered at $17.77. There had been no sale sign on the shelf and no sale price on the box.

"Excuse me, but is this exerciser on sale?" I asked in amazement. The cashier confirmed it was.

As we jubilantly carried our purchase to the car, I wondered if God had let our exerciser break just at the time He knew we could replace it at a bargain price. Or maybe He had held it together until He knew we could replace it. Then I remembered my prayer over our sack supper in the car earlier: "Lord, thank You for this food. And if it's Your will, please help us to find the right exercise equipment." He had answered and blessed us— with the right price, besides.

This was one more proof that the mighty God of the universe is interested in the small details of my life on earth, that He intervenes on my behalf in daily matters. If God cares that much about my body and my budget, I know I can trust Him with my big burdens.

Who is like You, indeed. I am so humbled by the marvelous things You have done for me. Help me today to share that kind of love and concern with those around me. KATHLEEN STEARMAN PFLUGRAD

CHRIST THE EVERLASTING EVERGREEN TREE

Jesus saith unto him, I am the way, the truth, and the life: no man cometh unto the Father, but by me. John 14:6.

Evergreen pine trees have long been thought of as symbolizing life because they keep their green foliage and remain functional from one season to another. The prophets Isaiah and Micah prophesied a long time ago that Jesus would be the Everlasting Father, the Prince of Peace, and the Ruler of Israel, whose existence has always been.

Christ does not symbolize life—He *is* life Himself. He said, "I am the way, the truth, and the life: no man cometh unto the Father, but by me" (John 14:6). He also said, "Therefore doth my Father love me, because I lay down my life, that I might take it again. No man taketh it from me, but I lay it down of myself. I have power to lay it down, and I have power to take it again" (John 10:17, 18). "I am come that they might have life, and that they might have it more abundantly" (verse 10). This wonderful testimony gives me the fullest assurance and opportunity to receive evergreen nutrients in their fullest measure for the new year.

As I face the new year I think about how I can have the evergreen presence of Christ in my home and my church. How can I maintain a sweet, evergreen, exotic aroma in my personality? How can I function from day to day in the coming year? I will have all the answers if I allow Christ, the Everlasting Evergreen Tree, to organize my agenda, focus my vision, and control my life.

Christ, the Everlasting Evergreen Tree, has provided much foliage for me for the new year. He has provided the foliage of peace, joy, health, understanding, wisdom, worship direction, forgiveness, hope, and full assurance of His overwhelming love. Yes, the most significant confidence I have for the new year is to know and trust Jesus, who is my Everlasting Evergreen Tree. I am soliciting the same confidence for you.

When this old polluted earth is cleansed and made new, by God's grace we will all receive evergreen nutrients from the tree of life. Trust Jesus. He is "the way, the truth, and the life."

The new year is started. I have already felt Your blessing. Help me to stay close to You so that I may continue to receive the gift of life eternal from You.

CECELIA LEWIS

I CAN SEE

Therefore I counsel you to purchase from Me gold refined and tested by fire, that you may be [truly] wealthy, . . . and salve to put on your eyes, that you may see. Rev. 3:18, Amplified.

I *really should get new glasses,* I thought one day, as things seemed to be a little fuzzy while I was driving. It wasn't as easy as before to read the signs from a distance, and the situation was a little more pronounced at night. *Soon,* I promised myself. *I must remember to make an appointment tomorrow.* Tomorrow turned into the next day, days turned into weeks, and weeks into months. Before I knew it, a whole year had passed. *But I see relatively well anyway,* I excused myself. *It's just my peripheral vision that's getting a little more fuzzy. I've just got to remember to make that appointment.*

But once again days turned into weeks, and weeks into months, and probably would have turned into another year if my frames hadn't broken. Now I had no choice. I might not have had time before, but I'd have to make time now.

I went through the exam, and even felt that my new frames gave me a chic look. I couldn't wait for my new glasses. When I returned a few days later to pick them up, the sales associate shined the lenses until the light reflected like stars. "Close your eyes," she said as she put them on me. After some adjustments, she asked me to open my eyes. I couldn't believe it! I could see the tiniest details on the sign on the other side of the room.

As I drove home, I felt as though I were truly seeing some things in my neighborhood for the first time. I couldn't believe I had settled for fuzziness for so long when I could have had this better view of the world.

God has offered me eyesalve so that I can see clearly—not only my sinful condition, but His loving grace. How often, I wondered, had I procrastinated or simply refused His offer?

Lord, help me to desire to "see" as You would have me see, and not settle for anything less. And help me do something about it today.

MAXINE WILLIAMS ALLEN

THE FLASHING SIGN

I can do all things through Christ which strengtheneth me. . . . But my God shall supply all your need according to his riches in glory by Christ Jesus. Phil. 4:13-19.

My daughter, Cheryl, her three boys, and I drove to Houston for my son's wedding. After the reception they flew back to Kansas City, but I stayed to visit friends. Five days later I headed home.

The long drive alone frightened me. At a traffic light I gave my fears to God in a tearful prayer, claiming His promises in Philippians 4:13 and 19. I thanked Him, and immediately a feeling of peace replaced my tension.

A short distance down the highway I saw God's name flashing from a bank's time and temperature sign. Over and over it flashed: *God . . . God . . . God.* I was elated! As I drove closer to the sign, I was stunned. The flashing lights were showing "6:00," not "God." But I knew God was with me; I had been given a message to keep my mind on Him.

Miles later I became confused in the darkness. Suddenly I caught a glimpse of a large sign directing me to stay in the left lane. To do so I had to make a sharp left turn. It seemed strange that the highway would have such a turn. I drove under the overpass and around a bend, where I came face-to-face with two sets of headlights coming straight at me. I was on the wrong side of the road!

O God, please help me! I prayed. I hit the brakes just as a car and a van separated as the Red Sea did for the Israelites, one going on each side of me. Both vehicles stayed under control and were gone as suddenly as they had appeared. I managed to get into the westbound lanes before any other cars headed toward me, and praised God for delivering all of us.

I learned later that the area had experienced a severe windstorm, which probably left the traffic sign twisted in the wrong direction.

My prayer had been answered. The flashing time and temperature sign had kept my mind upon God. The memory of the trip home from Houston lives in my heart and mind as an example of how God can strengthen us, meet our needs, and keep us safe, as He has promised, when we turn to Him for everything.   SHIRLEY GAST LYNN-SMITH

BROKEN HEARTS AND WOUNDED SOULS

The Lord is close to the brokenhearted and saves those who are crushed in spirit. Ps. 34:18, NIV.

I was in South America teaching family life seminars. One day I had the joy of distributing presents to children at a day-care center. Most came from homes headed by a single or alcoholic parent. For many, the only food they received all day was the noon meal at the center.

During lunch I asked Shelly, a student missionary, if it would be possible to see the home of one of the children. She enthusiastically said yes and told me that she had purchased a Bible for one of the mothers from her meager student missionary stipend. We could visit and deliver the Bible.

The conditions of the one-room wooden shack were so deplorable they defy description. Half-starved mongrel dogs and chickens freely roamed in and out. Mud, filth, and an outhouse completed the scene.

A woman wearing Reeboks stepped out to meet us, a dirty blouse hanging loosely on her shoulders and a dirtier skirt covering her distended abdomen. Her appearance matched the hopeless expression on her face. When Shelly presented her with the Bible, the woman said *"Obrigada"* (Thank you), but the hopeless expression never left her face. I thought, *This woman has a broken heart and a wounded soul.*

Urias, my translator, asked about her family. Without expression she told us about her four children and the husband who had abandoned her. She showed us a 10-day-old baby, fathered by a new man. He was demanding that she give away the four older children. Since she refused, she had no assurance that he would stay.

Later we delivered some basic food necessities. *"Obrigada,"* she said again, but her face told again of a broken heart and a wounded soul. The wounds were so deep it would take infinitely more to heal her heart and soul than a onetime donation of groceries.

I had done all I could for this poor woman and had to trust her to the Lord. For "the Lord is close to the brokenhearted and saves those who are crushed in spirit." Lord, bring relief to all the brokenhearted and crushed in spirit and grant them peace on this day. NANCY L. VAN PELT

THE PARENT THING

O Lord, open thou my lips; and my mouth shall shew forth thy praise. Ps. 51:15.

As I came up my driveway from my early-morning walk, I passed by a sight that made me retrace a few steps. On one of our flowering pear trees a cluster of tiny spring-green leaves foolishly peered out of their protective covering.

I did "the parent thing," unable to resist. "What in the world are you doing!" I demanded, blame and reproach dripping from every word. No answer.

"Don't you know winter is still ahead?" Still no answer.

"Here you've gone and done what you wanted to do. You've gone against what your Creator planned for you! Well," I continued in my most shaming voice, "you are going to freeze. You are going to die!" My haranguing hinted at not a smidgen of sympathy.

"You chose to do it. Now you'll just have to accept the consequences." With that final proclamation, I smugly marched into my house, satisfied with my little tirade.

Is that how I dealt with my children? I asked myself. *Please, God, I hope not.* But memory tells me I did use those tactics too many times. What withering effect we often have on our children! I'm so thankful to know that my plant condemnation in no way mirrors how Christ deals with His children. All those little leaves on my tree wanted was to feel warmth and love.

Ironically, today I once again walked down the same driveway, looking at the same Bradford pear trees. It's only the last of January, and those rebel trees are doing it again.

We are having an unusually warm, late winter. The little buds, supposedly blanketed away in their sleeping bags, have decided to peer out early. When I saw them, I was dismayed.

"What are you doing?" I cried vehemently. "It's not time yet! You are going to mess around and get frozen, and I won't have my beautiful explosion of blossoms when spring really does come." I actually broke down and cried.

These snafus of nature make me hungry for the perfect home, where we are soon to dwell. Nothing unruly, too early, or rebellious there.

Even so, come, Lord Jesus!   EULENE DODSON

THE PRICE OF PRIDE

Pride leads to destruction, and arrogance to downfall.
Prov. 16:18, TEV.

How much does pride cost? For Marie Antoinette, the queen of France during the French Revolution, the price was her head. When the royal family knew that their lives were in danger, a daring escape was planned. Everything might have gone smoothly if only the queen had been willing to travel as a commoner. Instead, she insisted on riding in a specially made coach, complete with ladies-in-waiting and large trunks of clothes. Her travel arrangements made people suspicious of her identity. The result of her pride was capture and eventual execution.

Pride cost another woman her dream of becoming a professional writer. In the writing class I teach, I am often impressed by the potential of my students. This woman had sold a story to a large magazine for $800. That is good pay for any writer; it is remarkable for a beginner submitting her first story. But her early success crippled her future efforts as a writer. She has not sent out a single story since her first story was published. She still takes classes and writes stories, but she doesn't try to sell them. She told me that she couldn't bring herself to submit any stories, because she knew that sooner or later her stories would be rejected, and she couldn't bear the thought of not living up to the promise of that first one.

Pride may not cause something as drastic as death, but it can keep you from making the most of your life. If you are nearsighted but refuse to be seen wearing glasses, life may pass you by in a blur. If you have to be the best at everything you try, you cheat yourself of exploring pastimes you might really enjoy. If you fight with a friend but are too proud to apologize, you may lose that friend. When you refuse to humble yourself and confess your sins to the Lord, you miss out on the assurance of being forgiven. When you realize the high price of pride, you may decide it's not worth paying for.

I want to be realistic today, not acting proud, but remembering what You have done for and through me. Help me to press on to new goals and feats, accomplishing new things for me, for You, and for those around me.

GINA LEE

SEE, I AM DOING A NEW THING!

See, I am doing a new thing! Now it springs up; do you not perceive it? I am making a way in the desert and streams in the wasteland. The wild animals honor me, the jackals and the owls, because I provide water in the desert and streams in the wasteland, to give drink to my people, my chosen, the people I formed for myself that they may proclaim my praise. Isa. 43:19-21, NIV.

The new year began with a rush, as time has a way of doing for me lately. What about a New Year's resolution? I wondered. Should I bother making any, since the year was already several days old? Resolutions seem to have a way of being quickly forgotten in the press of life. But still, I didn't want this new year to be just a repeat of the old year.

Lord, I prayed, *please do a new thing in me this year. May I allow You to do in me something that You have been wanting to do in me for a long time but that I have hindered You from doing. May I be so emptied of sin and self that You can accomplish in me and through me something wholly new!*

I never dreamed what new thing the new year would bring. On January 14 I was admitted into a hospital with a stroke. Even so, I now have renewed confidence that I can always trust God to supply all my needs. My husband and I were within four miles of an Adventist hospital when the stroke happened, and I was in the emergency room within a half hour. Hundreds of people began praying for me. My stroke was in the cerebellum, which controls the body's motor functions, yet I have full range of movement—no paralysis. My memory is intact, except for a few hours after the stroke. While I lay in my bed in the intensive-care unit of the hospital I repeated Scripture portions I had memorized over the years. Praise God, I remembered them all! My faith in God is stronger than ever.

I don't believe for a moment that my stroke was the new thing God planned to give me. But I do believe that my trust in Him throughout this trial is part of His preparation to receive the new thing He plans to give me. I confess before God my weakness and my trust in His care.

Even had my stroke resulted in crippling my body and mind, God would still have been with me and would still be answering my prayer. But what a joy it is to eagerly look forward to another year of being able to speak and write for Him.

CARROL JOHNSON SHEWMAKE

RUBBISH

Then Jesus said, "Come to me, all of you who are weary and carry heavy burdens, and I will give you rest. Take my yoke upon you. Let me teach you, because I am humble and gentle, and you will find rest for your souls. For my yoke fits perfectly, and the burden I give you is light." Matt. 11:28-30, NLT.

I enjoy my nature walks. One particular morning I was distracted by the rubbish beside the road. The next morning at 5:30, bags in gloved hands and with boots on my feet, I walked the ditches along the road, picking up aluminum cans, match covers, plastic wrappers, fast food containers, and mail.

I had not planned for the volume of rubbish I was collecting. I decided to fill the bags and leave them by the road to retrieve later. I carried them as far as I could, and when my arms became tired, I finally put them down.

A dresser that hadn't been there the day before must have been dumped from a moving vehicle. It was scattered in pieces along the ditch. I didn't have the proper tools to deal with it. How could someone do this to my beautiful road? This was not a landfill!

I was frustrated, overwhelmed, muddy, and tired; and it wasn't even 6:30 a.m. *Help, God; what am I to do?*

I had uttered these same words numerous times before, but not about something as mundane as rubbish—or had I? Parallels began to run through my mind. I began thinking about what God was trying to tell me. I was carrying rubbish I had picked up along the road. Much of it wasn't mine, but I carried it anyway. Gently God spoke to me, touching my heart: "Lay your rubbish at the foot of the cross. There you will find a different load to carry, one that is light."

I reviewed my morning's activities. Other people's rubbish had bothered me, and I had been determined to do something about it. And now other people's emotional garbage bothered me too. Was I willing to do something about it?

You promised to give me rest for my soul if I lay my load at Your feet. I need to get rid of other people's rubbish that I have been carrying. Thank You. Your load is light indeed.
DIANA PITTENGER

PLAYING WITH FIRE

The soul that sinneth, it shall die. Eze. 18:20.

It seemed that I had barely sat down to peruse the morning paper when the smoke alarm began to scream at me, loudly and clearly. Startled, I jumped out of my chair and ran to the kitchen, thinking my cereal must have boiled over and the burner beneath it was burning. Much to my surprise, it was my toaster. The bread had caught in it, igniting a sudden fire. Bright-red streaks of flame from two little pieces of toast were advancing up my cupboards to the ceiling of the kitchen. I was stunned.

I have tried to get wood burning in a fireplace, and if all the conditions were not right it would simply smolder and go out. But here was fire burning wood cabinets and a wooden knife holder. Even knife handles were ablaze. Every second it seemed to be gaining strength and burning faster, spreading at an alarming rate.

Fortunately, we were able to get the fire out without having to call the fire department, but there was considerable damage. Little flakes of greasy soot had floated all around the house. Amazingly, it had even settled on my living room drapes, at some distance from the kitchen. Almost all the blinds were covered too.

How could something so seemingly impossible happen so quickly and do so much damage?

When Satan tempted our first parents in the Garden of Eden, it seemed such a small thing, perhaps, but look at the damage it has done. How the insidious effects have spread over the whole world and have caused such destruction, misery, and death! No one can take lightly the devastating effect of sin without peril to their eternal life. Since that fateful day of the fire, my kitchen is a constant reminder of how easy it is for sin to entrap, like the caught toast, so silently and yet in so deadly a manner.

I cling to You because You know the dangers and temptations that face me today. You can see what I cannot see. Keep me close and keep me safe, I pray.

Pat Madsen

GERMAINE

I tell you, whenever you refused to help one of these least important ones, you refused to help me. Matt. 25:45, JEV.

The 81-year-old alcoholic, with her swollen face and foul breath, gray cape and moth-eaten hat askew on her long oily hair, was more than I could handle. I beseeched God to help me endure the nauseating stench of pus oozing from a nasty-looking infection on her left foot, and the smell of the alcohol I was using to treat it.

Germaine was so afraid of pain that she watched me closely, warning me she could not suffer one more pain in her life. "This time it didn't hurt; but watch out for the next!" Germaine warned as she left. There would be no next time, I vowed.

Then one morning her phone call startled me. "You must absolutely treat me! This time it's the right foot!" *This woman is imposing on me again,* I thought; but taken aback, I instinctively said, "OK, come!"

Germaine seemed milder this time. She ensconced herself in the armchair, flourishing a leaf of paper—the first of a long roster of poems she had written during her long, lonely hours. "Did you write that?" I asked, amazed.

"Yes!" she exclaimed. "I thought of all that might have been but never was!"

The poems were as fresh as the burgeoning spring. Suddenly, as I stood in total humility at her feet, Germaine appeared beautiful, a precious soul God wanted to reach.

Germaine shared with me the details of her unhappy life. Now, somehow, she knew she had an appointment with death. Our conversation was simple and direct. Not daring to lift her eyes heavenward anymore, she requested that I pray for her soul. I did—gratefully, and with conviction. We prayed for both our souls while shedding all the tears of our restored peace. We said farewell, and Germaine left forever.

Lord, I thank You that Your Holy Spirit helped me witness to Germaine during the critical moments when she needed to know how precious she was in Your sight and how much You loved her. Help me, Lord, always to see others as You see them.

RUTH FRIKART

A PLACE TO HANG YOUR HEART

He has planted eternity in the human heart. Eccl. 3:11, NLT.

Recently we moved from Cambridge to Cheltenham. Leaving what had been our home for six years was very difficult. Even though Jonathan and I had prayed about our move and knew that God had directed us to our new area of ministry, it was hard to leave our home, friends, and family. As my eldest daughter, Rima, and I drove out of our drive for the last time, I wanted to slam my foot on the brake and shout, "No! I am not moving!" But of course I couldn't, or my husband might have found himself looking for a new job—and I might have found myself looking for a new husband!

We spent that night with my parents before driving on to Cheltenham. On the hour's journey Rima and I spent most of the time sobbing. As soon as one of us would stop crying, the other would say, "And do you remember when . . ." And the crying would start all over again. We used tissues, tissues, and more tissues.

The move, however, has taught me something important. Home is not a house in Cambridge or Cheltenham. Home is where I hang my heart. I choose to hang my heart in God's home. To have a relationship with Him that is constant and growing each day is more important to me than where I will live today or tomorrow.

Tell me, where have *you* chosen to hang *your* heart? It is so easy to let the pressures, problems, and disappointments of life dampen our desire to be with God. It is so easy to let the scramble to achieve and to do blot out our view of God. It is so easy to hang our hearts in places other than God's home, especially when alternate things become more important than God.

Caught up with the stresses of a move and working in a new ministry, I had unconsciously removed my heart from God's home. I had not spent much time or effort in maintaining meaningful Bible study and prayer. Fortunately, God made me aware of that. Since returning my heart to God's home, I am enjoying my time with Him once more.

I want my heart hanging in Your home today, and I want to invite others to hang their hearts there too. Bless us, Lord, that we may come to know You better.

MARY BARRETT

"MOMMY, GOD LOVE ME?"

For God so loved the world, that He gave His only begotten Son, that whoever believes in Him should not perish, but have eternal life. John 3:16, NASB.

Life came full circle for me today. My daughter, Zoe, discovered that God loves her. But let me back up to the beginning.

Eighth grade was a critical year for me. I was the oldest child around who wasn't baptized. I felt pressure from my family and myself. But it wasn't until my teacher, Mr. Sorensen, studied the Bible with me that I truly met Christ for the first time. Something clicked, and I knew, actually knew, that God loves me. I discovered and accepted that He valued me and created me for the simple pleasure of knowing me. There was such an incredible and unfamiliar feeling in the pit of my stomach. I wasn't prepared for it. After all, I had been a Christian all my life. It was an integral part of my home and social life. But until that moment, Christ hadn't been a real part of me.

I fell madly in love with Jesus Christ. Christianity suddenly surpassed all the do's and don'ts. Christ was real in my heart, and I couldn't think of anything I wanted to do more than to show my love for Him through baptism. I picked December 24 as the day. It was my Christmas present to Him.

As I've grown with Christ I've discovered indescribable joy. I've discovered pain, too. Satan hits you most when you strengthen your relationship with God. I've had times when Satan has succeeded in tempting me to lose faith in God's love. But each time I've hit bottom, God has reminded me of the time I first fell in love with Him.

That brings me full circle. Today I was reading to my daughter, Zoe. As I read each line that had a "you" in it, she looked up and said, "Me?" Then I read, "Zoe, God loves you." Zoe turned her sweet face up to me and, with her hand on my cheek, said, "Mommy, God love me?"

Oh, Father! Yes, You love Zoe! Yes, You love me! I treasure the precious moments to fall madly in love with You all over again. Thank You for people like Mr. Sorensen, and even for the pain that sent me back to You. I also thank You for the love You've given me to share with my children. Let them "meet" You in me.

LISA D. INGELSE

HEALTH CONNECTIONS

Why art thou cast down, O my soul? and why art thou disquieted within me? hope thou in God: for I shall yet praise him, who is the health of my countenance, and my God. Ps. 42:11.

There is something wonderful about feeling healthy, and something challenging about being ill. But the greatest challenge is seldom the physical symptoms. Illness seems to bring with it a gloomy atmosphere that requires effort to resist. While remembering a lifetime of good health, I must acknowledge my few episodes of pain and fear: complications following surgery, a back injury, a delayed biopsy. When we are well and feeling great, we don't even think about our bodies and "wellness." Health is so comfortable that it produces an unawareness until it is breached by illness.

When I remember my illnesses, the physical sensitivities move back into the shadows, and the emotional and spiritual impact become the significant focus. Perhaps my focus is shaped by my faith. In reading the psalmist's acknowledgment of God as "the health of [his] countenance," I also recognize the significant role of faith. The pain, the unknown, and the fear of illness are generally relieved or intensified in proportion to my connection to my heavenly Father.

I remember the soothing presence of a caring parent and the sense of safety and comfort in feeling a gentle hand smooth the pillow or tuck in the sheet when I was a child and became sick. Perhaps it is this awareness of Another that makes the difference when I have wrestled with illness. Perhaps it is my confidence in the promise "I will restore health unto thee, and I will heal thee of thy wounds, saith the Lord" (Jer. 30:17). This promise whispers courage to me that embraces not only my physical illness, but also the injuries experienced by my spirit. When careless words or overwhelming experiences take their toll, leaving me wounded and hurting, "I will heal thee" echoes in my heart.

A caring heavenly Parent who smooths the pillows of stress and tucks in the sheets of my life when I am ill or discouraged, whose gentle hand and comforting promise remind me of His nearness, is perhaps my greatest health connection. In the darkness of pain, in a hospital room, or in the crowded but lonely moments of my life, the gentle hand of my heavenly Father promises healing and comfort in His time and in His way—but always through His presence.

STELLA THOMPSON

A WHOLE NEW ROOM

I will give you a new heart and put a new spirit in you; I will remove from you your heart of stone and give you a heart of flesh. Eze. 36:26, NIV.

I looked with dismay at my living room. Driving rain from the winter before had come in under the eaves and through leaks in the roof. The plaster was falling from the ceiling in some places, leaving holes through the turn-of-the-century lathe and plaster.

I was used to construction inside the house. Our home had been built in phases beginning in the late 1800s, and we have been the ones doing most of the upgrading and remodeling. Various carpenters have come and gone, most shaking their heads in dismay, but almost always saying "It will never be right" about some aspect of the construction.

Today a new contractor came to scrutinize, criticize, and then estimate how much it would cost to repair the damage. I braced myself for the usual carping, but this man was different. He looked around the room, felt the walls, and spoke briefly with his colleague. He then turned to my husband and me with a huge smile and said, "No problem! I will give you a whole new room!" For once someone had not seen the problem, only the solution. He had looked beyond the apparent reality and had seen the potential in the room, what it could be.

It did not happen overnight, and the mess was incredible. There were times during the following two weeks that I had trouble believing that the "whole new room" would ever materialize. Finally the work was completed, and truly it was a whole new room. Most of our friends did not come over during the construction phase, and the compliments we received from them were for superficial changes, such as the paint. Although the structural modifications were obvious to us, the intensity of the labor was unknown to them. But the beautiful result was evident.

It is often this way with us. God works on each of us in a different way to create "a whole new heart." The real work goes on under the surface; it is usually only the exterior that is noticed by others. When we are personally involved in change, we acknowledge the hand of God. My prayer each day reflects the personal desire to change: *"Create in me a pure heart, O God, and renew a steadfast spirit within me"* [Ps. 51:10, NIV]. *It may be messy and won't happen overnight, I know, but I want to give You my heart now for remodeling.*   CAREL CLAY

WHITE, SPARKLING, FRESH SNOW

Though your sins are like scarlet, they shall be as white as snow; though they are red as crimson, they shall be like wool. Isa. 1:18, NIV.

The weather forecast for my little town in western Washington predicted a heavy snowfall for several days. Everyone was talking about and preparing for the big snowfall. I dreaded it. I really have never been very fond of snow, and I drive long distances to work, so snow meant trouble.

A week later, on a Sunday morning, my husband and I awoke to a darkened bedroom. I lay still for a bit, wondering why the bedroom was so dark at that hour of the morning. Then I glanced at the skylight and realized that the weather forecast had been right. A quick dash to the window revealed the lawn, shrubs, trees, deck, and benches all covered with at least eight to 10 inches of the most beautiful fluffy white snow.

As I took pictures around my home and neighborhood, I saw perfection. Everything had been covered with a white blanket and glistened in perfect beauty. The trees sparkled, the streets were covered with white, the lawns were brushed perfectly smooth, and none of the underlying imperfections could be seen anywhere.

My eyes feasted on the beauty all around me—and I thought of Isaiah 1:18: "Though your sins are like scarlet, they shall be as white as snow." Sparkling, fresh, white, pure snow. I visualized my Saviour placing His cloak of righteousness around me and covering all my sins and imperfections. As I read verse 19, I heard the Lord inviting me and teaching me what my responsibility is in this partnership: "If you are willing and obedient, you will eat the best from the land." How easy— and what an award! More than I ever deserve, but an invitation too good and loving to ignore.

I thank You, Lord, for that snowy January morning. It helps me to better understand and appreciate what You have done for me. I need Your forgiveness and Your righteousness for today and each new day to come.

ERIKA OLFERT

STEADFASTLY ANCHORED IN FAITH

We should no longer be children, tossed to and fro and carried about with every wind of doctrine, by the trickery of men, in the cunning craftiness of deceitful plotting, but, speaking the truth in love, may grow up in all things into Him who is the head—Christ. Eph. 4:14, 15, NKJV.

The year 1998 was one of torrential rains, floods, hurricanes, tornadoes all over America, it seemed. It was the year El Niño dominated many parts of the country with inclement weather and devastation. The little town of Spencer, South Dakota, was wiped away by a tornado. Other parts hit hard by tornadoes were Pennsylvania and New York. Boston, Massachusetts, experienced destructive floods. Central California was devastated by strong winds and rains that damaged many crops.

One afternoon, as a very strong wind beat upon the trees in our backyard, I thought of the two cherry trees that had some fruit. The cherries weren't ready to be picked yet, but in a few days they would be. As I watched from the kitchen, I thought the branches were breaking. *The cherries must be falling from the branches,* I worried. I was feeling sad, because we had waited five years, and we thought there was going to be a good crop. Now it looked as though the winds would destroy it.

The day after the winds subsided I inspected the damage. Would there be fruit on the trees? Did the winds beat them to the ground? On the ground were a few immature cherries, but on the branches were the dark ripe cherries. How amazing that those good ones remained attached to the branches! They were the mature, sturdy cherries, still intact on the branches in spite of very strong winds that had beat mercilessly on them.

In our spiritual life we may be buffeted by the winds of trials and difficulties. Problems and hardships may seem to overwhelm us, but with our faith anchored in Jesus we shall overcome. There is nothing insurmountable with Him, the author and finisher of our faith.

Just like the mature cherries that stayed on the branches, if we are firmly attached to the Branch, Jesus, we will not succumb to the trials hurled at us by the enemy. Though winds of temptations and hardships—even devastation—assail us, we can still say with Job, "Though He slay me, yet will I trust Him" (Job 13:15, NKJV).

OFELIA A. PANGAN

LOOK IN THE MIRROR

So be careful. If you are thinking, "Oh, I would never behave like that"—let this be a warning to you. For you too may fall into sin. 1 Cor. 10:12, TLB.

I was scheduled for a taped interview downtown at 8:15 a.m., so I got an early start. I rehearsed my thoughts so that the interview would go smoothly. I arrived at the office building a few minutes before the appointed time. Confidently stepping into the elevator, I glimpsed my image in the mirror on the back wall. Horror of horrors, I had not combed my hair! *How could I have done this?* I thought with mounting panic.

Backing out of the elevator, I rushed to the car. *There is no time to go to a store and buy a comb. What am I going to do?* I thought. *I have to do something!* Seated in the car, I hurriedly tried to comb my hair with a ballpoint pen. I needed help—and the pen was not working. Reaching into the glove compartment, I fished out a plastic fork. In less time than it takes to tell, my hair was reasonably combed and I was out of the car, retracing my steps. I arrived at that appointment a changed person. Instead of focusing on myself, I was thanking God for that mirror.

Life is like that! Confident and assured, we plow ahead, thinking we have it all together. Moments later we are headed for disaster.

In His mercy God puts a mirror in our path so we can see ourselves as we are before we appear for another interview—one that will take place before His judgment bar. He has given us a mirror—the Bible—so we can know what we need to do to be ready. With our Bible, we can examine ourselves so that we will not be embarrassed when He comes. What if I had not known my true condition before I appeared for my interview? What if I had no way of knowing my true spiritual condition?

Oh, Lord, how You must love me. Not only have You saved me from personal embarrassment, but You have provided for me to be saved eternally. Help me to look into Your mirror early each day so that I may be prepared for what lies ahead.

BARBARA J. HALES

THE LOST CHORD

The kingdom of heaven is like a merchant seeking beautiful pearls, who, when he had found one pearl of great price, went and sold all that he had and bought it. Matt. 13:45, 46, NKJV.

When collecting scraps of material to put into comforter tops, I try to find combinations that match and blend the best. Not long ago I was collecting four pieces for the rail fence pattern, which takes one dark, one light, and two in-between colors. I had stacked enough sets to make a full-size comforter. I carefully placed aside each set for cutting and sewing, then further cutting down to proper size. One set especially caught my eye because the colors blended so well.

Then somehow, in all the cutting and restacking, the one set that I really liked disappeared. *Maybe I took one of the pieces and moved it somewhere else,* I thought. I searched through all the scraps, but the set didn't reappear. I sewed the other matching sets, mystified about where those lost pieces were and wondering if I would even recognize the set if I saw it again. It had been days since I had collected those scraps.

An old song that I enjoyed as a young girl, learning to play the piano, came to my mind. "The Lost Chord" is a euphoric song about an organist who struck a lovely chord, then couldn't remember the finger combinations that made the chord so beautiful. He struck different chords in an effort to regain that wondrous one, but just couldn't come up with it. His nostalgic song reveals the frustration of his search.

I'm sure there is a deeper meaning to the song, but that meaning never surfaced in my mind except to say that anything of great beauty is certainly worth looking for. I loved piano chords that used all my fingers, but I never actually hit on one so wondrous that it qualified for the frantic search for which the song is famous.

Such losses remind me of my own lost condition and how Jesus looks for lost sheep and sinners of the world. He told His disciples the parables of the treasure hidden in a field, the pearl of great value, and the prodigal son, all redeemed at great prices. When Jesus found me, I was looking for Him also. Maybe He thinks of me as a lost chord, worth looking for at any cost. And what a price He paid! With His own life He redeemed me, unworthy as I am. How thankful I am that He did!

GWEN LEE

ARE THEY LOST?

You have not strengthened the weak or healed the sick or bound up the injured. You have not brought back the strays or searched for the lost. You have ruled them harshly and brutally. So they were scattered because there was no shepherd, and when they were scattered they became food for all the wild animals. My sheep wandered over all the mountains and on every high hill. They were scattered over the whole earth, and no one searched or looked for them. Eze. 34:4-6, NIV.

Lost! Hopelessly and desperately lost! I knew I was lost as I wandered in the maze of fabric tables, too small to see over them. I wasn't interested in any of the cloth, no matter how soft or harsh or silky it felt. *I was lost!* Didn't my mother and grandmother know how desperate I felt? Where were they? I saw many legs, but none belonged to my mother or grandmother. No one seemed to care that this little girl was lost and close to tears! I tried to be brave as I crisscrossed the maze of display tables again and again, hoping, hoping; but I was frightened.

Sixty-five years later I can still feel the desperation of being lost. When I finally found my mother and grandmother, they were sitting on a bench around the corner by the restroom, calmly talking, completely unaware that their only daughter and only granddaughter was lost! Oh, I was welcomed, but I don't think they thought I was lost. They thought I was having fun, wandering among the fabric tables, feeling the different textures.

When I was a teenager I went out into the world and had my fun. Many times I was reminded that I was the only daughter and only granddaughter, so had to live up to the family's expectations for me. I know they prayed for me, but still I wandered. But I am so happy I was found and brought back to the fold, healed, and my wounds bound up.

I think about our youth who are wandering—testing and experiencing different activities and trails and paths. Sometimes we don't interfere because we think they may not want to be found. Maybe we don't realize they are lost and wishing they weren't.

I think of the church's "back door" that is swinging and want to do more than pray for our youth. I want them to know we love them and want them with us.

Teach me what to say and do, Lord.   JEAN HALL

ABOVE WHAT WE ASK

My God shall supply all your need according to His riches in glory by Christ Jesus. Phil. 4:19, NKJV.

The new job would be different from my previous position at the university, I knew, but I wanted to continue working for a few more years. So I determined to make the necessary adjustments. However, I didn't know how many adjustments there would be. I was used to being in charge; now I was being supervised. I had developed my own treatment plans and methods; now I had to use treatments that were new to me. I struggled to learn as fast and as efficiently as possible.

Soon some patients, preferring the treatment I gave, began to ask for me. This led to jealousy among the staff, making my task even more difficult. Thankfully, one of the aides befriended me, shielding me as much as she could without jeopardizing herself. But work continued to be unpleasant for me.

Please, Lord, I prayed, *give me strength to hold on, and help me to find another job so I can get out of this place.* On my days off I began looking for new employment.

I was glad for the privilege of attending an out-of-state workshop, and the time away did much for lifting my drooping spirits. There I learned more new techniques in a relaxed setting.

The day I returned, however, my friend whispered that I should resign before they fired me. I turned in my 10-day notice the next morning. My load was lifted, but I wondered about the future. What was going to happen? How would God answer my prayer?

Within a few days I was surprised by a telephone call and a job offer as department head, which I later accepted. God had answered my prayer. But I also discovered that He had been preparing me for the transition. Even though I had not enjoyed the previous job, I had learned skills that were required on the new job. Even the things I learned in the out-of-state seminar were necessary.

If I should go through unpleasant circumstances today, help me to know that You are preparing me for something. Help me to place my trust in You and to be grateful.

MILDRED C. WILLIAMS

WHAT'S IN A NAME?

I have called you by your name; you are Mine. Isa. 43:1, NKJV.

A young man called to make an appointment to research some of our historical film footage. Nothing out of the ordinary—this is what producers, writers, and directors often do. Oh, we had such fun before this young man arrived. On the morning he walked in, we soon all found some work that would take us into the reception area. But we saw no one unusual—just a serious young man who, nevertheless, sent us all back into our offices chuckling.

"How could they? How could his parents name him such an awful name?" I asked Joy.

"Oh, I asked him about that," his research assistant explained. "He was not born with that name." She told me that when he was younger and more foolish he had wanted to be rich and famous, so he legally changed his last name to "Famous" and his first name to "Rich." His middle initial? "N." He was surely known for his name!

When I was young, five cousins came to live with our family. On warm summer evenings we girls loved to sit on the wide front porch to watch the world go by. One evening a young man, a stranger, slowed his convertible. Singling out my eldest cousin, Sheri, he called out, "Hey, you're a Weaver, aren't you?"

Sheri, the coolest of us all, was flabbergasted. "I don't know you. How do you know me?" she demanded.

"You look like one. And those two"—he pointed to the twins—"are Weavers too, aren't you? You've got a brother, Art, right?"

Sheri nodded. Art had long since grown up, married, and moved away.

"Yeah, we used to run around together when we were kids. You have that family look." He waved cheerfully and drove on.

I peered at my cousins, trying to see such a striking family resemblance that someone who'd known only an older brother years before could stop and ask, "Are you a Weaver?" Would someone stop me on a corner today and ask, "Hey, are you a Christian? You look like one. You have that family resemblance"?

And when I ask, "How do you know?" I hope the person could reply, "Oh, you look like your older brother, Jesus."

LOIS K. BAILEY

THE PRICELESS WORK OF ART

The heavens declare the glory of God; and the firmament sheweth his handiwork. Ps. 19:1.

Before cameras came into being, drawings and paintings were almost the only way of making pictures or conveying images of how people or places looked. Pictures are looked at now for pleasure and used for book illustrations and advertising. Scientists and illustrators often use pictures to explain and illustrate facts. I have always admired those who have artistic abilities, especially those who can draw and paint.

During my years as an educator, I've known coworkers who drew pictures to illustrate a lesson or story. A teacher next door to me used to draw pictures on the chalkboard to illustrate stories and lessons to make them more meaningful and interesting. How I wished I could do the same! I was a little jealous until one day I came to the realization that drawing simply was not one of my God-given talents. It was then that I was able to look forward to the end of each day to go to her room to enjoy what she had drawn.

I enjoy and appreciate works of great artists in art galleries. I recall Audubon's famous pictures of America's birds. And Rembrandt, as I recall, was a master in the use of light and shadow. I think too of other great artists whose paintings depict landscapes with mountains, streams, and rivers. Whether visiting galleries or reading about great artists, I think of the greatest artist of all time, Jesus Christ, who created all things. Without Him, Audubon wouldn't be remembered for his beautiful paintings. Rembrandt could not have been a master of light and shadow.

Let's enjoy and appreciate the artistic abilities God has given. We can broaden our appreciation by looking for artistic beauty in museums, art galleries, churches, and other places where such beauty can be found. But most of all, let's appreciate, enjoy, and give thanks as we view God's art gallery while traveling by car, bus, airplane, and ship, when walking, or even merely when looking outdoors.

Today I want to bring You my thanks for the beauty You have created. "Thou hast created all things, and for thy pleasure they are and were created" [Rev. 4:11]. I intend to enjoy each one, because You made them just for me.

ANNIE B. BEST

SUPERWOMAN SYNDROME

Let us lay aside every weight, and the sin which doth so easily beset us. Heb. 12:1.

Her life probably started like most of ours. She was a typically precious newborn, precocious toddler, lovable little girl, and reserved adolescent. She blossomed into an intent young adult and became a focused, determined young woman. Somewhere along the path toward adulthood she picked up the cape and became superwoman. Why? We do not know. Was it society's demands? Or was it her destiny to be everything to everybody?

Does she sound like a woman you've known? Or maybe that woman is you!

Women today juggle parental roles with career, marriage commitments, civic duties, church responsibilities, and more. Too few of us make time for ourselves in our daily schedule to focus solely on self for spiritual and physical rejuvenation. The time we spend under the hair dryer or organizing the roster for the church department we serve in does not count. Nor does the shower that is shortened by the ring of the cordless phone.

We women become too busy—working, organizing, transporting, arranging, participating, overseeing, catering, cleaning, supporting, nurturing. Busyness stalks us relentlessly, while our acquired superwoman syndrome propels us into a continued frenzy. We are subconsciously under the impression that we can do it all—or that we should at least try.

We indeed have a dilemma. How do we release ourselves from this situation? With determination to change, we can remove the superwoman cape and reorganize and reprioritize. Unfortunately, though, we are soon back in our sad predicament of busyness. Why can't we learn just to say "No, I cannot do it. I will not do it. I owe myself some time today. I need time to commune with God—and I need it before I get busy with all my to do list." Why can't we say those words without feeling guilty, and then take that time?

Taking off our cape momentarily is not enough. As God's stewards, we are to "lay aside every weight, and the sin which doth so easily beset us."

I present this day to You, Lord. You know what is really important. Help me to prioritize and organize so I may have time with You and be a blessing to others.   BETTY ANNE LOWE

WHERE WOULD WE BE WITHOUT OUR SONGS?

He will rejoice over you with singing. Zeph. 3:17, NIV.

Music was an integral part of every day during our growing-up years. There was wake-up music, mealtime music, driving music, relaxation music. At first Mother played the piano, and Daddy, my sisters, and I sang. I'm not sure if it was my voice or what, but eventually I was assigned to piano-playing instead. As a result of all that exposure to music, I learned and internalized the words and music of hundreds of songs from our Christian heritage:

"Does Jesus care when I've said goodbye to the dearest on earth to me, and my sad heart aches till it nearly breaks—is it aught to Him? Does He see? O yes, He cares—I know He cares! His heart is touched with my grief."

"Whatever my lot, Thou hast taught me to say, It is well, it is well with my soul."

"In His arms He'll take and shield thee, thou wilt find a solace there."

I often wonder what I would have done through the years without these words of hope, praise, and comfort.

The first three years of my doctoral studies were relatively calm. Single and surrounded by a strong professional and social network, I sailed through course work and passed my comprehensive exams. With "only" the dissertation left, I confidently planned to finish this project in record time, 18 months at the most.

Shortly thereafter, I met the man who later became my husband. We dated, married, and in two years I had a husband, an infant, and his two children. I barely visited the campus. Choosing a topic and faculty members to direct my dissertation, doing the research, writing and rewriting, defending my results, and satisfying graduate school requirements all seemed overwhelming.

"Ponder anew what the Almighty can do if with His love He befriend thee." These words from "Praise to the Lord" dawned upon my consciousness. I cautiously began to apply my immature faith, pondering what the Almighty could do for me.

He is awesome! He used my husband, colleagues, acquaintances, parents, sister, and stepchildren to support and befriend me. Graduation day, two years later, was one of the most glorious days of my adult life, thanks to the Almighty. I wonder where I might be without the songs to inspire me.

DONNA DAVIS CAMERON

WAITING

Wait on the Lord: be of good courage, and he shall strengthen thine heart: wait, I say, on the Lord. Ps. 27:14.

After having lived most of my 11 years in Miami, I felt that there was only one thing that I had never had a chance to see—snow. Snow seemed so mystical compared to the liquid sunshine we were used to seeing in Florida.

The first Christmas after we moved to Maryland my parents surprised my little sister and me with a sled for Christmas. Unfortunately, it was not a white Christmas, and the sled stayed propped against the wall for several weeks. I would run my hand up and down the smooth lacquered slats and around the cold metal runners. Gripping the turning bar, I could almost imagine the cold air rushing past me as I slid down and round dangerous snowbanks.

When it finally did snow, not enough accumulated for sledding until after dark. My little sister and I had to do some heavy pleading to convince our parents to let us ride our sled in the dark. The wind made the snow swirl under the full moon's reflection, and I felt as if I were in a fantasy land. We all followed Dad as he carried the sled up the sloping sidewalk in front of our apartment building.

"Who wants to go first?" he inquired. My 4-year-old sister was the family's daredevil, so it seemed only proper to give her the honor. She did a belly flop on the sled and hung on for dear life. Dad gave the sled a shove with his snow-covered shoe, and Mom started to run along as coach. The sled went only a couple yards, sparks flying. *Wow!* I thought, *No one told me there would be sparks. This is neat!* Later I found out that if there had been more snow, the sled wouldn't have created the extra light effects that metal striking concrete produces. My family still laughs about the night the sparks flew.

I'm an adult now, and I am not much more patient about leaning my plans up against the wall while I wait on the Lord than I was about the sled. But I know from past experiences that if I don't wait on the Lord, my plans may come to a screeching halt, sometimes with the added attraction of sparks! "Wait, I say, on the Lord." JO ANN HILTON

WINTER BLUES

We, who with unveiled faces all reflect the Lord's glory, are being transformed into his likeness with ever-increasing glory, which comes from the Lord, who is the Spirit. 2 Cor. 3:18, NIV.

It was a nasty winter. Big gray clouds hovered over Southern Adventist University for weeks. The rain—sometimes driving, sometimes gray and dribbly—kept company with biting winds. Red, green, and yellow sunflowered umbrellas lined the halls of the dorms, but even their festive colors could not disperse the dismal mood that had descended on campus. Students were surly, teachers impatient. Even the normally perky receptionists had strained smiles. We all longed for the sun.

One Wednesday morning I woke up early and struggled through my morning routine: shower, hair, makeup, hair—again. *This is not my day*, I thought irritably. *And of course it's probably still raining.* When I peeked out my blinds to check, I stood transfixed. The world was white! And not just a little white. Great big gobs of white covered the ground, the trees, and the rows of cars.

"Wheeee!" I heard a girl scream in the hall. *That can mean only one thing*, I thought excitedly. *No school.* A quick phone call confirmed that classes were indeed canceled. I had a whole day to play, and I wasn't about to waste it.

I joined my friends on a big hill and went sledding for the first time in my life. I exchanged snowballs with some crazy boys in a convertible. I made an ugly snowman. And best of all, I couldn't stop smiling. Nobody could. A few degrees in temperature had transformed our campus.

Transformation isn't always good—the endless rain had transformed a Christian college into an irritated one. Snow brought the needed relief. If snow can change attitudes and brighten spirits, just think what the power behind the snow can do. Jesus is in the business of transforming lives, and you can believe that the transformation He gives is more lasting than snow. Ask Him today to give you His joy—the kind that will never melt.

SARI KARINA FORDHAM

FAMILY LIKENESS

Doesn't that privilege of intimate conversation with God make it plain that you are not a slave, but a child? And if you are a child, you're also an heir, with complete access to the inheritance. Gal. 4:7, Message.

While Australia has always been my home, England holds a special interest for me, because three of my grandparents were born and raised there. Among the highlights of a recent visit to England was the opportunity to follow up family connections. It was fascinating to see the outhouses and hop fields of Kent, where my grandmother used to go hop picking as a girl; to set foot in the farmhouse where my grandfather was born in 1892; to find my great-grandmother's grave beside a tiny stone church on a windswept hillside; and to tread the worn steps of the handsome fifteenth-century church where Baldwins and other relatives of generations past came to worship.

But perhaps most interesting of all was to meet the living connections—the relatives still residing in England. It was especially fascinating to see my mother and her English cousin side by side. They had grown up thousands of miles apart and met for the first time when both were in their 60s. Yet their common genetic heritage was confirmed by an obvious family likeness.

Even more wonderful than the complex workings of genetics is the heritage of the Christian family through which believers can experience a recognizable common bond, despite differences in age, culture, gender, and social circumstances. Conflicts may occur, but for me they are outweighed by the occasions when I have been surrounded by strangers, yet felt a sense of belonging, a sense of family, with fellow believers.

The family of believers has other significant advantages. Although I can trace my forebears back several generations, I have never inherited anything except flat feet and myopia. But as a Christian believer I have a fabulous inheritance to look forward to. No one "has ever seen, heard or even imagined what wonderful things God has ready for those who love the Lord" (1 Cor. 2:9, TLB). "And since we are his children, we will share his treasures—for all God gives to his Son Jesus is now ours too" (Rom. 8:17, TLB).

JENNIFER M. BALDWIN

HAVE I TOLD HIM?

Enter into his gates with thanksgiving, and into his courts with praise: be thankful unto him, and bless his name. Ps. 100:4.

As I sat in the emergency room with my 15-year-old daughter, waiting for yet another doctor to come by and give an assessment, I could no longer keep my emotions in check. I looked over at her with tears streaming down my face and wondered what she would be put through next. Severe tonsillitis had left her completely unable to speak and barely able to breathe. And while the medical team evaluated her condition, she had been subjected to needles plunged into her tonsils and into her arms, accompanied by numerous "looks" down her throat.

I picked up her one free hand and held on. She turned to face me, saw my tears, and mouthed the words "Poor Mama." I had to smile. Poor Mama? She was the one who had been through the mill, not I. She was the one being admitted to a hospital. I was doing fine. Or was I? Actually, I was in agony. And her concern for me helped, for it touched me deeply. I was able to face the next ordeal with her with renewed spirits and drying tears.

During the next four days, while my daughter was in the hospital, I was surprised at how many times I found myself thinking back to those two little words, and I drew strength. What a precious gift they were to me!

In the weeks following that experience I often remembered her kindness and was encouraged. I also began to realize that I am not the only parent who suffers when a child is in pain. I saw, in my mind's eye, a heavenly Father who turns a tear-streaked face my way when I am hurting; One who literally knows my every pain and feels my suffering. And not only mine, but that of every one of His children.

I wonder, could He possibly be encouraged by a kind word from me? What if I told Him how much it means to me to know that whenever my heart aches, His does too? What if I let Him know that His presence is my lifeline? That with His hand grasping mine, I have nothing to fear? If I were to just mouth those words, do you think He would hear?

RETTA MICHAELIS

DOG RESCUE

Whatever you did for one of the least of these . . . you did for me. Matt. 25:40, NIV.

That particular winter morning everything went wrong from the start. It was the end of a long, tiring, and busy week. The expression TGIF became more real as I got up two hours late. After all, it's my responsibility as mother to see that all three children are up, washed, and dressed; that breakfast is attempted; and that homework and belongings are ready for school.

Believe it or not, we made it into our van within an hour. I was feeling grand and praising the Lord. Five miles into our 12-mile morning journey, a beautiful but wet golden retriever was nonchalantly holding up traffic headed for the main interstate. I hollered, "That dumb dog is going to get himself killed!" Then I noticed how much it resembled my neighbor's dog. Could it be?

I put my hazard lights on and asked Mindy to call the animal by the name of our neighbor's dog. Sure enough, he jumped up and down, happy that someone would rescue him.

"Mindy," I said, "climb into the van and see if he'll follow." It worked!

"Mom, how did you know this is our neighbor's dog?"

All the way back home I wondered the same. And when I rang the neighbor's doorbell and heard a dog barking inside, I knew I had made a mistake. In my hustle and bustle I had neglected to look at the dog's tags. On my car phone I called a number listed on the tag. It was the dog's vet, who was able to tell me the dog's name and the owner's name and phone number. We all apologized to Max for calling him Cyrus and met Max's real owner four miles later. We learned that Max had left home the night before, and his owner had been looking for him.

Are we sometimes too busy to stop and assist others? Do we get so caught up in life and its rituals that we neglect to help even the "least of these," even an animal that might be lost or hurt?

Help us to lend a hand today in a way that might seem insignificant to us, but that can make a difference to someone else.

JULIE M. LYLES

GREAT PEACE HAVE THEY

Great peace have they which love thy law: and nothing shall offend them.
Ps. 119:165.

I can't get the code to work to unlock the gate to the storage area!" exclaimed my husband in desperation. Knowing he would arrive at the storage place after closing time, he had obtained the special code necessary to enter after hours. Why wasn't it working?

"I've tried calling the police, and they said they can't help me. I don't know what to do. The truck has to be unloaded so I can pick up the rest of the furniture. Besides, by 8:00 tomorrow morning the truck is due back!" I knew only too well the predicament we were in. The new owners would take possession of our house at noon the next day. What were we to do?

The incident was one more wrench thrown into our move. I thought I had made arrangements for a local mover to move our belongings into storage. But when he didn't arrive on the specified day, a phone call verified there had been a mix-up, and he would not be coming. It wasn't easy to find a U-Haul at the last minute, especially at the end of the month. Now my husband was responsible for the back-breaking job of loading and unloading all our things. To top it off, an unusual amount of snow had fallen, and he had gotten stuck twice.

A favorite verse from my childhood came to mind: "Great peace have they which love thy law: and nothing shall offend them."

"Call me back," I told my husband. I began praying as I called one friend after another, asking them to pray for a solution. I even called my friend in charge of the prayer meeting to ask that everyone pray for us. I was certain that if my husband punched in the code again the gate would open. I waited. When he called back, I was disappointed. The code simply would not open the gate. However, one of the men helping him had offered the use of his garage for storage for the next two weeks. The next day we learned that my husband had been given the code for regular hours, not the one for after hours. God had not answered our prayers in the way we had asked, but He did answer our prayers.

God's ways are not our ways, but we must trust that He is in control at all times. In many ways this move was the worst we had experienced in 25 years of ministry. Yet in other ways we saw the Lord at work and felt Him near.

VERA WIEBE

SCENTIMENTAL

Thou, Lord, art God, compassionate and gracious, forbearing, ever constant and true. Ps. 86:15, NEB.

Wednesday night is my time. My time to run business errands or window shop, to volunteer or escape, to spend with a friend or be alone, to read and think or daydream and reflect. The Lord always has a surprise treasure, a reminder of His loving care, hidden somewhere for me.

One particular Wednesday I started the day feeling a tiny bit sorry for myself. But I took control, and the day at work was positive and fun. That evening I decided to window shop, a budget-dictated choice. Valentine's Day was a week away, spring fever was taking root, and my gardening addiction was gnawing.

I studied the bare-root roses pictured on their packages. Then I noticed how fast they were leafing out. Another two weeks would be almost too late to plant them. Then one truly caught my eye. The colors reminded me of vanilla ice cream with red hot candies. I was captivated by the photo on the package wrapper and the description of its scent. I began to weigh the realities: Budget said NO! Not tonight!

While I was sorting these thoughts, a clerk offered to assist me. As we chatted, he mentioned the store's policy of replacing plants that did not perform the first year after purchase. In surprise, I indicated my unawareness of that fact. I told him that a rose I'd purchased there the previous year had not been true to its labeled color but that I enjoyed it and was happy with it. He paused momentarily, then said, "If you have a few minutes, I can discount this one down to zero for you."

I was stunned. I'm sure my face showed a swirl of emotions. I finally stammered a thanks.

As I walked to my car, I felt like crying and shouting for joy. I needed someone with whom to share. Then the quiet thought struck with an awesome force: *God had this token of joy waiting for me all day!* That fragrant gift of His love, mercy, and grace left me emotionally speechless and overwhelmed. It caused me to think of another gift that I had been given though I didn't deserve it—the gift of my Saviour.

Oh, the irony of it all. The name of this patent rose was Scentimental.

BEVERLY HELMSTETLER

PEANUT BUTTER SANDWICHES

Be not forgetful to entertain strangers: for thereby some have entertained angels unawares. Heb. 13:2.

Out of the corner of my eye I saw him quietly slip in and sit in the back. I couldn't believe what I saw—a White man in an all-Black congregation.

Brought up in the Deep South, I knew this wasn't customary behavior for the 1960s. Living in Michigan would take some getting used to.

After church services I caught sight of our unusual visitor by himself as people talked and greeted one another in small groups. Then a member approached the middle-aged stranger. It appeared that an offering had been collected for him. I watched as he studied the contents of his hand.

Suddenly a voice in my head cut through my thoughts: *Invite him to dinner. What? I—I—My house isn't clean,* I argued with the voice.

The message was repeated several times, then became an urgent command. Clutching my 12-month-old Delsey, I rushed to the last pew.

"Would you like to come over for dinner?" I heard myself asking the stranger with kind eyes.

My husband was in a state of disbelief. I was shy and a new Christian. I seldom, if ever, asked people over. Yet I had invited a perfect stranger who had come on foot. And he had accepted.

I set a meager table. As we ate cooked vegetables and tossed salad, I was filled with conviction that this was no ordinary man. I just knew he was an angel. After dinner my husband offered to take him to the main highway, and I gave him peanut butter sandwiches in a paper bag.

Years later I mentioned to my husband that I believed our guest had been an angel. He then gave me this startling account: "When I took him out to the expressway, the area was flat. No trees. No hills. No traffic coming or going. When I looked back, he was gone."

Hospitality is not one of my gifts. But I discovered that it doesn't take much to be kind—sometimes just plain vegetables and peanut butter sandwiches.

ETHEL FOOTMAN SMOTHERS

BLANKET THEOLOGY

He will cover you with his feathers, and under his wings you will find refuge. Ps. 91:4, NIV.

Recently it was necessary for me to move away from everyone and everything I knew as I began a new direction for my life. Feelings fluctuated between a hopeful eagerness and a sense of sadness and loss.

I unpacked and set up my new home between going to class and all the mundane, time-consuming activities associated with a new place. The process seemed to go so slowly. Finally one day I was able to put the bed together.

Putting on my favorite linens, I then decided to use, for a blanket, an afghan that my mother had knit for me, and over that I put a hand-pieced quilt my sister had made. Every night as I went to sleep I kept warm and snug with things made by people who loved me. It's a good way to sleep.

My youngest daughter has a favorite blanket that she called Pooh Blank when she was very young. One morning I woke to find her, now a teenager, asleep on my bed, covered with her Pooh blanket. That she came into my room was unusual, but that she came with the Pooh blanket was not. Apparently she'd had a bad dream and, being afraid, had wrapped herself in something that all her life had symbolized being safe and loved.

Being loved is so important, but *knowing* we are loved seems to matter even more. Kisses make the hurts feel better. Hugs cheer us up. Love that becomes tangible somehow reaffirms its existence, reminding us it's around us, close to us, and available to us. The concept of love has significance, but the love that touches is love remembered.

Beyond those times in our lives when we can feel God's presence, or when we look back and see that we have been directed to where we now are, is what can be called the knowing love—love experienced, inscribed onto our bodies and into our memories. If we can be vessels created by (and used by) a gracious God, then we can perhaps understand that a hug from a friend comes from the Friend as well. In the warmth of a blanket made or tucked in by someone special we also may feel tucked in by Someone very special. It's a good way to feel.   ALICE HEATH PRIVE

MY SISTER, MY FRIEND

[Treat] older women like mothers [and] younger women like sisters, in all purity. 1 Tim. 5:2, Amplified.

For as long as I can remember, my elder sister has given me advice just about the time I need it. During our teenage years my sister delightfully gave me vivid predictions of upcoming developments I would face, such as the "monthly cycle" and flirty boys. My sister gladly shouldered the responsibility of teaching me how to cope with those new situations. Being two years my senior, she prided herself in knowing about those matters.

Now as we grow older we seem closer again, and her advice becomes even more valuable. Having had two years of life ahead of me, my sister has passed each portal of the aging process that much sooner, and she tells me what to expect at each stage.

Since we have the same inherited tendencies toward health problems, my sister's advice is most helpful. She has learned well how to cope with the changing turns our lives take, and I have very much appreciated her sharing these findings with me. Her advice is not always about health matters only. It covers general living principles as well, such as ways to cope with difficult people, gardening tips, recipes, or household hints. I remember an especially trying time when my sister encouraged me with Bible verses and special quotations of good advice appropriate for that time.

My sister and I are very close, and I am so grateful to God for her. Those of you who have no older sister probably have friends who have filled that position for you. And I am sure those with younger sisters protect them as God would have you do. Of course, each of us can befriend our sisters in the church. I think our verse today considers women of the church our sisters as we edify one another in the faith, even as this devotional does. We are all members of the royal family, children of the heavenly kingdom. May your years be filled with the joys of true sisterhood as you comfort and edify one another in the Lord.

Father, we thank You that we are all members of the royal family, daughters of the heavenly kingdom, sisters in Your love. May our years be filled with the joys of true sisterhood as we comfort and edify one another in Your name.

BESSIE SIEMENS LOBSIEN

WHITE AS SNOW

Though your sins be as scarlet, they shall be as white as snow; though they be red like crimson, they shall be as wool. Isa. 1:18.

Snow covered the backyard, down to the park, and way beyond. I stood quietly, trying to take it all in. A brilliant sun blazed down on the fresh layer—so still, so inviting, and so pure. My thoughts turned to the promise given in today's text: white as snow. My sins! What a promise!

We know we can depend on this assurance. Each one of us. Soon I remembered that the beauty of this scene would be only temporary. Events quickly produce changes that mar the original loveliness, exactly as happens in our lives when we become tempted and tainted by sin.

As the morning wore on the changes became audible as well as visual. Out came the snowblowers, the snow shovels, the snowplows. The birds, rabbits, and squirrels hopped and scampered here and there. They tracked all over the magic white carpet. Rocks, stones, branches, and bunches of leaves began to show up. The slush and mush created by cars and other vehicles heaped dirty piles of mud over the white snow, covering much of it. A transformation took place that was not visually attractive.

Is that what happens when we become mired in the slush and mud of sin? Our "born-clean" characters become scarlet with sin, crimson red. We get discouraged and often forget what the Lord has promised us. He invites us to look again at what He says—even though these sins "be as scarlet, they shall be as white as snow."

Grasp it today and hold this promise to your heart. Think of it each morning as you start your day. Think of it each evening as you go to your sleep. It is the promise made possible because of God's great gift to each of us. His Son's blood can make us clean—white as snow.

The snow is gone again, but the lesson stays on. Help me to value and share what You have done for me. And throughout this day, with all that I see and hear, refresh my memory that You love and care for me and cover my sins—whiter than snow.

ARLENE E. COMPTON

BECOMING BEAUTIFUL

He has made everything beautiful in its time. He has also set eternity in the hearts of men; yet they cannot fathom what God has done from beginning to end. Eccl. 3:11, NIV.

Perception is a funny thing. Most of us spend our lives seeing only what we have been taught to see, and nothing more. Once we have viewed a situation, we form our opinion and stick with it. Sometimes a new focus is all it takes to see beauty where we thought there was none.

The first time I looked at the field it was ugly. All I could see was brown. The brown mud, one or two brown leafless trees, brown cornstalks. Even the sky looked brown. Another Nebraska winter was moving in for its annual visit. I couldn't stand the sparseness of the trees and the lack of life. This was not a beautiful place.

I had defined beautiful in my own mind a long time before, while living in Hawaii. Beautiful was the lush green Koolau mountains, ending in the blues, jades, and purples of Kailua Bay. Beautiful was the Hawaiian sky, a sky so deep I felt I could be drawn into space just by looking at it. No, this field did not match my idea of beautiful.

One day, however, I stepped into the field, leaving the neighborhood and developments behind. Snow crunched under my feet, and my nose tingled from the cold. The sun shone, lighting up each crystal of ice like a completely cut jewel. Even the frozen bits of moisture blowing around in the wind sparkled and flashed. A lone tree stood on the otherwise vacant horizon, emphasizing the emptiness. I felt small standing in the crushing expanse.

As I looked around I noticed the hundreds of little animal tracks crisscrossing the hill. Evidence of life sprang at me from everywhere, yet the field was silent, still, and vacant. I began seeing and experiencing something different. It was no longer a dead brown field; it was a storybook painted with golds, tans, ambers, and brilliant whites. It wasn't a horribly lonely place; it was a refuge of solitude. It had also become a place in which to expand my ideas and rethink my definitions. My field had become beautiful, for in the silence, in the stillness of this plain little field, I saw the magnificent handiwork of God.

MELISSA WYSONG

THE FAITH OF A CHILD

Without faith it is impossible to please God, because anyone who comes to him must believe that he exists and that he rewards those who earnestly seek him. Heb. 11:6, NIV.

My 7-year-old daughter, Kimberlee, desperately longed for a kitten. The only problem was that we already owned two adult cats. According to my husband, that was already one cat too many. Being a "supportive" mother, I suggested that she pray for a kitten. Since the problem seemed insurmountable, I thought a good solution would be to turn it over to God.

We live outside the city limits, down a long private driveway, and have very few neighbors. I felt fairly sure that my daughter could pray for a kitten, and it would take the Lord a little while to figure out a way to make that happen. In the meantime I tried to reason with my daughter about the huge responsibility of having another pet. A month passed, and I was beginning to believe that Kimberlee had given up the quest for a new pet.

Then came that fateful Friday night. When my husband went outside to get wood for the fire, I thought I saw a squirrel on the deck. But as I got up to look outside, I heard the distinct cry of a kitten.

"Honey, did you hear that?" I asked, not believing my ears.

Suddenly my daughter was on the scene: "Mommy, it's a kitten! I know it's a kitten!"

Reluctant to accept that possibility, I opened the door cautiously. In walked a tiny gray-and-white kitten with no hint of fear. It sat down in the entryway, looking up at me with big green eyes. The kitten ate hungrily and performed a crazy little dance on her hind legs that immediately endeared her to the whole family. She did not seem to mind when seven people crowded around to examine her. But she immediately attached herself to Kimberlee, who looked at me with the utmost trust and said, "See, Mommy, you don't have to get me a kitten because God has already sent me one."

To this day I have no idea where that kitten came from, but God really does answer prayer, even the simple prayer of a 7-year-old child.

"If you, then, though you are evil, know how to give good gifts to your children, how much more will your Father in heaven give good gifts to those who ask him!" (Matt. 7:11, NIV).   CAREL CLAY

THE VALENTINE CARD

I have loved you with an everlasting love; I have drawn you with loving-kindness. Jer. 31:3, NIV.

Did you get a valentine card this morning? My husband, finally realizing that I count these things important, surprised me on a recent February 14 with a carefully chosen card that he had bought in advance and kept hidden away one whole memorable year. It was so well hidden that at first he couldn't remember where it was!

My husband sometimes writes me a poem expressing his love for me. Some years he gives me flowers or takes me out for a special meal for Valentine's Day.

Was Valentine's Day created to ensure that at least once a year a husband would tell his wife that he loves her? I hope not. The years my husband forgot to send me a card, was it because he didn't love me? Not at all. He tells me every day, in one way or another, that he truly cares for me. Not just with words, but with actions that speak louder than words. He does it with help around the house (we both work full-time outside the home), a special smile, or a back rub when the going has been tough. He shows it with a daily early-morning drink accompanied by "It's time to wake up, love." So much nicer than the shrill alarm of the clock!

Over the years I have discovered that the more my husband expresses his love for me, the more I want to find ways to show my love for him.

This made me think about my relationship with God. Every morning He wakes me with the message "I love you. See? I have given you this new day." He has written me a whole book to tell me how much He loves me. It won't mean much to me if I don't open it up and read it, just as my husband's tokens of love would be meaningless if I didn't open them up and read them. God put love into action too. He gave the gift of His Son so that I might share eternity with Him. He wants me to love Him as much as He loves me. The more I find expressions of His love for me, the more I want to show Him how much I love Him too. How about you?

Lord God, I'm sending You a valentine—You sent me One. I know I should do this every day, but today I say thank You for the flowers, for special foods, for all Your gifts, but especially for Your love demonstrated by Jesus Christ. Happy Valentine's Day!   VALERIE FIDELIA

SON SHINE

I shall not die, but live, and declare the works of the Lord.
Ps. 118:17.

Writhing in agony, flat on my back in a hospital, I felt that the pain from serious injury was too severe for me to live another moment.

The auto accident that put me in the hospital occurred one evening when a lifelong friend was taking me home from a Christian retreat we had attended that weekend, some 300 miles away. Just three miles from my home a woman traveling at least 55 miles per hour with her headlights off slammed into our car, totaling it—and us. My friend did not survive, and my survival was in question.

It's amazing how a three-second accident can alter priorities so immediately. Before that, I had been described as the Pollyanna sort, always happy, carefree, and optimistic. Suddenly survival took center stage. If you've ever had so much post-trauma pain that one moment you think you're going to die and the next moment the agony escalates until you're almost afraid you *won't*, then you'll know my thinking. To increase the possibility of my pulling through, I wasn't even told that Ray had died. They were depending on my will to live.

Today's text urges us to choose life. Because I have a career in the health field, I know the importance of the will to live. This God-given trait is not to be used selfishly, but our text tells us why we should choose to live: it's so we can "declare the works of the Lord."

You certainly blessed me in that hospital years ago, Lord. You gave me the courage and the will to go on. I am grateful for that. Now I take this opportunity to declare Your goodness.

Has the "good" gone out of "good morning"? Is the daily grind overwhelming you at times? Then I invite you to look to Jesus, the author and finisher of our faith. Cling to Him for dear life. Tell Him exactly how you feel. Ask Him for strength to go on. You may even need to repeat today's text every morning until God's Holy Spirit comforts you with brighter days. Seek the help you need—He will gladly supply it. God can make your sun shine again. He can do it for you. Let the Son shine in!

JUDY COULSTON

THE MAILBOX

Thy word is a lamp unto my feet, and a light unto my path.
Ps 119:105.

When I was in about the fourth grade, I asked my dad to make me a little mailbox. We lived in the country, and there was no home delivery of mail. We had to go to the post office in town to pick it up. I had heard of people being able to get their mail delivered to the house, and I thought that would be wonderful.

My father, who always had plenty of things that needed to be done, took time from his busy day and fixed up a nice little mailbox for me. He put it at the end of the flower garden path that led to the back gate. Each day when I got home from school, the first thing I did was check to see if I had a letter. Almost every day my dear dad took time from his work to write me a little letter—letters full of encouragement and hope and love. Of course, I wrote him often. I would give a great deal to have some of those letters to reread now. When I left for college, the mailbox was still there. But while I was at school my parents moved, and I never saw my treasured mailbox again.

Now I have quite a different mailbox system, and my mail speeds from the sender to my e-mail address. Although I will never have the enjoyment that I derived as a child from the little mailbox my father so lovingly made and filled for me, I still have a "mailbox" where my other loving Father sends me messages of love. Some people call this the Bible. It has many letters for me, filled with encouragement and hope. There are letters that tell me that Jesus is coming in the clouds of heaven to take me to live with Him in a world where righteousness dwells. It also gives me the protective rules of life by which my loving heavenly Father wants me to live my life. This very special and precious guidebook makes every day safe, more productive, more peaceful, and more meaningful.

This mailbox contains the basics of eternal life! If you have not checked your mailbox yet today, I think this would be an ideal time to do so—a letter filled with love is waiting just for you.   PAT MADSEN

A LESSON ON WAITING

Why do you worry about clothing?. . . If God so clothes the grass of the field, which today is, and tomorrow is thrown into the oven, will He not much more clothe you, O you of little faith? Matt. 6:28-30, NKJV.

I just *had* to have that pair of shoes. Within the week, no less. The local department store didn't have my size. The catalog did, but I didn't want to pay the catalog price when I could get them on sale at the store. A quick call to a branch store in another town, 45 minutes away, confirmed that it had them in my size at the same price as the local store, and they would hold them for me. I persuaded my husband to go with me to get them, and we drove there that weekend.

Never considering that my information might not be accurate, I frantically headed to the shoe department, eager to make my purchase of "just the navy pumps I needed" to complete my wardrobe. When I spoke to the salesperson about the merchandise being held for me, she immediately went to the back to retrieve them. She returned wearing a puzzled expression. There was no such package in the back for me, she said. A couple searches and exasperated looks told me that my trip had been in vain. Still intent on owning those shoes, I gave in and ordered from the catalog.

About six months later, while shopping in a different town, I saw the very same shoes, in my size and color, on a sales rack for less than the catalog price and less than the former store price. I could not help seeing that God had taught me a lesson in a humorous way. I just stood there, shoes in hand, marveling at the frenzied effort I'd made months earlier to get identical shoes, and I had worn them only once.

No longer do I "just have to have" something that appeals to me right away. I've learned to wait on God, even for little things, because He is interested in every aspect of life. And although His timetable often seems totally out of sync with mine, the results of waiting are far more satisfying.

SHARON M. THOMAS

INSPIRING PANSIES

These things have I spoken unto you, that in me ye might have peace. In the world ye shall have tribulation: but be of good cheer; I have overcome the world. John 16:33.

Pansies are one of my favorite flowers. As I look into their smiling faces, I always receive a lift. Although you may think I'm ridiculous, I often tell my vivid pansy faces how precious they are to me. Then I thank God for eyes to see as I enjoy these staunch little flowers.

Only recently did I learn how truly staunch they are. I've heard someone say "Don't be a pansy," meaning don't be a weakling or a pushover. But this winter brought mild temperatures, and my pansies kept blooming through December and into January. Suddenly the mercury plunged, and 10 inches of snow fell.

How are my cheery little pansies going to survive this cold and snow? I asked myself.

A few days later a warm chinook wind melted the snow like butter on a summer day. With curious interest, I checked to see how my blooming friends fared. There they were—somewhat mud-splattered and tattered, but still smiling!

"You survived!" I exclaimed. "I can't believe this!"

Never again will I believe that pansies are weak and delicate. They are survivors!

At times I find myself, like my pansies, covered with the snows of trouble—emotionally strained after placing a loved one in a nursing home, numb after the loss of someone near and dear to me, overwhelmed by the destruction of a tornado, devastated by floodwaters, or weakened with failing health. Can I survive, plug along, and keep cheerful, like my precious pansies?

My Saviour tells me, "In the world ye shall have tribulation: but be of good cheer; I have overcome the world." I can claim this promise. Since I know He's overcome the world, I can face each storm that engulfs me—I can face tomorrow, no matter what happens. He is always near me.

Lord, help me glorify You by looking for Your lessons and messages in nature, and help me to develop the gift of wonder.

NATHALIE LADNER-BISCHOFF

BUNKY'S ONE AND ONLY SKI TRIP

There is a way that seems right to a person, but its end is the way to death. Prov. 14:12, NRSV.

I love to ski, and I finally talked my husband, Bunky, into accompanying me. Since he had never skied, I urged him to take a skiing lesson. He assured me that he didn't need any instruction.

Once at the ski resort, after much hilarious fitting of ski gear, we were ready to go to the beginner's slope, where Bunky could practice the fundamentals. We got in line at the tow rope, and one by one the skiers ahead of us grabbed the rope and began their slow ascent. When my turn came, I grabbed the rope and said over my shoulder, "Grab the rope, honey; it's your turn!"

About a third of the way up the slope, I heard a thud and screams behind me. When I turned, Bunky, with skis sideways, was mowing down every skier below him on the tow rope. Skiers toppled like dominoes! The tow rope operator halted the line and ran to assist the half-dozen or so skiers piled on and under, and seemingly attached to, my husband. I was laughing too hard to be of assistance.

After the tow rope operator had a serious talk with Bunky about the intricacies of hanging on to the rope, he blew the whistle, and we all latched back on and successfully made it to the top.

Once again I urged Bunky to get instruction in a beginner's class that was in progress at the top of the hill. He grinned and refused, saying, "Nah. Watch me fly like Superman!"

About halfway down the slope his skis encountered a large ice patch that catapulted him about 20 feet sideways, directly into a new group of skiers coming up the very same tow rope. Skiers seemed to fly in all directions as he plowed into them.

Bunky didn't get up. X-rays showed two broken ribs. I've never suggested another ski trip.

God has provided us with the Bible to guide us on the slopes of life. Each day we're offered "free" lessons with the greatest Instructor who ever lived. But many people see no need for instruction. "Nah," they say. "Watch me fly like Superman!" Bunky ignored instruction at the risk of some bones. We ignore God's instruction at the risk of our eternal salvation. How foolish it would be to pass it by.

ELLIE GREEN

FIG TREES AND GOOD FRUITS

The fruit of the Spirit is love, joy, peace, longsuffering, gentleness, goodness, faith, meekness, temperance: against such there is no law. Gal. 5:22, 23.

When I was a student at Spicer Memorial College in India in the early 1970s, a sturdy, massive fig tree stood on the front lawn of the women's hostel. It had strong branches and a profusion of green leaves. An important landmark on the campus, it occupied a lot of space. Often I was assigned to rake the dry leaves around this tree.

During the fig season the branches were loaded with fruit. Tiny green figs grew day by day, slowly turning red, and finally ripening to a dark, rich purple. The aroma of the fruit permeated the entire area near the hostel. Then the figs fell, just like the leaves, and nobody cared to pick them up and eat them.

I had always enjoyed figs—fresh, dried, or even baked. But these had worms and insects inside. *Strange,* I thought. *Beautiful and tempting on the outside, but ugly and repulsive on the inside.* I was disappointed with the fig tree.

Many times in subsequent years I passed this fig tree, and during the fig season it had many ripe purple figs. But the fruit was always full of worms and insects. I was angry at the tree for deceiving me, year after year.

After being away for about five years, my family and I again visited the campus. I looked for the fig tree and was surprised that it was gone. I was told that the estate manager had cut it down because of its uselessness. I felt sad.

The strong and healthy fig tree bore fruit that looked healthy but was rotten to the core. How am *I* on the inside? Am I also infested with worms and insects? Is my heart pure and sincere, or am I self-centered?

Sometimes Christians are satisfied to bear "worm-infested" fruit. May God help us always to bear the healthy fruits of the Spirit—love, joy, peace, patience, kindness, goodness, faithfulness, humility, and self-control.

BEULAH MANUEL

OF FURY AND FORGIVENESS

*A soft answer turns away wrath, but a harsh word stirs up anger.
Prov. 15:1, NKJV.*

It was Wednesday. Lauren, my 7-year-old, was at her riding lesson on another part of our farm, and our two younger children were napping. So I sat down for the first time all day. Suddenly the door burst open. In came Lauren, tears streaming down her face.

"Whatever is the matter?" I asked, surprised at her behavior.

The story spilled out. Her riding lesson over, she had stopped to help a neighbor with the goats. "I was just helping her when she started yelling at me," Lauren blurted out. "She said I talked too much and wasn't listening to her. I just started crying, and I don't ever want to go back."

I was furious! I wanted to stalk right up there and give that woman a piece of my mind. After all, our daughter is only a child, and I was ready to let her have it. But through my own angry tears I heard the Holy Spirit speaking. I stopped, took a deep breath, and asked Him to guide my thoughts and my response to Lauren. Immediately my anger began to melt away.

I took Lauren on my lap and told her that sometimes we can't understand why people act cruelly or say things that hurt us. There might be something bad or hurtful in their lives that has made them angry. Whatever the reason, Jesus tells us to forgive them.

"But I don't want to! I don't ever want to see her again!"

"I know, Lauren," I heard myself say. "But Jesus is in your heart, and He will help you want to forgive her. Just ask." We prayed together for love and forgiveness for the neighbor. Then Lauren jumped down and walked quickly out the door.

Thank You, Lord, I prayed silently, *for speaking to me about my anger and giving me words to calm Lauren and teach Your character.*

Later Lauren bounced in and said, "It worked, Mommy! I forgave her and told her I'd try to listen better, and now she's my friend." Lauren and I both received a powerful lesson that "a soft answer turns away wrath, but a harsh word stirs up anger."

Thank You for sending Your Holy Spirit to help both Lauren and me, bringing forgiveness and healing. Please stay with me through this day.

DAVA BENTON WHITE

THE BEST OF DRESSES

Fine linen, bright and clean, was given her to wear. Rev. 19:8, NIV.

Dressed in elegant finery, they crowded into every available seat in the National Sports Arena. The wealthy. The religious. Political leaders. Business magnates. Socialites. And so did we, although our apparel did not quite compare with that of the other guests.

We were all there to observe the enthronement of a prince who had just inherited leadership of a large socioreligious group headquartered in a neighboring country.

The band began playing. Escorted by a colorfully attired honor guard, the prince began a stately walk down the aisle to the centrally located dais. Young and handsome, he looked very smart in a Paris-tailored suit.

With the prince duly seated on an impressive "throne," a procession of potentates, presidents, prime ministers, and governors of neighboring nations began. Some were dressed in Western clothes, but most wore national costumes of shimmering silk, satin, and brocade, encrusted with gold braid, sequins, and tiny mirrors.

Each of these rulers had assistants who carried gifts for the prince. Those in the know told us it was hoped the jewels, wood and marble carvings, fine brassware, and priceless Persian rugs, if converted to gold, would equal the prince's weight in gold!

Amid all this pageantry and glamour my thoughts turned to the enthronement of another potentate—Jesus Christ, the ruler of the entire universe. Jesus, King of kings and Lord of lords, will be seated on a holy, glorious throne—in the splendor of majesty. He will be clothed in the soft but illuminating light of righteousness. And He will be surrounded, not by just a few hundred people in a limited area, but by thousands upon thousands from every land and every age. And we will sing, "Hallelujah! For our Lord God Almighty reigns. Let us rejoice and be glad and give him glory!" (Rev. 19:6, 7; see also Isa. 63:15; Ps. 145:5).

Jesus has graciously invited me to this enthronement too. And He has invited you as well. I have gladly accepted. To Him we all will be priceless jewels whose value was established by the sacrifice of His own life. For that occasion all of us will be wearing the best of dresses: fine linen, bright and clean—the robes of Christ's righteousness.

LOIS E. JOHANNES

ACTION!

You must be on the alert, for the Son of Man is coming at a time when you may not expect him. Luke 12:40, Phillips.

Lilian awoke in the early hours of a summer morning with a tremendous burning, searing pain around her eyes. Her first reaction was one of panic. When she switched on the light, she could see only dimly. What was it? What should she do?

As a very practical person and a retired nurse, Lilian was used to recognizing symptoms and coping with emergencies—other people's. Now, clearly, she had one of her own. Swiftly she ran through all the possibilities. Then she knew—glaucoma. Acute glaucoma. Not the slowly developing, systematically treatable kind, but a sudden blotting-out-of-light type that required an operation within 48 hours.

Lilian lived in a small seaside town in Cromwell; it had only a little cottage hospital with limited facilities. The nearest general hospital, the kind needed to handle her problem, was 60 miles of winding roads away. There was no time to lose. She got up, dressed, and awakened a friend who lived in the downstairs flat to drive her swiftly to the doctor's office.

Confirming Lilian's diagnosis and the need for speedy action, the doctor called an ambulance that sped off for the hospital in Plymouth. An operation carried out that same day saved her sight.

It was a testing experience with a happy ending. But what if Lilian hadn't recognized the signs? What if she hadn't acted on what she knew and hadn't done something about it immediately?

Lilian's experience says something very important to me. Jesus is coming. I know He's coming, and judging by the escalating signs, He's coming soon. I've read about the sleeping bridesmaids and the thief in the night. I recognize the signs. But what am I doing about them? Paul suggests matching actions to words: "Wake up . . . put off . . . put on!" (see Rom. 11:11, 12). Then by God's grace, we, like Lilian, can pass through the greatest test of all to the happiest of endings.

PEGGY MASON

JUMPING THE ROCKS

I am the Lord, your God, who takes hold of your right hand and says to you, Do not fear; I will help you. Isa. 41:13, NIV.

We were on a winter getaway holiday on the Oregon coast, and it was cold—several degrees below freezing. Wrapped in our winter jackets, my husband and I walked the almost deserted stretch of beach. Then we came to a place where a stream entered the sea. Water, too deep for us to cross in our shoes, stretched over the sands. It was too cold for wading, so we followed the stream inland and found a place where rocks enabled us to cross it.

My husband immediately jumped from rock to rock and stood on the other side, encouraging me to do the same. But I looked down at that dark, cold, swirling water around those rocks. It was only a few feet deep, to be sure, but falling in would have made me very wet and cold. I have never been very good at balancing sports. I was a failure at skiing and skating, and balancing on one foot on even a solid-looking rock in the middle of that rushing stream of icy water was not something that I wanted to attempt.

"Let's go back, or go up to the road," I suggested.

My husband encouraged and cajoled me, but I was still fearful. I stood forlornly on the other side of the stream. Then he got an idea. He picked up a stout stick and came back down to the water's edge and onto the far stone. Holding out the stick he said, "Hold on to this."

I looked up from the swirling water and saw his encouraging face and the extended stick. I grasped the stick and slowly and very cautiously planted a foot on the first rock, and then the other foot on the next rock. Trying not to think about the icy water, I continued across the remaining three rocks and grasped my husband's hand as soon as I could reach it. We continued our walk down the beach.

That event made me think of how Jesus holds out His encouraging hand to help us cross the difficult parts in our lives. When the icy waters of life threaten to chill us, Jesus says, "Come over to Me," and He puts out His hand and helps us over. If that fragile stick could give me courage to cross that stream, how much more courage can I get from the outstretched nail-pierced hand of my Saviour as He helps me balance in the dark moments of my life!

RUTH LENNOX

UNINVITED GUESTS

Before they call, I will answer; and while they are yet speaking, I will hear. Isa. 65:24.

Bone-tired, all I wanted was peace and quiet. But as soon as I lay down, 5-year-old Nickie whined, "Mama, I can't sleep."

Too worn out to move, I questioned her from my bed, trying to get to the root of the problem.

"I keep thinking about Satan. I don't wanna think about Satan. He's bad."

Still glued to my bed, I told her to ask Jesus to help her think about something good, like heaven. It didn't work.

"Ma, will you please turn my light on?"

That brought me to my feet. After switching the light on, I returned to my room. But the whimpering continued. Then an outburst of crying. "Mama," she muttered between sobs, "I can't sleep." Her little voice shook so badly with fear that I told her to come to my room.

Not one pair of feet obeyed the summons, but two. Three-year-old Dana sat on the bed beside me too. She wanted to know what was wrong "wit Nickie." I told her she was frightened.

"Jesus will take care of her," she consoled sleepily.

That bit of wee wisdom was all that I needed. I encouraged Nickie to pray. She brushed away a tear and started. "Dear Jesus, please don't let me think about Satan." Barely off her knees, she blurted out, "Mama, I'm still thinking about it."

I assured her everything would be all right, and just as I put them to bed for the second time that night my friend Bernie arrived with her two daughters. Reneé and Simone were nearly the same age as Nickie. They fell into each other's arms, giggling and squealing.

Bernie apologized for coming over so late. For some reason she was unable to shake the urge to come by directly after the evangelistic meeting.

Later Nickie giggled herself to sleep. God had sent special friends to take her mind off unpleasant thoughts and fill it with happy memories.

I knew that by impressing Bernie to stop by, God had answered Nickie's prayer before she even got on her knees.

ETHEL FOOTMAN SMOTHERS

GOD'S PUSH

Come to me, all you who are weary and burdened, and I will give you rest. Take my yoke upon you and learn from me, for I am gentle and humble in heart, and you will find rest for your souls. For my yoke is easy and my burden is light. Matt. 11:28-30, NIV.

I do a lot of backpacking with the kids from the school in Australia where I work as a volunteer. The seemingly endless energy of these teenagers amazes me. Although they use up much energy singing at the top of their lungs as they walk along the trail, they run up the hills that I struggle to climb. Their endurance makes me feel old as I trudge along behind, trying to keep up.

On one particular hike the trail wasn't excessively steep, but there were a few steady climbs and, as usual, I lagged behind on the hills. After lunch Sonja walked behind me as whip (the person designated to take up the rear).

As we were climbing a hill, suddenly my pack felt lighter. My feet picked up speed, for my burden was lifted. I felt as if I were flying up the hill. Sonia was pushing me! She said it was easier for her because she could lean forward as she climbed. I don't know if this was true, but it surely made it easier for me. I was so thankful that she was willing to help me carry my load. She said she enjoyed helping me.

God invites us to come to Him when we're weary and burdened. He says that if we take His yoke, our burden will become lighter as we share the load with Him. Although the purpose of a yoke is to carry burdens, when we take His yoke, He carries the burden. When we need a push, He is behind us to give it, and He will keep us from falling. It may not be easier for Him, but He always delights in helping us. Now is the time to bring our heavy loads and let our Burden Bearer carry them for us. He has promised to give us rest.

Lord, thank You for the gentle pushes that You give me. Help me to surrender my load to You. And today may I also be helpful in lifting someone else's heavy burden. HEIDI MICHELLE EHLERT

THE LOCKED DOOR

You should not pass judgment on anyone before the right time comes. 1 Cor. 4:5, TEV.

At 8:30 a family group met regularly for a little prayer meeting before church, and I joined them as often as I could. Usually I would be a couple minutes late.

One particular morning I had a Bible lesson to prepare, as well as the children's story for the worship hour. The weather was nasty, and by the time I arrived it was 8:40. The door of the room where we were to meet was locked. My reaction was both hurt and anger. But in the lesson I had just prepared, I had focused on feelings. We have a right to our feelings, I had planned to say. To have feelings is not sin. It's what we do about our feelings that matters.

You came to pray, I told myself, *now do that.* I went into the sanctuary and knelt in the empty room. First came feelings of self-pity. *I worked on my lesson, and now I'm not welcome in their prayer meeting,* I thought. But the Lord showed me I wasn't to pity myself. *Perhaps they felt it was not reverent to be interrupted while they were on their knees.* That was understandable. I explored my own responsibility.

By this time I had gotten my thinking in order and my emotions in hand. Now I could pray for people as we always did together in these early-morning meetings. When I rose from my knees I was at peace. Sitting in the still-empty sanctuary, I reread my children's story.

"Ruth?" a man's quiet voice questioned.

"Yes?"

"Did you come and find the door locked?"

"Yes."

"I am so sorry. Justin locked the door, and we didn't realize it. You know how little ones are, always into something. We certainly didn't want you to feel we were being exclusive."

Such a simple, reasonable explanation!

How often we assign to others unkind motives or behaviors that have no basis in fact. Is it not more charitable and less stressful for us to withhold judgment and let time bring the answers?   RUTH ANNEKE

PERFECT LOVE CASTETH OUT FEAR

Behold, what manner of love the Father hath bestowed upon us, that we should be called the sons of God. 1 John 3:1. Beloved, if God so loved us, we ought also to love one another. 1 John 4:11.

Today I met Edna. She sat on the edge of her hospital bed, swinging her legs back and forth, chuckling to herself. One eye had a patch over it, the other twinkled mischievously. In her hand she clutched Filmore, a stuffed mouse.

"You're my friend, aren't you?" she asked with a little nod. With my assuring "Of course I am," she resumed her leg-swinging.

Suddenly, without warning, she began to sob. The sobs grew louder and more intense. I got out of my bed and went to her. "Edna, what's wrong? Why are you crying?" It took some comforting, but finally we convinced her that four friends were sleeping in her room and that none of us would leave her.

When the nurse came in to take temperatures, Edna bounced on her bed with excitement. "Mommy," as she called the nurse, let her get up and walk with her if she agreed to be a good little girl. She jumped and skipped a little as a 3-year-old would, but Edna's 3-year-old mind resided in a 57-year-old body. In the hospital for cataract surgery, she would soon be returning to her institutional home, where once again she would be "too lonesome."

As I lay there I thought about Edna. If sin had not overtaken our world, she would be a happy 57-year-old grandmother. But her mind and body had been marred.

As the Father and His Son look in pity on this sin-sick world, on us, the beings they created to be so much like them, do we appear as "Ednas," having 57-year-old bodies with 3-year-old minds?

And then the magnitude of God's love began to seep through my thinking. At first Edna was difficult to love. But as I saw her innocence, her perfect trust, I began to see how our Father loves us. He understands our weaknesses, our infirmities, our childishness, but His love never changes. His love is so great that He gave His Son so that we poor, degraded beings need not be degraded forever. Praise God for a love like that, for the hope we have of rising above this life! JEAN REIFFENSTEIN ROTHGEB

MY PRIORITIES ARE IN GOD'S HANDS!

I will give them a singleness of heart and action. Jer. 32:39, NIV.

I am one of millions of people who commute to work five days a week. Most of them seem to use the same roads I do. While creeping along the same route in all kinds of weather, I have become a curious license plate observer. One of my West Coast friends refers to these special license plates that bear individuals' names, favorite sports, initials, and nicknames as "vanity plates."

One morning as I made my way along the familiar route, I was especially burdened by a list of "to do's" as long as my arm. Again and again I reorganized the list, each time coming to the same conclusion— there was more than I could accomplish in a day. And too many of the tasks had reached their deadlines. Just when I was about to admit to being overwhelmed, my eyes came to rest on the license plate on the car in front of me. It read "PR4PWR."

Thank You, Lord, I breathed with a sigh of relief. Thank You for reminding me that You are the only one who can prioritize my day. I will do just what the license plate reminded me to do. I'll "PR4PWR," and You will keep Your promise to give me a "singleness of heart and action."

One Christian writer describes our life energy as a pitcher of clear water that only we can decide how we will spill. We can choose to spill ourselves indiscriminately across a vast field, a dribble here and a dribble there, not making any real measurable difference. Or we can invite the Holy Spirit to place His hand over ours and show us where and when to spill ourselves today. I'm excited about a heavenly Father who speaks to me in creative ways, even through a vanity license plate on a busy day, and who reminds me of where my power comes from.

I am dangerous when left alone. I was born without a governor. I need the Holy Spirit's hand on mine as I lift my pitcher and spill myself today. How about you?

Father, keep me focused today by giving me the singleness of heart and action that You have promised. ROSE OTIS

PRESS ON!

The sins of some people are plain to see, and their sins go ahead of them to judgment. 1 Tim. 5:24, TEV. But now you have been set free from sin. . . . Your gain is a life fully dedicated to him, and the result is eternal life. Rom. 6:22, TEV.

OK, I admit it; I'm an ironer. I have a reputation for ironing almost everything. I'm not a fanatic, but I do enjoy wrinkle-free clothes. Not only do I like the pressed look; I actually enjoy the ironing process. I enjoy the feel of the iron handle in the palm of my hand, so smooth and firm. Ironing time can be a time of introspection, of reviewing and planning.

I have my favorite shirt on the board. I have ironed it many times before. How can it be wrinkled again? Can't I just press this thing once and be done with it? I'll even use a little spray starch so I won't have to iron it again.

Does God ever feel that way about me? Every day I come to Him all wrinkled again. *Yes, Lord, I'm the one with the perpetually folded and creased cuffs and collar. Please help me.* Once again He steams and presses me, prepares me for another day, knowing that tomorrow I will be creased and wrinkled again. But that's all right. I'm one of His favorites. He wants to perfect and crisp me up for His service.

When I was young, my mother showed me the proper order and procedure for ironing, over and over: "Iron the collar and shirt front last, because if you press it first, it will be wrinkled and mussed by the time you finish the arms and back." "What if I just iron the parts that people see?" I would ask. Then she would remind me that the rest of the garment needed to be pressed in case the sweater or jacket should be taken off.

In our Christian life we can do the same thing. We can spend our lives "pressing" and perfecting what people see; we can be ever so proud of the "ironing" job that we have accomplished by ourselves. No help required. But there will come a time in every life when the jacket comes off. To reveal what? A daily relationship with Jesus? A daily refreshing from His Word? A strong prayer life and an unwavering faith, or just a wrinkled back and sleeves?

I look forward to heaven, where I will have a wrinkle-free robe of light and the developed character of Jesus that will rival even the finest of permanent press.

SARAH COON

MY FATHER'S EYES

I and the Father are one. John 10:30, NIV.

I was fixing my mother's hair, a role I had had since I was a teenager. I have washed, rolled, cut, and colored her hair more times than I can remember.

"Mom," I asked, "did Dad ever wonder what color hair you were going to have when he came home from work?"

"Yes," she answered with a laugh. "And it was especially interesting that day my hair turned green! Remember?"

As I was putting the finishing touches on her hair that morning she looked at me thoughtfully and said, "You have your father's eyes."

I had never thought about having my dad's eyes. It was especially meaningful for me to hear it because my dad had died only three weeks before. Now I felt that I still had a part of him with me, and I felt very special.

The thought of having my father's eyes stayed with me for quite a while. As I drove to work, I would glance at my eyes in the rearview mirror and think, *I wonder what Daddy thought about as he drove to work. I wonder what Daddy was doing at my age. I wonder what Daddy would do in this situation.* My eyes had become a visual reminder of my dad.

I couldn't help thinking, too, about my heavenly Father. He created me in His image, and I am very special. But when those in the world see me, a Christian, do they see a reflection of the One whose I claim to be? Do I treat people as He does? Do I look at them through my Father's eyes—eyes of compassion, love, and understanding? Eyes that see beyond my expectations to their abilities? Eyes that see beyond a person's behavior to his or her needs? Jesus said, "I and my Father are one" (John 10:30). Oh, how I want to be one with my heavenly Father and view the world through eyes like His!

I am still working on giving my will to my heavenly Father each day so I can continually see others with His eyes. And I hope people will see my Father's eyes in me.

BONITA J. SHIELDS

MENDING TIME

A merry heart doeth good like a medicine: but a broken spirit drieth the bones. Prov. 17:22.

I enjoy my friend Diane. I have visited with her often through the years, and we shared the joys of motherhood. How I always marveled at her energy and efficiency. Her house was exceptionally well cared for, the yard and gardens were well groomed. She trained her seven children well and encouraged them as they worked with her. Each spring she faithfully worked in the fields, driving machinery that seemed much too large for her small body to handle.

Every time I see her she is bubbly and happy, ready to share a smile and a laugh. Complaining is not a part of her personality. Hard work never fazes her.

Wanting her children and family always to be well dressed, she took special care to wash, iron, and mend their clothes. One time when her middle daughter came home from college with her laundry, mother Diane quickly washed and mended it.

"Mother!" the daughter cried as she came out of her bedroom, holding her precious jeans, jeans of the latest style—full of holes. Or rather, they *had* been full of holes. Mother had patiently mended every hole!

We smiled and had a good laugh as she shared the story with me. I still feel the happiness and joy we shared over that experience.

Women need to find someone to share laughter and joy with. The medical community is quick to tell us of the benefits of laughter. Laughter shared will mend many a broken relationship. It is difficult to remain estranged when you can laugh together.

A merry heart does us so much good. We have a greater appreciation for our family and friends when our hearts are merry. Our countenance is able to reflect the love of Jesus when we are happy. Our health will be enhanced because we have a merry spirit. To avoid dry bones we need to choose to be like Diane—happy, cheerful, and full of joy. When we laugh at the little things in life, we will be better persons.

A merry heart—that's what I need today. I need the medicine of Your love and hope in my heart so that life will be more pleasant for those around me.

EVELYN GLASS

FOR WOMEN WHO'VE FALLEN AND CAN'T GET UP

You will be secure, because there is hope. Job 11:18, NIV.

One morning a friend called to ask for the name and phone number of a Christian counselor I had been seeing. I was getting ready for work and couldn't talk long, but I could tell immediately that things weren't going well. I passed on the information, praying that she would follow up and find the sympathy and direction she needed.

The next day I phoned my friend to ask how her day had gone. She said she was feeling better. The counselor had helped her to see that she needed nurturing. After caring for her patients, children, husband, and church members, she deserved to have her needs taken care of too. She needed to take time for herself. She needed to be able to accept help and special deeds from others. The counselor helped her to see life from a different perspective.

The same counselor has helped me in many ways. When I first went there, I cried for most of the session. I felt safe there, sure I wouldn't be criticized for being too emotional, wouldn't be called a wimp for crying. My makeup could run, but shame wasn't even an issue. My counselor emulated Jesus by listening, speaking words of hope, and praying with me. She put me in touch with the Healer.

Sharing with someone who understands is so comforting and freeing, like a mental massage. My "mind muscles" relax, and for a few minutes out of a busy, stressful week I can sit still and talk a while with someone who listens attentively. I can even finish whole thoughts without being interrupted! Sometimes in the process of speaking about my situation I find the answers I am seeking.

Are you feeling heavy laden, wound up, or worn down? A talk with God can make all the difference. Give yourself the gift of being heard and understood. Trust Him with your big and little concerns today, and you will be secure. If you have fallen and can't get up, there is hope.

I need to talk, Father. I need to tell You about my hopes and dreams, about my feelings. It feels so good to know that You love me no matter what I tell You, that You always listen. Bless me, I pray, so that today will be a good day.

DONNA DAVIS CAMERON

HOLDING OUR BROTHER'S HAND

Jesus called a little child to him and stood the child before his followers. Then he said, "I tell you the truth, you must change and become like little children. Otherwise, you will never enter the kingdom of heaven. The greatest person in the kingdom of heaven is the one who makes himself humble like this child."
Matt. 18:2-4, NCV.

My sister, who is much younger than I, is still a little girl. When she was even younger, she thought I was the absolute best and wanted to do everything like her "sissie." She still looks up to me as something pretty special. Sometimes it is a hard profile to live up to.

Like most toddlers, when she learned to walk she no longer wanted to be carried; she wanted to walk everywhere. As a general rule, she had to hold my hand when we went places together. But many times she would resist this, as she wanted to run free and explore. However, when she was given the choice of staying home or going for a walk hand in hand, she usually chose the latter.

Now she is older and doesn't have to hold my hand everywhere we go. But when crossing the street she willingly puts her hand in mine and trusts me to get us safely to the other side.

God tells us that to enter the kingdom of heaven we must become like little children. Humble adoration and trust in our Big Brother are the things that will lead us there. Daily we need to look up to our Older Brother, copying the things He does.

Many times we want to go our own way and explore the world. It seems that only at the crossroads of crisis do we reach up and take His hand, trusting Him to get us through. How much smoother our lives might be if we held His hand all the way! Where there's a hill, He can pull us up. He can see the invisible dangers that might harm us. He will hold and guide us, even through the darkest night.

I'm reaching up with my hand this morning, Lord. Hold my hand tightly. I need Your guidance through the day. Only You have the experience to guide me. I want to become more like You. HEIDI MICHELLE EHLERT

STUCK IN THE MUD

You listened and pulled me from a lonely pit full of mud and mire.
You let me stand on a rock with my feet firm. Ps. 40:1, 2, CEV.

As a first grader, I had such fun walking to and from school with my friend David. Often we would take the shortcut across a softball field in a city park directly across the street from where I lived. We had been warned not to walk across the field when it rained, because it would be too muddy.

One day, however, as torrential rains poured down and gusty winds blew, we left school and headed home. We made our way past the rippling brook and the woods near the softball field. David stepped into the area near second base and was starting to walk toward first. I was near second base. I attempted to catch up with David, but as I tried to lift one foot and then the other, I realized I was stuck in the mud. David, too, was having great difficulty trying to walk.

The usually dusty soil of the playing field was now an expanse of sandy mud, thick and heavy. No matter how we tried, we couldn't move. Lunch pails, book bags, and school papers were all practically swallowed up as one by one we dropped them. Slowly we were sinking deeper and deeper, and soon we were up to our knees in mud. Our yellow raincoats and black galoshes were caked with globs of the stuff.

I knew I was in big trouble for disobeying, and I was sure David was too; but we had no time to worry about that right then. We simply wanted to be rescued, but no one was in sight. Frightened out of our wits, we cried and cried for help.

Then, out of nowhere, someone was lifting me up and placing me firmly on the grass. Then that someone lifted David up and placed him firmly on the grass. Finally we were safe.

That someone was Mother, who had seen our predicament and had come to our rescue.

"You listened and pulled me from a lonely pit full of mud and mire. You let me stand on a rock with my feet firm."

Thank You, Lord, for hearing my cries and for lifting me out of the miry clay of sin and planting my feet on solid ground. IRIS L. STOVALL

A MYSTERY SOLVED

Be sure your sin will find you out. Num. 32:23.

As a child, I always wanted to open the new box of cereal after returning from grocery shopping with my mother. I would daydream about that first spoonful of crunchy, honey-flavored cereal, fresh from the box. I would think about how good it would smell and how good it would taste.

No matter how much I whined and pleaded, however, Mother insisted that I eat what was left of the old cereal before opening the new box. One day I mapped out a plan of action. I found the largest bowl in the kitchen, poured what was left of the old cereal into it, added sugar and milk, and sat down to eat. It really didn't look like a lot when dry, but soon it practically doubled.

It was more than my 7-year-old stomach could handle. Realizing my predicament, I began to think of ways to dispose of the cereal. I couldn't flush it down the toilet, for I had to pass my mother to get to the bathroom. I couldn't put it in the trash for fear my mother would discover it. So I did the next best thing. I dumped it behind the refrigerator.

When my mother saw the empty bowl, she couldn't believe I had eaten all the cereal and still had room for the new cereal. As promised, she let me have a small bowl of the new cereal. Yes! I had done it! I was delighted and well pleased with myself. I had deceived my mother!

Several months passed. It was spring, and Mother was conducting a total cleaning of the kitchen, which meant that every appliance was moved. As she began cleaning behind the refrigerator, she came across something strange. Carefully examining it, she summoned me to come immediately. I could tell by the tone of her voice and the look on her face that she had discovered my secret. I had to pay the consequences, for even though my mother loved me dearly, she showed me my erring ways by disciplining me.

When the day of judgment comes, our secrets, both good and bad, will be publicly proclaimed. The record will be there for all to read. Our heavenly Father gently guides us too, and when we go wrong, He corrects us because He loves us.

ARNITA REID

STORED TREASURES

Store up for yourselves treasures in heaven, where moth and rust do not destroy, and where thieves do not break in and steal. Matt. 6:20, NIV.

When I accepted a job in San Francisco there were so many uncertainties about moving to a large city. I didn't know if I'd share an apartment with others, rent a solo studio, or rent a room in a house with a family. This made it difficult to plan which household items and kitchen utensils to pack. California is much warmer than Michigan, but since the Bay Area is known for its damp, windy days, I wasn't sure which clothes to take.

Packing proved to be more emotion-laden than I'd expected. Since I couldn't afford a moving van, I had to fit all the belongings I'd need into the trunk of my car. I soon realized I couldn't possibly bring all I wanted and would have to start choosing.

The last weeks before I left presented agonizing choices between the practical things I needed and the sentimental objects I treasured. The Japanese china, gifts from students I had taught, or the functional fan for hot days? Sketches of English cathedrals that warmed my heart with memories of my travels there, or the rice cooker for the kitchen?

Utensils, appliances, books, clothes—I evaluated and prioritized every item in my life. Different objects took on more importance than I would have expected; I stored or tossed others that I had previously valued.

In the end I threw away, sold, or stored more than I had ever thought I could live without. I also compromised and mailed two boxes separately to meet me when I got there. But the impact of prioritizing the "stuff" in my life did not go away. I realized how much time, energy, and money I waste on earthly treasures, things I can't take with me, or would even care to, when I relocate to God's city someday. He has commanded me to travel lightly here and to store in heaven the incorruptible things that really matter.

Few will ever have to pack all their possessions in the trunk of a car as I did, but all of us need to evaluate what kind of treasure we're accumulating.

Lord, guide me in my choices today. KATHRYN GORDON

IN CONTROL

The human mind plans the way, but the Lord directs the steps.
Prov. 16:9, NRSV.

I handed the airline boarding pass to the agent. The instant she put it through the scanner I knew something was wrong. But what?

It had already been a long and stressful day, starting at 4:30 that morning. There already had been customs checks, passport checks, and rechecking baggage in one country. Now Miami—and customs again. Finally I found where to recheck my luggage. Then I was off to find which gate for Flight 2120.

As I ran through the terminal I wondered how there could be so many people who did not seem to be in a hurry. There it was—E-2. But the marquee listed Newark, not Washington's Reagan National. I checked the TV console behind me. No Flight 2120 to Reagan National listed. There were about 10 people ahead of me, waiting to check in at the gate, and time was running short. *God*, I said, *You are in control. Please. You know I can do nothing about the situation. You are going to have to take care of things.* It was beginning to be a familiar refrain from me, and I knew God would recognize it. *And please keep me calm and sweet.* Now that might be the hardest request of all.

As I stepped up to the counter I asked, "Does this flight go to Reagan National?"

"Yes, it does," the agent assured me as he issued a boarding pass. So when the flight was called a few minutes later, I stepped into line with confidence. And now there was a problem.

"Flight 2120 does not go to Reagan. It goes to Newark. Your flight is 2126," the agent told me firmly. "Check again at the desk."

"But the agent told me—" I began. Numb and stunned, I stared at the ticket. Then I saw something else. The boarding pass said Gate E-4. It couldn't be far, so I started to run. As I ran into the gate area they were making the last call for Flight 2126.

As I collapsed into my seat I looked again. Yes, my itinerary said Flight 2120, but the boarding pass said 2126. Both flights departed at the same time. But 2126 went to Washington.

God, You really were in control this time, because just about everyone else was wrong. Thank You so much! Please take control of all aspects of my life.

ARDIS DICK STENBAKKEN

A NEW LIFE FOR SONIE

Those who hope in the Lord will renew their strength. They will soar on wings like eagles; they will run and not grow weary, they will walk and not be faint. Isa. 40:31, NIV.

Sonie, a slightly built 15-year-old, had the most intense blue eyes I had ever seen. But the pain I saw reflected in them was hard to understand. How could God allow this just-starting-to-live teen to go through this grievous trial?

It had started with numbness and pain in her legs. My tests later revealed a dreaded diagnosis—multiple sclerosis. (MS is the more familiar term.) It was severe and quickly progressive.

The many prayers for her healing were not ignored, for God knew He could depend on this child. He knew what a picture of His love she would show. Sonie is now a 28-year-old woman with the same inspiring, trustful, blue eyes. She is a joy to everyone she meets. Whether "marching" down the aisle at her graduation on the arms of two strong young men (she was honored with a standing ovation), "marching" down the aisle on her father's arm at her outdoor wedding, or sitting in her wheelchair in the narthex of the church, she always has that same infectious smile that mists my eyes. One cannot spend time with Sonie without seeing her love for Jesus.

She has a priceless husband who never hesitates to be helpful to her in any way he can. It is beautiful to see him lift her easily in and out of her wheelchair. It has been difficult for her to accept the disappointment of not being able to have the family she had always dreamed of, but her own family loves her very much, and so does her church family; this gives her much happiness. And she has pets that her sweet husband feeds and cares for so she can have the luxury of their company.

I am eager for Jesus to come, and Sonie is too. Then she will "walk and not faint." We will finally run through the green grass and laugh and talk. I can imagine her "mothering" all the little ones who are there. That day is not far away. In the meantime, my friend will continue to show me how to love, what courage really is, and how much Jesus loves all of us. Her hope in the Lord is strong. How's yours?   JEAN REIFFENSTEIN ROTHGEB

THE REWARD

My God shall supply all your need according to his riches in glory by Christ Jesus. Phil. 4:19.

Because of a recession and home renovations, our financial resources were depleted. Each month our budget was stretched to meet many expenses. There was no money for the perm my hair needed so badly.

One Friday afternoon as a car pulled out of a parking lot, I noticed that the driver had left her handbag on the ground. When honking my horn failed to get her attention, I raced to collect the handbag and followed the car. Because the traffic lights hindered my progress, the car soon disappeared.

At home I checked the woman's handbag for identification. Her place of employment was given, but when I called, no one answered. Her home address was listed without a telephone number. The telephone operator confirmed that the number was unpublished.

I was able to track down the woman's husband, whom I knew only by reputation. Not long after my call, the woman arrived at my house to collect her handbag, which she had not even missed!

Monday morning I was again in the parking lot. The woman whose handbag I had recovered was speaking to her husband and pointing to me. Suddenly the husband was standing by my car window saying, "It was nice of you to retrieve my wife's handbag. We were so relieved that nothing was missing. My wife had plane tickets and other valuables in her handbag. You have been so kind; I would like to give you a reward!"

I protested vigorously, but he continued, "Here is my card. I would like to give you a free hairdo—anything you want done. Please call and arrange an appointment."

Recognizing the man as one of the most renowned hairdressers, I changed my tune and excitedly accepted his card. "Praise the Lord!" I exclaimed. "You have answered one of my prayers. Thank you!"

In my car I had a glorious prayer-and-praise service, thanking God for showing me that "our heavenly Father has a thousand ways to provide for us, of which we know nothing." *

BETTY ANNE LOWE

---

* Ellen G. White, *The Desire of Ages*, p. 330.

SUE'S TRAP

However you want people to treat you, so treat them, for this is the Law and the Prophets. Matt. 7:12, NASB.

Sue, our 5-year-old, was playing with Jack in the yard behind our building. Sarah Ann, who lived in the same building as Jack and usually played with them, was not welcome this morning, and Jack and Sue had told her so. She still wanted to play with them, however.

Knowing that Sarah Ann would come to their playhouse while they were gone for lunch and rest time, Jack and Sue decided to set a trap for her so she wouldn't bother them.

It was a simple trap: a string stretched out about eight inches above the ground between two trees near the door to their playhouse. They hoped that as Sarah Ann hurried to the playhouse she wouldn't see the twine and would trip over it, hurting herself. Maybe then she would stay away.

When Sue came in for lunch she told me all about it.

"That's not kind, Sue," I remonstrated. "Shouldn't you go out and take that string away?"

I reminded her that people often fall into the very traps they set for others and get hurt. But Sue was determined that the trap should remain, in spite of my warning. So I thought, *OK, we'll see what happens.* After lunch and rest time Sue, forgetting all about the trap, ran out to play with Jack. She tripped across the twine and fell forward. Looking out the window, I saw her sprawled in front of the playhouse, caught by her own trap.

As she came in to me, crying, she realized the truth of my warning, one of life's valuable lessons: Whoever sets a trap for someone else very often falls into it herself. Fortunately, she learned her lesson early and without great injury.

For all of us, young or old, this lesson really means that by practicing the golden rule we can avoid many pitfalls and heartaches. If we learn by precept and example, we can be spared many painful experiences.

Father, help us today to grow in grace and in the knowledge of our dear Saviour.   MAE E. WALLENKAMPF

FORGIVE

"It is mine to avenge; I will repay," says the Lord. Rom. 12:19, NIV.

The sensation was every bit as strong as it had been decades ago. How could that be? In the midst of a lecture tour I had taken a detour to do some family-of-origin work. The house was still standing, although everything looked so much smaller. The owners graciously permitted me to wander through the rooms and reminisce. Emotions nearly overwhelmed me in the doorway of the ugly incident room.

Over the years, whenever the memory had surfaced, I had bravely told myself *it only happened once. It can't have affected me much.* Wrong. The intensity of feeling was proof of that.

Returning home, I embarked on serious grief recovery work. Sharing with my two sisters-of-choice, I rehearsed the incident, looked at it with adult eyes, let go of any blame toward myself (a child cannot protect a child), cried tears of pain and frustration, and congratulated myself for the progress I was making—until I crashed headlong against the concept of forgiveness. I'm not the type to waste energy hanging on to a grudge, but suddenly the reality of trying to forgive the individual who had caused me so much pain was anathema.

Fortunately, God always makes provision for our weakness. Unexpectedly, I was invited to participate on a panel discussion about recovery and, wouldn't you know, we were asked a question about forgiveness. One of the other panel members responded immediately by saying, "Avoid confusing God's forgiveness with your role. All you have to do is give up your right to have the other person pay for what was done to you."

For the next few seconds I was oblivious to everything around me as I internally processed her definition of forgiveness. *I can do that,* I told myself. And right there on the platform, I did just that.

Immediately I felt a surge of energy, along with the recognition of how much it had required to keep the lid on that experience. How freeing to have stumbled through the last piece in my healing process—forgiveness.

Is there something in your life that you find hard to forgive? You can give up your right to have the person pay for the hurt you experienced—and leave God's forgiveness to God.

ARLENE TAYLOR

WHEN VICIOUS DOGS DIDN'T BITE

He shall give his angels charge over thee, to keep thee in all thy ways. Ps. 91:11.

Magazine sales were brisk in the little "aluminum town" of Alcoa, Tennessee, that Sunday afternoon. A few houses behind my partner and me a flower vendor was knocking on doors.

"Bernice, if that lady gets ahead of us people will buy the flowers and may not have enough money left to buy magazines," I worried.

Quickening our pace, we turned the corner and continued our work. Finally we reached the last street of our assigned territory. Midway in the block, I unlatched a gate that led into a large yard. A huge German shepherd lay stretched out in front of the door. Breathing a prayer, I bravely ascended the steps onto the porch. The big dog, head between his paws, lay peeping at me out of one eye. I pressed the doorbell, watching the dog for any suspicious movements. A woman came to the door and stared at me as though she were seeing an apparition.

"How on earth did you get in here?" she whispered. She explained that the dog always barks and sometimes bites.

The dog rose to his feet and stood beside me, staring at his mistress. Musing about the dog's change of behavior, she bought a magazine. The dog walked to the edge of the porch and watched me leave, not growling once.

About five minutes later I heard loud vigorous barking. Looking back, I saw the same dog clawing at the fence to get out. The flower vendor had stopped there, but when the dog tried to climb over the gate, she ran.

As I was leaving the last house on my side of the street, I was surprised to see a large mixed-breed dog under the porch floor. Praying, I kept my eyes on him, but he didn't notice me. I walked to the corner and waited for Bernice. The flower vendor was working her way toward me. As she attempted to turn into the yard of the house I'd just left, the dog burst out from under the porch and growled ferociously. The woman, afraid to move, stood as though frozen.

Twice in less than 30 minutes God had given His angels charge over me. I'm sure He had a special reason for wanting those two families to have the magazine, because He dispatched an angel each time to "anesthetize" the dog so I was not harmed.

MABEL ROLLINS NORMAN

THE PRAYER THAT SAVED MY HUSBAND

The prayer of faith shall save the sick. James 5:15.

Two days after my husband, Danny, left on a trip to Abidjan, Ivory Coast, West Africa, I was informed that he had been admitted to the hospital with malaria. They told me he would be all right after he got quinine medication. I was worried. I prayed hard, or so I thought, and even asked several friends to pray for him. However, it seemed that nothing was happening. The medication didn't work. His fever was still high, and he felt very weak. I called the hospital every day, hoping to hear something positive. But almost a week passed, and there was still no progress.

I will not forget that evening. He had been in the hospital for more than a week and was still very sick. I called at midnight my time and was informed that he was no better than when admitted. The doctor was worried. When I talked to Danny, I felt his fear of the unknown. He was worried for me and the girls.

"Don't be discouraged," I said, "because tonight the Lord will answer our prayers. You will be out of the hospital tomorrow. Just have faith in Him." With those words I said my goodbye, good night, and I love you.

Lord, You know how discouraged my husband is, I prayed that night. *He is so far away from us and must be very lonely. You know the pain he is suffering, and You know that I am also on the verge of becoming discouraged. I am pleading, Father, please let this be the last night of his sickness; please take away the fever and make him well.* I had a peaceful sleep the rest of that night. In the morning I went to the office. During our devotional time, I was asked how Danny was faring. I confidently told the group that he was OK and should be getting out of the hospital.

About 10:00 Danny called and told me what had happened after we'd talked the night before. After I'd hung up the phone, he had started to perspire. His hospital gown was soaking wet; the hospital even used newspaper to dry him as they didn't have extra gowns. He told me that he then had a peaceful and restful sleep. And sure enough, he was discharged that day.

I believe it was our faith—and not the medication—that healed my husband that night. God is faithful in fulfilling His promises—all we have to do is trust Him.

JEMIMA D. ORILLOSA

A SHORTCUT

Then they willingly received him into the ship: and immediately the ship was at the land whither they went. John 6:21.

I came across a "tiny" miracle in my Bible one morning. It lay hidden away by miracles of greater magnitude, overshadowed by five loaves and two fish feeding 5,000-plus people. All four Gospels mention the miraculous feeding, but only John tacks on this little-noticed additional manifestation of Jesus' divinity: "They willingly received him into the ship: and immediately the ship was at the land whither they went."

The village in the Philippines where my mother once taught lay about six miles (10 kilometers) from the public highway. In those days transportation was a big problem, especially when she had to attend monthly teachers' meetings. So my father always accompanied her. One weekend the teachers' meeting took longer than usual. By the time my parents got off the last bus at the junction, darkness had fallen. Seven miles (11 kilometers) still lay ahead. Heavy rain clouds shut off all light from moon and stars. As they passed a cemetery, rain started to fall. My parents' superstition about spirits and the state of the dead only added fear to fatigue. In the rain and darkness they noticed weirdly colored lights approaching. My mother clung harder to my father's arm as the lights circled them. She knew that they were against something that a man's physical strength was no match for. In the total darkness they couldn't know where they were. Then my father started to sing a Christian hymn he had learned:

"Lead, kindly Light, amid the encircling gloom, lead Thou me on;
The night is dark, and I am far from home; lead Thou me on.
Keep Thou my feet; I do not ask to see
The distant scene; one step's enough for me."

The song expressed exactly their desperate helplessness and need at the moment. Suddenly a flash of lightning lit up the place. They were amazed, because they knew they hadn't walked far, but now they found themselves just outside the door of their home.

Looking back, they marvel that God helped them, even though they did not know Him well then. Recalling this event encourages me to know that with Jesus, I too will realize my objective.   BIENVISA LADION-NEBRES

GOD SUPPLIES OUR EVERY NEED

Every one that asketh receiveth; and he that seeketh findeth; and to him that knocketh it shall be opened. Matt. 7:8.

My minivan had almost 200,000 miles on it when the engine gave out. While I waited for my son to find time to change engines, I drove an extra car we had. But one day it started acting up, and then on the way home one day it caught fire. Despite the efforts of several people, the car was totaled.

Between the insurance money and the trade-in of my still motorless minivan, I was able to get a nice little Oldsmobile (the operative word being little). It was a nice car, but I missed my minivan. There wasn't enough room for taking grandchildren and my teen group places in this five-seat car.

I didn't want or need a car payment, so I asked the Lord to help me find another minivan. I felt impressed to find out what the loan value was on the car. It turned out to be $4,600. I then asked for a minivan for $4,600 and started looking. But all of them were $1,000 to $1,500 more than the price I could pay. Then one Friday my husband said he saw a nice-looking minivan that I should go look at.

On Sunday my daughters and I drove over to see it. It did look nice, and when I read on the window the price of $4,600, I turned to my daughters and said, "This is my minivan!" Right then I thanked God for providing it. After I looked it over and had my son try it out, we decided it was a good deal—it was basically a one-owner car with low mileage. I didn't try to dicker the price—I just told the owner that I wanted it. He said I could have it for $4,300, which was another blessing, leaving me enough for tax and plate transfer. I took out a 90-day note and drove home with my "new" minivan. I sold my car a few weeks later.

It was a marvelous experience, Lord. It boosted my faith. You did exactly as You said You would. I know once again that You care for us and help us with every need. I want to trust You with my wants and needs of this day too.

ANNE ELAINE NELSON

EVERY PERFECT GIFT

You didn't hold back. You filled his arms with gifts. . . . You pile blessings on him. Ps. 21:3-6, Message.

"Y̶ou got more than I did," my granddaughter complained to her mother, pouting, as she helped load Christmas presents for the trip home.

I thought back to the months of anticipation when I had carefully selected her gifts and stockpiled them until they overflowed the closet and spilled along the wall of my bedroom. Now she was going home, and more than half of what I had for her was still in my room, hidden away from view.

It wasn't that I wasn't aching to give her those treasures, to see her face light up, and to imagine her delight in exploring the wonders chosen with such loving care. But my granddaughter has an intermittent affliction common to many children. At times she can't enjoy any of what she has because there is simply too much. At those times she wants more and more, but barely glances at what she gets before racing on to the next package. After the "feeding frenzy," she tosses everything down and is either bored with it all or distraught that there isn't any more. It isn't that there was one certain thing she wanted and didn't get, or that under normal circumstances she wouldn't be enchanted with any one of the toys or games or books. It is just that there is too much stimulation for her, and the more she gets, the worse is her condition.

There is no way to tell that to a child, so I winked at her mother, secure in the knowledge that during the year, one at a time, when she was ready, she would receive and rejoice in the lovely things I yearned to give her.

As we hugged goodbye, I recalled moments in my life when I am sure that God longed to give me some prize but couldn't because my attitude or situation would have made it harmful at that time. When I have wanted something other than God, when all I could think about was wanting husband or child or some other good thing, God has had to withhold those special presents until I was able to receive them in a time and a way that they would be the blessing He intended. No doubt His treasure chests are overflowing with even more that He wants to give me, to give you, just as soon as we are ready.

HELENE RABENA HUBBARD

JOINING TOGETHER

I gave them the same glory you gave me, so that they may be one, just as you and I are one. John 17:22, TEV.

I was thrilled to catch the feral kitten living under my house. With an infected wound on his head and a large population of fleas, he desperately needed a friend. Instead of being grateful to the person who had saved his life, Gilead was hissing and angry. My love was the last thing he wanted. I decided to make him part of me. I tucked a large smock into my waistband to form a pouch and carried him around inside while I worked around the house. Safe next to the warmth of my body, he would purr and fall asleep.

Ten years later, he is still my best buddy. While the act of carrying him around lasted only a few days, we are joined together for life.

Just as the kitten became a part of me, the Communion service gives us all the opportunity to become a part of Christ. Sometimes we come to His table angry over life's disappointments. We come to His table frightened and sick at heart. We come to His table knowing that we are unworthy to sit in the King's presence. "Take, eat, this is My body," He says. With a yearning to belong to someone, we respond to His loving invitation.

When we join in the Communion service, we are in a very real sense becoming one with our Lord. But Communion doesn't end with a simple ritual any more than baptism ends once we come out of the water. Both acts are only symbols of striving for a greater goal: walking, working, and living in communion with Christ.

We cannot count ourselves as His followers unless we are willing to admit that we are incomplete in ourselves and that only He can make us whole. We humbly acknowledge the part our sins played in His death. By symbolically making Him a part of our bodies, we are affirming our desire to let the Lord dwell within, a true communion with our Master.

Yes, Lord, we want to be part of Your family. I want that daily communion with You, so close that we are joined together for life. GINA LEE

I NEED A VACATION

He said to them, "Come away by yourselves to a lonely place and rest a while." Mark 6:31, NASB.

I felt physically and emotionally spent. I was tired of being someone's wife, mother, daughter, relative, friend, senior work associate, and coworker, not to mention the many other hats I wore from being involved in various church activities. I was just plain tired. This list was short when compared to those of others I knew who, like me, were striving to be superachieving, superliberated, modern women. *When will there be time for just me?* I wondered. I felt that I was lost, if not abandoned, on the fringes of my busy, productive life.

I tossed and turned. The clock read 3:00 a.m. *Why waste the time?* I thought. *Since I'm not sleepy, let me at least be productive and start on my "to do" list for the day.* I had made it a practice to put worship first on my list to ensure that I wouldn't forget. *Lord,* I whispered as I sank wearily into the sofa in the other room, trying not to wake anyone, *I can't keep this up. Do You have a little time for a one-to-one talk?* But I really didn't know how or where to begin, or even what I wanted to say.

I decided to read the Bible passages I had jotted down through the years. I came across Mark 6:31. It spoke to me anew, especially the "come away" part, for I longed to do just that. Sure, I had allotted time for the formal routine of studying my Bible lesson and reading my morning devotional, but I hadn't "come away" with the Lord. He was offering me rejuvenation, direction, and the affirmation of His love that comes from simply meditating on Him and listening to Him, that is, worshiping.

I was so busy giving, going, and doing that my personal spiritual reservoir had run dry, and I hadn't even noticed. And so as I basked in the personal attention of my Lord, and as He opened my eyes and heart, I continued reading and meditating on additional passages of His Word. I felt the warmth of His love. I knew I could once again pick up the torch of daily life and go on.

Now every morning I practice a little unabashed selfishness as I leave everything and everyone behind for a minivacation with the Lord. I "come away" with Him and simply rest a while. MAXINE WILLIAMS ALLEN

DEPENDENCE DAY

I stand silently before the Lord, waiting for him to rescue me. For salvation comes from him alone. Ps. 62:1, TLB.

I don't like this text. It is not my nature to stand silently waiting for someone to rescue me. From the time I could talk I was stamping my little foot and saying, "No! I want to do it myself!"

Independence is part of my nature—not dependence. I have never wanted to depend on anyone for anything. I worked hard selling religious books for eight years to earn my way through high school and college. I would do without before asking someone for help. I've walked many miles in freezing weather rather than ask someone for a ride. I have stayed up all night to get a job done by myself rather than ask someone to assist me.

I have prided myself in my ability to get things done without help. I've figured out how to move furniture around in the house by myself. I've even succeeded in moving the piano several times and rejoiced in my independence. I've always insisted on carrying my own luggage on a trip. I was self-sufficient until October 9, 1998, my Dependence Day. That was the day I had hip surgery, the day I had to learn to be dependent.

I had to depend on a walker for support. I began to let Ron bring me water instead of struggling to the kitchen myself. I learned to ask for help with my groceries. I asked for a wheelchair at the airport. I even let my husband do the washing when he offered!

Ron has been wonderful. The day I asked him to move a chair that was in my way, he cheerfully said, "What a pleasure it is to have my wife actually ask me to do something for her!"

However, it was not a pleasure for me. Each time I asked someone to help was an exercise in humility. I found it a great trial to depend on others. After Ron's remark, I spent some time dealing with my lifelong independence issues.

I like being in the driver's seat of my life. My surgery made me feel out of control, and I had no choice but to depend on others and to depend on God more fully than I had ever before. But I do believe He's happy about my new dependence on Him. When I cry out to Him for help, I can almost hear Him whisper, "I'm so pleased! My daughter is actually asking Me to do something for her!"

DOROTHY EATON WATTS

A SMALL MIRACLE

I will sing to the Lord, for he has been good to me. Ps. 13:6, NIV.

Have you ever been close to a miracle? Really close? I stood inches from mine and gazed in wonder. And no, it wasn't a private one that only I was aware of. Anyone passing by could see it—it was in my yard, outside my front door.

We lived down a gravelly lane. A short drive, also gravel, led up to our home. Where the drive met the lane, there was quite a rut, which jolted us when we drove over it. Some folk nearby had had their drive surfaced with tarmac. There was some left over in a pile, there for the taking, and we could see a use for it. We raked the lower section of our drive clean and spread the leftover tarmac on it and over the rut. We smoothed it off nicely and it dried, as tarmac does, hard and black.

Early one spring morning, about a year later, I was looking out our bedroom window and spotted something bright yellow at the end of the drive. Yellow against black, it was easy to see. Curious, I went to investigate. It wasn't *on* the drive, it was growing *in* it. A golden yellow crocus had burst fearlessly and perfectly through several inches of tarmac and was now gleaming in the sunlight. There it stood, erect in its alien environment. I felt a bit like the two disciples after the Emmaus road experience as I ran back into the house with news of our small miracle.

As we traveled to school and to work, one of us would call out as my husband backed down the drive, "Mind the crocus!" It was very precious.

The hymn that says "I sing the mighty power of God, that made the mountains rise" has always been a favorite of mine. I believe that He sends small miracles to remind us that our Creator God is just the same today.

Do you wonder that "I will sing to the Lord, for He has been good to me"?

Thank You for the miracle that You sent for all to see. Now help me this day to look for more miracles, some perhaps not so obvious. But I thank You for all of them.

PEGGY MASON

GIVE UP YOUR BURDENS

Come to me, all who labor and are heavy laden, and I will give you rest. Take my yoke upon you, and learn from me; for I am gentle and lowly in heart, and you will find rest for your souls. For my yoke is easy, and my burden is light. Matt. 11:28-30, RSV.

There is no more important, demanding, fulfilling, stressful, or rewarding job than the one we women have. But the laundry is never done. The house never stays clean. There is always another meal to prepare. There's yet another book to read aloud, a kiss and a hug to give, or a drink of water to get at bedtime. Even when the children are in bed, we are planning, studying, or catching up on the work. Many of us have jobs, are students, or have a home business or ministry besides. Most of us are busy with church activities. Those of us who are married are also striving to be good wives and support our husbands in their endeavors. Then there's always something we'd like to do for ourselves—read a book, take a walk, write a story. Everywhere there are things that we should be doing.

These all add up to a big burden. We've chosen it and we love it, but it is sometimes overwhelming. We can rejoice in all our duties, because we were chosen for this rewarding position of being women.

Has this prestigious position become burdensome to you? Some even may be facing burnout. Jesus promised in our text for today that if we take His yoke, it will be easy, and His burden will be light. We are not carrying this burden alone.

What are our burdens? Self, a strong will, children, spouse, business, ideas, plans, ministry, and expectations—anything not given to us by God can be a burden. Take all these burdens to Jesus. Give all of them to Him.

So how do we give up our burdens and our will? By becoming disciples of Jesus. By spending time with Him every day in Bible study and prayer. We need to give ourselves to Him and then listen quietly for His voice.

When we surrender our self-made burdens to Jesus, He will sort them all out and return a lighter, God-given burden, one suited just for us, God's real plan for us. Then we can praise and thank God for choosing us for the ministry He has chosen for us. (See 1 Timothy 1:12.)

JUDY MUSGRAVE SHEWMAKE

THE MULBERRY TREE

There is hope of a tree, if it be cut down, that it will sprout again, and that the tender branch thereof will not cease. Job 14:7.

As my husband, Andy, was planting a scrawny cutting from a mulberry tree, I wondered silently if it would grow, much less produce juicy mulberries. To my surprise, dark leaves started to roll out like miniature awnings. When the first mulberry appeared, it looked like a fuzzy white caterpillar. Then as it ripened, its color changed to shades of pinks and purples. But when it was fully ripe, the color was almost black.

As time passed, I realized why Andy had planted the little twig smack-dab in the middle of our backyard. The tree made the most beautiful canopy and provided a haven for the birds that came to feast on the berries. In the late summer we noticed patches of webs made by bag worms. As the leaves curled up, the tree acquired a haunted look; but each spring the new foliage showed no signs of the bag worms.

There was such an abundance of mulberries that we could not give them away fast enough to keep the ground clear of the purple globs. We couldn't even get close to the tree without having to spend a lot of time scraping and scrubbing our shoes.

It was a hard decision to cut the tree down, especially for Andy, who had been its only care giver. With ax in hand, he spent two weeks trying to cut through roots that were the size of a muscle man's upper arm. Finally, when the trunk was detached from the rest of its root system, it was so heavy it had to be hoisted out of the hole. I requested that it be rolled over to my garden so I could use it as a plant stand.

To our amazement, in no time the severed trunk was sprouting new limbs, and two little mulberries appeared. When we tried to remove the trunk from the garden, it was anchored solid once again.

We need to be like that old mulberry tree. No matter what came its way, it continued to do what it was designed to do. It took only what it needed and gave all that it could. Even when it was cut from its source of life, it used all of its hidden strength to become productive again.

JO ANN HILTON

GOD'S WAYS

"For My thoughts are not your thoughts, nor are your ways My ways," says the Lord. Isa. 55:8, NKJV.

I enjoyed working at the health center on the university campus with its neatly trimmed green lawns and attractive flower beds. I wanted to continue working there until I retired in a few more years. So I was shocked to learn that because of budget cuts, there would be some mandatory layoffs.

Because I was the only physical therapist on campus and my services were used by many students, I hoped and prayed that my position would not be eliminated. But after several campus meetings, I learned that physical therapy would be closed. I would be given a small lifetime pension and a health plan that would cover my husband and me.

I walked out on the grounds alone and wept. I hated to leave the students, my friends among the staff members, and my little department that I had personally decorated to make it homelike. I knew it was important to increase my prayer time, for I could not go through this difficult period alone.

Too soon my final day arrived. I knelt in my office and thanked God for the eight-plus years in such a wonderful place. Then, because I could not bear the goodbyes, I eased out through a side door.

While I was in the business office signing severance papers, a former patient walked in. When she learned that I was leaving, she threw her arms around me, exclaiming, "We love you so much, and we will miss you!" How comforting those words and the hug were!

On my way home a water hose in my engine burst. I tried to reach a gas station, but within minutes I had to stop. Shortly after I pulled to the curb, a couple students ran over to me. "Don't worry," the young men reassured me. "We'll patch you up so you can make it to the station."

This was a tremendous help to me. As I continued my drive home, I did not know what direction my life would take, but twice in one day God had given me evidence of His love and care, and I knew I could trust Him for my future.

MILDRED C. WILLIAMS

GOD'S WONDERFUL PROMISE OF HEALING

I will heal them. I will lead them and help them, and I will comfort those who mourn. I offer peace to all, both near and far! I will heal my people. Isa. 57:18, 19, TEV.

For eight months I had suffered from an ear infection that finally required surgery. After two surgeries I still suffered with constant pain and irritation. My doctor advised me to have one more surgery, but I had lost all hope of recovering. I was worried and kept thinking of the problem; for the rest of my life I might have to live without being able to hear clearly and with pain and discomfort in my ear.

I was down, especially after my mother called from India to say that my father, who had had a stroke, was getting worse. That weekend my entire family of four were down with the flu. The pain and agony got worse as we all lay in bed, unable to be in church.

Kevin asked, "What if all of us die?"

I explained that God, who loves us so much, would never allow such things to happen. We prayed for healing and comfort. Going in and out of hospitals made us aware of the larger picture of the suffering around us. I thought about how Jesus must feel as He looks down at the suffering and agony of His children.

On Monday morning, still down and discouraged, I went to the kitchen to prepare food for the family. As I was measuring rice, I accidentally spilled it on the floor. At first I was going to sweep the scattered rice. But on second thought I decided not to waste food. I tried to scoop some with my hands and then to pick up some of the grains. As I sat on the kitchen floor with a bowl in hand, trying to pick up the grains one by one, I began thinking of how much like the spilled rice my life was—scattered, shattered, and fragmented. Jesus had to stoop down to this earth to pick me up. I became assured of God's love and concern for me. His ability to pick me up, to put things back in place, to heal, comfort, and fix my life became real to me once more. I felt more willing to accept the fact that pain and suffering are inevitable in this sinful world. What made the difference was God's promise that He can heal and that He can pick up my problems, one by one.

I was happy I had spilled the rice that morning, for I experienced God's comforting arms around me one more time. BEULAH MANUEL

MURMURING

Search me, O God, and know my heart; test me and know my thoughts. Point out anything in me that offends you, and lead me along the path of everlasting life. Ps. 139:23, 24, NLT.

I've learned many things as I've walked along the roadside, appreciating the quiet of the early morning. I have been blessed with a home far enough from the city that animals roam freely and without much regard for the dangers of people. Seeing the birds of the air and the creatures of the land has always been of special enjoyment, and I have often been blessed by their company during my early-morning times of solitude.

One spring morning I started on my walk a little later than usual and found things different and distracting. I'd missed the first peek of the sun in the east. The birds had performed their aerobic dances without me. Scampering squirrels and rabbits had returned home with their morsels of nourishment. I'd missed the shrieks of the hawks as they captured their breakfast. It wasn't the same. Instead, a speeding car went by, splattering water from a puddle left by an early shower. Through an open window I heard a baby crying. Students gathered to catch the bus to school. A jogger ran past me with a hurried "Good morning."

I felt cheated. I was having to share my morning solitude with others, and I didn't like it! I was comfortable with things the way they were in my very early morning walks. I murmured my complaints to God, but He didn't answer.

Have you ever noticed how quiet God can be when you're murmuring? I was complaining of the changes to my routine and not grasping the new opportunities. I was having trouble with I-sight. I could have thanked Him for the much-needed rain, prayed for the troubled baby and her household, taken a moment to encourage the students to have a great day, or returned a pleasantry to the jogger. Instead, I murmured in discontent.

Now I claim the promise of today's text. In the stillness I recall these timely words and praise my God for consistently reminding me of His love and desire for me to become as He is!

God, You have a way of teaching me things when I least expect it. May I walk the roads faithfully and gladly welcome every opportunity to share Your love along the way.
DIANA PITTENGER

EVEN TO GRAY HAIRS

Even to your old age, I am He, and even to gray hairs I will carry you! I have made, and I will bear; even I will carry, and will deliver you. Isa. 46:4, NKJV.

My sister and I were admiring her gladiolas. Getting her garden shears, she cut me a dozen two-foot spikes of coral, salmon, peach, and apricot. I brought them home, arranged them in my tallest vase, and centered them on my dining table.

The individual flowerets of the gladiola begin opening at the base of the stalk and continue all the way to the tip. In a few days the lowest flowerets had faded. I pulled them out of the sepals, cut four inches off the stems, and rearranged them in a smaller, lower vase. Finally there were only two or three flowerets on each stalk, definitely more pastel, but still quite striking in their beauty. To secure their stems, I put a frog in a round five-inch glass bowl. I wanted to enjoy these very last blossoms, which by this time I had transferred to the windowsill above my kitchen sink.

It strikes me that life is like that. We begin our productive 20s, managing both work and children, making an impact on the world, watching dreams unfold and blossom. By middle age many dreams have faded, but there is still richness and color to life. Retirement finds us continuing to bring beauty to our world, albeit a much smaller world.

When we took English III from Mae Lay in high school, we were required to learn some significant lines from each of the English poets, including this from Robert Browning's "Rabbi Ben Ezra":

>Grow old along with me!
>The best is yet to be,
>The last of life, for which the first was made:
>Our times are in His hand
>Who saith, "A whole I planned,
>Youth shows but half; trust God: see all, nor be afraid!"

Let those of us in the last bloom of life give glory to God, helping others to enjoy His beauty through us each day that we live for Him.

RUTH ANNEKE

LESSONS FROM THE CATERPILLARS

He has made everything beautiful in its time. Eccl. 3:11, NKJV.

My students and I had been carefully observing five caterpillars for our science project. I was fascinated with the caterpillars and glad for the opportunity to actually witness the changes taking place. Each morning when I arrived at school I went directly to the observation container to see if my new "pets" had made it through the night. I found myself making the following analogies to the human spiritual experience.

1. When the caterpillars first arrived, they were very small, but each day they feasted on their wholesome diet of leaves until they doubled their size. Likewise, if each day we feed our minds with spiritual food, they will develop beyond what we can imagine; some will more than double their present capacity.

2. After eating to their stomach's content, they slowly crawled their way to the top of the container, one by one. They did not go all at the same time, neither did they all spin their chrysalises at the same time. Like the caterpillars, changes do not occur among us at the same pace. Some of us struggle through the changes, while others adapt quite easily. We do not need to compare ourselves with others and be overcome with anxiety. The change will come.

3. The caterpillars hung from the lid, and no matter how we shook the container, they held fast. How I wish I did not give up as easily as I sometimes do when things in life shake me up! I need to hold on steadfastly to the promises of God.

4. The cocoons clung to the lid for 10 days. My students became impatient when there were no apparent changes. We get despondent and discouraged when things just seem to stand still. That's when we need to exercise faith and believe that the change will come.

The caterpillars survived the changes, and now we have five beautiful butterflies. The most profound lesson is that if we survive the changes and the delays that come into our lives, we will emerge as attractive as the butterflies, with characters fit for the kingdom.

I pray for patience this day. You are not finished with me yet. Help me to hang on because You are making something beautiful—me. Thank You.

ANDREA A. BUSSUE

THE GIFT OF TEARS

I have seen thy tears: behold, I will heal thee. 2 Kings 20:5. Thou tellest my wanderings: put thou my tears into thy bottle: are they not in thy book? Ps. 56:8.

W hy are my tears sometimes briny and free-flowing and sometimes heavy and nondescript, as they slide down my cheeks? Each one marks a defining event in my history, blending experiences of joy and sorrow.

I have no desire, no ability, to collect these markers for future reference, but there is One who does. My Creator gave me the gift of tears, knowing just how important they would be to me as I pass through life's valleys and mountain ranges. I am seldom aware of the beauty of this gift while struggling just to move past the darkness of the moment. My Designer, however, with His gentle thoughtfulness, knew that tears would map my history as well as His. None of my tears escape His notice. They are precious to Him. His own journal records my emotional journey, because I am never far from His mind. Each incident in my history is also an incident in His.

My tears never fall unmixed with God's own; they are a blending of our experience. They are a link, reminding me of who I am and who He is, reminding me that I never suffer alone, never celebrate alone. God notes my sadness, and He will one day wipe away all tears generated by sorrow, pain, and loss. On that day my tears will have a role in the celebration of peace and victory over every sorrow and loss. The container of my tears will stand in its place, next to God's own. Perhaps the quality of that special moment, when my tears have completed their ministry, can best be symbolized by the fragrance of the world after rain.

Tears of pain and sorrow were never meant to exist in our world, but their presence reflects the Creator's infinite wisdom and infinite love in dealing with the detours and delays that mark His experience and ours. The freshness of the world after rain and the strength and courage of a face washed by tears are demonstrations of a love that mends what is broken, that heals what is injured, that brings joy out of sorrow.

STELLA THOMPSON

INFLUENCING OTHERS

*Ears that hear and eyes that see—the Lord has made them both.
Prov. 20:12, NIV.*

It was alumni homecoming at the small boarding high school our two sons had attended. I had gotten to know many of the students who went to school with my sons because we live in the community where the school is located, and some of them had become "our kids."

This alumni homecoming, however, was especially fulfilling for me. During the time my sons were attending the school, my husband and I owned a photography studio, and we usually had at least one student working for us. One of these students, Anna, was in my older son's graduating class, and she was very special to us. We've tried to keep track of her through the years and were there to do her wedding pictures. So naturally I was very happy to see Anna at the alumni weekend.

At this school it is traditional for the current students and the alumni to have a baseball game on the last day of homecoming. So on Sunday I went to watch my son play ball. I saw Anna, and we began talking. After we had talked a bit she said, "You know, I've always meant to tell you how you helped me. I'm an auditory person as a rule, but when I was working for you at the studio you taught me how to visualize."

"Oh? How did I do that?"

"You would always say 'Oh, isn't that pretty?' or 'Look how nice that looks,' and as a result I began to see things in a different light. I am now a more visual person. I've always wanted to thank you for that."

I didn't care that I hadn't changed the world or moved mountains. Anna's statement might have meant nothing much to anyone else, but it surely made my day. And I had not even known I had been making a difference.

Talking with Anna gave me a lot to think about. It made me realize that one cannot avoid being an influence in this world.

Lord, I wonder how I might have influenced others unknowingly. I pray that it will always be for the good. And help me to say thank you to those who have influenced me.

DONNA SHERRILL

TEACH THEM DILIGENTLY

These words which I command you today shall be in your heart. You shall teach them diligently to your children. Deut. 6:6, 7, NKJV.

When our children face possible frightening situations, it is heartening to know that they remember to call on Abba, our heavenly Daddy, our Father, and trust in His power to protect and deliver them.

One winter evening our daughter took the bus home from school as usual. That evening, however, she was tired, and before long she was fast asleep. She was still asleep when she reached her stop, and by the time she awoke, she was a long way from home. Her first reaction was to panic. She jumped off the bus and took another bus in the opposite direction. This bus, however, made a short turn, and she was forced to walk about three miles before reaching home.

Imagine what was going through the minds of two anxious parents and a host of relatives and friends three hours after this child should normally be at home. The police had been informed, and just as a search party was about to be mobilized, our weary, wet, weeping wanderer came walking along the street to our house. The police asked their usual questions, made their routine checks, and waited around just to ensure that all was well.

After a shower, more tears, and some close questioning, the story emerged. The part that interested us most, though, was Kamila's response to our question "What was going through your mind when you were lost and it was getting darker?"

"Psalm 23. I was praying and repeating Psalm 23," she said.

Visions of an angelic party being dispatched to the side of a terrified child came to our minds. As we all talked about that experience, it became clear to us that our little one was beginning to internalize the faith of her parents. She remembered what we had taught her about God as we sat in our house, walked by the way, lay down, and rose up (Deut. 6:7). This was a comforting thought.

I have no idea, Abba, Father, what any of us will face today. But we are fortifying our minds with Your Word. Now please walk with us, even through the valley, because You love and You care. MARIA G. MCCLEAN

SINGING IN THE RAIN

Behold, God is great, and we do not know Him. . . . For He draws up drops of water, which distill as rain from the mist, which the clouds drop down and pour abundantly on man. Indeed, can anyone understand the spreading of clouds, the thunder from His canopy? Job 36:26-29, NKJV.

Morning was still buried deep in the night. No fingers of dawn yet traced the sky. The house shivered in a gust of wind; the windows creaked. Lightning brightened the sky for a moment and was followed by a tremendous quake of thunder and another shudder of the house.

Then came the rain. Not the gentle drops I was used to on a summer night, but water like a gigantic pitcher pouring over the house. Water gurgled from the eaves, surged over the windows, and splattered on the lawn. The lightning flashed again. Thunder shook the heavens, and the rain poured down harder.

I was fully awake by now. Seldom do we have storms of this magnitude in southern California, and I enjoyed lying in the predawn darkness, listening to the sounds of a spring thunderstorm. Then as the rain lessened, suddenly from the garden came the sweet song of a mockingbird. Loud, clear, precise notes with all the nuances and variety stored in its little heart flung melodies heavenward. I could imagine that little gray mockingbird tottering in the wind—tiny feet clinging tightly to a rough brown branch, wet feathers clinging to a shivering breast, eyes closed for protection from the rain, head and bill reaching high to sing every note it had ever heard.

Why is the mockingbird singing? I wondered. *Is it thrilled to have a bath? Delighted to swing in the wind? Out of a grateful heart, is it singing to the loving Creator who sends the wind and rain to water the earth? Or is it singing to encourage its own little heart or to encourage the other birds? Is it singing in the darkness, hoping that daylight and peace will soon return?*

I do know its song brought me joy in the dark rainy morning as I lay listening to the downpour fade into the steady beat of raindrops on my roof. Its music gladdened my day.

I thought that if a little bird can sing in the storm, I too can learn to sing in life's storms, because the God who takes care of the sparrows and mockingbirds and wrens has even more regard for each of us.   EDNA MAYE GALLINGTON

APRIL 4

THE ENVIES

God said, "I give you every seed-bearing plant on the face of the whole earth and every tree that has fruit with seed in it. They will be yours for food." Gen. 1:29, NIV.

I never expected to get struck with a case of the envies at the grocery store, but there I was, turning a nasty shade of green as I watched the man ahead of me unload his cart. He had stuff like Rice Krispies Treats, in a box, already made. The only thing you could consider premade in my cart was the cheese, and that was a stretch. His cans and boxes weren't dented and taped up like wounded soldiers. I'd been shopping in discount food stores for so long I'd forgotten that some people ate food out of cans and boxes that hadn't been through World War III.

It was all I could do not to burst into tears right there in the checkout aisle. If only I could afford . . . If only I had . . . If only . . . I tried to think back to a time when I had been able to enter a grocery store and buy whatever I wanted, convenience food and all, without agonizing over every last dime. Had I ever?

Then it dawned on me: I hadn't. Ever. Growing up, we got sugar cereals only on our birthdays. Most of our food was grown in our own garden. Most of the packaged stuff stayed on the grocery shelves during our shopping trips. We loaded our cart with staples that Mom would slave over to convert into healthful, nutritious, but essentially unspectacular meals.

During nursing school I got by on $20 a week, living on Raisin Bran and a conglomeration of home-canned tomatoes, carrots, and noodles that I named Italian Garbage Soup. The early years of marriage were the closest I ever came to carefree grocery shopping. But even then I remember lots of Ramen noodles and canned vegetables. After the children arrived, the discount food store quickly became our main grocery store.

Standing there thinking about it, I realized that Satan was pretty slick indeed to have me mooning over food just because it was in a pretty package. When I thought about it, I realized that it was like everything else he tried to pass off as good: a whole lot of hype. No matter how hard he tries, he'll never top the pure, natural food God created just for us. Sure, maybe our food looks as if a black belt used it during a practice session; but God provided it, and I am grateful that He did. CÉLESTE PERRINO WALKER

RETIREMENT

To every thing there is a season, and a time to every purpose under the heaven. . . . He hath made every thing beautiful in his time. Eccl. 3:1-11.

So it begins—the countdown to retirement. For more years than I care to actually remember there has been a specific job to get up for each morning. Fortunately, in recent years alarm clocks were not a necessary part of those mornings. Before sleep overtook me at night, my mental clock would be set, and I would awaken within a few minutes of the predetermined early morning hour.

Within a few short days it will not be necessary to set that clock so early each day. It will be unnecessary to decide what to put in the "brown bag." No more running out early on frigid winter mornings to warm up the car; no more driving to work in the dark nor driving home again in the darkness of our short winter days. No more calculating whether the gas gauge will allow another day of driving to work, or if I must stop to refill before the homeward drive.

When next spring comes, early-morning walks will replace that dash to work at the last minute because I lingered too long at the clothesline, listening to the singing birds and watching the play of sunbeams dancing on the new blades of grass. Funny how hanging up clean sheets and socks always makes my heart sing praises to my heavenly Father.

No more cheerful "good morning" greetings from friendly coworkers. No more hung-up print jobs or computers or problem-solving. No more filing endless pages in big black books because Congress changed the rules on something again. No more fun break times with 3-D puzzles and popcorn and shared confidences. If I'm not careful, tears will soon come if this train of thought continues! It saddens me in a way—yet I am happy.

Wise old King Solomon said, "To everything there is a season." My seasons have been fruitful, whether in plenty or in drought. A new season is upon me; what will it bring?

Father, I am skin-tingling excited. What do You have for me to do for You and those around me? In every age You have a purpose for me. Please help me to find and enjoy that purpose today, this new season of my life.

BETTY R. BURNETT

REFLECTIONS OF HIS LOVE

We all, with unveiled face, beholding as in a mirror the glory of the Lord, are being transformed into the same image from glory to glory, just as by the Spirit of the Lord. 2 Cor. 3:18, NKJV.

On the last day of the women's retreat in Webster, New York, the director was closing the celebration with a special gift, a beautifully wrapped mirror, for someone in the audience. She asked us to close our eyes so it would be a personal experience for the recipient.

I listened as she described a woman who had difficulty loving herself and did not see her self-worth. I recognized that person—it was me! I was a Christian, but no matter what, I could not see Christ's reflection in myself. It was a malady that incessantly plagued me.

As the director asked for a raised hand, the Holy Spirit beckoned to me. The tears flowed quietly as I surrendered to His will. As heads were bowed, the director came to my side, placed the mirror in my hand, and hugged me. I could not open my eyes—it was truly a special moment between my Saviour and me. I hid the mirror under my coat.

Upon my return home I unwrapped the mirror, looked at myself, and felt my healing begin. I wept tears of relief. I saw the little girl who was damaged at such a tender age, but I also saw that she gave her heart to Jesus. I realized how much Jesus loved me, and I knew I no longer had to attempt to be patient through my own efforts. He loved me unconditionally. Just as I was—I was still His child. At that moment I felt His loving arms surround me, and I caught a glimpse of His reflection in the mirror.

The healing process has been slow, but my special mirror is an encouragement to me. It is tucked away for now, but when I get to heaven, I can climb into my Father's lap, place my cheek next to His, and together we will look in the mirror. Then He will say, "See, My daughter, I was in the mirror all the time."

Satan would have us believe that our heavenly Father does not love us. God, however, reminds us that Satan is a liar. No matter our past experiences or childhood traumas, He loves us, and He paid the price to "restore" us. He empowers us through His Holy Spirit to become the women He desires us to be.

EVELYN BOLTWOOD

THE PLANE THAT RETURNED

While they went to buy, the bridegroom came; and they that were ready went in with him to the marriage: and the door was shut. Matt. 25:10.

The spiritually uplifting sermons, the inspiring music, and the excitement of seeing old friends had come to an end; the church conference became history.

We were scheduled to depart for New York at 12:30 p.m. the next day. It was important that I not miss the flight. We stopped at the hotel's information desk to ask what time we should catch the bus for the airport. The clerk politely informed us that the 11:00 a.m. bus would be just fine.

We went up to our rooms, packed, and checked our tickets and other travel documents. Everything was ready, so we settled down for a good night's rest. We had plenty of time.

At 10:45 the next morning we were in the lobby with our luggage, and the bus arrived minutes later. We boarded, and it left promptly at 11:00. About 15 minutes later it made its first stop at a hotel, then another and another, picking up passengers at each hotel. The minutes were ticking away.

It was about 12:15 p.m. when the bus arrived at the terminal. We had only 15 minutes! Asking the other passengers to excuse us, we went directly to the head of the line. We explained our situation to the clerk and asked for help. He quickly checked our tickets and labeled our luggage. "I don't think you're going to make this flight," he said, "but you can try."

We ran, but when we reached the gate the plane was moving away. The attendant looked at us pityingly and asked, "Were you to be on that flight?" He spoke into his radio, and the plane came slowly back to the gate.

In my seat I closed my eyes and thanked God for this miracle. I thought of the time when a door was shut by heavenly hands, and Noah could not open it. I thought of the 10 virgins and of the five for whom the door was shut. In both cases the people had been given plenty of time. I thought also of an important flight I plan to take and for which I have been given plenty of time to be ready, watching, and waiting. When that heavenly flight takes off, I must be ready to go, for there will be no returning for me. Oh, that I may be found ready and waiting!   MAUREEN O. BURKE

LISTEN FOR GOD'S WHISPER

In all thy ways acknowledge him, and he shall direct thy paths.
Prov. 3:6.

When my husband received military orders to move to Bamberg, West Germany, our 10-year-old daughter and 6-year-old son were eagerly looking forward to the tour. Once my husband left, it was my responsibility to prepare for departure as soon as school was out for the summer. Four sets of packers descended upon us with the precision of a military formation. Everything was duly sorted and packed according to their categories—the storage items to be left behind, the air freight, the household goods, and the accompanied baggage.

After what seemed an eternity we departed from Fort Bragg for our cross-Atlantic trip to Frankfurt. By the time we arrived in Bamberg we were relieved to be "home." We were welcomed by a beautiful German woman, and we began to visit and enjoy the German hospitality. Because we arrived in the middle of the afternoon, however, we had lost a full night's sleep. Our bodies were weary, and we just wanted to sleep, regardless of the time of day.

Yolande decided that she was going to bed, even though we had been advised to stay up until Germany's bedtime. She wanted to take a nice warm bath before going to bed, so bath water was prepared, and she was happy to jump in.

We continued to visit while Yolande enjoyed her bath. She must have been in the tub at least 15 minutes when I heard a small voice whisper in my ear: "You must check on Yolande." Without hesitation I jumped to my feet and went into the bathroom. To my dismay, Yolande had fallen asleep in the tub and the water had reached up to her chin. I was horrified when I realized what could have happened had I not heeded that small voice.

We were happy that the Holy Spirit whispered in my ear at just the right time. Fortunately, I responded without questioning.

The Holy Spirit still speaks to us. We must heed His voice.

Father, help me always to discern the voice of Your Spirit and to obey the nudge. You have directed my paths, and once again I thank You.

YVONNE DONATTO

THE CROCK-POT LID

Before they call I will answer. Isa. 65:24, NRSV.

At the church-sponsored fund-raiser for our small church school, I had been assigned to sell veggie chili dogs. So I borrowed my daughter-in-law's Crock-Pot to keep the wieners hot. Sales were brisk.

Later I arrived home with praises on my lips for our success in spite of the poor turnout because of the weather. As I began unpacking the boxes, the Crock-Pot lid crashed to the floor, breaking into many pieces. I quickly swept up the mess.

Well, I thought, *this is another unexpected expense to add to our already stretched budget. I will have to purchase a complete Crock-Pot. Where on earth will I find a Crock-Pot lid to fit?* I had forgotten so quickly about the One who made the fund-raiser a success. He also knows where everything in the world is.

The following Thursday I went into a Salvation Army thrift store to look around. After browsing for a few minutes, I was impressed to ask the clerk if she would possibly have a Crock-Pot lid. (Of course, I knew she didn't.)

To my utter joy and surprise she said, "Wait a minute. I think one came in on Tuesday, and I didn't put it out here on the shelf." As she headed for the back room, she said that the lid might not fit.

"Oh, no," I said, finally coming to my spiritual senses. "If God kept the Crock-Pot lid in the back room, it is the right size."

As the clerk handed me the new-looking glass lid, I knew it would fit! I praised God for giving me a surprise and paid the clerk a dollar. It fit better than the old one. When I finally told my daughter-in-law the whole story, she praised God with me.

Each time I use the Crock-Pot, I smile when I think of how He worked through the person who donated the top, the clerk who left it in the back room, and the Holy Spirit, who impressed me to visit the store and ask for a Crock-Pot lid, even though my faith was less than strong. How precious we are to our Father God, who delights to give us surprises!

EUNICE VERRETT HUGHES

BUTTONS AND BOWS

I will instruct thee and teach thee in the way which thou shalt go: I will guide thee with mine eye. Ps. 32:8.

When she was a toddler, my daughter Kelly's personality showed a streak of independence that was matched only by her determination. Even at that early age she was eager to tie her own shoes. And she did not want any help.

"Let me show you how to do it, Kelly," I offered. But no, she didn't need help. Not even a beginner's lesson.

After struggling with several frustrating attempts, she finally consented to let me show her how it was done. But before I could get to the final tuck-and-pull stage, she insisted, "I know how! I'll do it myself." But then the laces would dangle as she moved her white high-top shoe to and from my lap. Her frustration increased with each unsuccessful attempt. Kelly could not understand what she was doing wrong. She was so impatient to do it herself that she never allowed me to get to the crucial step of securing the bow.

Believe me, the big problem had nothing to do with tying her shoes! I could teach her how to tie her shoes, but I could not teach her patience, which was required for all lessons.

I wondered if there have been frustrations in my life that could have been prevented if I had taken the time to learn something completely. Such as reading the instructions before attempting a project, rather than waiting until I was stuck and totally frustrated. How many of my problems have I snatched back from the Lord before He had a chance to show me completely how to fix things His way? Or how many times have I rushed into the day without first taking time to get the instructions—either by reading His instruction book, the Bible, or by sitting quietly enough to hear the Holy Spirit? I can't even use the excuse of not having the time. I know that on the days I do take the time I accomplish so much more. When I spend time with Jesus, it always feels as if my day has been handed to me in a package tightly secured with a bow of His love.

Lord, help me to be a willing learner in Your school.   JO ANN HILTON

RENA

Inasmuch as ye have done it unto one of the least of these my brethren, ye have done it unto me. Matt. 25:40.

Who is it?" Mother asked as I answered the phone.
"It's Rena. Do you want to talk to her?"

Mother wrinkled her nose and shook her head. Meanwhile, Rena continued to talk. She would talk to anyone who would take the time to listen, even if it took an hour. I knew Rena was lonely. For 35 years she had dedicated her life to taking care of her retarded son, Richard. Her husband had left her because he couldn't handle the responsibility. Mother had befriended her when she lived next door. Mom would take care of Richard while Rena did her shopping or visited the doctor. Ordinarily Richard was afraid of strangers, but for some reason he took to my mom.

Richard died shortly after my mom moved, and Rena was alone and very lonely because she couldn't drive and, for the most part, was confined to home. When I moved in with Mom, I was the target for these phone calls.

One night the phone rang about 10:30. I was surprised to hear Rena at that hour.

"Margaret," she whispered, "I have a terrible pain in my chest."

"Hang up and call 911!" I ordered. I was frightened for her. A few moments later I called, and Rena was able to answer and inform me that the paramedics were on the way. The next morning the doctor told me that Rena had had a massive heart attack. Ten days later she died.

I was very sad for Rena. I also had a guilty conscience. I had never talked to Rena about God or invited her to church with me. I had wasted the countless hours on trivia.

I asked the Lord to forgive me for wasting a golden opportunity. I was so sorry it was too late for Rena.

How many lonely Renas are out there? I'm sure most of us know at least one. Let's remember that these dear people need the Lord as much as we do. You may be the one who can influence that certain person to accept the Lord as her personal Saviour.

"One of the least of these . . ." *Today I may meet one of these children of Yours. Help me to do for him or her what You have done for me.*

MARGARET E. FISHER

THE LIFE THAT GOD GAVE TWICE

The Lord is nigh unto all them that call upon him, to all that call upon him in truth. He will fulfil the desire of them that fear him: he also will hear their cry, and will save them. Ps. 145:18, 19.

Eight-month-old Joshua could not tell me how he was feeling, but the moment I touched his hot dry skin I could tell he had a high fever. I immediately prepared to take him to the doctor, but before I even knew what was happening, Joshua suddenly went into severe convulsions.

Having no idea what to do, I did the only thing I could think of. I took him in my arms and held him tightly. I cried and prayed, sure that he was dying. I could not think of anything else.

A neighbor came in and took Joshua from me. She held him for a while, then laid him on the bed. I felt that I must hold him at such a critical time, so I took him in my arms again. Then another neighbor took him. She held him, and then she also laid him on the bed. Later I learned that they believed the old superstition that it is bad luck for a baby to die on its mother's lap. They didn't have the courage to have him die in their arms either, so they laid him on the bed.

Samuel, my 11-year-old, saw what was happening. "Mommy," he reminded me, "let's pray."

Little Joshua lay limp in my arms, panting, too weak to make even the tiniest sound. Samuel, the neighbor women, and I knelt, and I poured my heart out to God. No sooner had I said "Amen" than Joshua gave a little cry. That cry was a sign of life, an immediate answer to prayer.

Today Joshua is a dedicated nurse, who daily participates in spreading the love of God. He is the son God gave me twice.

God has also given me life twice—He created me, and He has redeemed me. When I was close to eternal death because of sin, He held me in His arms, loving me and giving me life to serve Him.

I do not have words to express the gratitude that I have to You, our great and faithful God, who gave us life. What a privilege to serve You!

MARIA FREIRE SOUZA DOS SANTOS

FRIDAY THE THIRTEENTH

Now to him who is able to do immeasurably more than all we ask or imagine. Eph. 3:20, NIV.

Looking at my calendar one Friday morning, I smiled as I noticed that it was the thirteenth. *So what?* I thought. *My text this morning promised that the angel of the Lord would be with me today, so I have nothing to fear.* It was a beautiful day, and I fairly skipped to work.

I needed to enter nearly 400 names and e-mail addresses into my computer address book so I could mail a "Good News From India" bulletin before the day was finished. I saw no reason that couldn't easily be accomplished by the time the office closed at 1:00 p.m. *This is a cinch! I'll get this done!*

I closed the door to my office and concentrated on the task at hand, carefully double-checking each entry. I zipped right along, and by noon I had entered all the names. I closed down the address book and copied the newsletter to the first name on my address list. Going down the list, I clicked on each name that should receive it.

But where were all those names I had just spent four hours entering? Not one name was there! I was sick. What could I have done wrong? I checked the process for adding names to the address book and realized that I had missed one important step: after entering the names, I was supposed to click on "OK" to save them. Because I hadn't done that, they had all disappeared. I had to begin all over. What a chore! *What happened to my guardian angel? How come he let Friday the thirteenth be such a disaster day?* I thought. *Why did he let me do that! Why didn't he stop me, or at least hit the "OK" button for me!* Then I smiled as I pictured him smiling his understanding and encouragement.

My good humor returned as I realized that I had been careless in my hurry to finish the task. It had nothing to do with Friday the thirteenth, nor was it the responsibility of my guardian angel. *Charge it to tuition, Dorothy,* I told myself. *There's no use to cry over spilled milk. What's done is done. Now get busy and see how quickly you can redo it.*

After lunch I finished the task much more quickly than I had imagined it could be done. The news bulletin got out on time, and I had a real sense of the presence of the Lord with me, doing for me more than I could ask or think.

DOROTHY EATON WATTS

MY GARDEN

He will satisfy your needs. . . . You will be like a well-watered garden. Isa. 58:11, NIV.

I've been bitten by the gardening bug again. It happens every spring. Not that I've ever had anything that remotely resembles a flourishing, healthy garden. But I still get caught up in an overwhelming desire to make something—anything—grow.

This year I've decided to do a little more reading on the subject than I get from the seed packages. A master gardener from England said that pruning and weeding are very important, because a garden is a careful balance of plants that must be allowed to grow and spread freely, and those that must be strictly controlled. H'mmm . . .

My personality reminds me of a garden. I have weeds, roses, and a lot of thorns. There are rocks in the soil and old roots left by the one who used to be the gardener here. But I have a new Gardener working in me now, and I'm trusting Him to turn this wasteland into a plantation.

Sometimes I get impatient because I want to be perfect *now*. But the Master Gardener knows what He's doing. It takes time. He's taking out rocks here and there, digging up roots, softening the soil, planting more seeds, pulling out weeds, cutting off dead branches, fertilizing, and all the other things a good gardener knows how to do. And when I am patient and focus on how far I've come rather than on how far I have to go, I can see that, season after season, there are a few more roses and a lot fewer thorns.

I take comfort in the thought that my Master Gardener is much more patient than I am, and that He can see what I'm going to be when He's finished. He knows that beneath this rocky, weedy ground there is a heart waiting to break forth in blossoms of love for Jesus. After all, I'm the one who asked Him to take over and do His work in me. And every day, before He picks up His shovel and hoe, He makes sure that I'm still ready to yield to His tilling. I ask Him to please weed and prune, even if it hurts. That's my part. He does all the rest. And then He shines on me with His love and rains on me with His Spirit.

The best part is that after He has done all the work, and I have yielded up the harvest that He Himself has cultivated, He will say to me, "Well done." I'm so looking forward to offering my crop to Him.   Lynda Mae Richardson

WHITER THAN SNOW

Wash me, and I shall be whiter than snow. Ps. 51:7.

I was 62 before I had my first experience at a women's ministries retreat. I was assigned to a cabin of "giggly girls" (grown, mature ones, you understand). They were great women, and I loved them all, but I decided early on that it was a little too late for me to start a life of camping and bunk beds.

Ask me what I learned. In the bathrooms I learned that "Jamie loves Jason" and "Michelle loves Sean." I was happy also to learn from the same location that "Jesus loves you" and "I love Jesus." I learned that "20,000" wads of gum decorated the frame of the bunk above me. I learned that daddy longlegs also love the women's retreat. I am not afraid of daddy longlegs, but do detest wads of secondhand gum. I had to roll into bed with my eyes shut.

The meetings were inspiring, and the group singing was stimulating and moving. The speaker brought us special blessings, and I met some great new friends.

But one of the last night's meetings was a kaleidoscope of emotions for me. We were sitting in the open air on the side of a hill above the lake. A large wooden cross stood behind us.

As the sunset glowed across the sky, the speaker invited each woman to use the red liquid coloring provided to write her name on a small square of white cloth and nail it to the cross with a large spike. Many joined in nailing their "sins" to the tree.

Next morning I drove down to get one last glimpse of the lake. Turning toward the cross, I was awed to see that the moisture from the lake had made the red stains run on the white pieces of cloth. The sun had been up only a few hours, but it had bleached the red into a light pink as it faded toward white.

From my vantage point, the cross had been transformed from a stark reminder of sin and death into the soft promise of resurrection. Love's covenant appeared as blossoms springing from every inch of the splintered cross. The Sun of righteousness was turning the crimson stains into white . . . whiter than snow!

As I drove away, I was softly singing, "Jesus paid it all. . . . Sin had left a crimson stain; He washed it white as snow." EULENE DODSON

WHAT ABOUT MY NAILS AND HANDS?

She extends her hand to the poor, yes, she reaches out her hands to the needy. Prov. 31:20, NKJV.

Recently I read a statement that advised, "Trim your nails. They tell a lot about you." My first thought was *What do my nails and hands say about me?*

I look at my nails after I have come in from gardening and see how the dirt under the nails has pulled the nails from their bed—not a pretty sight. Then there is the rash on my hands from contact with weeds. The old Norwegian expression "Uff da!" certainly says it all. What will people think of these hands? I quickly scrub them and put lotion on to soothe the soreness, but the damage doesn't go away quickly. Will people understand the nails of a gardener?

When my friends see that my hands are all red and sore and that my nails are broken and torn, will they know that I spent some hours scrubbing and cleaning for my elderly friend?

At times my hands show the remains of stain and varnish. Will others know how much fun I had making a beautiful piece of furniture out of a scarred and battered table? It isn't easy to remove wood stain from hands and from under nails, but I try.

Scars from getting too close to the oven grate remain, reminding me of the many loaves of bread and other things I have baked. The cuts from a slipped knife when preparing vegetables to feed family and friends are unsightly. Yet they remind me of the many pleasant meals we have shared through the years.

My nails will never win a beauty contest. My hands often show signs of wear and tear. I take comfort in knowing that I have used them to give pleasure to others, to help lift a heavy load for another, and to create things of beauty. They have soothed a crying baby and stroked loved ones in their last moments. Some nails are less than beautiful because they are attached to working hands.

Jesus has hands that bear the marks of His suffering and pain. Hands that show He was willing to give all for you and me. There is no way to remove those scars. Because He wants our days to be days filled with comfort, pleasure, and joy, Jesus was willing to go through eternity with hands that say a lot about Him. May I always use the gift of my nails and hands to exemplify His love, no matter how scarred and soiled they may become.

EVELYN GLASS

IT'S YOURS, GOD!

Humble yourselves under the mighty hand of God, that He may exalt you in due time, casting all your care upon Him, for He cares for you. 1 Peter 5:6, 7, NKJV.

It was becoming a joke with my friends. Luckily, I could laugh about it too, though it could have been very frustrating. Every Friday as I prepared for Sabbath something would break. One week it was the washing machine. I turned it on, filled it with dirty laundry, and set off to do more things. When I came back to put the laundry in the dryer, it was still "filling." Later it was still filling. Finally I turned it off.

The next week it was the dryer. I closed the door, but nothing happened. I tried several times. Checked the fuses. Made sure the vents were clean. Nothing fixed it. On Sunday it worked!

Every Friday, it seemed, something different broke down. One week it was the vacuum cleaner. Then the dryer broke again. The washer took another turn. On several occasions the appliance worked fine when I tried it again on Sunday. Most times my husband had to do a little repairing. It became such a regular habit that when I headed out one Friday for a women's retreat, my mom joked that since it was Friday, maybe it wasn't a good idea for her to lend me her van.

This could have been frustrating. I could have been angry. And I guess I could have tried getting everything done on Thursday. But I didn't. I responded the same way every time: *It's Yours, Lord! This is Your washing machine. If You want me to get the washing done, You'll need to take care of this. I can't do anything about it. If You don't do anything about it, then this chore will just have to wait till another day.* Then I went about my work. No grumbling. (Who grumbles about not having to work?) No complaining. Just letting God have it and trusting Him to know what's best. Even about broken appliances. Eventually, I knew, the item would be fixed or replaced and the work would get done. Until then, I chose to give it to God and go on.

God invites us to cast all our cares upon Him. He wants anything that frustrates us, causes us worry or pain or fear. There's nothing too small or too insignificant for Him. He wants to give us rest and freedom. We each have a choice about how to respond to the breaks and problems of life. God invites us to cast them all on Him, because He cares.

TAMYRA HORST

TO ALL TREMBLING CHILDREN!

Can a mother forget her little child and not have love for her own son? Yet even if that should be, I will not forget you. See, I have tattooed your name upon my palm. Isa. 49:15, 16, TLB.

On a sunny April afternoon our 2-year-old son, David, was excited to run around the little pond all by himself, chasing butterflies and doves, watching as little ducks had fun in the water. He went farther and farther away from me. Each step made him more confident. Of course, we needed to watch him from a distance, but he was so happy, so proud to be able to run around and do more and more things without help.

When it was time to go home, we had to cross a busy street. David ran ahead. When I finally managed to catch him, he firmly crossed his arms and said, "Don't take my hand!" I disappointed him by not taking notice of his firm signs.

As soon as we reached home a fierce spring storm hit us with pouring rain, thunder, and lightning. My brave, independent "big" boy became a crying baby in a second. He was frightened by the sudden loud sound. I had to lift him up, and he clung to me with all his strength. He held on so tightly I could hardly move.

Suddenly I realized how similar my own reactions are to those of my little boy's. At times I feel so independent, as if I were telling God, "Don't take my hand! I am good enough to take care of myself. I know how to handle this." But my confidence can be shaken so easily, and then I'm trembling, crying, my heart full of fear. As I read the Bible I meet others with the same quick change of mood. Yes, this is so human! We are so fragile, so vulnerable alone! How can we ever think we can run ahead without holding His hand!

How reassuring it is for me to know that God loves us with such tender care that He used the mother's example to illustrate this point. Maybe a mother can get tired of her own child, but our Father loves us with unfailing love. If only we cling to Him with all our strength, as a little child clings to a parent! He gave His dearest, only Son, to save us!

Let us all grasp the promises of God and feel His protection day by day. Storms and problems come and go, but our God is always there, stretching out His protecting arms.

God, do take my hand. I need You.

CHRISTINA ZARKA

ONLY BELIEVE

He said to them, "How foolish you are, and how slow of heart to believe all that the prophets have spoken!" Luke 24:25, NIV.

The disciples were experiencing the darkest moment of their lives. The cruel death of their Leader, Friend, and Saviour had left them feeling hopeless. Even though they had spent much time with Him and had read the prophecies, they still couldn't understand, and they didn't believe that He would rise again. Doubt and fear gripped their hearts. As they walked along the road to Emmaus, they discussed the headline news of the weekend. Tongues were ablaze with the incident. When a stranger joined them in their walk, they couldn't believe he had not heard what had happened. Hadn't he heard the angry crowd shout, "Crucify Him!" Hadn't he been to Golgotha? And even if he was new in town, didn't he hear the gossip? How could he be so uninformed? They were so stricken with grief they did not recognize the stranger to be Jesus.

Before I criticize them for being so despondent and skeptical, let me take a deep breath. Not for one moment should I judge them when so often I find myself in the same dilemma. I can't count the number of times that I have read and claimed the promises, but as time elapses and the answers to my prayers seem not to be forthcoming, I abandon the very promises that I need to embrace for hope and comfort. I become consumed with the problem, and my eyes are blinded to the might, power, and very presence of a God who can take me through any situation.

It is consoling to know that when Jesus revealed Himself, He guided the two disciples through the very Scriptures that were so familiar to them. Later, when He appeared to them in the upper room, He even invited Thomas to touch Him, because the mere account of his colleagues did not satisfy Thomas's curiosity. Sometimes I am just like Thomas; however, I must realize that continuously harboring doubts and demanding a physical sign can stunt my growth of faith. Yes, sometimes He will make allowance for that, but I must learn to take Him at His word. I must believe that even in my darkest hour, Jesus will be there to comfort and reassure me of His presence. May you have peace in knowing that His word is true and unchanging. ANDREA A. BUSSUE

THREE WISHES

For God so loved the world, that he gave his only begotten Son, that whosoever believeth in him should not perish, but have everlasting life. John 3:16.

I remember how warm the sun was one April day as it glittered on the amber water. I was leaning on the railing of the old bridge that crossed the brook flowing past our house while my 15-year-old mind wrestled with the problem of wishes. At school that day we had read the old story of Jacques and Yvette, who had lost their three wishes because of greed and carelessness. *I wouldn't have been so foolish,* I decided.

But what would I do with three wishes? I mulled the problem over as I watched the water bugs skating on the surface of the water. Not one of them ever sank. We should be so lucky. I couldn't remember a time when we hadn't been poor. With enough money we could have a new house, one with a bathroom. Wow! And my sisters and I could each have our own room. It was hard to imagine such luxury.

A song sparrow in a tall tree warbled an intricate tune, but he didn't mention money. H'mmm. Money wasn't everything. What good would money be if I were blind or crippled or always in pain? I'd better be smart enough to wish for perfect health.

I envied an iridescent dragonfly, hovering and swooping over the water. It seemed to have not a care in the world. Then a passing bird snapped at the dragonfly. No, perfect health wouldn't mean perfect safety. I could be killed by a truck, as Marlene's brother had been. That was the trouble with life on this earth. It wasn't sure. Would I dare to wish for a life that wouldn't end?

This wishing business could be rather scary.

Everlasting life. But hadn't God already promised it to us if we believe on His Son? Jesus died, but He didn't stay dead; and somewhere He said that we would live also. Then came a luminous thought: *I don't need three wishes as long as I trust God.*

From the top of the elm the song sparrow dropped its silver notes. *God is good,* I thought. *God is forever. I have nothing to fear.*

And that assurance has kept me to this day.   OLIVINE NADEAU BOHNER

BEAUTY ALL AROUND

In thy presence is fullness of joy; at thy right hand there are pleasures for evermore. Ps. 16:11.

Our day's activities began early. Sleep hadn't been very restful for the group of teenagers and their adult counselors, who had bedded down on the floors of a school gymnasium and a classroom the night before leaving on a mission trip. But we had no time to think more about that. We had to eat breakfast quickly and board the buses that would take us to the airport. Then one bus broke down. The other bus had to make two trips to the airport at the height of rush hour. Hurry was impossible. The second busload would have missed their flight if the airline hadn't held the plane for them.

Then followed the long flight. The attendants served a light fruit lunch that only partially satisfied the cravings of growing young people. Finally, there were the long lines and formalities of immigration and customs, followed by a two-hour bus ride before we finally arrived at our destination.

Night had fallen by the time we arrived at our camping area. Without many lights it was hard to make out the surroundings where we would be living for the next 10 days. About all we could see was that it was very dusty and that there were a few desert plants. We tried to pitch our tents in the darkness and prepare for a night of sleeping on the ground. Then came news that the restroom facilities weren't ready. That didn't make us feel any better.

Just then a slight breeze on the night air brought the most beautiful fragrance. It smelled like orange blossoms. In the midst of all the dust and tiredness, God had sent something to lift our spirits, something for which we could give thanks. The next morning we learned that, indeed, there was an orange grove just over the fence from our compound. But in all the rest of the time we spent there, I never again noticed the perfume of the orange blossoms as I did that first night when it was so much needed.

Thank You, God, for sending joy in the midst of stress, and the promise of pleasures forevermore when we remain in Your presence. BETTY J. ADAMS

GOD WAS TAPPING ON MY SHOULDER

Fill me with joy and gladness; let the bones which thou hast broken rejoice. . . . Create in me a clean heart, O God, and put a new and right spirit within me. Ps. 51:8-10, RSV.

As this date rolls around each year I always think about something my father told me: "God is tapping you on your shoulder." He said it after I had experienced a tornado, and also after an accident.

At first I didn't get it, and life went on. My few wounds from the tornado healed. Then came the more serious vehicle accident on April 22, 1995. I suffered broken ribs, a collapsed lung, and a broken clavicle. I had a long road of rehabilitation ahead of me and a lifetime of pain. "God is tapping you on your shoulder," my father repeated.

This time I told my father what I was thinking. "God has hit me a whole lot harder than the last time, and I now understand why."

My life was nowhere near what it should have been. I had grown apart from my Lord God and Saviour, even after all that He had done for me. I no longer depended on Him for what I needed. So He allowed the tap on my shoulder. Even though the accident was life-threatening, I feel that it saved my life, for it gave me time to think about my relationship with God.

Since then I have sought to be closer to my Lord and Saviour in everything I do. I pray every day and night, and sometimes throughout the day. My mother and father also pray for me. My mother especially gives me spiritual wake-up calls on occasion, and I suppose I do not mind, because that is just what mothers do, and I love her even more for it. I have also begun some new and better habits that glorify my Lord. I am in no way perfect yet, but I'm trying. I am so grateful for both of my fathers—my earthly father for telling me, "God is tapping you on your shoulder," and my heavenly Father for doing the tapping.

Lord, help me to stay close to You this day. It makes my life so much better! I want our relationship to grow, because I know You love me even more than my earthly parents do. Fill me with Your joy and gladness.

MILANE Y. TODD

EXPOSED ROOTS!

Our God is in heaven; he does whatever pleases him.
Ps. 115:3, NIV.

D id I dare? I was such a novice at the gardening business. Yet the temptation to transplant that lonely little marigold that had come up from a seed was so tempting!

I had been getting a crash course in Gardening 101. Dad (my father-in-law) had carefully explained the correct mixture of dirt and potting soil and had shown me how to "firm" the plants in the ground. But he wanted this plant left on the edge of the patio where it was adding color to the gray cement. However, my ideas of a well-kept English garden and Dad's much more natural look in gardens were at odds over this single but beautiful marigold.

Then the moment arrived (as it does for any good child who thinks she knows more than her parent). When Dad went with our son to get a load of topsoil, I quickly took the trowel and carefully dug a wide dirt ball around the plant and lifted it out of the ground. Mission accomplished! I was exhilarated for all of about 30 seconds. Suddenly the "dirt ball" around the roots fell off and left the roots exposed. I could hear Dad's voice. He had given two "thou shalt nots" of gardening: first, leave no air pockets when planting—always firm the soil; and second, do not let the roots become exposed. I started to throw the plant away, then I thought, *So it dies; it didn't cost anything.* At my preselected planting spot I discovered the ground had too many roots to plant my precious marigold. Behind me was a good location, and Dad might not notice it in this spot, because by the next day it might be dead.

After I finished planting, I watered the plant, which already looked half dead. Yet for some strange reason I felt a sense of joy and a belief that my orange Majestic Wonder would survive. Later, from my bedroom window, I looked at the plant, struggling to survive. I realized that plant was like me sometimes. In my foolishness and selfishness, often my "roots" get exposed; but Christ never leaves me unassisted if I reach out to Him. Even in my most embarrassing moments Jesus has let me know there is always a way of escape in Him.

It has been a week since the experiment, and my magnificent marigold is beautiful and strong. Dad says God blessed my ignorance. Well, I think he's right. Christ has covered my "roots" with His glory.   VALARIE YOUNG

THE PARKING SPACE BLUES

Why are you downcast, O my soul? Why so disturbed within me? Put your hope in God, for I will yet praise him, my Savior and my God. Ps. 43:5, NIV.

As much as I liked giving Bible studies, the hassle of finding parking was certainly dimming my joy. You see, the Far Rockaway neighborhood in which my church is located is not the prettiest or—much more important—the safest part of town, especially for a woman alone. Many members have been assaulted or robbed; two have been badly hurt.

And the other problem was time. One particular night, for example, I had a church board meeting at 8:30 after the study in the Villaltas' home. What were the possibilities of getting a spot close to my Bible study that would save me time, and also one close to the church? Being late would mean having to park on a dark, empty lot one block away.

To many, my worry was insignificant. But for me it was a big deal. I don't like to be late. I always try to manage my time in the most efficient way. So I asked the Lord for two parking spots—and felt very greedy.

When I reached my destination that night, a spot was waiting for me right in front of the apartment building. And when I drove to the church one hour later, the closest parking space to the church was free. Since that night I have always prayed for convenient parking places, and He has not failed me once.

Going to a women's ministries meeting in Manhattan not long ago, my friend and I prayed before leaving Queens. We asked for traveling mercies and not much traffic, but it wasn't until we were almost there that I realized we had not asked for a parking place. If you have ever driven in the uptown part of Manhattan, you know how difficult parking is. We had not been to this house before, and we had to carry boxes with the materials—and we were wearing high heels!

But the Lord answers before we ask. My friend and I smiled gratefully when we saw a parking spot on the corner, but we had tears in our eyes when we looked at the number on the nearest door and realized that it was exactly our destination.

God, You are so good!

ALICIA MARQUEZ

"HERE AM I! SEND ME."

By faith Abraham obeyed when he was called to go out to the place which he would receive as an inheritance. And he went out, not knowing where he was going. Heb. 11:8, NKJV.

When we were called to go to Laos, my husband and I didn't even know where the country was. We didn't know the people's culture. Neither did we know what language was spoken there. We really didn't know anything about Laos. But we felt the call was from God, and we accepted the challenge. Like Abraham of old, by faith we left our country of birth.

When we were in college in the Philippines, as part of the ministerial training, groups of two or three theology students were sent to churches around the metro-Manila area to be trained to preach. One student said, "Send me anywhere in the world except Tala Leprosarium," a big place where lepers are quarantined.

My daughter Lynda home-schools her daughter Lauren. One day the Bible lesson was about Abraham leaving Ur of the Chaldees. After explaining that Abraham and his household had left by faith, Lynda asked Lauren to draw a picture of Abraham and his household. Lauren drew a chariot with Abraham and Sarah inside. She also drew a tent. As Lynda expounded on the meaning of faith, she asked Lauren, "What if God asks you to go to another country, or perhaps to another state, to be a missionary for Him?"

"But I don't want to go. I'd rather stay here," Lauren replied.

"If God is calling you, won't you leave California?" queried Lynda, to make sure the 6-year-old understood what she was driving at.

Not to be outsmarted, Lauren answered, "Let me draw where God is sending me." She drew herself lying on her bed, then she added a bubble in which she wrote the words addressed to her: "Lauren, I want you to go to Hawaii."

When God calls me to go somewhere, am I like my 6-year-old granddaughter? Do I try to rationalize and give excuses? Do I say, "Lord, I want to be a missionary, but please, not to a leprosarium. Not to an inner city. Not to a remote area."

Lord, help me to be like Abraham of old. Help me to respond willingly, like Isaiah, and say, "Here am I! Send me" (Isa. 6:8, NKJV).   OFELIA A. PANGAN

CHOICES

If it seem evil unto you to serve the Lord, choose you this day whom ye will serve; whether the gods which your fathers served that were on the other side of the flood, or the gods of the Amorites, in whose land ye dwell: but as for me and my house, we will serve the Lord. Joshua 24:15.

The telephone call came early one Saturday morning. It was a reminder of a period in my life that I thought I had forgotten. It resurrected guilt over past failures and anger at someone who had deceived me. Later I became angry at myself for allowing past mistakes and hurts to haunt me. As the day progressed I concluded that I had not completely forgiven myself for my mistakes or the individual who had hurt me. Finally God's voice got through to me through my Bible reading and observations of others in similar circumstances.

As a middle manager in the volatile health-care industry, I have met individuals who had reasons to be angry, bitter, and resentful. They have faced demotions and frequent job changes with grace and patience. One man made an indelible impression on me. He had started working at a large medical center at age 16, immediately after migrating from the Caribbean. He swiftly rose through the ranks to become assistant director of his department. Administrators changed; his department was outsourced. To use his words, he was relegated to a position without functions. He shared with me that he had made a decision to shed resentment and anger.

I realized that I had three choices in dealing with my situation. They included: 1. Serve the gods that the Israelites worshiped: I could choose to dwell on past mistakes and hurts. That would lead to a life of suspicion and bitterness. 2. Serve the gods of the Amorites who lived in this land: I could continue in my current emotional seesaw of guilt and worry about my failure to forgive. 3. Serve the Lord: I could accept God's forgiveness completely and accept His grace to forgive the one who had wronged me.

I chose the third. It was not always an easy choice. Frequently I yearn for the gods of the Amorites, but each day, as I choose the God of Joshua, the load gets lighter. I do not know what life's experiences have brought you, dear reader, but do remember that you too have a choice.

ERICA JOAN CHARLES

JUSTICE AND MERCY

He hath shewed thee, O man, what is good; and what doth the Lord require of thee, but to do justly, and to love mercy, and to walk humbly with thy God? Micah 6:8.

I was vaguely aware that my license tag and inspection sticker were two months out of date. But my car was only one year old, I was a good driver, and besides, who would ever notice?

I had given myself the luxury of having my nails done. The polish was not quite dry, and the oil was on my cuticles. Back in my car, I feared that I might mess them up, so I decided to delay fastening my seat belt. On the interstate a few minutes later, a highway patrol officer drove up beside me. He started around my car, then fell back behind me. As I watched in my rearview mirror, his ominous blue light came on, and he put on his hat. I knew I was in trouble and quickly pulled over. I rolled down my window and smiled sweetly as he approached.

"Ma'am, do you realize that your tag and inspection sticker are outdated?" he asked.

"Really?" I replied innocently.

Then he added, "And you weren't wearing your seat belt either, were you?"

"You're going to give me a ticket, aren't you?" I asked weakly.

"I'm going to have to give you something," he said as he took my license and returned to his car. He was there for what seemed like a very long time, and when he returned he had an official-looking paper.

"I am writing you a ticket only for your outdated tag and inspection sticker. This will not cause any point against your license and will not affect your insurance. I am not charging you for not wearing your seat belt, but I am telling you that it is very important for your safety."

"But my nails are wet." My reply sounded weak and foolish, and it was. I thanked him for doing his job and for being kind and merciful.

As I drove on to get my tag and inspection sticker renewed, I was reminded of how our heavenly Father deals with us. He allows us to make choices that break His laws, but when we reap the just consequences He is oh, so merciful.

I humbly come to You today, again asking for Your justice and Your mercy. And please help me to extend that justice and mercy to someone else this day.   ROSE NEFF SIKORA

THE PROMISE

*Your Maker is your husband, the Lord of hosts is His name.
Isa. 54:5, NKJV.*

Tall and brown-skinned, with the high, proud cheekbones and
luminous eyes of her African ancestors, she sat slumped on the hard
seat outside the little desert bus stop, her sleeping child cuddled against her.

The air was stiflingly hot as she sat alone, abandoned by humanity and
by God. She'd lost her job, been evicted from her apartment, and all she'd
gotten from her son's father was a bus ticket to nowhere. He'd said, "I
don't want you and the boy to jeopardize my new family."

She looked down at the child for whom she would fight and endure so
much. He hadn't eaten since the morning of the day before. The bus stop
was shut and would not open until noon the next day. She stared down the
shimmering empty strip of concrete—no shelter, shade, or water. There
was no complaint from the boy, though he was hot and thirsty. She
awakened him, but he was too weak to stand. She lifted him and, stopping
only to look under the drink machine for lost change, trudged over to the
dumpster. Empty. Carefully she looked all around it. Nothing. She'd heard
of people dying of heat stroke in the high desert, and she now realized they
wouldn't live through the long, searing, waterless afternoon. With the child
clutched close, she slumped down and, in her despair, prepared to die.

A cool breeze touched her cheek as a cloud covered the sun momentarily.

"Ma, what's that?" asked her son. "Is that water?"

Dear God, she thought, *are we now to suffer delusions from the heat?* Now
that she had given up, could they not just quietly die?

"Look, Ma," the child whispered through cracked lips. She looked.
Where nothing had been before, she now glimpsed two bottles of
water—cold water.

The clouds stayed as she held a bottle to her son's lips. "Oh, God!" she
wept. "You do see me." She remembered a text she'd read long before: "For
thy Maker is thine husband." And she heard the added words: "And I'll be
little Ishmael's Father, too. He'll grow up to be a great man."

For the first time in days, Hagar, the Egyptian, looked up and smiled.

LOIS K. BAILEY

HEAVEN IS MY HOME

As it is written: "Eye has not seen, nor ear heard, nor have entered into the heart of man the things which God has prepared for those who love Him." 1 Cor. 2:9, NKJV.

My day this spring morning started with joy as I looked out my kitchen window. We live in the country with near neighbors but a lot of space. Behind our house are towering Douglas fir trees and a few oak trees. Our three quarters of an acre blends into a forest of similar trees.

Thank You, Lord, I whisper. *This is almost like heaven to me.* There is something about a forest that invites worship. I praise Him as I watch the hungry birds at the feeders and as I see the vibrant colors of dahlias, pansies, and roses in the garden.

As I continue my reverie, I hear a loud thump at my window—I've heard that sound before—and hurry out the sliding-glass door. On the deck is a pine siskin—one of my favorite birds—lying quietly with closed eyes. I hurry to find a box and a piece of flannel. Maybe if it has a chance to be warm and still it will recover from the stunning blow.

Placing the tiny body on the cloth, I cover it and put the box in a safe place. Later I check to see if the bird will greet me with bright, open eyes. It is not to be. *Dear Lord,* I moan, *did I say this is like heaven?*

All about me I can still see the loveliness, but the enemy, death, threatens us and tries to rob us of joy.

A song invites itself to my lips and heart:

> "I'm but a stranger here, heaven is my home;
> Earth is a desert drear, heaven is my home;
> Danger and sorrow stand round me on every hand;
> Heaven is my Fatherland, heaven is my home."

Thank You, Lord, that the words of this song speak to us today. There is still much for which to be thankful. We have sunshine and rain. There are thorns on the roses, but that does not take away the fragrance.

Our pain or heartache is tempered with the beauty here and the promise of a real heaven that will be beyond our wildest imagination.

MARY FOLKES WALTER

SLEEPLESS NIGHTS

I will lie down and sleep in peace, for you alone, O Lord, make me dwell in safety. Ps. 4:8, NIV.

Each day I arrived home from work, flipped on the evening news, exchanged my stiff business clothes for my favorite T-shirt and shorts, and plopped onto the sofa to hear what was going on around me. Day after day I carried out the same routine. As I watched the news and heard which neighborhood had been the scene of murder, rape, or vandalism, I breathed a sigh of relief that it hadn't been mine.

Then one evening the news focused on my neighborhood. In a nearby apartment complex a single female had been burglarized and assaulted in her apartment. My heart began to thump, and my palms became sweaty. *Not my quiet neighborhood!* I thought. *Nothing like that could happen here!* I felt sorrow for the victim, then my imagination began to run wild! *Oh, Lord, what if I'm next?*

After that, each evening as I arrived home I scoped out the parking lot before getting out of my car and tiptoeing to my apartment, not wanting to alert anyone that I was home. Once inside, I flipped on all the lights and swung the closet doors open like a detective on a desperate hunt for a fugitive. After feeling that everything was safe, I would then let down my guard, but only until it was time to retire to bed. In my distorted thinking, I felt that if someone were to burglarize me, it would be better if I could hear them coming. So for weeks I took my pillow and pulled the blanket from my bed and slept on the sofa.

Finally, one day I came across 2 Timothy 1:7: "God hath not given us the spirit of fear; but of power, and of love, and of a sound mind." There was no need for me to fear the devil and the evil that goes on around me. Because of the fear that I had allowed to creep into my heart, I had lost my good reasoning powers! My Father in heaven wants me to be at peace at all times. "Thou shalt lie down, and thy sleep shall be sweet" (Prov. 3:24), He promises.

How foolish of me to lose faith in God's promises that He will protect me. He is ever watching over me, for He never sleeps! He sees all and knows all!

Oh, Father, thank You for Your promises! I needed them so badly, and I still do. Today I will walk and sleep in peace because You alone make me dwell in safety.

PENELOPE S. SMITH

WHEN YOU'RE READY

Every good and perfect gift is from above, coming down from the Father.
James 1:17, NIV.

God delights in giving me wonderful surprises. But He often has to hold back because I'm just not ready for them.

One thing I've wanted for a long time is a soul mate, a kindred spirit, a bosom friend. I've longed for a special friendship in which we help each other to grow spiritually and emotionally, one in which we both give and take spontaneously and hold each other accountable. A friendship that is emotionally consistent, open, and intimate.

As a teenager I didn't have this all figured out, but I knew I wanted a spiritual friend, one who was uniquely mine. I searched for many years and finally decided that such a person didn't exist. I learned that it was good to have a variety of friends because of my varied interests, so I acquired many treasured friends. But I still secretly longed for that unique friend.

God longed to give me this precious gift too, but had to hold back because I wasn't ready yet. He knew that I needed to grow and mature and heal before He could trust me not to misuse this gift. Knowing that I would stuff this person into the void in my heart, God waited until my void was healed and completely filled with Him. The wait has made the gift that much more rare and precious.

I didn't recognize God's gift when we first met. She wasn't the type of person I'm usually drawn to. But as we interacted we both saw the potential for a special friendship and pursued it.

In every level we explored, we uniquely clicked—spiritually, emotionally, mentally, and experientially. We frequently thank God for the gift of each other. And we thank God for teaching us both not to misuse our friendship.

Is there a void in your heart? What do you stuff into it? I encourage you to seek healing and allow God to completely fill your needs. There are so many wonderful gifts He longs to give you when you're ready.

HEIDE FORD

THE STRANGER

Be not forgetful to entertain strangers: for thereby some have entertained angels unawares. Heb. 13:2.

A stranger sat alone in the last pew, next to the middle aisle, just watching. The meeting was over and most of the people had left, but some were visiting, totally ignoring him.

As my husband, Ralph, and I walked out the door, my concern grew. Who was he? Did he need help? Why wasn't someone doing something? He didn't wear the world's latest fashions, but he was clean. I turned to my husband and asked, "Did you see that man sitting in the back row of the church, all alone?"

"No," he answered.

"I wonder if he needs help. He looks so alone." The thought crossed my mind that we should take him home and give him a bed, if he didn't have a place to sleep.

"Let's go back and see," replied my husband. So we turned around and went back into the church. He was still sitting there, just watching. My husband asked who he was and if he needed anything, possibly a ride.

A smile came to his face, just a faint one, but someone at least was paying some attention. He said that he was staying at a mission and would like a ride there. Ralph went to talk to someone who would be passing close to the place and asked if he would give the man a ride.

As I stood by the stranger, I briefly put my hand on his shoulder and told him we were glad that he had come that night. Another smile!

I went to find my husband, and when we returned to the man, I looked into his eyes. Oh, those eyes! *Could he be an angel,* I wondered, *checking to see if anyone cared enough to reach out?*

How often we walk past those who need a kind word, food, a warm coat, shoes, or maybe just a hug. How about those people who sit alone in church, hoping someone will talk with them? Is someone you know hurting? Have you telephoned her recently, or sent her an e-mail or a letter? Are you so in tune with our Saviour that you hear Him as He tells you to reach out to help someone?

CONNIE HODSON WHITE

THE 25-CENT LESSON

What woman having ten pieces of silver, if she lose one piece, doth not light a candle, and sweep the house, and seek diligently till she find it? Luke 15:8.

I couldn't find that 25 cents anywhere! I racked my brain, trying to figure out where it could be hiding, spending what seemed like hours going over every transaction in my checkbook—twice! Each month as I try to reconcile my bank statement, I seem to go through this whole traumatic experience. And since I have some unique and creative methods of recording transactions in my checkbook, there are many ways that money can get "lost." But even if my balance is off by one cent, I still have to go through the entire process of reconciling until I find it. Some have counseled me to just add the one cent, or even 25 cents, to the figure in my checkbook to make it balance. It surely would save a lot of time, and I've been tempted.

But I know that wouldn't really correct the situation. So I keep searching—adding, subtracting, comparing, double-checking figures—and praying. Then, suddenly, when I finally find the error and my 25 cents, I rejoice and let out a loud "Thank You, Lord!" What a relief!

Even though my 25 cents is not as valuable as the lost coin of the Bible, finding it is almost as joyful. I can empathize with the woman who lost her coin in her frantic situation. I can also understand her emotions at finding it. Yes, I even understand why she would invite all her neighbors to come and celebrate with her.

But what I can't understand is the depth of love that Jesus has for the lost sinners in this world. That He would leave all the riches of heaven to come looking for a "lost coin" is a mystery to me. He could have just erased this little planet with its sin and started all over. He could have given up the search long ago. Satan tempted Him to do just that, but I'm forever grateful He didn't take the easy way. He went through the entire process, doing everything painstakingly right, until He found His precious coins. And all heaven rejoices. What a wonderful God we have!

Thank You, Jesus, for coming to search for Your "lost coins" on this planet and for not giving up on us.

NANCY CACHERO VASQUEZ

A CHOSEN INSTRUMENT

He knoweth the way that I take: when he hath tried me, I shall come forth as gold. Job 23:10.

My husband and I have two very dear longtime musician friends. Orpha plays marimba, and Henry plays violin. For many years Henry's skilled hands also built violins. He says, "God furnishes the wood; I just put it together."

Henry would take two blocks of wood and knock them together as he listened. "That," he would say, "is a definite A tone." Or a C, or an E. He searched the world for just the right wood—spruce for the front, curly maple for the back. In his studio he would carefully select a piece and place it in a frame. Then the long process of carving, chiseling, and polishing would begin, and after some 200 hours, a beautiful violin would emerge. Not only was it beautiful; the tone was exquisite. And the same hands that chiseled and carved and polished the violin finally nestled it under his chin and brought from it music angels would delight to hear.

As I recall how Henry searched for that special wood for his violins, it comes to me that we too are unsightly, of no apparent value, and unable to change ourselves. But the Master Designer comes to earth to search for us, and with joy He takes us to His heart as His very own. Oh, how loved and cherished we feel!

But then the fashioning process begins. Trials and perplexities chisel away at our lives. Discouragements and sorrows cut us to the quick. Unable to understand the reason, we sometimes question how God can allow our troubles. Oh, we're not alone. Job too questioned God. But in time, like the block of wood, we begin to take on a new character; and finally it dawns on us that God's loving hands are at work, patiently and skillfully shaping us into something beautiful. It takes time to build character. Lots of time. But God invests in us because He sees something special that He values and loves.

One day very soon the process will be complete, if we allow it. Then those same caring hands of God will tenderly lift us up before the universe, and the beauty of our perfected lives will bring forth music such as unfallen worlds have never before witnessed. And we will forever remain cherished children of the King.

LORRAINE HUDGINS

NEW CREATION

If anyone is in Christ, he is a new creation; old things have passed away; behold, all things have become new. 2 Cor. 5:17, NKJV.

Watching a monarch butterfly (that had been a crawling caterpillar before its metamorphosis) crawl out of its chrysalis puts our verse for today into fuller focus. First the wet butterfly pushes open the now dry and brittle chrysalis with its fighting feet. It is becoming stronger by the minute as it stretches its long black legs, one by one, and slowly sways its drying body. Its great orange wings begin to uncurl and gradually dry in the life-giving sunlight. Its long black tongue curls and uncurls into its mouth. It will use it to draw nectar from many flowers. The veins in its wings begin to fill and swell, making the wings grow larger and brighter, standing on its black-and-white body. Watch carefully, because soon, very soon, it will take to the sky and begin its new life as a new creature, doing the activities programmed within it by the Creator, flying from flower to flower, bringing pollen and beauty to the garden. Following its God-given instinct, it will join with thousands of other monarch butterflies in the migration south to an ancient ancestral wintering ground. One of these is Pacific Grove, California, where the monarchs find the same eucalyptus and pine trees each year. Some monarchs even go farther south to Mexico's Sierra Madre to winter.

I too can become a new creature, as our verse illustrates today. But only "in Christ," my Creator, can I be renewed in all things, leaving the old behind. As with the butterfly, my newness is a gradual process, a stretching of my mind to God's ways. It is a filling of the life-giving Spirit by the Creator's words in my thoughts as I read His Word. And soon, with my new spiritual "wings," I will be lifted up into heavenly "gardens," bringing beauty and hope to my associates and God's children within my range of flight as I let God's life-giving sunlight into my life, giving color to my new "wings" by His grace. And I will become new every morning by remaining in Christ through His Word. Like the migrating butterflies, I may even go to faraway places to fulfill God's assignments. Then, when my Creator returns to claim His creation, I will be given a new body and real wings to soar to worlds unknown with my Creator and all His new creations who have also been renewed by His grace through the study of His Word. Will you be among those new creations? I hope we can fly together! BESSIE SIEMENS LOBSIEN

SIMPLE CUSHIONS

Always giving thanks to God the Father for everything, in the name of our Lord Jesus Christ. Eph. 5:20, NIV.

I decided to make some pillowcases, but as I was going through my supplies I saw some leftover foam and thought what fun it would be to make large floor cushions for the living room too. Not only would they look good, but I remembered how much fun the children had with such cushions when they were small. They had crawled over and around them, even hiding behind them. Now, as adolescents, they liked to join friends and family on Saturday nights for games and fun. The cushions would make perfect seating, scattered around the floor.

I found some lining, left over from making curtains, and was soon busy making five cushions, one for each member of the family. But when I finished, I wondered if I had made a mistake. Instead of sitting on them as I had envisioned, the children had pillow fights with them.

Three months later I underwent surgery. I asked my husband to please bring along two pillows to the hospital to support my head and legs. (There is nothing as comfortable as one's own pillow!) He laughed. "All five cushions are already here in the car!"

I had to laugh too. "Two will be fine, thank you. I have a feeling they will be very comfortable." And they were. They worked perfectly, alleviating many pains. I thanked God for those cushions.

When I made the cushions, I had no idea that I would find them so useful. In fact, I had no idea that God was planning ahead for my future. But He was. He provided comfort long before I had pain. Before I was fully recovered, I found all five cushions useful. Each size and shape had a special use. What a friend He is!

I thought of the text in Psalm 147:1: "Praise the Lord. How good it is to sing praises to our God, how pleasant and fitting to praise him!" (NIV).

I do praise You, not just for the cushions, but also for being my friend. The simple cushions remind me of Your love and care for me. Hold me close today.

NELMA MARQUARTDT TOCHETTO

VOICE OF THE SHEPHERD

My sheep hear my voice, and I know them, and they follow me: and I give unto them eternal life; and they shall never perish, neither shall any man pluck them out of my hand. John 10:27, 28.

It was a glorious morning. The sky couldn't have been bluer. Birds' songs seemed sweeter than I had remembered, and the grass was greener than any green I had ever seen before. All of this beauty beckoned me outside to work in the garden, next to the south pasture fence, where my precious two sheep and two goats grazed.

While thoroughly engrossed in weeding, I became aware of something nudging my shoulder. Honeylamb, my Suffolk ewe, had found me and was pushing her black velvet face through the fence. Her soft brown eyes seemed to beg for attention. I can never resist spending time with these sweet animals, so I stood up and talked to her while I stroked her under her chin and above her nose.

"You know how to get my attention, don't you, Honeylamb? Are you enjoying this gorgeous day too?"

When they heard my voice, the rest of the menagerie appeared, and I had to repeat the routine with each of them. After I returned to my gardening, they stayed by and moved wherever I moved. They wanted to be near their shepherd. They wanted to stay close.

I thought, *I too want to be near my Shepherd, Jesus. I want to hear His voice and to feel safe as He leads me.*

My husband and I recently passed through some very dark valleys, but because our Good Shepherd was with us and we trusted Him, we were guided to safer pastures. As His sheep, we have nothing to do but to trust ourselves completely to the Shepherd's tender care and leading. "He tends his flock like a shepherd: He gathers the lambs in his arms and carries them close to his heart" (Isa. 40:11, NIV).

Dear Lord, I want to continue this loving and trusting relationship with You. I want You as my Shepherd. I want to be close to You, to lean my head against You and be stroked by Your hand. May I always listen for and know Your voice.   ALBERTA BENNETT CICCARELLI

A SPIRIT OF TIMIDITY OR ONE OF POWER?

God did not give us a spirit of timidity, but a spirit of power, of love and of self-discipline. 2 Tim. 1:7, NIV.

We have to move!" I screamed hysterically at my husband. "I can't live here anymore!"

My bemused husband replied, "Don't be silly. We've been here only a week. I'm not about to repack all those boxes. We have to live here."

What caused my irrational outburst? Five furry creatures parading in my back garden—a family of cats. The proximity of five cats is enough to throw this usually calm, composed woman into a state of extreme agitation, as she has a phobia about anything connected with the feline species.

From my earliest days I had an uncomfortable feeling anytime a cat and I had the misfortune to meet. And as I grew older, the problem grew larger. Meeting a cat took on dramatic consequences—I would either scream uncontrollably or become rigid with fear. It was totally irrational, I knew, but it was, nevertheless, reality.

However, Jonathan was right. We couldn't possibly move. I had visions of my 2-year-old daughter and myself becoming prisoners in our own home. I didn't want to leave the protection of my four walls and encounter one of my four-legged neighbors! I had no choice but to ask God to deal with the situation. I knew that no amount of self-control or positive thinking about these furry animals would help.

God did not miraculously answer my prayers overnight. Instead, every time I encountered a cat, He urged me to give my fear to Him, and in time courage replaced that negative emotion. I cannot honestly say that cats and I are ever going to be bosom pals, but I am no longer afraid of them.

I have often wondered why God put me in that situation. Why did He allow me to go through such emotional stress and trauma? God does not want us to be hampered by our fears, no matter how silly or serious they may be. So He puts us in situations that invite us to rest in His fearlessness, which is more powerful than our greatest fear. He wants us to be radiant with His power, His love, His self-discipline, instead of cringing in our timidity. It is exciting to give our fears to Him and watch His power in action.

MARY BARRETT

PRESSING TOWARD THE MARK

No matter which way I turn, I can't make myself do right. I want to but I can't. . . . Who will free me from this life that is dominated by sin? Thank God! The answer is Jesus Christ our Lord.
Rom. 7:18-25, NLT.

She wrinkled her little brow and lurched forward, intent on the toy I dangled just inches from her trembling hand. Time after time she swiped right past her goal. Finally I placed the toy gently in her hand. Instantly she grasped it and, in bringing it to her mouth, bonked herself on the head. She didn't cry. She just tried again, and this time she made it.

I raised my eyebrows in silent communication with the physical therapist examining the child with me. The baby was old enough to be starting to walk, but she couldn't even sit steadily. Each time she tried, she would suddenly stiffen and fall backward, or sit for a few seconds, then collapse forward. When she tried to reach out with her hands, they would shake and veer from their course. At nearly a year of age, she couldn't hold her own bottle reliably.

I am a developmental pediatrician, and my job is to examine children who may not be developing just right, and to suggest ways to help the child and the family overcome and/or live more comfortably with the difficulty. Sometimes it is a challenge for all of us. When parents hear the words "cerebral palsy," they often imagine it means "stupid," because it is obvious to any casual observer that the child can't do the things other children can at that age. But what it really means is that the brain and muscles aren't able to cooperate. The brain sends signals the muscles can't obey.

Now that she is nearly 2, even though she may never walk or talk so you can understand, little Karen can recognize colors and match animals to their sounds; she comprehends nearly anything you say. She is a bright child in an uncontrollable body.

I'm that way myself. I want to obey God and to follow His instructions. His goal is my goal. But so often I fall down or veer past or suddenly jump in a ditch for no particular reason. Because He loves me, no matter what, He helps me exercise those weak, vacillating muscles and get stronger. When I can't leap into His arms, He picks me up. Better yet, He promises a whole new nature, a glorious obedient body, perfectly able to do His will—forever.

HELENE RABENA HUBBARD

FRIENDSHIP

A friend loves at all times. Prov. 17:17, NASB.

For the first 10 years or so of my married life my world largely revolved around my immediate family. With four children, life was busy and satisfying.

One day, on the kitchen phone, I was explaining to my friend Mary why I couldn't go to her home party. "Oh, I'm sorry, but I already have everything I need, so I really can't come." Hanging up, I noticed that my husband had come in.

"You know," he commented, "I think you should go."

"Why?"

"For the sake of friendship."

Taking his advice, I called Mary back and assured her I would go. That lesson my thoughtful husband taught me then has stayed with me through the years. Friendships are treasures to be cherished and valued. I think back over the years . . .

There's Joyce, and wonderful early-morning walks with our dogs. We've moved away since, and how I miss those conversations, the problem-solving we did, the experiences we shared, and the spiritual discussions we enjoyed.

And Irene, whose lovely singing voice I admire so much. When I confided to her my dream for a church choir and for special music programs for our church, within a few months Irene laid the groundwork that made our lovely choir possible. What a friend!

Recently my husband and I shared a lakeside bench with friends we've known and loved through the years. We shared a special closeness as we watched the evening sun sink gloriously below the horizon. A moment that memory will hold! I thought back to the words of advice—"for the sake of friendship."

Thank You, dearest God and Best Friend, for those words. I want to thank You too for Your gift of friends and friendship. It seems so important, to us women especially. Help me to build those friendships today for You.

MARILYN KING

MY PASSPORT

That is what the Scriptures mean when they say, "No eye has seen, no ear has heard, and no mind has imagined what God has prepared for those who love him." But we know these things because God has revealed them to us by his Spirit, and his Spirit searches out everything and shows us even God's deep secrets. 1 Cor. 2:9, 10, NLT.

The hour was already very late, and I had yet to pack our suitcases before I could sleep. We were leaving on a Christmas holiday early the next morning, so I made a list of the things I must not forget to take. My husband caught a glimpse of my list—(1) money, (2) drugs, (3) Blue Cross, (4) pink slip—and snickered. "If customs sees your list," he commented, "we'll be searched for sure!" We took a minute time-out and laughed together.

We were 12 hours from home, nearing the United States-Canadian border, when I realized I hadn't put my passport or our son's birth certificate in my purse. They had not been on my list. These valuable documents were home in my jewelry box. Would my husband's word be sufficient? If asked by a customs agent for ID, I had absolutely no way of proving my U.S. citizenship and Canadian Landed-Immigrant status or Sonny's dual citizenship.

As always, at the border we were asked our citizenship—but we didn't have to prove it. Be assured, however, I learned a lesson. Next time, when traveling and crossing borders, my passport will be the first thing on my list.

For me, vacations are a foretaste of what heaven will have in store for my family and me. I'm a positive thinker, and I'm trusting that all my loved ones will reach the golden shore.

Just think! Someday we'll travel the universe as redeemed ambassadors for Jesus, sharing our personal testimonies with God's other wonderfully created beings and with one another. Perhaps our traveling companions will be our guardian angels for a while, until we learn our way around up there. They too will have awesome testimonials to share.

There is only one thing that could make my smile bigger than it is now—if I were chosen to be Jesus' personal traveling companion throughout eternity. Jesus is our passport to eternity, and the only thing we will be taking with us to heaven is our character; which is being engraved in our hearts and minds right now.

DEBORAH SANDERS

HANDS THAT SPEAK

Behold my hands and my feet, that it is I myself. Luke 24:39.

As I read my daughter's essay describing her mother, I had to smile when I came to the sentence about my hands. She portrayed them as "the hands of a worker." I glanced down at the hand that held her paper and observed the swollen knuckle on my index finger. That was where the sliver had become embedded while I was sanding some oak molding. I couldn't deny it. Mine were the hands of a worker. Not much to look at, to be sure.

I considered the hands of some of my girlfriends, many of them quite different from mine. Hands that were taken to the manicurist regularly and had nails done to perfection.

My hands are only the outward indication of who I am on the inside. I like to do things myself. This is partly because my mother taught me to work at an early age. And it is partly because I love the sense of accomplishment. Mostly, however, it is because it saves money. Unlike my girlfriend with the glamorous hands, a gardener, two housekeepers, and the services of professional decorators, I keep up those tasks myself. And my hands tell the story.

This desire to do things myself is fine when it comes to projects around the house, but it's not such a good idea when it comes to working my way to heaven. The simple truth is that I don't have what it takes. No matter how hard I work or how beat-up my hands may become, the job is simply out of my realm.

Thankfully, there is Someone who will do the work for me. And the wonderful truth is that He charges nothing! All I have to do is get to know Him and enjoy His company while He works to remodel my character and renew my heart.

How can I be so sure? Just look at His hands! They give Him away. They carry permanent scars as reminders of the incredible work He does for me—obtaining my salvation. And because of the story His hands tell, I can pull weeds and scrub floors and hang wallpaper with a song in my heart and His praise on my lips!

RETTA MICHAELIS

A LIFE LIKE A GARDEN

Feed the hungry! Help those in trouble! Then your light will shine out from the darkness. . . . You will be like a well-watered garden, like an ever-flowing spring. Isa. 58:10, 11, TLB.

My great-aunt Jess was a special person. She could not boast of any spectacular achievements or overwhelming obstacles surmounted, or anything else of heroic proportions; but Auntie Jess was special nonetheless. She didn't profess any particular church affiliation and was never overtly religious, yet she had a way of touching people's lives that was somehow Christlike.

Anyone who needed a friend could count on Auntie Jess—from a lonely young farmer's wife to a neighbor dying of cancer. I recall too the old gentlemen from down the road, for whom Auntie Jess prepared a hot dinner every day for more than 10 years. Many a friend and neighbor, or anyone with a need, was invited to share the produce of her flourishing vegetable garden. The whole tennis club came to share in the enjoyment of her beloved flower garden—a regular site for the annual garden party. Taking roses to her neighbors on Christmas Eve was also one of Auntie Jess's favorite rituals.

Ever eager to see improvements to her community, Auntie Jess would sometimes couch her suggestions in the form of a humorous verse submitted to the local newspaper. In fact, when the road past the farm was finally sealed eight years after her death, Jess's efforts were still so well remembered and appreciated that a plaque was set up in her honor. Even more appropriately, a tree was planted in her memory.

Needless to say, Auntie Jess had many friends. Just how many may never be known, although her funeral revealed something of her capacity for touching people. All in good faith, the kindhearted woman who helped prepare refreshments for the mourners put out 50 cups and saucers. Jess's daughter, with a better knowledge of her mother, quietly added 100 more.

Cheerful, practical, and unassuming, Auntie Jess was the kind of person who will be genuinely surprised when the King says, "Come, you who are blessed by My Father, for you were there when I needed you. You fed Me and clothed Me and visited Me."

Today I want to be there for You. Help me to reach out to those in need around me. Strengthen me that I may flourish for You, like a well-watered garden.

JENNIFER BALDWIN

GROWING UP

When I was a child, I spoke like a child, I thought like a child, I reasoned like a child; when I became an adult, I put an end to childish ways. 1 Cor. 13:11, NRSV.

"Mom, I don't need you anymore." Leslie's voice on the other end of the phone sounded cheery enough, but the message was strange.

I encouraged my college daughter to develop that thought. "What do you mean?" I queried.

"You remember what I said when I left home the last time?" Leslie asked.

I couldn't say that I did. "Well, I'm not sure what you mean." I quickly thought of all the things I used to do for this nearly grown daughter. When she was a baby I did everything. As the years all too quickly rolled by, Leslie gained her own autonomy, dressing herself, learning to cook, graduating first from eighth grade, then from high school. She learned to drive a car and obtained gainful employment. She developed both female and male friendships.

"Mom, are you listening?" Leslie's pleasant inquiry interrupted my reverie.

"Oh, yes," I answered. "I was just trying to figure out what you meant when you said that you don't need me anymore. Does that mean you're grown?" I asked the last question with a chuckle.

Leslie simply went on with her thought. "When I was home last, you put a relaxer in my hair. I told you then that I still needed you. Well, this evening I did my own hair!" She said the last statement with pride, evidencing a successful job.

"It must have turned out fine if you don't need me. Right?"

"Oh, it looks great!" Satisfaction exuded through the phone.

As parents, we look forward to the time when our children gain independence. In the spiritual realm, we also need to grow and mature, but this side of heaven we will never outgrow our dependence on our heavenly Father.

Lord, please be patient with me. Help me to stay close to You. Guide me until I become like You.

ELIZABETH DARBY WATSON

WATER OF LIFE

When you pass through the waters, I will be with you; and when you pass through the rivers, they will not sweep over you. Isa. 43:2, NIV.

No one would ever have known that I was recovering from major depression—I was an excellent actress. After a particular series of events, I had cried out to God in anger. Finally I found my way to a competent therapist. With the Holy Spirit's guidance, I found my way back and now feel healthier than ever. Not always perfect, but better equipped to see the signs of depression, tackle them with appropriate help, and turn them over to Christ.

Have you been there? Was it difficult to reveal to your family and friends the waters or rivers you faced? For me it was paralyzing. Who would understand? Furthermore, I would worry, *What kind of Christian am I?* In recovery I learned a valuable lesson: Christians will pass through the waters—sometimes torrential floods—and will react, because we're free to do so.

Our wonderful Jesus understands our depression and wants to help us draw closer to the Father as a result. Today's scripture implies with certainty that there will be waters, not *"if* you pass," but *"when* you pass." He may not originate the floods, but in His great love and infinite wisdom, He can calm the waters. God is in control. No matter what we want to say at the time, He bids us, "Call to me and I will answer you" (Jer. 33:3, NIV).

If the Christian life were carefree, a walk in the park, a continual romp on cloud nine, we might feel less compelled to call upon Him, even for praise and thanksgiving. What irony! Sometimes it takes spiritual two-by-fours to bring us to our knees, shaking our fists. Yet it is Jesus and His answers we seek.

The enemy would have us believe we are abandoned. Don't believe it. It's when we feel that way that our heavenly Father comforts the most and rescues us from the flood. In retrospect, I can mark exactly where God was leading when my floodgates were opened. What an awesome revelation! How real He became to me! "In everything give thanks" (1 Thess. 5:18) has taken on a new and spiritually refreshing meaning.

If you're down, hang on. Confide in a trusted person, and then quietly reflect on where you've been. Somewhere in the floods you will find the Water of Life.   ROSALYNDA "GINA" KOSINI VORMELKER

A BETTER ANSWER

Delight yourself in the Lord and he will give you the desires of your heart. Ps. 37:4, NIV.

I look forward to going to free clothing distribution sites. I like browsing through the selections and finding something just right for me. Unfortunately, the only site I know of now is open only once a month for two hours. It's only 20 minutes away, but I have to depend on my friend Donna to drive me there. This month she could not take me, and I rather selfishly felt that she had let me down. I even prayed that she would change her mind. I told God this was a simple pleasure I enjoyed. I am also grateful that such ministries are available, because a recent illness had set me back financially, and I was unemployed.

Please, Donna, please, I pleaded silently.

I looked at the clock. The clothes closet was open. The afternoon dragged on, and I was becoming more and more disappointed. God hadn't answered my prayer. Dejectedly, I did a little cleaning in the apartment, but I felt forsaken. Why would God deny me this small pleasure?

After cleaning for a while, I took the garbage to the basement. There, near the recycling bin, was a cardboard box. It was graduation weekend, and college students were moving out, disposing of many of their things. Many times in the past they had not even bagged the stuff they left behind. I peered into the box. It was filled with interesting stationery store items, things I love. I brought the box back upstairs and with great pleasure examined its treasures. It was full of things a writer loves: a ream of typing paper, a three-hole paper punch, a pencil case with a woman's watch inside, blank greeting cards, manila envelopes, self-stick memo pads. My spirits lifted. This was better than free clothes!

I then realized that I had been praying the wrong prayer. Rather than allowing God to meet my needs in the way He saw best, I had been telling Him exactly what to do and how to do it. God surely is the ultimate source through whom we receive countless unplanned, undeserved, and immeasurable blessings each day.

Lord, remind me that You are my sovereign, not My servant, and that I must let You respond to my needs in the way that is best from Your perspective.

ALEAH IQBAL

SEEING THROUGH A CHILD'S EYES

Whosoever shall not receive the kingdom of God as a little child, he shall not enter therein. Mark 10:15.

Whenever I'm in the car, I listen to a Christian music station, alert for songs that my son, Terry, can sing in his church work. I had heard "Shepherd Boy" several times and knew it would be just right for Terry's voice. But I wasn't sure of the title or the vocalist. It took me a year and a half to find it.

Terry was born with a natural love for music. At five months he was keeping time with any music around him with his little hands. People noticed and remarked about it whenever we were out shopping. At age 4 he was singing "Amazing Grace" with his brother at church. As he began evangelistic work it seemed only natural for him to combine his singing with his preaching.

Terry sang "Shepherd Boy" several times at church for me, and each time I just loved hearing him sing it. But then he was transferred to another city, about an hour away, and I could not hear him sing regularly.

One week a young woman, Rebecca, sang "Shepherd Boy" at our church. She had just begun singing when Ashley, my 8-year-old granddaughter, leaned over to me and asked, "Isn't that Uncle Terry's song?"

I nodded and whispered, "Yes." I had mixed feelings about someone else's singing the song I had found for Terry.

Rebecca did a wonderful job. When she finished, Ashley leaned over again and said to me, "Wasn't that nice of Becky to sing that song for Uncle Terry?"

Suddenly it all snapped into focus for me through the eyes of a child. No more resentment of Becky for singing the song, but a real joy that she could deliver the message in song for Terry, for all those who needed its blessing.

We need to have the eyes of a child in order to focus on the important things—especially on our goal to be ready when Christ comes to take us home.

Today I can share Your gifts, or I can hold them close to my heart, where no one else can enjoy them. Help me to be willing to do something for someone else, sharing Your love.

ANNE ELAINE NELSON

THE BEST JOB IN THE WORLD

Thanks be to God that, though you used to be slaves to sin, you wholeheartedly obeyed the form of teaching to which you were entrusted. You have been set free from sin and have become slaves to righteousness. Rom. 6:17, 18, NIV.

I've found a wonderful job—probably the best job in the world—working for a universal, multinational corporation!

I used to work for my boss's main competitor, and I ended up hopelessly in debt to the evil tyrant. I had no career prospects. No job satisfaction. Only guilt and meaningless activity.

Then I heard about a boss who took on anyone who wanted to work for him—immediate acceptance into the workforce, equal opportunities for everyone, exciting and enjoyable. Each person was offered a tailor-made position, designed around her own skills, gifts, and potential.

Initially I was worried about the old boss's response when I handed in my resignation. He isn't exactly known for tolerance and caring, and I was concerned about my massive debts. But I discovered that my new boss had paid off my debts before he'd even employed me! Also, he gave in-service counseling and treatment to help me recover from my previous traumatic experience. I received a comprehensive study manual, complete with daily on-the-job training.

I am in constant contact with the boss through a brilliant intergalactic communication link—far beyond the dreams of any phone company, and simpler, more reliable, and less expensive than a mobile phone.

We also have the best pension plan available. Every loyal worker is entitled to a luxury house in the most beautiful retirement complex of the universe—Club Paradise—complete with an exciting all-expense-paid space voyage!

Although the immediate pay may not match the salaries of executives of other multinational companies, our boss makes sure that all our needs are perfectly met.

Sometimes the work seems hard, and the workers feel lonely and unappreciated. But we never forget whom we're working for, and how much He loves us. And one thing I know for sure: I never want to work for anyone else. Do you?

KAREN HOLFORD

GOD IS ONLY A PRAYER AWAY

Cast all your anxiety on him because he cares for you.
1 Peter 5:7, NIV.

Nineteen-year-old Natalie's dreams for life were shattered when her boyfriend dropped her after finding out she was pregnant. Her greatest fear was telling her parents. When her older sister had become pregnant at 19, she had been given an ultimatum—terminate the pregnancy, or leave home. She had not left home.

When a tearful, frightened Natalie arrived at the day hospital where I work, I pleaded with her to keep the baby. I told her God was prepared to help her in her dilemma if she would only give Him a chance. I read 1 Peter 5:7 to her, assuring her that God cared for her, and asked her to claim the promise. I then suggested that together we pray for her situation for two weeks. After that she could make her decision.

Two weeks later she was back, smiling. She had decided she would trust God and keep the baby. But she still had not told her parents. The next day she called me. Sadly, the response was what she had dreaded: "Get rid of that baby, or go."

I said, "Natalie, God answered your first request and gave you the courage to make your decision. Trust Him for the rest. Now keep on praying, and don't leave home until your dad actually puts you out. If you're really stuck for accommodation, you can stay with me for a while."

When she told her parents of her plight, her father bundled her into the car with her clothes and dropped her off at her ex-boyfriend's house, where she received scant welcome. I arranged to take her to my home in two days' time. In the meantime, we continued to pray.

When I went to get her two days later, her smile was radiant. "My dad has just told me I can come home. I've met God through this experience, and He has answered even this erring newcomer's prayers."

Ours were the hands of faith, prayer the key, and heaven was the promised storehouse!

I want to cast all my anxieties on You too. You have promised to care for me, and I have seen that promise fulfilled. Please give me even more faith.

JUDY BORCHERDS

LEAVING OUTCOMES TO GOD

For we walk by faith, not by sight. 2 Cor. 5:7.

One morning I asked God to lead me to someone whom He could bless through me that day. I am not sure what I was expecting, but I anticipated an experience that would put a glow in my heart when I said good night to God at the end of the day. Throwing my books into a bag, I headed to catch a bus for the university library in downtown Johannesburg, South Africa. Suddenly, up ahead, I saw him—the answer to my morning prayer.

"Do you know where the nearest petrol station is?" he asked in a distressed voice. He'd run out of gas nearby, he said, and the one station he'd found wouldn't accept his bank card. So he'd walked to an ATM, which reportedly shredded his card.

I sized him up. Clean-cut, middle-aged, nice suit—yes, he probably was rushing to an important meeting. "Would you like some money?" I asked, remembering my prayer. He looked relieved and nodded. I was already feeling good.

When he asked for the equivalent of almost $40, I felt a twinge of suspicion, but he immediately offered to deposit the funds in my account as soon as his meeting was finished. I was thrilled at how God had so directly answered my prayer. Thrilled, that is, until the next day when I checked and found that no one had deposited a cent. Although happy to help with gas money, I was on a tight budget and had counted on being reimbursed. I checked the account daily. I didn't mind losing the money as much as I could not tolerate that someone had intentionally taken advantage of my generosity.

I started listening to the Holy Spirit. He reminded me that I'd asked God for an opportunity to help someone, but I had not said that I would help only someone who would return the favor. For all I knew, God may use that man's dishonesty (if in fact he was dishonest) to reach him somehow. I believe God uses circumstances and events to reach people in ways that we will never know about this side of eternity. Perhaps that is one reason we walk by faith and not by what we can see.

ALICIA WORLEY DE PALACIOS

THREE OPEN DOORS

Jesus beheld them, and said unto them, With men this is impossible; but with God all things are possible. Matt. 19:26.

I had developed asthma, and at the suggestion of my physician I moved to Oceanside, California. Daily walks on the beach were wonderful, and all symptoms of asthma disappeared.

Then my brother-in-law, Harry, became very ill. How I wanted to be with my sister before the inevitable happened. But there were two problems: I didn't have the money to make the move to Murrieta, California; and if I were to live in that desert community, perhaps my asthma would return.

"Lord," I prayed, "I love my sister and want to be with her during her time of trouble and heartbreak. You know there is a lack of money, and possible asthma, should I move to the desert. All things are possible with You, Lord. If I am to move, I know You will open doors to make the move possible."

Three days later I received a letter from a magazine saying that it would publish an article I had submitted, and that a check would be coming. "Lord," I asked, "is this an open door?"

I called my sister with the news. She offered to find an apartment for me.

"Not yet, sis. I must save enough money for the move and for the first month's rent."

She called back 10 minutes later. "Harry will pay for half the moving charge!"

"You've opened another door! Thank You, Jesus!"

By July 1 I would have the rent for the first month and the deposit refund from my present apartment to cover the deposit on the new place. Then my niece, Kathy, called. "If you move in on June 1, the first month is free!"

Door number three! "Thank You, Lord!"

The Lord has answered countless prayers over the years, but never again in such a short time. Twelve days after my prayer, He had thrown three doors wide open!

I never tire of telling how rapidly our wonderful God opened three doors. And I have never had asthma again!   Dorothy Anne O'Reilly

FORBIDDEN FLOWERS

Blessed is anyone who endures temptation. Such a one has stood the test and will receive the crown of life. James 1:12, NKJV.

Recently our family spent a day in an African game park. While my husband and son scanned the bushes for animals, I was more interested in the wildflowers. There were many beautiful varieties in the most delicate colors peeping out from among the weeds and grass. What a wonderful example of God's care and provision for His creation that those flowers thrived under such harsh conditions.

Then I saw an exquisite flower—a cluster of bell-shaped blossoms in a deep pink. I had never seen such a beautiful flower before. I have a profusion of mauve and white agapanthus in my garden, but I had never seen a pink one before.

We soon saw masses of them growing all over. I begged my husband to stop the car so that I could dig up just one little plant to take home. His answer was No. Picking wild flowers was prohibited.

Each time I saw "my" pink agapanthus as we drove along, my heart ached for just one. I tried again. "No one will miss it. Think how beautiful it will look. It would bring joy and happiness to many." But for all my rationalizing, all I got was another definite No.

The desire for one of those plants was so great that nothing else interested me for the rest of the day. Later, when I thought about the whole sorry saga of my forbidden flower, I realized that Satan often uses attractive things to capture our interest in what is forbidden. He tempts our senses with desire. Desire turns to covetousness and intense longing. We rationalize and find hundreds of reasons we must have what we want. We rebel against better judgment and the voice of conscience. We pout and fret and make ourselves miserable.

I am grateful for the voice of my conscience, even if it came through, loud and clear, in the voice of my husband!

Thank You for deliverance from temptation!

FRANCES CHARLES

I KNOW THE JUDGE

He is able also to save them to the uttermost that come unto God by him, seeing he ever liveth to make intercession for them. Heb. 7:25.

Speeding 15 miles over the limit, I had my mind more on getting to work on time than on looking out for government traffic enforcers. Reality hit when I saw flashing blue lights in my rearview mirror. My weak excuse availed nothing, so I was obliged to take the ticket that the officer handed me. My day was shattered.

What should I do? What could I do? I thought about it all that day. Traffic school, pleading for mercy in court, hiring a lawyer, or just sending in the fine and forgetting about it. So what if my insurance went up astronomically. It did not seem as though there were any appealing options.

Several days later someone mentioned to my brother-in-law that I had gotten a substantial ticket. "Tell her to give me the ticket. I know the judge," he quickly offered.

I smile now as I go over the events and the conclusion. My brother-in-law spoke to the judge, and the fine was reduced. More incredible than that, while paying my fine, my brother-in-law found that my ticket had been completely absolved. No insurance hikes, no points on my record, no deserved consequences!

Funny how God turns ordinary happenings into extraordinary object lessons. Grace was manifested toward me by the action of my Brother, God's only Son, in taking my sins. It was as if He had taken all of my life's tickets, if you will, saying, "Trust in Me; I'll take care of it. After all, I know the Judge!"

I come to You again, Lord, asking for Your continued grace and love. I don't know what pressures and stresses I will face today, but I know that with You as my elder brother, all will be well. I once again thank You for the incredible and undeserved gift of grace exhibited to me in so many ways.

CHARLOTTE VERRETT

TIME

There is a time for everything, and a season for every activity under heaven. Eccl. 3:1, NIV.

It was the best of times, it was the worst of times," Charles Dickens wrote many years ago. That about summarized the first six years of my married life. We had planned it perfectly: Kevin would get his bachelor's degree in civil engineering in two years, and then we would start a family. Ah! The innocence of the young and newly married!

Six years and two unplanned-but-very-much-wanted children later, I sat in the auditorium at University of California at Davis with tears in my eyes as I watched Kevin receive his master's degree. Tears of relief? Yes, and much to my surprise, tears of sorrow.

I remembered all the hardships of student life: living from one student-loan paycheck to the next; spending nights, weekends, and holidays alone while Kevin worked and studied; and of course those dreaded midterms. (I called them "mean-terms.")

Yet I also remembered all the happy times during school vacations—decorating the house with balloons and homemade signs whenever Kevin aced a test; visiting him on campus; and how much our daughter, Lauren, loved going with me to Daddy's office, located next to the agriculture department, with its cows and pigs. There were those annual celebration bonfires in our fireplace, when Kevin burned all his school papers for the entire year. I also remembered the funny times. Kevin once passed me on the freeway and held up his lab book, in which he'd written "I love you" in huge block letters—and then forgot and turned it in to his professor. We never laughed so hard as we did the day it was returned, and his professor had written in red pen, "I didn't know you cared!"

Lord, help me keep my eye on the goal, but help me enjoy this day with You, too. Help me to remember and treasure how You have led me in the past, and how You care for and love me today. I look forward to a future with You, but I want to relish this day before it too is gone.
STACEY KENNEDY

GOD'S PAINTINGS

Do not cast me from your presence or take your Holy Spirit from me. Ps. 51:11, NIV.

Supper was going to be late because my husband and son were not in yet from cutting corral poles in the timber west of the cabin. I decided to saddle up our big paint horse and go looking for cattle I had seen in Canyon Creek earlier in the day. I made a big loop and found 12 head, which I rounded up. Leaving them by the spring on Prospect Creek, I headed back to camp. I would gather them back up in the morning and take them into Leigh Creek, their last pasture until we took them off the high mountain country for the winter.

As I rode the trail high on Prospect Ridge, something below caught my eye. Grazing with her back to me was a cow elk. A young bull stared at me from a stand of aspens. Quiet, except for the clatter of the big paint's feet on the rocks, I rode on. It had been a beautiful day, and I had enjoyed many beautiful unspoiled evidences of God's love. Joy filled my heart.

While cooking dinner later that evening, I looked out the window and feasted my eyes on one of the most brilliant western sunsets I have seen painted by the hands of God. It was rich in glowing pinks and purples, and brushed over with just the right touches of orange and yellow. Brilliant colors danced on top of the knobby peak west of the cabin. Then the colors started to fade, the brilliance leaving slowly at first, then faster, as if God were withdrawing His presence from the earth. Panic swelled up within me. "No, God, don't go!" A profound loneliness engulfed me. I hungered for the brilliance of the sunset because it represented God's awesome presence in my life. The darkness represented the sin of the world and its overwhelming sorrow.

How thankful I am that until Jesus comes, He will be painting the skies morning and night as a sign of His love for us!

Lord, for the hours of this day, help me to look for evidence of Your constant love and assurance that You will never forsake me, Your daughter, and that You are by my side, no matter where life's trail may lead.

KAREN FETTIG

BUBBA

Before they call I will answer; while they are still speaking I will hear. Isa. 65:24, NIV.

Many people believe that animals have no feelings and therefore do not need any Christian consideration. I believe that God, who created them, cares for the animals. I know He cares about the sparrows, and He certainly cares for dogs, cats, and other domestic and wild animals.

Over the years we have had a number of cats, dogs, and miscellaneous other pets that all children like to have. For years we have been partial to Boston terriers, and a number of ours have grown old and died. It is always hard to lose them, but they give so much joy while they live that it is worth the sorrow.

For the past nine years we have been connected with a rescue committee of the Boston Terrier Club. We have found homes for some and kept others. At present we have three, all males. One is completely blind, another completely deaf.

One of the rescued Bostons was named Bubba. His 84-year-old master couldn't cope with his exuberance and asked us to find a home for him. Since he was only 6 months old, we didn't know if he would cry most of the night from loneliness, or if he would adjust. In the meantime, we called members of the club to see if we could find a home for him. We always ask God to help us find homes for these dogs.

Bubba was a delightful dog and adjusted with little trouble. At first we prayed, "Dear God, please find a good home for Bubba." By the next morning our prayers had changed to "Dear God, Bubba is such a good dog. Please find him a home with children [Bostons love children], a fenced-in yard, and a woman who doesn't work." Now, you may think that was a tall order for God, but God has answered many of our prayers for our dogs with perfect ease.

By the next evening we had a home for Bubba. The woman didn't work. They had a fenced-in yard and three young children who loved Bubba on sight. And he loved them.

If God can do this for a little orphan dog, think how much more He can do for us! We often limit what God can do by not asking. He may say no, yes, maybe, or wait a while; but He is always concerned for our welfare. We need only to lean on Him and ask for what we need.

LORAINE F. SWEETLAND

EVERLASTING FRIENDSHIP

Now you are my friends, since I have told you everything the Father told me. John 15:15, NLT.

Because I am naturally shy, sometimes I do not appear to be friendly. In my heart, though, I long for good friends because I haven't had many, even as a child.

My only friends in high school were classmates with whom I worked on activities. In college I had three outstanding friends, and we still communicate occasionally. I now have three additional friends whom I met in places I have lived. I also have casual friends with whom I share the same likes and dislikes, common activities, similar problems, and similar backgrounds and philosophies.

Friends enjoy togetherness and supportiveness, and they understand each other's problems. That, after all, is what friends are for.

It is difficult to maintain friendships when we get too busy or move far apart, so some friends come and go; but others stick like sisters—or even closer than sisters.

I found a friend, though, who exceeds them all. He finds me when I am lost. He talks to me without hesitation. He knows where I am and what is on my mind. He assures me when I am in doubt. He responds to my requests, according to my needs and what is best for me.

I did not recognize His intentions early in life. I never really responded well to His longing to be my friend. I easily lost sight of Him. Yet He never lost sight of me, even in times of danger and in times when my spirit was the lowest.

All I need to do is call Him. I cannot overburden Him, and I can talk to Him anytime, anywhere, at no charge. I can even tell Him about humorous incidents. And He will listen to my sad stories. He lets me express my deepest feelings and heals my hurting self. There is no price He cannot pay. Just ask Him.

I would like to share this friend with you. He has already said that He wants to be your friend. Let Him know you would like His friendship.

O, Jesus, You have said, "I have loved thee with an everlasting love: therefore with lovingkindness have I drawn thee" [Jer. 31:3]. Thank You for that everlasting friendship!   ESPERANZA AQUINO MOPERA

THE POWER SUPPLY

God has the power to help or to overthrow. 2 Chron. 25:8, NIV.

One Friday my husband and I were driving from Hosur to Trichy, nearly 300 kilometers away. We hoped to reach Trichy by midafternoon.

Unfortunately, around noon the engine suddenly stopped. My husband made several attempts to restart it, but it wouldn't budge. A driver from a nearby taxi stand tried to find the problem but couldn't. He took my husband to a neighboring town to get a mechanic. Nearly two hours later he completed temporary repairs, and we drove to a garage. But nobody there could find the problem. Whenever we slowed down, the car stopped, right in the middle of the road. We were embarrassed. Someone had to push the car to restart it. In one place a couple men came to our rescue. "We sensed something was wrong and came to help," one said.

The last place the car stopped was a police checkpoint. We were afraid to ask the police for help, so my husband tried to push and steer at the same time. A police officer asked what was wrong, but when we explained, he moved away. Another said, "Come, let's give him a hand." Others joined him. The engine roared again.

When my husband took the car to a mechanic in Trichy, he said that the condenser, an electrical fitting that supplies electricity to the engine, was worn out. The engine could not receive the power it needed, especially when the car slowed down.

Sometimes when I feel that all is going well, unexpectedly some disappointments and difficulties come, and I become discouraged. My spiritual condenser doesn't work. My relationship with God comes to a standstill.

Just as the engine needs the electrical supply to keep the car going, I need God's power and strength to go forward in my heavenward journey. I am so glad that God does not throw me in the junkyard when I am disconnected from Him, knowingly or unknowingly. Instead He offers help through various sources, such as His written Word, my husband, parents, pastors, relatives, and friends. He does this for me because He wants a relationship with me, and He wants me to reach the eternal home He is preparing for me.

Thank You, Father, for Your love.   HEPZIBAH G. KORE

GIANTS OR DWARFS

Whoever desires, let him take the water of life freely. Rev. 22:17, NKJV.

For years we had read of this enchanting area, and now was the time to visit the giant redwoods and majestic mountains of the Pacific Northwest that beckoned us. My husband and I planned a camping vacation in Washington and rented a small Toyota camper. We traveled along winding mountain roads to the heart of a rain forest. Prolific ferns grew in lush display, their fronds forming a tropical cover for the valley floor. Moss and lichen hung like cords from tree branches. Sitka spruce, 250 feet tall and more than 12 feet around, dwarfed us. The moisture-filled air and lush growth, we were told, was caused by an almost daily rainfall that amounted to between 120 and 180 inches a year.

A few hours away lay the desert areas of northern California, where shrubs and trees lift withered and stunted arms from the dusty earth that provided little nurture for their growth. The stark contrast was vivid—one area produces giants, the other dwarfs. The difference is the rainfall.

In our lives and in those of our children we need an atmosphere overflowing with the Water of Life, in which our souls can be bathed constantly with life-giving power. If this does not happen, we will be dwarfed and stunted like the desert shrubs. We can grow to be giants in spiritual power, or be dwarfed purely by the atmosphere in which we are nurtured. The lesson spoke clearly to our hearts.

We also observed giant Sitka spruce that had fallen decades before and lay horizontally on the ground. As their timbers decayed, they became hosts, or "nurse logs," to seedlings that had fallen onto their moist exterior and sprouted to become saplings. These small trees stood in rows along the trunk of the fallen giants, taking life and nourishment from their timbers. We stood quietly to absorb this sacred moment.

Jesus Christ became the fallen giant who provides nurture and nourishment to all who fall upon Him and draw life from His body. He died that we might live.

Dear God, I thank You for providing the sustenance I need to grow. I want today to draw life from Your body and to place myself in the "rain forest," where the Water of Life may cause me to grow into a spiritual giant for You.

JOAN MINCHIN NEALL

HOW WELL DO WE SEE?

Now we see through a glass, darkly; but then face to face: now I know in part; but then I shall know even as also I am known. 1 Cor. 13:12.

After visiting my mother-in-law in a nursing home, I was walking down the hall toward the exit when I heard another patient talking animatedly. A little woman with nicely permed silver hair and wearing a colorful flowered housecoat reached out her hand to someone invisible to me, and said, "So nice to see you. I'll run into you again soon, I hope."

As I came closer, I noticed she was conversing with and holding out her hand to her own image reflected in the long mirror.

Most of us don't have any trouble recognizing our physical selves in a mirror. But how good is our spiritual eyesight? Is it possible to be so spiritually nearsighted, so wrapped up in ourselves, that we fail to see there are others who need our help and encouragement? Or might we be the opposite—farsighted to the point of concentrating on helping others so much that we neglect our own spiritual welfare? Are we sometimes plagued with an astigmatic condition—unable to focus well enough on ourselves to perceive our faults and failures? Or maybe we can't see how others may be seeing us? Likewise, are we able to look at others the way God does?

The Bible addresses all these conditions. The first part of Matthew 7 says that we should not judge others, and that we ought not to try to fix someone else, pulling the speck out of her eye, until we get rid of the plank in our own. We also read that "the Lord seeth not as man seeth; for man looketh on the outward appearance, but the Lord looketh on the heart" (1 Sam. 16:7).

The same Book also reveals the remedy. While saying that we are unaware that we are wretched, miserable, poor, blind, and naked (Rev. 3:14-18), God offers us His advice: "I counsel thee to . . . anoint thine eyes with eyesalve, that thou mayest see."

We all have spiritual blind spots, but we don't have to stay that way! God can give us the wisdom and spiritual insights that we need.

BONNIE MOYERS

THE ANGELS ENCAMPED

The angel of the Lord encamps around those who fear him, and he delivers them. Ps. 34:7, NIV.

M ama, what does 'the angel of the Lord encamps around us' mean?" asked our 6-year-old son, Steve.

I was busy preparing breakfast and kept about my work. "It means that angels are always near to protect us from harm," I answered. I didn't know the text would become real that very morning.

Seated in her high chair, 8-month-old Audrey impatiently banged her spoon on the chair's tray. As I continued stirring the cereal I was cooking, Audrey managed to spill the milk on the floor, so I sent Steve outdoors for the mop. Suddenly a loud sizzling noise interrupted the morning quietness. Steve burst through the door, eyes stretched to capacity, shaking with fright.

"I tried to get the mop off the gas tank, and it got caught on the top," he stammered. The sizzling sound was that of escaping gas!

"Run! Quick! Ask Mrs. McDonald to call the gas company!" I urged. She didn't have a phone, but I knew she would go for help. While waiting for her to return, I continued cooking, "serenaded" by the sizzling sound of escaping gas!

Finally Mrs. McDonald returned and reported that someone would come soon. Just then we heard a truck speeding up our road. It jerked to a stop in our front yard. The serviceman leaped from the cab and ran to the back of the house. The sizzling noise stopped. Then he asked if the pilot light was still on and if I had used any of the burners. I told him I had finished cooking breakfast while waiting for him to come. In stern tones he warned, "Next time this happens, turn all the burners off and blow the pilot light out." In unprintable words he warned, "You could have been blown to bits!"

After the serviceman left I lifted the baby from her high chair and called the other three children to follow me into the bedroom. My legs wobbled, and I trembled to think of how close we had come to tragedy. We knelt beside the bed and thanked God for sending His holy angels to protect us. And Steve prayed, "Mama cooked while the gas leaked, and we didn't get blown up, because angels encamped around and protected us from being blown up."

MABEL ROLLINS NORMAN

AWESOME

Before the mountains were born or you brought forth the earth and the world, from everlasting to everlasting you are God. Ps. 90:2, NIV.

I had heard about it. I had seen pictures of it. I had even seen television clips and movies using it as background in a scene. Nothing prepared me, however, for the "awesomeness" of Niagara Falls. The thunderous rumble could be heard and felt literally a mile away; and as the sun flirted with the clouds, a rainbow arched the expanse.

The sightseeing boat seemed so small and vulnerable as it bobbed in the water a good distance from the pounding deluge. I, along with a few hundred other blue-poncho-clad tourists, stood in muted amazement as we were bathed in the spray from the falls some quarter-mile away.

The announcer had given a running commentary on the falls as we boarded the boat and traveled closer to get a better view. He had gone through all the usual statistics—"The American Falls stands 165 feet high. The Horseshoe Falls, to which we are heading, stands 161 feet high and is 2,600 feet along its crestline. The fall is as deep as it is high."

Once we stood before the massive Horseshoe Falls, he said simply, "This is Niagara."

What more could he say? Yes, this is Niagara! Such power! Such beauty! How humbling it all was. In my mind I could hear the familiar words of the well-known hymn:

> "O Lord my God! when I in awesome wonder
> Consider all the worlds Thy hands have made,
> I see the stars, I hear the rolling thunder,
> Thy pow'r thro'out the universe displayed."

Before us rose an unending display of the mighty power of our awesome God. The falls echoed the mighty thunder of God's creative voice and would not be stilled. His awesomeness was wonderfully evident.

Lord, help me each day to realize anew how great You truly are and to take time each day to reflect on the awesome wonders that You created for me to enjoy. MAXINE WILLIAMS ALLEN

THE ADVERSARY AND THE ADVOCATE

God demonsrates his own love for us in this: While we were still sinners, Christ died for us. Rom. 5:8, NIV.

The car landed upside down, headed in the opposite direction. As the dust was settling, the driver climbed out and announced, "I'm OK."

The highway patrol officers witnessed the spectacular accident on their way to answer our 911 call about the weaving car we had followed for 40 miles. When they stopped at the scene of the accident, I rushed to meet them. The adrenaline that had been building finally boiled over, and I voiced my accusations loud and clear. "He's the one! He's guilty; he deserves all he gets. That's the license number I phoned to you!"

In the interest of safety, the officer asked us to move back while they questioned the very fortunate driver who had survived the amazing crash. He admitted that he had been drinking and sat quietly on the bumper of the patrol car while one of the officers came to ask us for a statement and our telephone number.

We were thankful for several things. First, there was no serious injury or death, even though the car had been swerving into oncoming traffic. Second, justice had been carried out. He had been caught. Third, it was an excellent firsthand lesson for the three teenagers and the 10-year-old in our car who had witnessed the event.

As we drove the remaining distance to our home, I thought about our accuser, the adversary, who is always there, ready to shout, "She's guilty! She's the one who did it! She deserves everything she gets! She deserves death!" Yes, I do. Everyone deserves death.

The following morning we thought it would be interesting to see the site of the accident. We went there, but it was difficult to see that anything had happened. Some faint skid marks were all that were visible. Very few people would even notice them, and no one could tell where the car had ended its wild journey.

It reminded me of our Saviour, the Advocate, who stands by with a loving arm around us, and an even lovelier voice, saying, "Yes, she's guilty. She did it. She deserves to die. But Father, I love her. I died for her, and I forgive her. Please accept My sacrifice and My blood." He removes all the evidence, and no one knows what happened. All the stain of sin is gone.

LILLIAN MUSGRAVE

BLOOMS IN THE DESERT

Even the wilderness will rejoice in those days. The desert will blossom with flowers. . . . There the Lord will display his glory, the splendor of our God. Isa. 35:1, 2, NLT.

Having always lived in Sidney, on Australia's eastern seaboard, I was delighted when at last my family and I had the opportunity to visit Perth, the capital city of Western Australia, more than 2,000 miles (3,000 kilometers) from Sydney, on the other side of the continent. Our visit would be in the spring—"wildflower time." Good winter rains had been reported, so the season was expected to be an excellent one.

Western Australia is a huge state with an area of almost 1 million square miles (more than 2.5 million square kilometers). Apart from the fertile southwestern corner, there are vast tracts of arid land that get only scant rainfall. Yet Western Australia is home to an enormous variety of wildflowers, many never seen in the eastern states. Given a little rain at the right time, they grow in tremendous profusion.

We delighted in the colorful carpets of everlasting daises with their delicate papery petals in pink, white, or yellow. There were bushes of Geraldton wax in many shades of pink, as well as the distinctive kangaroo paw, the state's floral emblem, vivid in red and green. And hidden among the hardier plants were fragile orchids of many hues. But especially fascinating to us were the wreath flowers (*Leschenaultia macrantha*) that favored seemingly inhospitable dry soil. We found some of these plants in an unused gravel pit near a remote township. From a central point, the cluster of stems radiates out along the ground, covered in fine, firlike foliage. At the circumference come the flowers, tinted in delicate shades of lemon and rose. Each plant, about 30 centimeters across, looks exactly like a freshly prepared wreath someone unaccountably discarded on a patch of bare, stony ground.

God did display His glory, a glimpse of His splendor.

I am so glad that the God I worship is a Creator-God with the mind, the power, and the artistry to create such beautiful things as wildflowers in such infinite variety—a God who can make the desert bloom. I can't wait to see what else He has in store for me when I reach that "far country," my heavenly home.

JENNIFER M. BALDWIN

THE RESCUE TEAM RESCUED

For God so loved the world, that he gave his only begotten Son, that whosoever believeth in him should not perish, but have everlasting life. John 3:16.

L ying on the street was a badly wilted chrysanthemum stem. The parent plant was close by, and somehow the little stem had been broken off and left to perish. As I walked by I noticed it. Then I did a double take. *I'm going to pick that up and see if I can bring it back to life,* I thought. After all, it was doomed for the trash, and what did I have to lose, except a bit of time. It was so limp that I wondered why I should waste the effort.

When I got home I made a friendly plant nursery for the little casualty, watered it tenderly, then waited. I was very happy the next day to see that it had revived and was showing tiny signs of life. Weeks went by, and it began to look alive. I pinched out the top as it started to grow and stuck that in the ground beside it. Finally, when the starts began to show some real growth, I transplanted them to their very own pot.

I was most eager to see what color my new plant was going to be. All of my other chrysanthemums were blooming merrily—all but my little rescued plant, which refused to put on any buds. But grow it did—big and beautiful—except that there were still no blooms. Then, when all the other chrysanthemums had quit blooming, it started budding out—and out, and out! It was a gorgeous, fluffy, dark-pink shade. And what a flurry of blooms it produced! I had never had such a prolific plant.

In the Bible we read about the dry bones that had no life, but life was breathed back into them. "Thus saith the Lord God unto these bones; Behold, I will cause breath to enter into you, and ye shall live" (Eze. 37:5). So it is with all of us. We have been rescued by the heavenly rescue team that was dispatched from heaven to come to this earth to enable us to have life eternal. God alone can see in each of us the potential for everlasting life.

"For God so loved the world, that he gave his only begotten Son, that whosoever believeth in him should not perish, but have everlasting life." *Thank You, Father!*

And when He transplants, anything beautiful can happen!

PAT MADSEN

BIGGEST SUMMER SURPRISE

The Lord said unto Samuel, . . . man looketh on the outward appearance, but the Lord looketh on the heart. 1 Sam. 16:7.

As I boarded the airplane to return to California following an international convention in Albuquerque, New Mexico, I was glad to settle into my window seat and anticipate my flight home. A boy, about 14, settled in next to me. Soon absorbed in my reading, I took no note when the third passenger sat down in the aisle seat of our row.

How startled I was, when I finally glanced over, to discover sitting there a gangster-type man with very long, thick, bushy, unkempt black hair—mere inches away from me, looking straight ahead. At least I assumed it was a man. His hair was so thick and out of control that it concealed his entire face and upper body. Actually, frightened would be a more accurate description of my reaction. Where I live, a person can be killed by a gang member simply for wearing the "wrong" colors. To my knowledge, this was the closest I had ever been to a gang member. At 20,000 feet up, I felt trapped.

Finally I got up the nerve to speak to him, even though I had not yet seen his face. As I addressed him, he turned and leaned toward me. Suddenly I was gazing into the kindest, sweetest eyes I can ever recall seeing in a man. What a stark contrast to the "gang-banger" image his clothing and hair projected! Those kind eyes were an outward expression of his even gentler heart.

What a great conversation we had. The flight time flew by. By the time we landed, both my traveling companions knew that I love the Lord, and we all enjoyed a wonderful season of sharing.

That incident was a memorable one. How often I've thought of that young fellow and how totally I had misjudged his character by his "packaging."

Lord, help each of us to see past the imperfections and stereotypes of the outward appearance and to look for the genuine goodness of each heart.

JUDY COULSTON

GOD'S SENSE OF HUMOR

He that sitteth in the heavens shall laugh. Ps. 2:4.

Have you ever wondered if God has a sense of humor? I'm sure He does. In fact, there have been times in my life when I have perceived the Divine chuckle at my expense! On one such occasion, however, He had a providential purpose behind it all.

One warm Sabbath my husband left home early to check on his patients at the community hospital. After feeding Taffy, our dog, I was to get dressed, prepare a talk, and fix a dish for potluck. Then I was to follow on to church.

The back screen door was faulty and never locked, so I closed it behind me to keep out flies before giving Taffy her food. When I tried to reenter, that old screen door was locked. Every attempt to unlock the screen proved futile and increased my predicament. With only the "bare essentials" on, I was in a bit of a dilemma. Draping myself in an outdoor rug, I circumnavigated the entire house, hoping one of the six entrances—or even a window—would yield to my desperate efforts. No such luck.

Our nearest neighbors were a couple blocks away and definitely unapproachable in my state of undress. So I turned my gaze heavenward and pleaded, *Dear Lord, I realize the humor of my condition, being locked out of my own home without clothes. I too will find this very amusing in the future. But You know time is of the essence, and I must get on with Your business.* There was nothing to do but sit and wait and listen to the phone ringing inside. Finally, at noon, I tried the screen door again. It slid open with the greatest of ease. "Thank You, Lord!" I blurted out as I dashed inside just as the phone rang again. A voice more desperate than mine implored me to transport a woman and her small son from the Domestic Violence Safe House to the hospital. The youngster had developed pneumonia and needed immediate medical attention. Could I be the "good Samaritan" in this case? Of course I would.

Dressing quickly and thankfully, I completed my assignment and hurried on to the church. *So that's the reason I was locked out, Lord!* I summarized. *You had a Sabbath-day social welfare mission for me to perform that took priority over church obligations. Thank You for that opportunity—and for the humor in my own situation. As always, You are all-wise and all-caring!*

JILL WARDEN PARCHMENT

I'LL BE WHAT YOU WANT ME TO BE

[Be] confident of this, that he who began a good work in you will carry it on to completion until the day of Christ Jesus. Phil. 1:6, NIV.

I'll go where You want me to go, dear Lord, O'er mountain, or plain, or sea; I'll say what You want me to say, dear Lord, I'll be what You want me to be."

The familiar words of this favorite old hymn bring tears to my eyes whenever I hear them sung. They have become the focus of my prayers in the past few years. But I have a problem: knowing where God wants me and what He wants of me.

Life has brought many shattering changes to me—an unwanted divorce, a midlife career change that required my going back to school at age 39 (a real shock to my system!), children growing up and leaving home, loss of identity and self-worth.

However, time has been a great healer. God has brought into my life a wonderful friend who lends untiring support and encouragement. School turned out to be a great blessing. My new soon-to-be career is helping to restore my identity and sense of self-worth. Although I've missed my children greatly, it's been a blessing to see how God is leading in their lives.

Yet I feel lost. I know that God has a plan for my life, but I feel as if there is a haze over my eyes and I just can't quite see what He wants of me. So here is where faith comes in. Praying for wisdom, I take one day at a time, one step at a time, believing that when the time is right He will remove the film from my eyes and make the way crystal clear.

Sounds good, right? Oh, yes! But when you get down to the nitty-gritty, it isn't as easy as it sounds. Days of doubt-filled pity parties come all too frequently. Fear of the unknown creeps in through the window of my soul. When this happens, I cry out to the Lord, sometimes with literal tears, asking Him to help me, to give me faith to hold on.

That's when that still small voice very softly comes through the recesses of my brain: "I will never leave you nor forsake you" (Heb. 13:5, NKJV). Praise God! He won't ever change His mind about me! He will see me through!

Lord, help me to have the patience to wait on Your time. Give me the faith to believe that You will reveal to me just what You want me to be, and give me the strength to see this through "to completion until the day of Christ Jesus."

CAROL BRACKET KASSINGER

FIRST THINGS FIRST

Seek first his kingdom . . . and all these things will be given to you as well. Matt. 6:33, NIV.

Laura had waited a very long time for the appointment. It was her last hope. Although officially retired, the eminent consultant had finally agreed to one visit. Sitting in the secluded patio, Laura finished her story and sat back, waiting expectantly for a response.

The consultant rose to her feet and began collecting items that she placed on a large wooden table. When everything was assembled to her satisfaction, she took a large widemouthed earthen vessel and placed it in front of her bewildered client. One by one the woman carefully placed thumb-sized rocks in the vessel until it could hold no more. "Is this vessel full?" she asked.

Laura responded that it was.

Shaking her head no, the woman began to add tiny pebbles, shaking the vessel to work them down into the spaces. Again she asked, "Is this vessel full?"

Laura answered, "It is now."

The woman picked up several handfuls of sand and dumped them into the vessel. The sand went into all the tiny spaces. Once more she asked, "Is this vessel full?"

This time Laura responded, "Um, probably not."

Nodding, the woman took a dipper and poured water into the vessel until it was filled to the brim. She asked, "What does all this mean to you?"

After some hesitation, Laura ventured, "That if you try really hard, you can always fit something else into your life."

The consultant reached into a cabinet under the table and took out an agate of rare beauty. It caught the rays of the sun and sparkled, dazzled, and shone. "Is there room for this precious stone in the earthen vessel?"

"Not unless you clean out the rubble," Laura answered.

"Exactly," the woman confirmed. "This agate represents your relationship with God, your core uniqueness that you largely have abandoned, and the really important things in life that only you, from the position of your innate giftedness, can contribute. Clean out your earthen vessel. And put the agate in first, or you'll never get it in at all."

ARLENE TAYLOR

A HUM OF UNDERSTANDING

God does not see the same way people see. People look at the outside of a person, but the Lord looks at the heart. 1 Sam. 16:7, EB.

Birds, blossoms, and sunshine beckoned us to eat breakfast on our back porch. My husband and I were soaking up the peaceful springtime beauty while munching on our granola, when suddenly the air was filled with fire and fury. The peaceful Anna's hummingbirds were being attacked as they swooped into their feeder for breakfast by the marauding rufous hummingbirds, who were passing through. I was somewhat irate. How could these explosive intruders be so vicious to our year-round inhabitants? As they whirred past our heads, aiming their sharp beaks at our friendly Anna's, I verbally attacked them for their rude behavior.

A couple weeks later I had to retract my animosity and substitute admiration for those fireballs. I read that for their 3½-inch size they migrate farther than any other bird in the world. They may travel from western Alaska into Mexico. Their tiny wings beat 50 or more times per second. Their metabolism is 50 times that of a human. Their dive-bombing behavior seemed so selfish, but it was a matter of survival. If they don't eat every hour, they may die. Scientists have discovered that many of these rufous hummers are found dead where droughts have kept the wildflowers from blooming along their migratory route.

Yesterday I spent most of the day in the emergency room with my husband. In the curtained cubicle next to us was a very disturbed young woman. She was ranting and raving and yelling obscenities and curses at the medical staff. A security guard paced outside the window.

The lesson of the rufous hummingbird popped back into my mind. I also pictured Jesus with the demoniacs of Gadara, Mary Magdalene, and the woman at the well. Jesus did not write them off as the rest of society had done. Jesus saw them clean and whole, sharing the message of hope and love He would give them.

I began praying that this hurting woman would find Jesus as the solution to her problems. Before long her demeanor changed. When the nurse discharged her, it was with a warning to stop playing Russian roulette by mixing alcohol with her incurable chronic disease.

Dear Jesus, open my eyes to see people as You see them, with Your understanding and vision of the potential of each hurting person who touches my life.

DONNA LEE SHARP

CASTING ALL YOUR CARES

Casting all your care upon him; for he careth for you. 1 Peter 5:7.

I was excited, because for the first time I was going to be just a guest at a women's ministry retreat. This time I was not one of the committee who had to work long hours in preparation, as I had done so often in my home conference. I was looking forward to a weekend of relaxation and of being pampered.

I was, however, carrying a heavy load of three distinct problems that had burdened me for the previous four months. They continued to weigh heavily on me. I had spent much time in prayer, but I wasn't seeing any answers. All this overshadowed the meetings. What was God trying to teach me?

The meetings were Spirit-filled. I was richly blessed. But it was a chorus we sang Sunday morning that struck a chord. I had sung it many times, but this time it seemed to lighten the load I had been carrying. A sense of peace flooded over me.

I flew home, arriving late at night. The first answer to prayer was awaiting me when I arrived. Before the month ended I received the second answer. It took four months for the slightest evidence that the Lord would answer the last prayer. But the answer did come.

I found myself singing the chorus again and again before going to bed, upon waking, while in the shower, while driving the car, and while at work. No longer did I feel the weight of the heavy load. When troubles come my way now, I recall that experience and begin singing my favorite chorus.

"I cast all my cares upon You.
I lay all of my burdens down at Your feet.
And any time that I don't know what to do,
I will cast all my cares upon You."

Father, my burdens are too heavy for me. I accept Your promise to take them, every one, and care for them according to Your will. Thank You for the joy that this brings into my life today. VERA WIEBE

"HELLO, GOD. ARE YOU THERE?"

The Son of Man has come to seek and to save that which was lost. Luke 19:10, NKJV.

The sun gilded over the cresting lake waters as our college class pulled our canoes ashore. We were exhausted and hastened to make camp. I was sick with a high fever. But even more, I was heartsick. Friends offered to help, but I scorned their pity.

When night fell and all had snuggled into sleeping bags, I quietly slipped back to the waterfront. I sat alone on the soaked pier, my arms wrapped defensively around my knees. The tied canoes whipped about in heavy waves.

I could set out in one and never be found again. What reason had I to live, anyway? Eventually I leaned my head back and gazed at a brilliant star display. Just days before, my brother had felt the same despair and ended his life.

Now I screamed in silent anguish. *Where were You, God? How could You let this horror happen and dare call Yourself a God of love?*

It was now well into the night. I'd done a thorough job of pushing everyone away. Yet a lone figure appeared out of the mist, just to see if I was OK. I said I just needed fresh air. Silence. He hesitated, then left. How could I share what I couldn't understand?

Hours later I crawled into a cold sleeping bag. I felt nothing. But I knew for certain that never again would I believe in God.

Everyone was too nice at breakfast. I felt guilt over my secret; yet I also felt a strange sense of freedom. Soon we headed up the lake for some spectacular scenery and lots of tomfoolery. I couldn't join in. Sacred songs kept playing over and over in my head. I frantically pushed them away, but they kept returning. Memorized verses came from nowhere.

That entire day I fought a raging battle as I was plagued by reminders of God's love. God just wasn't willing to let go of me. He'd witnessed my brother's death and mourned it too. He didn't kill my brother. In fact, He'd given His own life because of His revulsion of sin.

God continued to love me that day until I finally broke and confessed His reality. Our Redeemer seeks to save all those who are lost. Someday all things will be made clear. Until then, I can only trust a loving God.

DAWNA BEAUSOLEIL

A JEALOUS HUSBAND

I, the Lord your God, am a jealous God. Ex. 20:5, NKJV.

Tim was mad at me again. He was withdrawing, becoming silent. And I knew why. It wasn't the first time. But it frustrated me. I really thought I was trying.

We were at camp meeting. I was busy leading the women's ministries meetings in the mornings and working at the locating booth in the afternoon. Tim's only commitment was taking care of the sound system for an afternoon seminar. We were attending two seminars together, but it wasn't what he wanted. He was jealous of my time. Jealous that I was spending so much of it without him, working on something, or talking to someone. He wanted me to spend that time with him—not to do anything in particular, just to be with him. He was proud of all that I was doing and of how God was using me, but he still wanted me to spend more time with him. It was our "vacation."

I thought I was spending time with Tim. I prayed about my frustrations, talking to God about how I saw what Tim wanted. A thought suddenly struck me. It was as if God had said, "I understand what Tim is feeling, Tami. I'm jealous of your time too. How much time are you spending with Me? Not just putting in time so that you can say that you are. Not necessarily doing anything but spending time with Me. Enjoying each other's company. You're so busy doing things. Good things. I'm glad that you're doing it. I've called you to do much of it. But I never want your service to take away from your time with Me. I enjoy your company. I long to spend time with you. I'm jealous of your use of time too."

God wants me to spend time with Him even more than Tim does. And while Tim may get jealous and become silent, God gets jealous and waits, trying to show me and remind me of how He longs to spend time with me. Even using a jealous husband to remind me.

As Tim and I finished off our week at camp meeting, trying to work out compromises and deciding what we need to do next year in order to make it a better time for all of us, Tim's feelings were a constant reminder of a God who is also jealous. I was reminded that God and Tim love me so much that both enjoy my company and long for it.

Is God jealous of your time too?

TAMYRA HORST

TRICKED

We know that all things work together for good for those who love God, who are called according to his purpose. Rom. 8:28, NRSV.

Three years after our marriage, my husband, David, received a call to return to mission service in Africa. Because of his previous mission service and because of his love for it, David wanted me to have the same experience. We applied for a position in Africa, preferably West Africa. Our request was granted.

David would be working with USAID, an organization that worked hand in hand with the church to help feed the starving populations of developing countries. I would assist as needed. We packed, said tearful goodbyes to family and friends, and prepared to leave for Ethiopia. After an orientation, we were on our way. I was becoming excited too.

Joy soon turned to sorrow. Because of the political situation, all work visas to Ethiopia were canceled or denied. Our call was canceled. Tears of disappointment rolled down my cheeks. What were we to do now? We were unemployed and had nowhere to go. Our family and friends were waiting for us to embark for Africa.

Soon we were offered a call to London, England. We didn't want to go, but there was no choice. We reluctantly accepted, not knowing that God had a marvelous surprise for us.

David was assigned to pastor three churches. Almost immediately we also found a rewarding ministry helping young people to get a Christian education. God has allowed us to witness products of this education. Our joy is refreshed each time we hear from any of these jewels. One young woman has become a pastor and author in the United States. Others became missionaries, teachers, musicians, and pastors.

Dear Father, thank You for "tricking" us into going to England. You knew that we would not have accepted the call before we left California. I cherish the memories that You helped us make and trust my life to You, because You will make "all things work together for good" (Rom. 8:28).

EUNICE VERRETT HUGHES

REBUILDING INDEXES

Be renewed in the spirit of your mind. Eph. 4:23.

As usual, the first thing I did when I reached my office was to turn on the computer to deal with my e-mail. I tried sending my messages, but they wouldn't go. I couldn't get into my files. Nothing worked. It was as though the whole system had shut down and nothing moved.

I tried a friend's connection, but I found it difficult to operate. For every urgent message possible I sent faxes. For several days I struggled. I felt so cut off from the world without my usual e-mail connection. This was especially trying for me since my husband was in the United States for three weeks while I was half a world away in India. I might as well have been on the moon.

Then another friend suggested, "Try rebuilding your indexes. I think that might help. Go to 'Session Settings' and click on 'Rebuilding Indexes.'"

So I did. And when it was finished doing its job, I tried to open my files. No problem! I tried connecting to my e-mail server. No problem! Communication was restored. It felt so good to be in touch with everyone once again.

This past week was a hectic one. I worked night and day to finish jobs before a Friday deadline. I finally got to the place where I could no longer think straight. People's names I should remember would not come to me. I would walk into a room and wonder why I had come there. It was plain that my own computer system was locked up.

Friday afternoon arrived. I left my office and piles of work. I shut off my computer and took my dog for a long walk at twilight. I enjoyed the sunset and sat for a long while on the front steps, enjoying the quietness of Sabbath's arrival. After some special cinnamon rolls and a hot drink, I curled up on the couch with several copies of my favorite Christian magazine. I went to bed early and got up to enjoy a two-hour bird walk before getting ready for church. The music was great! The Bible discussion was stimulating. The sermon was just what I needed to hear. I spent time in the afternoon writing in my prayer journal.

My internal computer is working again. I'm ready to face a new week. I've spent time with God "rebuilding my indexes."

Thank You, Lord, for the Sabbath, which gives us time to renew our minds and establish communication with You again. DOROTHY EATON WATTS

INTENSIVE CARE

God shall wipe away all tears from their eyes; and there shall be no more death, neither sorrow, nor crying, neither shall there be any more pain: for the former things are passed away. Rev. 21:4.

My mother and I stayed day and night at the hospital while Dad was in for heart surgery. Mrs. Barker, an elderly woman, also came every day to visit her husband in the intensive-care unit. I was impressed by her dignified smile, day after day, especially after she told me that her husband was in a coma and not responding even to her familiar voice.

One morning she and I were alone in the waiting room, watching a talk show that was featuring wedding apparel. It was delightful to watch the satin and chiffon twirl as the wedding dresses were being modeled. I glanced over to see if Mrs. Barker was enjoying it and was surprised to see her eyes welling up with tears when, just a few seconds before, she had been smiling. Thinking she might be the sentimental type, I asked, "Do weddings make you cry?"

She took a moment to wipe the tears from her eyes, then replied, "No. It's just that the bride doesn't know what she is getting herself into!"

The way she blurted it out caught me off guard and I started to laugh. She couldn't help laughing at my reaction, and we both ended up with a much-needed break in the stress level. We parted on that happy note.

I never saw Mrs. Barker again, because my father was transferred to the progressive-care unit. But what she said has stayed in my mind. Because her love for her husband was very evident in our conversations, I didn't think she was referring to the hard work of being tied down. Maybe she was wondering if it would have been easier if she had never loved at all.

When I returned home, I had a greater appreciation for my husband. I tried to see things through his eyes. One thing is sure: When he says, "Let's go and have a fun day," he doesn't have to say it twice.

I think of the wedding of the Lamb, a time of beginning again. Oh, the joy! We will know exactly what we are getting into—an eternity of joy and pain-free, tearless happiness. Only it will be even better than we can imagine.

JO ANN HILTON

ENID'S TESTIMONY

When I came to you, brothers and sisters, I did not come proclaiming the mystery of God to you in lofty words or wisdom.
1 Cor. 2:1, NRSV.

Enid and I work for the same health facility, but each in a different department. For years we've worked the same hours, so we park our cars and walk to the building together. We seldom hold a very long conversation before one of us begins to testify about the goodness of the Lord.

One morning I listened to Enid praising God for enabling her to get to her job through another winter, despite her car being on its last legs. A few weeks ago she had had to leave church in an emergency, and she hadn't been able to get her car to start. One of the members had lent her his car to make the trip.

"The Lord is good," she said. "I really needed a car. Also, my church is undergoing renovation, and I wanted to make a contribution. I had no money, so I borrowed $3,000 from the credit union. I prayed, 'Lord, I really need a car. I want to give some money to the church. I can't afford to spend the whole $3,000 on the car. Please help me.'"

The following weekend the same man who had lent her his car during the emergency had approached her and said, "I am selling my car, and I am not selling it to anyone but you."

Enid acknowledged being in total shock. "How much are you asking for it?" she had asked.

"You tell me," he had answered.

Enid laughed as she told me how her legs had felt as though they would not hold her up and that she had been speechless. "Angels held me up and God gave me words," she told me.

"Will you accept $2,000?" she had asked.

"It's yours," he had responded.

"I couldn't believe it!" she told me. "The car has low mileage, and he has kept up the maintenance on it himself. Now I can give the church $500, in addition to my tithe, and have some left."

As we entered the building to start our new day, we parted, giving God all the glory, thanks, and praise. He truly blesses. What a joy to give our testimony to His goodness daily.   CORA A. WALKER

ANTIQUE IN A BIRDCAGE

If anyone is in Christ, there is a new creation: everything old has passed away; see, everything has become new. 2 Cor. 5:17, NRSV.

When I entered Ann's Texas home for the first time, I heard strange scratching and chirping sounds coming from the back of the house. Later I discovered a bluejay living in a walk-in cage that took up half the enclosed back porch. Rescued as a baby by Ann's mother, that bird has lived on the porch for years. Only a screen separates him from the master bedroom, where Ann's mother spent her last years.

I was chatting with the bluejay through the screen when I saw behind him an old spindle-legged table. Although it looked as if it had once been a lovely table, its round top was now blotchy white with bird droppings. The delicately turned legs were wired together, and half the lower shelf clung tenuously to two legs. The other half was long gone. The clawed feet were a nondescript metal. The whole table looked gray and tired. It appeared useless.

Recently Ann sent me a picture of that same table. But now it is a rich, dark walnut table with gleaming brass feet. Even the shelf underneath is full-sized, touching all four legs. It's a handsome table, worthy to be cherished.

What made the difference? Well, in this picture there was also a master woodcrafter, standing beside the table. He had a contented smile on his face. With his skilled hands he had restored this table to its original luster and beauty. The table is once again useful—a family treasure, a thing of beauty.

God promises to work the same miracle in our lives. "If anyone is in Christ, there is a new creation: everything old has passed away; see, everything has become new." We too have value, but until He transforms us, we look much like the table did when still in the birdcage.

Dear Lord, You are the Master Craftsman. Re-create me with Your sweet Spirit; renew me so people will see Your perfection and Your love for them shining through me. Help me to be useful for You.   SANDRA L. ZAUGG

MY PEGGY DOLL

I will never leave you nor forsake you. Heb. 13:5, NKJV.

On my fourth birthday I received a very beautiful doll from my father. I named her Peggy, and she was very precious to me. As I grew older, Mom and I made pretty dresses for her.

Many years later, when I got married and had my own daughter, Heidi, I taught her to handle Peggy carefully. Heidi was a friendly child, who made friends with Pandora, an older girl down the street. One day when Pandora came to play, she sneaked the doll outside as the girls played "housie-housie"—which included making mudcakes. When I checked on the girls, they and the doll were unrecognizable. I was really upset. Pandora ran home, and I had to clean up my precious daughter and doll.

Sometime later Pandora came back to play. She begged and pleaded to play with Peggy, promising she would not take the doll outside. Before long I heard my door bang as Pandora left. Heidi was in tears, and beside her lay my precious doll—beheaded!

My father, who had given me Peggy, was due to arrive shortly. In my state of panic, I couldn't think what to do with this beheaded doll. Hide it? It might still appear. So in my bewilderment and fear, I quickly dumped the doll into the garbage bin. I have never ceased to regret that day.

We females are pretty and precious in God's sight. He made us beautiful. We are His treasure. When we fall into the mud of sin, our heavenly Parent picks us up, cleans us with His blood, and redeems us. He puts on us a clean white robe. Satan, our archenemy, poses as a friend, but then leads us into various temptations. He tries to behead us, either with lack of good judgment or with temptation.

Satan is even happy to see us dumped into the garbage bin. Then he runs away, leaving us in trouble.

But I am glad for today's promise: "I will never leave you nor forsake you."
Thank You, heavenly Father; thank You.   PRISCILLA ADONIS

GOD MAKES THE ROUGH PLACES A PLAIN

Every valley shall be lifted up, and every mountain and hill be made low; the uneven ground shall become level, and the rough places a plain. Isa. 40:4, NRSV.

One of our favorite Sabbath afternoon activities is going to the mountains, particularly when it is hot in the valley. We like to hike or drive a four-wheeler over back roads and generally enjoy nature. I tease my husband, Gil, that the rougher the road, the better he likes it.

One Sabbath afternoon we decided to explore just such a 26-mile road. Up and up we lurched over the rutted, rocky road that seemed barely to cling to the edge of the mountainside thousands of feet above the valley floor. As we enjoyed the ever-expanding panorama and the oak trees glowing yellow against dark green pines, I tried not to think about how long it would take to find us if we went over the edge.

Nearly 20 miles later, after going down several unusually rough rockslides and landslides, we came to a place where the road ahead was completely obliterated by slides. There was a road down toward the valley, but we did not know if it went through, and we would not be able to get back up it if it did not. Sundown and dark were drawing perilously close, and in the shadows it was already quite cool.

"I guess we will have to go back the way we came," Gil informed me, "but we have two slides to go up. If we can't make it, we will have to try the road down or spend the night on the mountain." We had only two sweaters and one down jacket between us.

We had gone about two miles when we discovered that Princess, our dog, wasn't with us. We didn't want to go back, losing precious time backtracking to retrieve her, but we had no choice.

We turned and headed back up the mountain. As we approached each rockslide, I prayed fervently that God would help us over them. Gil stopped, gunned the engine, and up we went! One more landslide to go. Again, up and over we went.

Thank You, Father, for making the rough places a plain. There may be some rough spots ahead of me today. Please help me get over them, just as You did on the mountainside.
JOYCE WILLES BROWN-CARPER

LOST!

The Son of man is come to save that which was lost. Matt. 18:11.

It was 5:45 p.m. I had to get home. My 17-year-old son was due at work by 6:00. I walked quickly through the mall with my 7-year-old son and 6-year-old daughter. They were skipping along proudly in their brand-new sneakers, in no great hurry to get home. I glanced back occasionally as the distance between us grew.

"Where's Voni?" I asked J.T. when I turned to look and saw only him.

"I don't know," he said.

"You didn't see her?" I questioned impatiently.

"Back there I did," he answered.

My heart sank. This area had many exits leading to other parts of the mall, as well as to the outside. I thought about my daughter—lost! Had she been distracted by something fascinating? Frantically I retraced my steps and finally, in desperation, tearfully asked a store clerk to call security. With instructions on where to meet them, I began sprinting toward that location.

Then I saw her standing alone, crying. A wave of relief swept over me. I grabbed her. "Voni, where have you been?"

"Where were *you*, Mommy?" she whimpered. Tears flowed freely as we hugged tightly. I had done all that was humanly possible to find my child. It was my fault that we got separated, for I had strayed too far from where she could see me.

How often we move too quickly or perhaps too slowly along life's pathways. We wander in strange or dangerous territories, not knowing which way to turn, turning the wrong way, distracted by something fascinating, or lingering where we shouldn't—our eyes completely off the Master. We're lost! And many times we do not even realize it. How sick at heart our heavenly Father must be as He, in anguish, cries out to us, "Child, I'm right here. Don't you see Me?"

How wonderful that our heavenly Father is always there when we need Him. In His infinite wisdom and love, He patiently seeks to find each wandering child and lovingly enfolds us back into the safety of His arms.

IRIS L. STOVALL

JUNE 21

ASK AND BE FAITHFUL

The faithful will abound with blessings. Prov. 28:20, NRSV.

When I went to my friend's home for a visit, I saw something beautiful. Right under their tree, on the lower branch, hung a bunch of orchids in full beauty and glory. I stood there, looking at the delicate yellow and orange flowers. I marveled to myself over the wonder of God's creation that we mortals can appreciate and enjoy.

Knowing the family was transferring, I ventured to ask my friend if she could leave the plant for me to take home to my garden. To my delight, she gladly agreed. So that is how the plant was transferred to my garden, right under my Jackfruit tree.

We cared for it oh, so tenderly. We watered it faithfully so that the plant had enough moisture during the dry spell. And we were glad to see that the plant responded to our loving care. In fact, the first season it awed us with its beautiful, delicate flowers. It was only natural for us to congratulate ourselves over the success. We then looked forward to the next season for another display of its rare beauty.

Time passed. I do not know whether it was our carelessness or that we took it for granted that the plant was surviving, but we seemed to forget that it was a tropical forest plant, not used to the dry heat. You can guess what happened. Yes, one day as I walked over to the tree I found my beloved orchid all dried up. As if to say farewell, it and the stump to which it was attached fell to the ground with a thud.

Jesus said, "Ask, and it shall be given you" (Matt. 7:7), and He keeps His promise. We know this is true, because we have received countless blessings from Him. Many times we take these blessings for granted—and even fail to appreciate them. We become unfaithful to God, the source of these blessings. Then suddenly we realize we have lost all the blessings. When we come to this place, we must remember that God allows the loss in order to draw us back to Him. The blessing is not lost altogether—God is still waiting to give it to us.

I want to be faithful; I appreciate the blessings with which You continue to bless me. May my life today be such that I may continue to receive these blessings.

BIRDIE PODDAR

THE CAMP MEETING TORNADOES

The angel of the Lord encamps around those who fear him, and delivers them. Ps. 34:7, RSV.

Storm warnings had circulated around Minnesota all day, causing uneasiness. Now the heat and heavy humidity were stifling. In the distance loomed ominous-looking cloud banks, interlaced with heat lightning.

We felt blessed to be at camp meeting, as the message reminded us of God's loving care and protection and of our need to trust Him with everything. The evening service closed with a hymn and a prayer for God's protection as the storm approached. As we left the meeting for our dormitories, we were concerned for those camping in the north woods. They were assured they would be evacuated if things worsened, but could remain in the main building if they wished. It did not look as though it would be a restful evening.

About 10:30 a sudden and strong gust of wind knocked the fan out of our window and across the room. Then we heard camp security knocking on doors and telling us to go to the basement. Tornadoes had been sighted and sirens were blowing. People (many still in their nightclothes) moved from all three floors to the basement.

Lights went out and rain came down so hard it forced its way through the window edges, ran onto the floor, and rushed down the stairs in waterfalls. We began to sing "A Shelter in the Time of Storm." Soon the water was midcalf-deep in the hallway.

A loud crash told us that the large window in the stairway hall had smashed to pieces. Many had passed in front of it on the way to the basement. Long after midnight all-clear signals finally sounded.

In the morning we were shocked to see dozens of uprooted trees. We learned that one woman in the woods had been missed in the evacuation. She had prayed for protection, gone to bed, and fallen asleep, never hearing the goings-on. Surely an angel had stood by her tent.

Four tornadoes sighted south of town had been heading straight for our campground. They had jumped over us and touched down some 15 miles away. What we had experienced was merely the tailwinds of those tornadoes.

Thank You for the angels who were with all of us that night!

DARLENE YTREDAL BURGESON

WAITING AND WAITING

Those who wait on the Lord—shall renew their strength; they shall mount up with wings like eagles, they shall run and not be weary, they shall walk and not faint. Isa. 40:31, NKJV.

I love cats. Those who know me very well will often ask me, "How are the girls?" referring to my two cats, Pumpkin and Buffy. Pumpkin, the older one, is almost 15, and I seldom let her outside because I am afraid she would not be able to defend herself.

One day I let Pumpkin outdoors with every intention of keeping a close watch on her. But I got absorbed with something and forgot that she had been outside for some time. I rushed to let her in, but there was no cat. Again and again I called her name, but no Pumpkin appeared. I figured that she had wandered beyond hearing distance and would be along shortly.

About 15 minutes later I called her again. I repeated this scenario at intervals throughout the day. Worried, I started thinking of all the possible tragedies that could happen to my poor, defenseless cat.

As I searched the neighborhood, it seemed that all the cats I saw looked like Pumpkin. *How foolish could I have been to let her out, even for a little while!* I thought.

Throughout the day I prayed, but it reached the point where a gentle whisper of a prayer was not enough. I agonized with God to deliver Pumpkin so that my worst fears would not be realized. Tears streamed uncontrollably down my face as I began to realize that all the waiting and praying was possibly in vain. It was beginning to get dark, and the thought of Pumpkin's spending the night somewhere outside was unbearable.

"Please, God, deliver Pumpkin before evening comes" was my constant prayer.

As I searched the neighborhood one last time, I passed a little boy sitting on the steps in front of his house. I asked him if he had seen a small gray cat. I will never forget what he said. But the most peculiar thing was how he said it. With great assurance he replied, "Don't worry, lady. Your cat will come home." Somehow, his words comforted me, and when I returned home, there was Pumpkin, sitting on the front porch!

Such an encouragement that little boy was! Help me to speak an encouraging word when given the opportunity so that someone else's strength may be renewed.

DONNA A. SMITH

FRIENDSHIP AND FORGIVENESS

Jesus said, "Neither do I condemn you; go, and do not sin again."
John 8:11, RSV.

They dragged the terror-stricken woman to Him and left her in a trembling pile at His feet. She had been the object of lust, and no one in the group of accusers was blameless. But they showed no mercy. She was not allowed to wash, to dress, or to walk on her own. They dragged her through the dusty streets, gloating that they had her—and that they finally had *Him*. If He said to let her go, He would be disregarding a commandment. And if He pronounced the death sentence, they could report Him to the Romans for insurrection. But they didn't know Jesus!

He knew the law; He gave the law. He knew the spirit of the law; and He knew their hearts. He knew hers was broken, and He wasn't about to crush more life from her. He had come to restore life.

But first He dealt with all those hard, cold faces. "What does the law say? What should we do? Stone those caught in adultery? All right! But there is more to the law. The guilty should not be punished by the guilty." He stooped and began to write the sins of the group in the dust, with details so exact the accusers trembled. He knew. They knew He knew, and they melted away. But the woman did not know. She had not lifted her eyes. She took the piercing silence as a death sentence and waited for the first crushing stone.

Finally she looked up. Only Jesus was there. He knew the worst about her, but His face was filled with compassion and forgiveness. He knew there was more to her than someone to be used, then tossed aside. He knew her. He knew there was a real person there. He had made her—for a better life than this.

"'Woman, where are they? Has no one condemned you?' She said, 'No one, Lord.' And Jesus said, 'Neither do I condemn you; go, and do not sin again'" (John 8:10, 11).

He believed in her. He forgave her. She felt clean from the depths of her heart and soul and spirit. She would never forget. She gathered up the tatters of her clothes and began to walk in newness of life.   KYNA HINSON

MY RAINBOW PROMISE

I know the plans I have for you . . . plans to prosper you and not to harm you, plans to give you hope and a future. Jer. 29:11, NIV.

M y wedding was only a week away. I should have been the happiest woman in the world. But I had just gotten off the phone with my husband-to-be, who was at his home in Canada and having second thoughts. "What if we wait another year, Steph? What do you think about that?"

My first thought was *No way! The invitations have already been sent, the caterer is cooking away, and the horse and carriage have already been booked. Why didn't you think of this before we set a date for the wedding? Why would you want to embarrass me like this?*

My heart was breaking. How could he do this to me? How could he doubt my love and dedication? What was wrong with me? I got into the car and started to drive, something that always calms my nerves. I kept praying, "Lord, what are You doing to me? Are You telling me that he isn't the one? Or are You telling me just to trust in You and things will work out?" My emotions ranged from anger to feeling sorry for myself to heartbreaking sadness and then back to anger and feeling as though I'd been betrayed. "I thought I knew him, Lord. Why are You letting me go through this painful experience alone?"

After I'd mentally exhausted myself with all the arguments, I said, "OK, Lord. You handle this one. Give me a sign, and I'll do whatever You want me to do." At that moment I came over a hill and saw the most beautiful rainbow I had ever seen, every color clearly distinct, the sun's rays beaming through the clouds. It seemed to be saying, "Stephanie, just trust Me. I promise you that things will work out for the best. I love you and would never hurt you. Remember My promise: ' "For I know the plans I have for you," declares the Lord, "plans to prosper you and not to harm you, plans to give you hope and a future." ' "

A sudden peace came upon my heart, and I knew that He was in control of my life. I knew that things would work out for the best. Harry and I have been happily married since June 25, 1995. We plan to be married forever. I can't wait to take my husband's hand when we are in heaven and stand at the feet of Jesus to thank Him for keeping His promise.

STEPHANIE YAMNIUK

GETTING THE VIEW FROM THE TOP

He gives power to the tired and worn out, and strength to the weak.
Isa. 40:29, TLB.

"Why did I ever decide to do this again?" I asked myself as I sat down for the umpteenth time to catch my breath. Here I was on vacation, climbing a mountain. However, this was no ordinary hill. With its peak at 13,455 feet (4,101 meters), Mount Kinabalu is the highest mountain in Southeast Asia. The climb is as famous for the beauty of its route as for the view from the top. Kinabalu's slopes possess a wealth of plant growth and a large variety of birds.

I had scaled this mountain once before, when I was younger and more energetic. Now married, I wanted my husband to experience and see the wonders of nature God had given us on the island of Borneo. After listening to my "sales pitch" for more than a year, Dan consented, and we started arrangements to spend our vacation in Malaysia.

Dan, my aunt Sabeda, and I began the climb at 5,944 feet (1,812 meters) above sea level. We planned to climb to 12,500 feet (3,810 meters) and stay overnight at the Sayat Hut. The second phase to the peak would begin at 3:00 the next morning in order to catch the spectacular sunrise over the mountain.

But here we were, taking another break for my benefit. I was huffing and puffing and feeling as if I were carrying a load of rocks in my backpack. Once again I looked forlornly at Dan and asked, "Why are we doing this?"

He smiled encouragingly and said, "I'm tired too. We'll just rest awhile."

Aunt Sabeda, who had made this trip to the peak six times before, kept us going. "You're almost there; don't give up now. The view from the peak is beautiful. Come on; you can make it."

She was right. Struggling in the early-morning hours in the high altitude, Dan and I suddenly gasped in awe as we glimpsed the granite peak. Strangely, we were energized again. We could see it, and we were going to make it.

The Christian's road to heaven is not easy; at times we feel ready to give up. *Sorry, Lord; this is as far as I can go. My legs are just about to buckle under me. Please, not another trial. I'm so tired, Lord.* Yet the Lord does not yet give up on us. He puts in our paths someone who is going our way, who encourages us to go on. He knows the journey can be difficult, but when we see the peak, we will know He is worth it, and together we will rejoice in His heavenly kingdom.

LYNNETTA SIAGIAN HAMSTRA

THE WALLS CAN STILL FALL TODAY

Now Jericho was tightly shut up. . . . No one went out and no one came in. Joshua 6:1, NIV.

We rented one of two houses on a big compound, enclosed by a very high wall with barbed wire. Julie, the owner, lived in the other house. She was a caring and loving landlady, and we got along very cordially—until my husband resigned from Barclays Bank to work for Ford Motor Company.

My husband resigned for religious reasons, but that had no meaning to Julie. Unknown to us, she had hoped to benefit in extraordinary ways from the financial services of the bank because my husband was a manager. She was a businessperson. As matters stood, she had no need for a manager of Ford Motors. She therefore wanted us out of her house.

One week when we returned from church, the lock to the gate had been changed and we could not get into the compound. We had to wait outside until 8:00 in the evening when Julie returned from the market. She refused to give us a new key and continued to lock us out. We had no recourse to the law because the military of the country had just seized power, and during the interval conventional law had taken a holiday.

We began praying for the Lord to soften Julie's heart till we found a new place. Then one Sabbath evening we returned from church with a friend who wanted to visit with us before going on home. But when Julie came to open the gate for us, she told our friend that if he entered the compound, he would not be let out until the next day. Wondering how long the Lord would allow such humiliation and harassment to continue, we prayed more fervently.

The next day the sun was shining brightly, and a pleasant cool breeze was blowing. We were going about our normal chores. As usual, Julie's gate was locked. Suddenly a big *Boom!* startled all of us, and we rushed out to see what had caused it. To our astonishment—and Julie's—that monstrous and invincible wall had come crashing down—torn down with no human effort!

The Lord has promised that He will be with us, even to the end of time, and the falling of Julie's wall is a testimony to me that God is certainly with us. It does not matter what the trial is, if we remain faithful to Him, He will work all things out for our good. He has done it again and again in our lives.

MABEL OWUSU-ANTWI

EVEN IF I SUE?

I have loved you, my people, with an everlasting love. With unfailing love I have drawn you to myself. Jer. 31:3, NLT.

We were driving down from the Rockies to a weekend getaway on a tiny island off the coast of British Columbia, Canada, when my 12-year-old nephew asked, "Auntie, will you pay my way through law school?" Delighted that he had begun giving serious consideration to his tertiary education, I responded, "Of course, darling."

"Even if I sued you for every time you've mentioned my name in your writing or in your talks or your preaching?" Benign mischief put a sparkle in his gray eyes.

I had to smother a smile. "Absolutely, my dear."

"But why would you do that?" He seemed genuinely puzzled.

Before I could answer, his sister looked up from an entry she was making in her blessings journal. "Unconditional love. That's why," she said matter-of-factly.

"She'd really take her hard-earned money to pay my way through school, and then pay again when I sued her? That's a rip-off—a royal rip-off!" His whisper was incredulous.

She nodded. "She said she would, didn't she?" (The muted conversation was clearly reserved for those in the back seat.) "I think she's trying to be like Jesus. He did something like that. He came to us with so much love and we . . ."

I strained unsuccessfully to hear her words, but the wind from the open window blew them away.

After we arrived on the island, my niece lingered beside me for a few minutes of sunshine. "We experienced a parable in the car yesterday, didn't we?"

I started to answer before I understood that her question was rhetorical. Basking in the summer sunshine, I began to meditate with my pen. I watched the words almost form themselves into a prayer: "Dear ever-loving Redeemer and Rescuer! Thank You for helping us earthborn sinners understand—even if only on a minuscule level—the greatness of Your saving love for us. And thank You for children who remind us of who You are."

GLENDA-MAE GREENE

DON'T EVER LET GO!

God is our refuge and strength, an ever-present help in trouble.
Ps. 46:1, NIV.

G rand and awesome in size, they stood all hazy and pink in the cool morning mists—the Great Sand Dunes of south central Colorado.

"Let's see who can get to the top first!" my friend challenged, and we were off. At first it was easy, but as the incline increased and our pace slowed, we soon realized something quite important: For every two steps we took upward, we lost one step sliding down in the moving sand. And if we dared to stop and rest, we continued to lose ground, slowly slipping downward. If we hoped to make it to the top, we had to take small steps, pace ourselves, and avoid stopping.

I have long since compared that climb to our struggles in the Christian's upward climb. The first part is relatively easy. We are taking big steps and moving quickly. Then the climb becomes steeper and our pace slows. The devil is constantly tempting us to stop and take a supposed rest or to be satisfied with the height we have achieved. But herein lies the glitch. The minute you rest, you stop moving upward. And to compound matters, you begin to slide downward, slowly at first, but gaining momentum quickly. There is no such thing as standing still on the steep side of a sand dune or in the Christian's upward climb. It's either up or down. I learned that the way to stop the downslide in my Christian walk was to stop resting immediately. No matter how far back I slide, I grab hold of the Saviour's outstretched hand and start climbing again.

If you look around, you'll see your brothers and sisters struggling upward too. Each has his or her own obstacles, but each is firmly holding the Saviour's hand and moving steadily upward. Speed is not important; only the direction of movement is. It has taken a long time for me to learn this lesson, and I'm still tempted to rest here and there. But when I keep hold of the Saviour's hand, I always move upward, and there is no describing the sense of thrill and adventure as I, along with my Christian brothers and sisters, climb higher and higher.

What looked like an easy 15-minute climb to the top of those dunes turned out to be a sweaty hour-and-a-half workout! Yet running and sliding from the top to the bottom of those great dunes took only seven minutes!

VALERIE F. JACOBS

A FRIEND IN NEED

Thou art my rock and my fortress; therefore for thy name's sake lead me, and guide me. Ps. 31:3.

When I was 13 years old my mother decided that I should attend the mission boarding school 37 miles (60 kilometers) away. I didn't want to leave my parents, but I knew they were focusing only on my good. My mother told me there are more things to learn than those considered a formal education, and she was right. "You have to develop your potential, learn to adjust, to accommodate, tolerate, and understand different types of people," she said.

My trunk was packed with my clothes and other necessary articles. It was time to go. The monsoon rain was pouring down mercilessly, and when my mother and I arrived at the school, we were both in dripping saris. After I was oriented and settled, my mother left. Later, as I sat on a small stool in the corridor, anxious thoughts gripped me. I began to imagine many possible calamities that could happen to me. I could understand only my own language—how was I going to answer my teachers? Maybe my cousins and classmates would think I was dumb. Maybe they would find a nickname for me. What would happen to me if I never picked up English? Would all the money be wasted? When would I get a letter from home? Who would guide and share my problems? Could I successfully face and solve my problems?

Slowly I got up from the stool to get my Bible from the tightly packed box. I found the verse, "Be not afraid, . . . for the Lord thy God is with thee" (Joshua 1:9).

Suddenly there was a tap on my shoulder. A girl with a kind face hovered over me. She said, "Don't be so sad. I can understand you. Come with me to supper."

"I don't know anyplace around here. I am glad you are able to understand my loneliness," I said. She became a close lifelong friend. It appeared to me that she could read all my thoughts. She took me to the dining hall, chapel, and classes. Sabbath morning we went to a secluded place to read our Bibles. From then on I could understand that God had sent that friend to me to console me in my despair. Confidence returned to me. I decided to face the world with the help of God, because He sees me and provides for all my needs.   SOOSANNA MATHEW

LAND OF THE FREE

Where the Spirit of the Lord is, there is freedom. 2 Cor. 3:17, RSV.

I sat in the dining area, paperwork spread out before me, as our three young children marched in circles around me and through the living room. Our son, David, had a tape of patriotic songs they were attempting to learn.

As they marched, I laughed with them—until they came to the part of our national anthem that says "the land of the free and the home of the brave." My eyes began to water as I tried to explain "the land of the free" to the children. We had been studying other countries, and I thought of all those who have never known a "land of the free." I thought of those who have known freedoms and have lost them, and my mind hung on thoughts of the freedoms that seem to be slipping away around the world.

How can we justify the freedoms not extended, the pain caused when freedoms are stripped away? Surely God never meant for us to be subjected to the selfish whims of other people! He never meant for us to be bigoted, fighting, murdering, warring, imprisoned by sinful habits. I turned back to the children and their innocent march as they whirled around the room, shouting those words. My thoughts wandered, searching for an answer before resting on "God will wipe away every tear from their eyes; there shall be no more death, nor sorrow, nor crying. There shall be no more pain, for the former things have passed away. . . . Behold, I make all things new" (Rev. 21:4, 5, NKJV).

Here was my answer. A smile crept onto my face and the lines of sorrow softened. There is a "land of the free" available to everyone! No matter what kinds of slavery or imprisonment we have endured here on earth, God offers eternity in freedom. I admitted to God right then my slavery to things of this world, my sorrow over freedoms lost to humans everywhere, and thanked Him for an invitation to heaven, land of the truly free. I stood and joined the children's happy march, placing my confidence in God's land of the free, remembering that as long as I had God's Spirit within me, I would always be free.

DAVA BENTON WHITE

UNSAFE ASSUMPTIONS

[Woman] looks at the outward appearance, but the Lord looks at the heart. 1 Sam. 16:7, NIV.

It was great fun standing just above the beach, watching the windsurfers cutting back and forth, over and through the waves. What grace! What strength! I could not even imagine what it would require to hold that big sail up and keep the whole thing balanced. The riders flipped their sails and skimmed out to where the breakers were forming, then they turned and rode toward the rocky shore with great speed. Suddenly one of them turned and almost jumped back across the wave. Then, instead of simply turning, the rider and board did a beautiful flip—a complete somersault.

"Come quick!" I called to Dick. "Watch the rider on the left. He just did an incredible flip! And there—it happened again!"

We watched for some time. In fact, the surfer who had been doing the somersaults tired before we did and rode one wave all the way to shore. I watched as he brought the sail around, picked up the board, and pulled off his wet suit headpiece.

I gasped. How could it be? The strong and graceful one who had been putting on such a show was not a he at all. She shook her long hair out, unzipped the wetsuit, and stepped out in her bikini. Very much a female.

I, of all people, an advocate for women, had assumed the wind riders were men. I'm not even sure why I thought it must have been a man—I have seen women windsurf before. I know women are strong. I know women are brave. And I certainly know women are graceful. So why couldn't it be a woman riding and flipping over those waves? I had made an assumption because I could not see all the facts. And for some reason I had expected a man. And I was wrong.

I dread to think of the times I have made an assumption about a person or event when I did not have all the facts. I have no idea how many times I may have been wrong. I hope that has never happened to you, but I fear it happens more often than we would like to admit. Assumptions are seldom safe, even when we base our conclusions on past experience.

How glad I am that when You judge me, You will have all the facts. You know my heart—and don't make assumptions. I can feel safe with Your conclusions and judgments. ARDIS DICK STENBAKKEN

THE BEST BIRTHDAY GIFT

Thanks be to God for his indescribable gift! 2 Cor. 9:15, NIV.

As Christians, we know that the best gift of all time is the gift of Jesus—given not once, at His birth, but again at His death and resurrection and continuously through His high priestly ministry for us. But we grow up learning about the value of gifts, even the gift of God, from what is given us. Growing up during the Depression years in a poor family in which gift-giving was meager, I learned that it isn't the number of gifts or the money spent on them that creates the spirit of giving.

One of the best gifts I received was the present my mother gave me for my sixth birthday. Although my father worked when he could find a job, and always managed to pay the $5 monthly rent on our house and buy a few staples, there was seldom anything for extras. Our small herd of goats gave milk and cream; our laying hens produced eggs. We had a good garden that kept us supplied with vegetables, and our strawberry patch was a joy in springtime. Mother canned hundreds of quarts of fruits and vegetables each summer.

I went to bed the eve of my birthday with an expectant heart. I knew Mother would bake me a cake. Mother was a marvelous cake maker, and the birthday girl always got to scrape out the bowl. Since I have a July birthday, we usually made homemade strawberry ice cream, my favorite. But I wondered if I would receive a gift. I went to sleep that night with sounds of Mother at the treadle sewing machine. Was she sewing something for me?

Morning came quickly, bright and sunny, as my birthdays always were. As I entered the living room, I spied a golden vision of loveliness—a baby doll clothed in yellow silk! To a doll lover like me, this was the very best gift possible. Upon examination, I discovered she was my very own Sally, who had suffered a bashed-in head several months previously. Mother had carefully stuffed her head with batting and fashioned a tight little white cotton cap to keep the stuffing in and to cover the rough edges of the break in her composition head. Over it all, Sally was crowned with a ruffled yellow silk bonnet. New yellow silk panties and dress completed her outfit. In my sight she was better than a new doll.

God's daily gifts are often like that—disasters turned into golden gifts.

CARROL JOHNSON SHEWMAKE

THE BIGGEST
FIREWORKS SHOW EVER SEEN!

As the lightning cometh out of the east, and shineth even unto the west; so shall also the coming of the Son of man be. Matt. 24:27.

The dense darkness came late on that Fourth of July night—Independence Day night in the United States. Seated on the wide grassy meadow in front of the civic center, we waited a long time for the show to begin. Finally the announcement was made that the city had spent $55,000 on the evening's fireworks, and we were sure it would live up to its reputation of being the biggest and best in all the western states. People came from many regions around, paying enough entrance fees to cover the cost.

Suddenly the sky lit up with horizon-wide designs of color and light, one on top of another, so fast that our eyes could hardly keep up with the changes, each one popping and booming so loud we could hear nothing else. Only occasionally could we hear the "oohs" and "ahs" of the people very near us. Thousands of people crowded the area, sitting on blankets or folding chairs. We knew thousands more were watching from hills and buildings all over the city and its suburbs.

"This show is spectacular!" I declared. "I have never seen any like it!"

The whole sky lit up from side to side, making visible all the thousands of faces lifted skyward. The displays came rapidly, nonstop, for an hour and a half. My neck was tired of bending backward to see it all. Finally the show ended as abruptly as it had begun. Overcome by it all, people began to silently gather their belongings and leave.

During that display of light I tried to imagine what it would be like to see the coming of Jesus. How many times brighter that will be! And talk about fireworks! The trumpet, the shout, the bright colors of the spectrum—what a show! I doubt that anyone can imagine that brightness. We have no idea what that will be like until the time comes. We read Bible stories about persons who could not endure the brightness of the presence of God. The brightness of His coming will destroy all evil.

Only the sealed saints will be able to endure that brightness. I want to be among the elect group who can look up with no fear into the face of our coming Lord as we behold Him in all His glory! BESSIE SIEMENS LOBSIEN

MY CHILD, TRUST ME

I will instruct you and teach you in the way you should go; I will guide you with My eye. Ps. 32:8, NKJV.

We had waited with anticipation for the central California ministerial couples' retreat; however, the weekend preceding the retreat was a busy one for my husband. He was to preach in one of the churches, but the bigger responsibility was to officiate the following day at his nephew's wedding in Loma Linda, about eight hours from the retreat center. So after the church service we headed for Loma Linda, eating our lunch in the car while driving.

That night and the next morning it rained very hard, leaving puddles everywhere. I became concerned about our trip north to the retreat center after the wedding. I tried to brush off my worry, but it kept nagging me.

With much apprehension we left Loma Linda at 1:45 p.m. We had been to the retreat center before, but it had always been in the daytime. We had lost our way then. What would happen at night with inclement weather? When the rain poured in the valley, snow usually accumulated in the mountains.

As we traveled that afternoon I was very quiet, praying and pleading with God to direct us so that we would not miss any turn on that long journey. Something inside me said, "Oh, you of little faith; why don't you trust Me?" Then I remembered the promise: "I will instruct you and teach you in the way you should go; I will guide you with My eye." Then like lightning Isaiah 41:10 flashed before me: "Fear not, for I am with you; be not dismayed, for I am your God. I will strengthen you, yes, I will help you, I will uphold you with My righteous right hand" (NKJV). I also remembered reading Proverbs 29:25, "The fear of man brings a snare, but whoever trusts in the Lord shall be safe" (NKJV). How my fear became a snare to me! Why couldn't I trust Him who knows me?

Remembering those promises, and without speaking with my husband, I prayed earnestly, "Father God, please help me to trust You implicitly. Take away my unbelief, and please direct our path." Soon peace flooded my soul, and we reached our destination safely, without missing any turns. Amazing!

OFELIA A. PANGAN

GOD'S WATCHCARE

The angel of the Lord encampeth round about them that fear him, and delivereth them. Ps. 34:7.

*B*ang! Bang! Bang! Bang! I was in a deep sleep and thought I was dreaming, correlating the sounds with leftover firecrackers from the Fourth of July that had just been celebrated a few days earlier.

"Wake up! Wake up!" my husband shouted as he stood at the window at 4:00 a.m. "I heard six gunshots. There are police surrounding the entire street over there; they have cordoned it off. It looks as though they have covered someone with a sheet."

"Mike," I implored, "please step away from the window. There may be more shots, and a stray bullet may kill you."

He returned to bed, and we were left to wonder about what had just taken place.

A couple hours later we arose to prepare for the day. After worship my husband, the amateur detective, headed for the terrace to get a better look at the crime scene.

As he entered the living room on his way to the terrace, I heard a piercing scream, then his excited call. "Darl! Darl! Come quickly!"

I rushed to the living room. He pointed to a bullet hole in the wall. We were stunned. After the initial shock wore off, the reality of the incident set in. First, the area where the shooting took place was at least a mile and a half from our house. Second, if the bullet was going to lodge anywhere, the law of averages dictated that it should have lodged in our bedroom, where we were sleeping, since it was the closest to the shooting. But God in His mercy sent the bullet past us and into the living room, which was unoccupied at the time.

We worshiped again in thanksgiving for our spared lives. We had a testimony for everyone we saw that day, and not only that day, but every day since then. What a mighty God we serve. Truly our heavenly Father watches over us!

Obviously an angel watched over us when we did not even know we were in danger. You delivered us. For that we give thanks. I thank You too for all the other times You have delivered and ask for Your protection for this day.

DARLENE SIMMONDS

191

HELP!

Do not fear, for I am with you; do not be dismayed, for I am your God. I will strengthen you and help you; I will uphold you with my righteous right hand. Isa. 41:10, NIV.

One Sunday afternoon as I sat staring at my week-at-a-glance schedule, what I saw produced fear, anxiety, and defeat. How would I ever make it through the week? Besides working full-time, I was attending classes in preparation for a state exam, managing day-to-day home chores, caring for two elderly parents, and serving in several church offices.

My schedule showed after-work appointments for a visit to my doctor, accompanying my mother to her doctor, an exam, the need to request a day off from work to accompany my dad to the hospital for eye surgery, and an out-of-town assignment that would get me home late Friday afternoon. The physical and mental stress overwhelmed me. *I can't do this,* I thought.

As I sat feeling sorry for myself, a still small voice said to me, "You're right; you can't do it. But I can help you, if you let Me." Feeling ashamed that I had not asked for help first, I replied, *Lord, I need help! Please help me!* I folded the schedule and put it aside, then I took up my Bible and turned to Isaiah 41:10. After reading the text several times, I felt calm and began to study for the exam.

On Monday morning things began to happen. The doctor's office said it would be necessary to reschedule my Monday appointment. On Tuesday my cousin called and offered to accompany Dad to his surgical appointment. Since he'd had a similar surgery, he knew what to expect. There would be no need for me to take time off from work. The change of these two appointments relieved me of a significant amount of fear and stress, enabling me to prepare for the other appointments. I couldn't believe it—but then I should have. I had tried to carry the load of life's responsibilities all alone when there was One who was waiting to help me, and all I had to do was ask for help.

Today, if you are feeling exhausted, afraid, overwhelmed, and concerned, remember that there is One who has promised to help you. He is *waiting* to help you. All you have to do is ask.   MAUREEN O. BURKE

MY TESTIMONY

In all things God works for the good of those who love him, who have been called according to his purpose. Rom. 8:28, NIV.

It's been more than 12 years since I had a stroke at the young age of 40. I'm so glad the hard part is over. God has brought me a long way since nearly dying, the feeding tube, the respirator, and even the mistreatment at the nursing home. The stroke caused me to lose the use of all my limbs and my voice. I was in shock for quite some time and cried almost all the time. The staff at the nursing home I am in now has been kind and patient with me.

The Lord has been good and has blessed me tremendously. I now have some movement on my left side, and the feeding tube has been removed. I can even hold my head up now; before, my head hung to the side. Most of the improvements have occurred during the past two and a half years. God has His own perfect timing, and I am still improving. I believe His timing in restoring me is somehow drawing more people to Him. It is a great honor to be God's instrument!

I enjoy life in spite of my disabilities. God's numerous blessings to me include wonderful friends, good health, and more knowledge of Him through the Bible study I started here in the nursing home. A motorized chair and a little computer that talks and prints are added blessings.

Through the sale of my house I was able to get many things I needed— a large-print Bible, new clothing, furniture, and decorations for my room. All are more of God's blessings. I had great fun picking out a whole new wardrobe. I have decided to give 10 percent to the Lord from my proceeds, since He has done so much for me.

I've made several improvements lately that have really excited me. I can now chew my food. I can suck on little pieces of candy without choking, and I can push the buttons on my radio/cassette player. I can also turn over the cassette by myself. God has proved again and again that nothing is impossible for Him. We have an awesome God!

Heavenly Father, thank You for life and for Your numerous blessings to me. I am greatly honored that You have chosen me to be Your instrument to draw people to You. I pray that I will always do Your will. I am so grateful that You gave Jesus, Your Son, to die on the cross so I can have eternal life.

ARDELLE BJORALT

GRATITUDE OVERWHELMING

They sang a new song: "You are worthy to take the scroll and to open its seals, because you were slain, and with your blood you purchased men for God from every tribe and language and people and nation." . . . [And] the four living creatures said, "Amen," and the elders fell down and worshiped. Rev. 5:9-14, NIV.

What's he doing that for? I wondered as a stranger fell prostrate, touching my feet, as we waited to board a train at the Karmatar railway station. Bending down, my husband touched the man and asked him to stand up. As I looked into the stranger's eyes, I recognized him as the father who had brought his 8-year-old daughter to our home.

When I had looked at her swollen and badly bruised face, I knew I would not be able to treat her with the meager facilities available at the mission dispensary. I counseled the father to take his daughter to the doctor. He pleaded that he had no money. So I gave him some and told him to get to the doctor as soon as possible.

For several weeks he continued to collect payments for the doctor. When his daughter was well, he brought her to see me. In his hand he carried a gourd, a gift of appreciation, grown on his own vine. I didn't see him again till that morning at the railway station.

I dreamed once of Jesus' second coming. When I met Him face-to-face, I fell at His feet and worshiped Him. Tears of joy and gratitude filled my eyes as I realized what He had done for me. Throughout my journey on earth He had protected me and guided me. He gave up so much, suffered so intensely, and purchased my pardon with His spilled blood on Calvary's cross so that when He comes to claim me as His own I can inhabit the mansion He has prepared for me.

I know when we shall see Him face-to-face we all shall fall prostrate at His feet, expressing our love and gratitude, like the man who fell at my feet at the train station. The gourd was not in payment for what I had done; it was a token of his gratitude. He was not aware of, nor did he care about, the crowds around him. He just wanted to express his thankfulness. Whatever we give God now is like that gourd. No matter how many gourds or shekels we bring, they will never be enough to pay the ransom price. But when we fall in sincere reverence and gratitude at Jesus' feet, God accepts us into His family.

BIROL CHARLOTTE CHRISTO

THE MIRACLE HOME

My God will meet all your needs. Phil. 4:19, NIV.

I watched as the real estate agent hammered a "For Sale" sign into our front yard. We were on the move again. As a pastor's wife I was used to the complicated procedure of buying and selling houses in England.

We found a buyer for our house almost immediately, and then realized we had only a couple days in which to find a place to buy in the new district, where houses cost twice as much. Praying, I called real estate agents in the new district, collected faxes on potential properties, tried to evaluate them from the photos and sketchy information, and then scheduled a string of appointments. One house in particular struck me as being perfect for our needs. When I looked at the price, however, I knew it was beyond our budget, but I booked a visit anyway.

The house was easily the best one for our needs. The price was a problem. But my husband, Bernie, had noticed that the present owners were Christians because of the music they were playing and the plaques on the walls. He shared with them our vision for a house that would have space to minister and provide hospitality. He told them he wanted to make an offer for their house, but it would be low—not to insult them, but because it was the best house we had seen, and this was all we could afford. They said they would pray about our offer.

I went to bed excited, hoping above all that we would be able to live there one day. I prayed and eventually felt a deep peace that the house would one day be ours. Because Bernie had asked our church members to pray for our move, he too felt convinced that God would enable us to live in the house we liked so much.

Finally a phone call came from the real estate agent to say that the owners had accepted our pitifully low offer. We were delighted! Bernie told the agent that the deal was a miracle. Hesitantly the agent admitted that it must be so, because the family had turned down an offer much higher than ours!

After we moved in, we discovered that God had added a number of wonderful and unexpected blessings to our life by finding us this special house, our miracle house!   KAREN HOLFORD

MAKE ME LIKE A MOTH

Jesus replied, "My light will shine out for you just a little while longer. Walk in it while you can, and go where you want to go before the darkness falls, for then it will be too late for you to find your way. Make use of the Light while there is still time; then you will become light bearers." John 12:35, 36, TLB.

Lord, make me like the moth that flew in my door tonight. I don't know how long it had been imprisoned in my dark garage, clinging there as close as it could get to the sliver of light beside my door. But I do know that the moment the door opened, it beat its fragile wings and came straight into the brightness of my dining room.

Lord, make me like a moth, ready instantly to follow Your light. Help me to find the glimmers in times of darkness and cling patiently there, waiting on You to open the door, no matter how long it takes. Keep me watching for Your light to stream forth with sudden abundance so that I will be prepared to follow in the moment of opportunity.

Lord, I need the perception of a moth. Give me the ability to sense light from You as readily as the moth sensed the beam of light that shone from my doorway. Help me to recognize light in whatever form You send it, at unexpected times, in unlikely circumstances, or in the darkest of places.

Lord, I need the fearlessness of a moth. When the light comes, make me bold to follow it to its Source, even if it means changing my course. The moth does not worry about its appearance or about tomorrow. I need that kind of peace. Give me courage to enter new territory. And let me not hesitate to come alone, if I must.

Lord, please grant that I be as single-minded as the moth. May I put all my energies into the pursuit, heading straight toward Your light, never wavering over distractions or hesitations. Keep me focused on the goal.

Father, today I ask You to forgive me for the times I've feared truth and been reluctant to follow. I pray that You will teach me to follow light as naturally as that moth, and that You will grant me a share of its soaring joy in the pursuit. Amen.

KATHLEEN STEARMAN PFLUGRAD

POLISHED STONES

That our daughters may be as corner stones, polished after the similitude of a palace. Ps. 144:12.

The restless water beckoned us as our little Toyota camper wound its way down the narrow curvy mountain road to the Pacific Ocean, where we hoped to observe a sunset. Heavy clouds overshadowed the view, but as we approached the shore the golden ball dipped into the molten waters of the mighty ocean, and shades of pink and orange burst forth, low on the horizon. We parked our vehicle and walked toward the beach. In the gathering darkness large rocks and intriguing shapes of driftwood became silhouetted along the shoreline. Restless waves ceaselessly rolled ashore to the music of their own symphony. We sat on a piece of driftwood, absorbing the aura of the moment.

Our eyes were drawn to the beach beneath our feet, where a myriad of pebbles, large and small, covered the gray sand. Those rocks, once jagged and rough, had been part of the ocean bed. But they were driven from their nest by the waves and pummeled, tossed, and turned until their rough edges were rounded.

We picked up some stones and saw that not all were smooth. Some had hard substances in them that did not yield to the action of the elements. Their surfaces were still rough and jagged in places. They lay in stark contrast to those that were perfectly round and smooth.

How like our lives! The rough and jagged edges of our characters, exemplified by the unkind word, the hasty remark, the harbored hateful thought, God allows to be washed and pummeled by the circumstances around us, the trials, the knocks of adversity. But if our characters have not been changed by our acceptance of the work of the Holy Spirit in our hearts, the trials of life will not accomplish their purpose, and the hard places in our lives will remain.

God, grant me today the patience and insight to see the molding of Your forces on my life. The trials and adversity that I experience can be the very forces that polish the rough, jagged places of my character. May I yield the hard places to the work of the Holy Spirit. Continue to polish me "after the similitude of a palace." Thank You, heavenly Father. JOAN MINCHIN NEALL

JULY 13

BUS DEPOT ENCOURAGEMENT

Encourage one another daily. Heb. 3:13, NIV.

Passengers and friends crowded the waiting room of the bus station. Finally the door to the loading area opened to indicate that the bus was ready for us to board. As goodbyes were said, husbands and wives hugged and kissed. A mother and daughter hugged, and I could see tears in the eyes of the older woman. One by one the passengers went through the door to the loading area, waving last farewells to their loved ones, who then left the depot.

But not all went away. One little girl, probably about 8 years old, slipped through the door and stood waving and smiling at someone on the bus. She kept on waving—first one arm and then, when that tired, the other. At times she needed to hold up the waving arm by supporting it at the elbow with the other hand. It was obvious that someone she loved and cared for was on that bus, and she was not going to leave that person until the very last minute.

For 10 minutes she waved and smiled and jumped up and down as only a child can do. She brought smiles and encouragement not only to her own departing loved one but to all of us passengers on that side of the bus.

Eventually an official came and ordered the little girl back through the door to the waiting room. The door closed, the bus pulled out, and we were on our way. The vision of that little girl with her smiling face and waving arm was with me throughout that three-hour journey.

In many texts Paul admonishes the early Christians to "encourage one another."

If one small girl can spend 10 minutes bringing encouragement to others, can I not do something each day to give a lift to those around me?

Please, Lord, grant me a childlike radiance to spread a word or note of encouragement to my daily contacts, loved ones, friends—and even to those I do not know. By word and deed and smile, may I shed Your love around.

RUTH LENNOX

BRIGHTEN THE CORNER

A cheerful heart is good medicine. Prov. 17:22, NIV.

I love to make a person's day, and I find it's not at all hard to do. Furthermore, the reactions I receive make *my* day.

Once when I was in a Denny's restaurant, the man in the next booth had on a most attractive tie. As I left, I stopped beside him. "Excuse me, sir," I said. Startled, he looked up from his newspaper. "I like your tie!" His face lit up as he thanked me. When I told a server that I appreciated her service, she smiled and said, "A compliment like that makes my work easier."

A lovely sweater, an attractive pantsuit, a pretty pin, good service—I can't help myself. I have to comment, and the smiles and thank-you's are worth it.

Then there's the other side of the coin. It also makes me happy to have someone make my day. Several incidents come to mind.

One woman told me, "You have a sweet smile." Another told me she liked my laugh. How about that?

I have a purple, V-necked, long-sleeved sweater that has silver flecks all through it. People have told me the flecks look like raindrops or moon dust, and such comments and compliments make my day.

Since I find it hard to cook for one, I frequently eat out at noon, and I've become acquainted with a number of restaurant managers and quite a few servers. I'm not especially good at making conversation, but I am a good listener. These dear folks tell me about having gone through a divorce, girlfriend problems, or their children. Then I let them know I'll be praying for them. They all seem to appreciate it. And I try to follow up: "Are things going better for you now?"

In his book *Try Giving Yourself Away*, David Dunn wrote about his niece's reaction to compliments: she passed them on. If someone said her dress was lovely, she'd say "Thank you. My mother bought it for me." Not only was her own day made, but so was her mother's.

Yes, I love to make a person's day. As the old song goes: "Brighten the corner where you are." And it's so easy to do! PATSY MURDOCH MEEKER

AT THE SOUND OF HIS VOICE

My sheep hear my voice. I know them, and they follow me.
John 10:27, NRSV.

H e breezed into my office one summer morning and just stood there. I looked up expectantly. Wordless, he stood in the doorway. I smiled. His eyes telegraphed a message to me. I was clueless about either the message or his identity. His shoulders sagged almost imperceptibly, and then he spoke. "You mean I made a 200-mile detour just to see you, and you don't even know who I am?"

At the sound of his voice, the fog cleared. Springing up from my desk, I greeted him warmly. He had been one of my best friends more than a decade earlier. We had worked together, counseling high school students. We had spent hours arguing about biblical perspectives, philosophies, current events, and dreams of ideal spouses. But we had not seen each other for years. The occasional phone call was the single link in the chain of our communication. Without the signature timbre of his baritone, I would have passed him off as a total stranger.

Lunching with my girlfriends the next day, I regaled them with the story of our meeting. "I can't believe you!" one of my girlfriends chided. "You've talked about him so much, and then you couldn't even recognize him when he came to visit!" I gave several reasons that had happened. He had lost more than 50 pounds and had shed the beard I had never seen him without. No one was convinced. Gradually the resemblance between that friendship and our heavenly friendship emerged in our discussion. "Clearly, there was eyeball-to-eyeball communication keeping your friendship alive. When you were in the same location, you both could recognize the change in each other," one sage opined. "But when you moved to separate sides of the continent, that was it. With our heavenly Friend, nothing can separate us. We don't need eyeballs or even eardrums. We need only hearts. He never changes. We can always recognize Him."

"And He always recognizes us. Now, what are we going to do differently?" The friend's question stunned us all into reflective silence.

Eternal Friend, I will hear Your voice. Help me to recognize it in the gentle breeze, in the hesitant request of a timid soul, or in a call for extraordinary service. Thank You, loving Lord, for showing me that with You the lines of communication need never be broken.   GLENDA-MAE GREENE

IN NEED OF RESCUE

The Son of man is come to save that which was lost. Matt. 18:11.

Before I was born, my parents lived on a farm in northern Canada with a dog and a cat. Neither of these pets accepted their first baby—me.

As a toddler, I was allowed to play in the fenced yard around the cabin. Shuffling up to Shep, I would reach toward him. He would growl, rise from his resting place, and move to a spot farther away from me. I tried to befriend Shep frequently, but always got the same reaction.

One day I discovered Kitty and reached out to touch her. She arched her back, hissed, and ran away. At 2 years of age I was too young to understand that sometimes pets become jealous of a new baby.

Perhaps Kitty decided to get rid of this pesky new family member. Whatever her thinking, when the yard gate was left open one day, I followed Kitty to the barnyard. I wanted so much to pet her, but she kept just out of reach. However, she would turn and meow at me as we passed the barnyard animals. Her pause and meow lured me to follow her through the pasture. I scrambled to keep up with her in the high grass. Skillfully she kept out of reach and led me into a thicket of tall willow bushes. Suddenly Kitty stopped, turned, meowed harshly, and disappeared into dense underbrush.

Then I discovered that thick bushes held my foot tightly. Squirming and wiggling, I could not move forward or backward; nor could I get down to crawl out of my predicament. Frightened, I screamed at the top of my lungs for a long time. Suddenly strong arms parted the bushes, and Daddy's smiling face beamed at me. He untangled my foot and scooped me into his arms. All the while he carried me home, I sobbed into his shoulder.

This experience helps me understand the Bible story of the Good Shepherd, searching for His lost sheep. No matter how lost we become or how severely problems entangle us, He sees and hears when we cry, scream, or pray; and He longs to rescue us, just as my father rescued me from the thick willow bushes long ago.

Thank You, Father in heaven, for that comforting thought. We are caught in the brambles of this sinful world. Please come to our rescue soon and take us home to live with You!   NATHALIE LADNER-BISCHOFF

YOU ARE MY SUNSHINE, LORD

The Sun of Righteousness will rise with healing in his wings. And you will go free, leaping with joy like calves let out to pasture. Mal. 4:2, TEB.

After long hours sitting at my desk in Hosur, India, I decided to take a walk. Matt, my golden retriever, joined me. We went outside the mission compound and headed south past the temple, toward the eucalyptus grove where we often walked. The sky was blue when we started, but suddenly dark clouds rolled in, blocking the sun. It was monsoon season and rain was on the way, I knew. We headed back home, where I picked up an umbrella.

Light showers fell softly on my umbrella. I found the soft patter of drops soothing to my weary heart and mind. I thought of how the rainy, dark weather matched my mood of the past few days. I longed for sunshine to chase away my gloomy thoughts.

Just then the sun came out. Dripping leaves glistened. The marigolds seemed a brighter gold. I turned to look behind me. There was a rainbow over the village of Navadhi.

Rain is falling just now in our family, I thought. *Dark clouds hide the sun. Calvin's operation is a concern for all of us. The death this week of Ron's younger sister, Sharon, has been a time of darkness for our family. Yes, the rain is falling, but the sun is shining at the same time. God is good, and there is the promise of the rainbow that we will not be destroyed.*

Then my mind turned to the situation in India. *Rain is falling now in Southern Asia on Your church, Lord. Dark clouds of financial problems, staff stress, and reports of religious persecution have blotted out the sun.*

Yes, the rain is falling; but still the sun is shining too. Your Holy Spirit is at work opening hearts, opening doors, building churches, impressing people to give to meet the needs. Miracles are happening everywhere. Yes, the sun is shining through the rain, and the rainbow of Your promise is there. Your work will not be washed away by the tide of evil.

My heart was light as I shook the water off my umbrella and went inside my house. Picking up my journal, I wrote:

"You are my Sunshine, Lord. All my rainbows come from You!
Your presence illuminates every droplet, bringing me love and hope."

DOROTHY EATON WATTS

I SURRENDER ALL

You are a forgiving God, gracious and compassionate, slow to anger and abounding in love. Therefore you did not desert them. Neh. 9:17, NIV.

Several years ago I was invited to play the organ for a friend's wedding in Bermuda. On the last day before my return to the United States, I walked along the shores of that beautiful island with its pink sand, interesting sea shells, and clear waters, longing to go swimming. More than once my conscience warned, "Lorraine, don't go swimming!" but after surveying the scene and observing no impending danger, I proceeded to go into the ocean. I reasoned, *If I don't go now, I probably will never have the opportunity again.*

It felt so cool, refreshing, relaxing, and invigorating on that hot summer day. I swam farther and farther from the shore, but then something went wrong—I was unable to move my legs. Leg cramps! The harder I tried to swim to shore, the more the huge waves that seemed to come from nowhere pushed me out into the deep. I became frantic. My head was continually being covered by the waves, and uncontrollable coughing resulted when the salt water entered my nostrils and burned my throat. I dared not ask the Lord to help me after I had directly and deliberately disobeyed Him. I called for help the best I could, but nobody heard me or even noticed me. I was overcome by complete exhaustion.

Lord, forgive me and save me! I cried as I went under, never to rise again—I thought.

But the Lord still loved me and answered my plea for help. A young man pulled me to the reef. As we waited for the strong wind and huge waves to pass, I worked on regaining my composure. A high wave almost pushed me off the rock, and I scraped my right knee. In spite of the salt water burning my open wound, I was determined to cling to the rock.

The Lord could not save me until I surrendered all to Him. As long as I struggled to save myself instead of allowing God to save me, there was no hope. The Lord wants our total surrender and for us to cling to Him, the solid rock, Christ Jesus. Jesus is our rock in a weary land. A shelter in the time of trouble.

Lord, help me always to be consecrated fully to Thee. My daily commitment is Lord, I surrender all. You are so gracious in Your forgiveness.

LORRAINE JAMES STIGGERS

MAINTAINING THE ENTHUSIASM

What is our hope, or joy, or crown of rejoicing? Are not even ye in the presence of our Lord Jesus Christ at his coming? 1 Thess. 2:19.

I am sure all Australians have imprinted on their memory the excitement they felt when the Olympic Committee announced, "The winner is Sydney!"

What a buzz it was to know that Sydney would host the games! Sydney-siders watched the metamorphosis of a functional and aesthetically pleasing games site at Homebush Bay. Gone were old industrial buildings in favor of modern arenas for sport, surrounded by tree-covered wide green areas in preparation for countless athletes and guests.

The three adorable mascots, cute characters developed from Australia's delightful native koala, platypus, and echidna, are now well known. Thousands of these figures and other souvenirs were prepared as mementos of the games. The hospitality industry geared up to provide everything the visitor could possibly desire. The athletes in Australia were delighted to have the opportunity to perform in their own country. It was inspiring to have athletes from around the world arrive, seeking victory and glory. Oh yes, this was an exciting event! There was no doubt about it. Or was there?

Sydney was like hyped-up little children who become a bit tired of waiting for a party to begin. So the organizers launched a program to pump up enthusiasm, to keep the collective adrenaline level high, right up to the games.

It is amazing how we humans keep looking for new things to interest us so that yesterday's mind-absorbing item fades dully as we grasp for something more dazzling. That is probably why Jesus admonished us to be ready for His coming, to "watch and pray" (Matt. 26:41); to stay awake, for "in such an hour as ye think not the Son of man cometh" (Matt. 24:44). What He is preparing for us cannot be imagined, for He delights to indulge us, His children. The accommodation and hospitality will exceed the creativity of our little gray cells to visualize, for our Friend will give us "hope," "joy," and a "crown of rejoicing." When I think of Him, it's easy to maintain my enthusiasm.

Dear Jesus, help me not to lose my enthusiasm, excitement, and sense of expectation while I wait for You.   URSULA M. HEDGES

WORTH THE WAITING

*If we hope for that we see not, then do we with patience wait for it.
Rom. 8:25.*

W ait" is a short word in the English language, but one that plays on all of our emotions as we encounter experiences from day to day.

Thinking back, I can recall a few encounters in which the word "wait" played heavily on my emotions: in college, waiting in a long line at the dining hall for breakfast; waiting in line to renew my driving permit; waiting at the airport after a delay in the flight schedule; and waiting for my first grandchild. The list could go on and on, but watching my 2-year-old grandson has taught me a lesson in waiting and exercising active patience. It's amazing that at certain times in the afternoon, when my grandson's thoughts are focused on his father's coming to pick him up, his desire to be ready increases to the extent that he wants to be totally prepared—shoes, clothes, and hat must be on. From that moment on, the excitement begins to mount so much that he wants to look out the window for Daddy.

During the waiting-and-watching period by the window, Brandon begins asking such questions as "Which way is Daddy going to come?" "Will he be driving fast?" "Will he blow his horn *beep, beep?*" "What will Daddy say to me?" The waiting and watching continue with each passing car. Finally one car doesn't pass by, because it's my grandson's father's car turning into the driveway. Oh, what joy and excitement there is! Squeals of delight, jumping, running back and forth to the door as his father gets out of the car. The front door opens, and with outstretched arms Brandon leaps into his father's arms. Without a word his actions plainly show that it was surely worth the wait.

Am I awaiting Christ's return with a similar excitement and joy? Am I doing those things that Christ would have me do while I wait for Him? Or am I so preoccupied with the cares of this world that I have begun to lose patience and lose my anticipation of His coming?

Lord, give us all patience to work, watch, and wait so that we can be ready when You come.   ANNIE B. BEST

SACRIFICES MADE IN LOVE

Be full of love for others, following the example of Christ who loved you and gave himself to God as a sacrifice to take away your sins. And God was pleased, for Christ's love for you was like sweet perfume to him. Eph. 5:2, TLB.

My mother ate the burned toast so her husband and children could have the golden brown slices. She ate the broken cookies, the hard crust, the piece of cake with little or no frosting, and the smaller piece of everything, so we could have the biggest and best. She didn't mind taking the piece of pie that plopped upside down on the plate or the egg with the broken yolk. She salvaged the biscuit that fell in the gravy and served it to herself. While we enjoyed fresh bread, she rolled up leftover pancakes for herself.

As a child I wondered how Mother could enjoy a leftover salad on burned toast for breakfast. "It's too good to throw out," she'd say. I had yet to learn the principle that love knows no bounds.

Why did she do it? It may have been for reasons of thrift during hard times. But more than that, I believe her great love for us negated any burden attached to these simple acts of kindness. Since we hadn't yet learned the pleasure of giving love, we selfishly and blindly accepted her sacrifices for us. As I matured I recognized Mother's love and understood that anything done in love is not a burden. I have wondered if we ever showed her enough appreciation. God bless her!

If I can appreciate the small acts of kindness demonstrated by my mother, how much more should I appreciate the greater sacrifice of Jesus on my behalf. He left His heavenly home to become a man on this sinful planet. He received no honor in His hometown of Nazareth. He endured starvation in the wilderness for 40 days. He knew weariness with no place to go for a luxurious rest. He felt pain and sadness. Some of those He loved most denied, forsook, and betrayed Him. He suffered mockery, beatings, and the shame of being spat upon. And finally, He suffered a criminal's death on the cross so that you and I might have eternal life.

How is it in our Christian walk? Are we still immature children, who do not perceive God's love through His Son?

Let us grow in grace and love.

EDITH FITCH

GOOD DEEDS WON'T TAKE YOU TO HEAVEN!

By grace are ye saved through faith; and that not of yourselves: it is the gift of God: not of works. Eph. 2:8, 9.

I was working in the office while Pam, one of my coworkers, was typing. She left to go to lunch while I watched the office. Moments after she left, I happened to look on the floor where she had been sitting. I could not believe what I was seeing. Cash! I picked up the money and examined it.

There were three $20 bills—two old ones, and one new one. I noticed the new bill first. For a moment I thought it was fake because of its new look. Then I came to my senses. I had $60 in my hand. I concluded that it was a blessing from God. *Thank You, Lord!* I screamed within myself.

I started having second thoughts. More than likely this was Pam's money. Then I started to reason with myself: *I'll just wait to see if anyone asks for it. If no one does, I'll keep it.*

Ten minutes later a very upset Pam came into the office. She was frantically searching the office. I asked her what the matter was, even though I had a pretty good idea. She explained she had lost $60. It was then I admitted I had found the money and gave it to her. She thanked me.

On my way home that afternoon I was involved in an accident. I couldn't believe it! I told myself, *Earlier today I did a good deed despite my financial need. How could this have happened to me?*

For a moment I was tempted to blame God and take my anger out on Him. I felt He had let *me* down after I had done such a "Christian" deed. I questioned Him. Then I realized it could have been worse—it was just a fender bender.

After more careful thought I also realized that just because I did a good deed earlier that day didn't exempt me from trials, much less get me to heaven.

I praise You, God, for reinforcing this lesson we Christians sometimes may take for granted. Help us do right just because it is right. And thank You for the wonderful gift of salvation.   LINDA DUNCAN JULIE

HE CARETH FOR YOU

Humble yourselves therefore under the mighty hand of God, that he may exalt you in due time: casting all your care upon him; for he careth for you. 1 Peter 5:6, 7.

We have a beloved pet named Noel—a black, brown, and orange striped cat. She got her name because of her arrival at our home shortly before Christmas. Noel has been the perfect pet for two preschoolers. She has endured with patience and an occasional dignified "meow" everything from being dressed in doll clothes to being picked up by one front leg. In fact, the only bad habit Noel had was testing her young growing claws on the kitchen wallpaper. So as soon as the vet said she was old enough, we had Noel's front claws removed.

A few weeks after she'd been declawed, Noel grabbed the opportunity to dash out the front door. We looked for her for several hours. It was early spring and the nights were still quite cold, so we were worried when we were unable to find her before bedtime. Another day passed. My husband and I were afraid that some harm had come to her. We thought that we had seen the last of our Christmas cat, especially since she was without front claws with which to defend herself.

Our 5-year-old son, Grant, was sure that Noel would be home. He asked if we could pray for our cat's safety and return. We prayed together and asked Jesus to bring his kitty back safely. Then he fell asleep, sure that his cat would be home soon.

The following day two magazine-selling college students stopped by our house. As we chatted I mentioned that we were missing our cat, in case they saw her while they were going door-to-door. About 20 minutes after they left our house, they were back—with Noel. She had been huddled in the corner of a porch three houses down our block. A little boy's prayer was answered, and Noel was safely home with our family again.

In the grand scheme of things one missing cat isn't a big issue. The only lasting consequence would have been one very sad little boy. And yet our God cares enough about one child's feelings to send two salespeople at just the right time to provide a way home for a cat.

If God loves us enough to be concerned about a child's pet, how much more He must long to comfort us when we experience hardships. Cast all your cares upon Him today, however big or small, for He cares for you!

SANDRA SIMANTON

WITNESSING AT HOME

Rise up, ye women that are at ease; hear my voice, ye careless daughters; give ear unto my speech. Isa. 32:9.

I heard God give me a warning one morning as I sought to be in His presence. I wondered if the Lord wanted me to do more for Him. I went to church every week. I was a responsible wife and mother, catering to the needs of my friends and family. But as I continued to meditate on Isaiah 32 the Lord spoke to me, saying, "Oh, My daughter, do your children see the work of righteousness that shall be peace, and the effect of righteousness—quietness in your life?"

I had to admit that all my children saw in me was a mother who very often yelled or murmured. Many mornings, when there was a mad rush for all to leave the house, they heard something very different from what I really wanted them to hear.

I started praying about this area of my life, for I needed a little more patience. The Lord helped me realize that I need to be careful, because my children are watching me every day. "Lord, give me a little of Your patience each day that I may first be a witness at home," I prayed.

The change has been gradual but wonderful. One day my son said, "Mommy, you are so good to me." My daughter very often asks me to bend so that she can reach my ears, and then she whispers, "I love you, Mommy," and runs away. These are moments I treasure. It is so much better than the regrets I had before for being a fretting and fuming mother.

We parents consecrate our children to God. But do they see Jesus in our lives every moment of each day? And what about those who see us at work or in other aspects of our daily lives as women? Let's ask Him to help us each day to walk in the Spirit so that body, mind, and spirit will be in harmony with the Spirit of the living God. Then will our children, family, and friends see the fruit of the Spirit—love, joy, peace, long-suffering, gentleness, goodness, faith, meekness, and temperance—manifested in our lives. May the Lord help us women to be witnesses at home, and then we will definitely be witnesses to the world.

I am listening, Lord; speak to and through me. I want to represent You today.

JEAN SECILIA

QUEEN OF THE NIGHT

Man born of woman is of few days and full of trouble. He springs up like a flower and withers away; like a fleeting shadow, he does not endure. Do you fix your eye on such a one? Job 14:1-3, NIV.

In the 1960s my uncle took a leaf of a plant from Brazil to my grandmother in Finland. She put it in a jar with water, and when it had enough little white roots, she planted it. The plant thrived and grew, filling a whole corner of the room. One night Grandmother called, "Come see the queen of the night. She has about 25 flowers that are beginning to open." They were wonderful!

When I got married 30 years ago, my mother-in-law saw the plant and took a leaf back to Germany. The queen of the night bloomed in her home every now and then until she could no longer keep it. So finally I got a leaf and started growing my own queen. The first time it started blooming I watched the bud grow every day, and every evening I would wonder, *Will it open tonight?* Then one evening I came home at about 10:00 and sat down in the armchair to watch the news. A strong perfume came from somewhere behind me, and I turned to look. Lo and behold! The first flower of my queen of the night was opening up! I had completely forgotten about it, and if it hadn't been for the fragrance, I would have missed the wonderful sight. I can't describe the beauty of this flower—every time I see it I am filled with joy.

Last summer my queen decided to produce a flower just in time for my fiftieth birthday. What a thrill to watch it open up in company of friends! The next night there were three more flowers. As it was a warm summer night, I went across the street and invited all the neighborhood women who were still sitting outside to come and see my treasure.

But this beauty lasts only one night. In the morning the petals droop and the perfume is gone. The beautiful flower wilts as soon as daylight dawns. I treasure the memories and marvel at God's extravagance in placing so much beauty in such a short-lived flower. But the Bible reminds me that my life will pass just like my beautiful flower. Yet God's generosity tells me that during the short life I have on this earth I should live as beautiful a life as I can. I hear the apostle Paul whisper in my ear, "Let us fix our eyes on Jesus, the author and perfecter of our faith" (Heb. 12:2, NIV). He is the beautiful Rose of Sharon who will never wilt.

HANNELE OTTSCHOFSKI

ONE SIZE FITS ALL

To her [the bride of the Lamb] was granted that she should be arrayed in fine linen, clean and white: for the fine linen is the righteousness of saints. Rev. 19:8.

It was a beautiful two-piece summer dress, on sale for half price, but it was a size smaller than I usually wear. However, I tried it on and found that it fit. I jokingly said that when I wore it I would leave the tag outside so the label would advertise the size to all who saw it.

The first time I wore it in a public place I ran into an acquaintance from long ago. Imagine my chagrin when she graciously and kindly tucked the label inside my dress! I had accidentally done what I had threatened to do.

In years gone by I made most of my clothes, but because I had sons instead of daughters, I had done very little sewing for my family. Once I took a sewing class at a community college. The teacher was an expert; carried away by her enthusiasm, I decided to make a pair of pants for my husband. I found a pattern that purported to be the right size, chose a nice fabric, and started pinning, cutting, marking, and sewing. The day came when I proudly took the almost-finished garment home for him to try on. To my dismay, the pants were at least two or three sizes too big in the waist. Grimly I set to work to alter them by taking up the back center seam, but by the time they were small enough, the hip pockets almost met in the back. My loyal, long-suffering husband bravely wore them a time or two before they disappeared in the back of a closet.

Yes, some garments are too big, some too small, some too long, some too short. For Christmas my son sent me a luxurious velveteen robe with flowers on it, all in black. The label says that it is size small, but it is very roomy and could be worn by a person larger than I am. We also bought two fluffy pink robes for gifts. We were not sure what size to get, but they were labeled "one size fits all," so we decided to risk it. We were happy that both recipients could wear them and enjoy them.

Jesus wore a robe too when the soldiers, mocking Him, clothed Him in purple. He wore that robe for you and me that we might someday wear special robes, robes of fine linen, clean and white. Unlike the robes we bought, these are available to everyone, free of charge and guaranteed not to wear out. We won't have to check labels, for it can truly be said that "one size fits all"!

MARY JANE GRAVES

LEMONS TO LEMONADE

Rejoice in the Lord alway: and again I say, Rejoice. Phil. 4:4.

It's easy to rejoice and praise the Lord when things are going well, but when difficulties, accidents, or sickness unexpectedly come upon us, do we complain and become discouraged, or do we rejoice and continue to trust the Lord in all things? My mother was one of those who could always rejoice. She reminded me of the saying "When life gives you lemons, make lemonade." Hers was not an easy life, but she had a trusting relationship with her Lord and taught us to do the same. One particularly trying situation I'll never forget.

Early on a Monday morning my children and I were getting ready for school when the phone rang. A hospital in a neighboring city was calling to inform us that my mother, stepdad, and aunt had been in an auto accident while traveling to church the previous evening. My mother had been thrown into the windshield and was the most seriously injured.

When we arrived at the hospital my mother was conscious, and we were so thankful that all three of them had survived. Later we learned that my mother had received more than 100 stitches on her face and had suffered other head injuries.

As the days and weeks went by she continued to heal. In time the scars on her face were barely noticeable, and she had no recurring headaches. The doctors had feared the headaches might not go away.

Not only was there physical healing that took time; there were also insurance claims. Although it took a while, when their case was finally settled they were awarded enough money to buy a small, modest house. Through the years Mother continued to be thankful for her comfortable home, which she considered a gift from the Lord. She rejoiced always, in adversity and in blessing.

Not every trial has a happy ending on this earth, but we know that our Lord is with us as we go through each one. He can help us change "lemons to lemonade," just as my mother always did.

Father, in times of adversity and trial, help me to remember past blessings and to trust You on the basis of those favors. PATRICIA MULRANEY KOVALSKI

KEEP CONNECTED

Abide in me, and I in you. As the branch cannot bear fruit of itself, except it abide in the vine; no more can ye, except ye abide in me. John 15:4.

One beautiful summer morning not long after Hurricane Andrew, while I was enjoying my daily walk, my attention was drawn to a bird sitting on the top of a tree, swaying in the morning breezes and singing heartily. I stopped and watched the little creature, so undisturbed, singing so sweetly. I wondered in what language that song would be translated in heaven. Then I noticed that although the tree had a fairly large trunk and was full of foliage, the trunk was split to the ground. Apparently it had been damaged by Andrew. Then I noticed, to my surprise, that large steel spikes were driven through one part of the tree, connecting it to the main trunk. After looking more closely, I noticed that the higher branches were also tied with strong cord to hold that section of the tree in place.

The tree appeared green and beautiful. There was no sign of damage—everything seemed perfect and beautiful. It was only when I investigated more closely that I realized what someone had done to save the mighty tree.

I thought about the many times our lives become damaged by the storms of life and by the cares of this world, with its problems and allurements. Sometimes we get disconnected from the main trunk, the Source of life. But our loving Father, with His strong cords of love, binds us back to Him through the power of His Holy Spirit. There are times when He has to use strong spikes of disappointments, sickness, or loss of possessions, to get us reconnected, but in the end we always blossom and bloom as if we had been always connected.

Let us remember that we always have to abide in Him. Without Him we will be damaged, and our lives will not be what He planned for us.

The winds of this world have damaged me, too, but I cling to You. I need You to hold me, keeping me close with those cords of love. Your promise sustains me this day.

PEARL MANDERSON

INTERESTED PARTY

Even the hairs of your head are all numbered. Luke 12:7, RSV.

When I first saw the cat at the animal shelter, I wanted to take her home with me. She was so friendly that it was as if we already belonged together. She had a funny white stripe around her mouth that made her look as though she was always smiling. Her coat was a gray-and-white tuxedo affair. I knew this was going to be my cat the minute I touched her.

I told the attendant that I wanted the cat. Unfortunately, there was a three-day wait. Previously I had picked out a lovely little long-haired cat, but by the end of the waiting period, he had already been put to sleep. The workers at the shelter told me that when a cat gets sick they put it to sleep right away. Knowing how easily stressed cats catch diseases, I was afraid this cat wouldn't make it past the holding period either. Now I begged for her life, telling the attendant that I didn't care if the cat was sick. I wanted her, no matter what.

The attendant said that would be no problem. She would just mark the cat's card for me. She took out a pen and wrote "I.P." on the cage's card.

"I.P.?" I asked. "What's that mean?"

"Interested Party," she told me. "If he knows there's an interested party, then the vet will go ahead and treat the cat instead of killing it."

Such a simple act—two little letters on a card, and the cat would live!

I named her Gilah, which is Hebrew for "joy." When the waiting period was up, I redeemed her from the shelter hospital. She had, in fact, become very ill, but because I was an I.P. she had been allowed to live. Eleven years later she is still my joy.

We all have at least one Interested Party—Jesus Christ. He cared enough to write "I.P." on our cards—only He wrote it not in ink, but in blood. He is willing to do whatever it takes to save us. He is the one who offers us life eternal. Because there is an Interested Party, we have a future, and a chance for something more—to become Christ's joy.

I feel as though we belong together—You and I. I want You for my Forever Master. I praise You for being my Interested Party—I have no other future. You are my hope for today. Praise God!

GINA LEE

INSPIRATION OR PERSPIRATION

Study to shew thyself approved unto God, a workman that needeth not to be ashamed. 2 Tim. 2:15.

On an island south of the Australian mainland I took a position in a school that was to begin four days of celebration to mark its 100 years of service to the community. It was interesting to witness and to take part in the parades, church service, open day, and drama presentations. Because the headmaster was not well, I was given his class, which was required to sit for a state examination at the close of the school year.

It was a joy to work with the class, and I thoroughly enjoyed the experience. Over the years I have forgotten the names and physical features of most of the students. There is one who will never be erased from my memory, however.

Nick was a slim freckle-faced boy of average ability, who did not stand out from his peers. But after a few months Nick began to make his presence felt. Every few minutes up would go his hand. "How do you spell that?" Then there would be a rustle of pages as he looked up the meaning of the word in question. No matter what subject we were discussing, Nick was always asking question after question. At times the other students and I felt frustrated with his interruptions, but we all benefited from his search to gain a thorough knowledge of all subjects.

The end of the year came too quickly, and the state exam was over. The students were excited at the prospect of going to secondary school the following year. I too was excited, as I was going on to the mission field.

Not long after that the headmaster asked, "Remember Nick?"

How could I ever forget Nick!

"Well, he has recorded the highest score ever in the state exam in the history of the school's 100 years."

Nick had searched his subjects well and was rewarded for it. I was reminded of the common saying "Success is 1 percent inspiration and 99 percent perspiration." The experience with Nick keeps fresh in my mind another thought: *Do I search the Scriptures with such fervor?* The reward for getting to know my Jesus as a personal friend would be a high pass indeed.

JOY DUSTOW

FOR I KNOW THE PLANS

I know the plans I have for you, . . . plans to give you hope and a future. Jer. 29:11, NIV.

I started life with two major problems: I was born in an atheistic country, and I was not very healthy. As soon as I started school my health began to deteriorate. I was bothered by strong headaches, and no one knew the reason. In the fall and winter I often spent two or three months in hospitals.

I missed my friends and my family so much. For a shy girl from a village, staying with strange nurses and doctors was difficult. Living in a hospital, however, forced me to communicate with strange people. I learned to love them, and they loved me. I sought something good in each person so I could learn something from them.

Being in the hospital didn't help much with my health, but there I found a lot of friends and gained knowledge that has been useful my entire life.

I learned something else, too. I realized that children, as well as adults, die. I began to worry about my future. But my mother told me about the love of Jesus and His promises. Although I was not quite 9 at the time, I determined to read the whole gospel story so I could know Jesus better. I accomplished this by the time I turned 10.

Once when I was feeling really bad I heard the doctor say to my father, "Why are you worrying? You have three more children." I knew then that I was very sick.

But Dad replied, "You have five fingers. Which one do you want cut off?"

What love! As a result of overhearing that conversation I decided to give my life and my heart to the Lord immediately, hoping for His mercy, power, and healing.

The mockeries of atheist teachers couldn't poison my heart in the following years. For me Jesus was—and is—alive. He helps me so much. He says, "My grace is sufficient for you, for my power is made perfect in weakness" (2 Cor. 12:9, NIV).

I am looking forward to that moment when I see the Lord, who created a miracle in my life. "There will be no more death or mourning or crying or pain, for the old order of things has passed away" (Rev. 21:4, NIV).

Strengthen my faith, Lord. LUDMILA M. KRUSHENITSKAYA

SHARING WHAT YOU HAVE

She did what she could. Mark 14:8, NIV.

It was a simple little Indian village, located on the hillside several miles off the main road, reached by traveling over a rough and winding track. But we didn't mind the drive, because we had friends at the end of the road. We made the trip almost weekly to hold special services for the children. The children looked forward to our coming—this was a bright spot in their lives. Our carryall vehicle was always filled with others from the nearby mission school who helped with the singing or told Bible stories. Even the adults enjoyed the illustrations on the felt board as pictures were a rare thing in their homes.

We sometimes brought a lunch, but usually we made the half-hour drive back home to eat there. Then one day as we were preparing to leave the village, one of the women invited us to come eat with her family. I hesitated to accept, as I had visited in her humble hut many times; it consisted of a dirt floor and a little cooking fire for a stove. I knew there was barely enough to feed her family. All of that didn't matter to her—she was willing to share the little she had with our group of six people. She insisted I sit on their only chair (there was no table). No one seemed to mind sitting on stones or boards and holding their plates in their laps while they ate the simple fare of beans, tortillas, and sweet potatoes. We all had an enjoyable time together, and I'm sure she was blessed by her willingness to share.

I think of the times I haven't invited visitors for dinner because I thought my house wasn't good enough or I didn't have a special meal prepared. This humble Indian woman taught me a lesson that I'll never forget as she shared the little she had with her friends.

Like the gift of the widow in the Bible who put her last two coins in the offering, my friend's gift was more than I could ever give, because hers was not taken from abundance, but from her simple store. She "did what she could."

I have so much, and I do thank You, my gracious God. Please help me to be more willing to share with those around me—whether they need food, material things, or my love and encouragement. She did what she could. Help me to do likewise.

BETTY J. ADAMS

ANGEL COVER

He shall give His angels charge over you, to keep you in all your ways. In their hands they shall bear you up, lest you dash your foot against a stone. Ps. 91:11, 12, NKJV.

I closed my Bible and prayed. I felt energized and ready to take on the challenges of a new day. While getting dressed for work, I meditated about the angel story I had read for my devotion. *I would like to have an angel story,* I mused.

After breakfast my brother volunteered to take me to work. He was going on a trip that morning and wanted me to do some things for him. Even though we were engaged in conversation as we drove along, we were well aware of what was going on around us. We observed a car coming down the hill on the left. At the intersection we expected the driver to obey the four-way stop sign, so we proceeded through. She did not stop.

I braced myself for the thunderous grating of metal. My brother tried his best to maneuver the car to avoid hitting her, but it was either hit her or crash into the iron bridge we were headed straight for. When the other driver realized what she had done, she panicked.

Suddenly our car made a 90-degree turn, missed the bridge by inches, and came to a sudden stop. I tried to regain my composure and still my racing heart as I momentarily relived what had just happened.

"It must have been an angel. There was no way I could have avoided hitting her and missed the bridge at the same time!" my brother exclaimed.

"I agree," I breathed in amazement. Breathing a sigh of relief, I said, "Thank You, Jesus. I wanted an angel story, but I didn't expect all the drama."

We both praised and thanked God for His protection and intervention that morning. His angels bore us up and prevented us from dashing (smashing) our foot (the car) against a stone (the bridge) and injuring ourselves.

Thank You again, God, for angel cover! ANDREA A. BUSSUE

ASK AND IT SHALL BE GIVEN

Ask, and it shall be given you; seek, and ye shall find; knock, and it shall be opened unto you. Matt. 7:7.

When I was very young my mother and grandmother taught me to trust in God consistently for all my daily needs, and they introduced God to me as my heavenly Father. I go to Him for all my spiritual and physical needs. He is very personal to me, and I talk to Him constantly—not just in the morning when I get up or in the evening before going to bed. At times I even ask Him to help me with traffic lights. When I am a bit late for work and want to make it on time for morning worship, I ask God to help me get green lights for the two traffic lights that I have to pass, and believe me, He has answered my prayers.

As Christians, the greatest joy and blessing we experience is that we worship and belong to a God who is almighty, and there is absolutely nothing that our heavenly Father cannot do.

My daughter, a biology major, had to start applying to medical schools before her final year of college if she wanted to start classes in the fall. After applying to all the schools she was interested in, she was confident God would help her get into a medical school. However, when her friends and classmates started hearing from medical schools in September, she became a bit anxious about her situation. By January, when she had not heard from any of the medical schools, she really became apprehensive.

I encouraged her. "God knows what is best for you, and you need to have complete faith and trust in Him."

In the meantime, my prayer request to my heavenly Father was to keep my daughter's faith strong and to choose the right school for her. I asked that she get the acceptance before her birthday on February 16. I told God that this would be His birthday gift to my daughter. I wrote this request in my prayer journal and earnestly prayed every day.

On January 23 a big brown envelope arrived in the mail. Inside was the answer to my prayer—my daughter's acceptance to Loma Linda University Medical School, my heavenly Father's birthday gift to my daughter!

I praise God for *all* His blessings. He is my personal and caring heavenly Father, and He will be yours, too, if you invite Him to be.

STELLA THOMAS

A WORD IN SEASON

*A word fitly spoken is like apples of gold in pictures of silver.
Prov. 25:11.*

To this text we can add, "A word fitly written . . ." We can't all be eloquent speakers. In fact, many of us can't think of anything appropriate to say when faced with certain situations. A friend confided that she simply could not visit someone we both knew. "She's dying of cancer, and I know I should go, but I just don't know what to say to her."

"So what do you do?" I asked.

"I don't do anything. I know I should, but . . ."

This is an all-too-common scenario. Many people, like my friend, wish they could help, but they don't know what to do or say. So they do nothing. They don't visit, telephone, or write.

I find that sending a greeting card saves me the embarrassment of perhaps saying the wrong thing. It takes only small amounts of time, effort, and money and gives great amounts of comfort or pleasure.

Most shops sell a variety of cards, most of which are expensive enough to make a big hole in my budget. So I watch for the bargain basements, where pretty no-message cards can be purchased at less than half price. Attractive notepaper with matching envelopes is equally suitable.

If you can find an appropriate Bible text, quotation, or short verse, write that on your card and add a few words, such as "So sorry to hear of your sickness [accident, misfortune, bereavement]. My thoughts [prayers, sympathies] are with you. May God give you comfort. Sincere love from ——."

Of course, you will have to adapt the words to suit the circumstances or your relationship with the person, but there is no need to write a long message. Knowing that you are thinking of them is joy enough.

You can also include short poems, fillers, poignant articles, stories, even suitable humor, cartoons, or news from the daily paper. Send one of these to your sick friend.

Everyone feels a certain amount of excitement when the mail carrier arrives, so I let my letter do the visiting for me. It can work for you, too.

GOLDIE DOWN

REMEMBER THE TIME

Remember how short my time is. Ps. 89:47.

I had brought along the empty tube to remind me of my purchase. I needed to get some sewing needles for my machine, and without hesitation I walked straight to the counter for them. I searched carefully, but to no avail. I looked and looked for the number on the tube but could not match it.

I hurried to the cashier and told her my plight. She summoned a clerk for assistance, and he produced the match in no time. I thanked him and returned to the front counter.

When the cashier gave the total, I was startled. "You forgot these," I said, pointing to some other purchases.

"Oh," she said. "I sure did. Just put them in your bag and go on."

"I can't." I replied quickly. "You are getting me in trouble with heaven, and I must pay for all my supplies."

"Heaven?" she asked.

"Yes," I answered. She laughed, embarrassed, as she began to correct the error. I paid the additional amount, and we parted, smiling.

Not long after that I saw her in the neighborhood. We chatted about topics that ranged from home and family to college, sewing, and mutual friends. Then the topic turned to religion and God's love and purpose for our lives.

Some time later I stared at the television in shock. The news anchor gave a woman's name, description, and place of employment. It all fit. My new friend had been shot and killed by her estranged husband.

My mind raced to the supplies I had bought from her. How had those moments affected her for eternity? Had my determination to be fair with heaven made a difference? I bowed my head and thanked God for the opportunity to witness for Him.

Life is so uncertain. Today I may meet someone who needs to hear about You. Send Your Spirit to guide me in all my words and actions.

MARGARET B. LAWRENCE

HE LED ME

The Lord alone did lead him, and there was no strange god with him. Deut. 32:12.

I know that the Lord has been leading in my life over the years, but I have felt it especially during the past several years.

I was due to retire in nine months, but I felt that I could still be useful. *Lord,* I prayed, *what do You want me to do for You yet?* I wrote to church headquarters to find out if there was a place where I could volunteer. The reply seemed positive. I waited. Then a second letter said they knew of nowhere I could serve. They did say that if there was a particular part of the world where I wanted to go, I could apply directly. I prayed again. *If there is a place I am needed, I know You will send me. I don't have anything particular in mind, only further service.*

Then I waited. One month left before retirement. Then two weeks. Then the miracle happened. I received a letter from a hospital asking if I was interested in serving in Pakistan. *Thank You, Lord. I am willing!*

So much to do and so little time. I packed, stored my goods, and found someone to take care of business while I was away. Soon I had a two-month visitor's visa and was on my way.

I enjoyed my service for 27 months. Then it was time to go home and see my daughters again and find a place to live. Would the Lord lead again as He had done before? I placed my needs before Him.

My three daughters live thousands of miles apart. While I visited each of them I tried to find a place to live that I could afford. After five months of traveling, praying, and, I must admit, some deep frustration, I again went to the Lord. *Please give me the courage to pick up the telephone again and ask for accommodations.*

He answered my prayer. I called a place I had applied to several years earlier but without response. This time the manager said I could move in in about three weeks!

I thanked the Lord often. How grateful I still am that He allowed me a small place where I could still be of service. And He cared for me, allowing me to settle comfortably into retirement close to one of my daughters. I know for certain that where God guides, He provides. Will you allow Him to lead you where He wants you to be today?

PHYLLIS DALGLEISH

I AM NOT DISORGANIZED

Don't be impatient. Ps. 27:14, TLB.

On my office wall hangs a statement that says, "I'm not disorganized, just flexible." What does that really mean? I like the *Oxford English Dictionary's* explanation: a flexible person can easily be changed to suit new conditions. The word *flexible* became particularly intriguing during my attendance at a Mission Institute training session at which we expatriates were counseled concerning expectations for life situations outside our home countries.

As life in a foreign country progressed, flexibility became even more significant. I prepared my daily class outline for an entire term only to find that the president of the country could add an extra holiday whenever an appropriate occasion arose. How was I to accomplish the goals I had set for the class? A little voice inside me reminded, *Remember to be flexible.*

I intended to finish preparing an examination to be given in the next day's class. I was on a tight schedule, but if all went as planned, I would make it. Then I got a memo from the vice chancellor's office for an unscheduled committee meeting that afternoon. My presence was required. Now what was I to do? Something inside of me said, *Remember to be flexible.*

I had left instructions for a task to be accomplished. I had even written out the instructions. It had been a whole week and still things had not progressed. Many excuses were given. So the project was carried over to another week.

Sundays are good days to plan for the rest of the week. But then a close friend in a nearby village died. Naturally, I went to the funeral—on a Sunday. A funeral in this part of the world is an all-day affair. Once again my well-planned schedule ended in disaster. No, I'm not disorganized, but life teaches me that I must be flexible.

Lord, what are You trying to teach me? That my plans must give way to Your plans? That I must keep the ultimate goal in mind and not just my immediate plans? Help me today to allow You to lead in every aspect of my life. Keep me flexible through Your Spirit.   FONDA CORDIS CHAFFEE

A PAINTING

Its branches will spread out like those of beautiful olive trees, as fragrant as the cedar forests of Lebanon. Hosea 14:6, NLT.

I once saw a beautiful painting that showed a pathway so barren, so deserted, yet had a charm that nothing else in the picture had. Beside the pathway three jacaranda trees in full bloom spread out in an exquisite violet carpet, as if to pave the way for a king. In the background, behind the pathway and the jacaranda trees, a mountain loomed, large and intriguing. The painting was perfect in every way. I could find no fault or imperfection.

Yes, it was perfect; but if I took away the jacaranda trees it wouldn't be a perfect painting. If I erased the pathway, the painting wouldn't look the same. If I got rid of that big mountain, it wouldn't be as beautiful. The artist used the jacaranda trees, the pathway, and the mountain to create a painting. He knew he needed all three to make the picture unique, to make it perfect.

We live in a painting created by the Master Artist. It is a beautiful painting with many things that are ravishing in their own way. We need each element in the painting, because without one of them the painting wouldn't look the same. Without flowers the world wouldn't look as dainty; without trees it would look dull; and without each of us it wouldn't be as exciting. When God painted our world He knew what to put in it. He knew He needed the butterfly to make the world brighter, children to tickle the world, and friends to put smiles on faces.

The picture God painted is very beautiful. There are pretty flowers growing all over the place, bees in their hives, ants minding their own business, the sun peeping through the clouds, people wearing smiles on their faces, and love wrapped up with big bundles of hugs. If something were missing, the world wouldn't be the same anymore! I am glad that God, the greatest artist, put every single thing in the picture, because each one is important. I am glad God put you and me here to give life to the painting. Aren't we proud that He used you and me to give beauty to the world?

CHRISTINE JEDA ORILLOSA

THE CALENDAR

Jesus answered him, saying, It is written, That man shall not live by bread alone, but by every word of God. Luke 4:4.

"That cannot be," I said emphatically to the person on the phone. "My calender shows that the twenty-third is Tuesday, not Monday."

"Are you sure you're looking at the right month and year?"

"Yes," I said. "I have it right here in front of me, and that is exactly what it says."

There was a long pause, then, "Well, I have my calendar right here, and it shows that the twenty-third is Monday."

After I hung up I checked my calendar with others, and yes, there truly was an error in the calendar. It looked correct, but upon close scrutiny it turned out to be wrong!

Have you ever looked for a street address only to find that some prankster had changed the signs? You could look forever and never find the address because you were on the wrong street.

Every day magazines and newspapers are full of information about everything from our health to how the nation is going. Quite often one discovers that each one may have a totally different outlook from the others. Have you listened to the weather forecast on two radio or TV stations? Sure enough—they differ, even though the forecast is for the same place and same time. Certainly they cannot all be right.

How can we possibly know what is right and what is wrong? What do we have to refer to? How can we know for sure what is truth? Do we read the Bible, the expositor of truth, every day to learn for ourselves? Although there is much falsehood in this world, we can know what is truth and never be misled if we follow the Word, the Truth.

Father, thank You for Jesus, the never-changing, never-ending Truth. He is the Word made flesh. You have also given us the Bible to guide us. Help me today to study diligently so I can know it and You better.   PAT MADSEN

THE BUTTERFLY

And we know that all things work together for good to them that love God, to them who are the called according to his purpose. Rom. 8:28.

A butterfly is a fragile creature. One day my husband called me to come and see one by the edge of the road.

"How long do they usually live?" he mused out loud.

"I don't know. I'll have to look it up in my encyclopedia." (I found out later that our roadside butterfly was a monarch, and that they can live as long as 18 months. They sip nectar from flowers and migrate long distances.)

The butterfly was alive but appeared to be injured. I held out my fingers, and to my surprise and delight, it climbed onto my hand. I took it to our backyard and placed it on a bush near some tall flowering phlox. I knew it would be safe from the cars flying by and would be near food if it was able to feed.

It was midafternoon when we found the monarch, and after placing it on the bush I went about my work. Later that night, about 9:00, I remembered the butterfly. Was it still there or was it gone? Was it still alive? I took the flashlight and went out to see. Yes, it was still there and still clinging to the bush. I asked the Lord to watch over it and went to bed.

The next morning when I let the dogs out, I went to see about the butterfly. It was gone. I could see no evidence that a bird had eaten it, and I could find no place where it had fallen. Apparently it had gained the strength it needed and had flown on its way. I prayed a silent thanks to God for helping it.

Many of us are like that butterfly. We are very fragile. We need Someone to help us climb out of our dangers, Someone to help us find a place of refuge until we gain our strength and can go on. And that Someone often uses us to help one another. I want to be used by that Someone for others each day.

Please keep me close to You so that You can choose to use me, not just for today, but for all my days. Strengthen me and help me to reach out to others, that they too may learn of Your love. LORAINE F. SWEETLAND

THE TEST

If you think you are standing, watch out that you do not fall.
1 Cor. 10:12, NRSV.

One of my most necessary possessions is my little gray Ford Tempo. It's about 10 years old and has acquired a few dents and scratches here and there, but I tolerate them because it gets me where I need to go. I enjoy the security the car affords me. Since we don't have public transportation in our city, I need my car. I like to make sure everything is in good shape, so I am faithful in having it checked out regularly.

As my seventy-fifth birthday approached, I knew I would have to take a driving test, a law in my state. I dreaded it; but then, I've been driving for more than 50 years, so what could possibly go wrong?

The day of the test arrived, and I was quite apprehensive. After we completed the drive around the designated city blocks, we returned to the parking lot in the mall and sat for a few moments while the instructor completed her paperwork. Then she gave me the bad news: I had failed the test. Along with that unsettling news, she informed me I had ignored not one but two warnings from her while in the car.

Through the years I apparently had developed the very bad habit of failing to come to a full stop at stop signs. They call it a "rolling stop," but a complete stop is required by law—one in which you count "One, two" before proceeding.

All I could do was reschedule the test and try to unlearn a bad habit. I tested again and passed without incident. I now come to a complete stop at all stop signs (much to the distress of some impatient drivers behind me). Bad habits are hard to break. I've heard it said that a groove is made in the brain by repetition and to reroute that path takes time and patience. It's difficult, but not impossible. First we must acknowledge the fact that the habit is out of control, then take action to correct it.

As I discovered the hard way, it's much easier to stem a tiny stream than try to rechannel a raging river.

CLAREEN COLCLESSER

THE GARDEN OF MY HEART

He also that received seed among the thorns is he that heareth the word; and the care of this world, and the deceitfulness of riches, choke the word, and he becometh unfruitful. Matt. 13:22.

When we moved in, the small garden in front of our house was full of weeds. I considered gardening a nuisance, but because everyone would see the garden, it was necessary to start weeding. Soon I became more interested and spent all my spare time there.

The more time I spent in weeding, the more I realized the dreadfulness of sin. Weeding was not as easy as I had thought it would be. Often we are unmindful of the danger of sin. We think we can overcome easily. Soon we find it is not so. I also learned that while there are different kinds of weeds, they all spoil the beauty of the garden. Likewise, sins spoil the beauty of holiness that God has given us.

It was easier to pull out the young weeds, because they were not deep-rooted. The deeper the roots, the more difficult it was to uproot them. So it is easier to overcome sin completely at the early stage than after a long period.

I discovered that weeds grow faster than vegetables or flowers, hindering the growth of the desirable plants. So does sin. We feel guilty the first time we sin. If we continue sinning, the guilt disappears, and we begin to justify our sins. This causes our spiritual growth to deteriorate.

The garden needed constant weeding. Whenever there was a lapse, it looked awful. One day as I was weeding, one of the youngsters on the campus said, "Aunty, there is no use weeding. We tried, but we failed and gave up. Soon you will also give up." I smiled at him and thought, *I will never give up. This weeding has taught me the dreadfulness of sin and the importance of constant communion with God if we are to have a clean heart, free from sin.*

How often do we feel that we can never overcome sin—that we are unworthy to come to the Lord, that He will not hear us or care for us? So we give up.

Friends, "Come now, and let us reason together, saith the Lord: though your sins be as scarlet, they shall be as white as snow; though they be red like crimson, they shall be as wool" (Isa. 1:18). Isn't that good news? He will remove the weeds from the garden of your heart.   HEPZIBAH G. KORE

THE BEST IS YET TO COME

Behold, I make all things new. Rev. 21:5.

Melissa and I slipped into the reception room. It was Bette's ninety-eighth birthday. Along with others, we were there to recognize a beloved near-centenarian and to support her goal to live to be at least 100. I wanted Melissa to meet this unique woman.

In the place of honor at the front of the room, Bette was a trifle unsteady as she leaned on her walker. Her knees trembled as if they might give out, but her eyes twinkled and the million wrinkles on her face curved upward. Waving a utensil dramatically in her free hand, she said in a chipper voice, "Remember to save your fork!" At that moment a masterpiece in the shape of the Eiffel Tower (Paris was Bette's favorite city) rolled into the room on a silver tea cart. With eyes like saucers, Melissa groaned aloud when the baked sculpture fell to the serving knife.

The festivities wound down. The birthday lady struggled to her feet again. Smiling broadly, she thanked us for the celebration and repeated, "Remember to save your fork!"

"Why did she say 'Remember to save your fork' again?" Melissa asked. "We've already eaten the Eiffel Tower."

"Ask her," I suggested. "You'll never know unless you do." I felt sure there would be a response as unique as Bette. There was.

"My dear," the birthday celebrant explained, "when I was your age, we were poorer than the proverbial church mice. On those rare occasions when I heard that special phrase, I knew the best was yet to come." She paused a moment. "I made those words my motto for life. Living them has made all the difference. In fact," Bette continued, her face molding into the wry expression many of us had grown to love, "when I die, I want a giant fork displayed at my memorial service. Even then, the best is yet to come."

My eyes misted. Bette's personal history had not been without deep dark valleys, but she'd always bounced back up to the next mountain peak. No wonder, with an outlook like that!

It was no surprise to hear Melissa tell her mother later that evening, "I've got a motto for my life—'Remember to save your fork.'"

They will have plenty to talk about on the way home, I mused as I watched their car pull away from the curb. *And that would be a great motto for me, too.*

ARLENE TAYLOR

RUTHIE MEETS HER FATHER

Surely goodness and mercy shall follow me all the days of my life. Ps. 23:6.

Nightly wishing upon the first star that she saw, little Ruthie did not realize that she was actually praying. Only 9 years old, she had just spent a week at camp in southern Indiana. To earn money to go there she had sold greeting cards, looked after younger siblings, and for weeks had wished upon the first star she'd seen every night. But the money came very slowly. In the late 1940s folks didn't have much to share with a little girl and her pipe dream of going to camp.

Ruthie had heard about camp in the children's class she had recently begun to attend at church. The woman who picked her up each week was so good to Ruthie. Sometimes she gave her pretty ribbons to wear in her thin, straight hair. She encouraged Ruthie to be clean, brush her teeth, comb her hair every day, and be obedient.

One day the church lady and her best friend stopped by and asked to take Ruthie with them to town to go shopping. Shopping! Ruthie had never been "shopping" in her life! Before the afternoon had passed, she owned three lovely new dresses, pretty little undies, and—in a hankie all tied up— enough money to go to camp for the first time.

To Ruthie, camp seemed like heaven. Why, there were great mounds of mashed potatoes, luscious corn, more sliced tomatoes than even she could eat, and all the milk she could drink at every meal! Every day there was flag raising, nature study, crafts, swimming, and best of all, campfire in the evening under the stars. The stories always pointed the children to the God who made the starry heavens above, and who loved each child as though she were the only child in the whole world.

There at camp young Ruthie learned about God, her heavenly Father, because two young women unselfishly gave of themselves. And because God does work in mysterious ways "His wonders to perform," a couple years later the "church lady" actually became Ruthie's foster mother.

Ruthie eventually learned that it was not the star upon which she had wished that had granted the longings of her heart, but her wonderful heavenly Father, who had created the star—a Father who loved her, protected her, and led her to a saving knowledge of Himself. And she loved Him "all the days of [her] life."

BETTY R. BURNETT

LIFE'S MUSICAL MILESTONES

O sing to the Lord a new song; sing to the Lord, all the earth! Sing to the Lord, bless his name; tell of his salvation from day to day. Declare his glory among the nations, his marvelous works among all the peoples! Ps. 96:1-3, RSV.

I once read about a group of music educators who published a list of 42 songs that represented American culture. Alphabetically, it began with "Amazing Grace" and ended with "Zippity-Doo-Dah." I grew up with many of the songs on the list, and as I contemplated the really significant music in my life, I could recall several musical milestones along the way.

The first really significant songs were hymns. Learning that "Jesus Loves Me" early in my life helped me in making my decision to follow my Saviour. At the age of 15, tears streaming down my face, I went forward during an altar call. I can still hear the congregation singing "Just as I Am." Each time I hear it I recall my entire born-again experience.

The usual songs followed along in my life, including graduation's "Pomp and Circumstance" and wedding songs and marches for my wedding and for my children's. Lullabies are high on the list as I fondly remember many hours that I spent rocking and singing to our own little ones, and now to grandchildren.

All these songs bring back wonderful recollections of special times. But there is a song of greater significance that I recently experienced. Our home had been empty of homemade music for well over a year while my husband battled cancer. A few days ago, however, I heard him singing in the shower. It was only a few bars of "The Holy City," and it was not perfectly rendered; but after all he had been through, his song of victory was truly the sweetest music in all the world to my ears.

Ultimately, the only music that will top this will be the song of redemption when in heaven we will sing a new song, praising our Saviour and King: "Worthy, Worthy Is the Lamb."

You put music in my heart and soul, Lord—songs of praise and thanks for the way You have led. The future, even today, is uncertain. But I look forward to joining that mighty choir someday and singing praises with the redeemed!

ALBERTA BENNETT CICCARELLI

LICENSE PLATES

Let your light shine before others, so that they may see your good works and give glory to your Father in heaven. Matt. 5:16, NRSV.

Before being allowed to drive a vehicle on a public road, one must obtain a license plate for it. In Wisconsin we are required to put plates on both the front and the back of our vehicles. There are several plates we are allowed to choose from: ones that support endangered species, or education, or the 150-year celebration of the state of Wisconsin.

Upon moving to this state, we decided on the standard plates: three letters, space, and three numbers. Both of our cars have the three letters RRR, which my husband, Rick, says represent him and his two brothers, Ron and Randy. Those three letters caused me to think about other license plates.

Often people personalize license plates. Some use their name or an important date. Others have messages for all to see. One I saw read "THKS DAD," which I assume meant "Thanks, Dad" (perhaps for the car?). Not long ago we noticed one that read "I Doctor." I'm guessing that person is an eye doctor. One plate we liked read simply, "DABULLS." The owner of that vehicle was obviously an avid fan of the Chicago Bulls.

What would happen if we as humans were required to wear license plates? Maybe our clothes would have Velcro on the back, and each morning before heading out the door we would be required to attach the license plate to our back. Some of the choices for personalization might include *kind, courteous, thoughtful, rude, demanding, cheerful, happy, gloomy*—or simply *Christian*.

What would be written on your human plate? Would your Christianity be visible enough that without being given a test you would be given a plate reading "Christian"? Or would you be required to take the test and hope for the best?

In Matthew 5:16 we find, "Let your light shine before others, so that they may see your good works and give glory to your Father in heaven" (NRSV).

May we each have the assurance that our human plate would read "Christian" and that everyone would recognize it as appropriate.

MARSHA CLAUS

GRACE IN AN ENVELOPE

My grace is sufficient for you, for power is perfected in weakness.
2 Cor. 12:9, NASB.

Not so long ago a very kind gentleman on the other side of the country from where I was living won my heart—something I'd vowed never to give away again. The wedding took place a few months later, even though we knew it would necessitate living apart for a time until God revealed which of us should relocate. Jim lived in Oregon, and I in Maryland.

Two weeks after the honeymoon, after he'd returned to his responsibilities in Oregon, my thoughtful new husband sent me an envelope containing a credit card with a note. It read "I don't want you to be worrying so much about struggling with your bills. We're in this together now. Use my card."

That credit card was a tremendous relief! It couldn't have come at a better time. So I carefully tucked it away and continued wrestling with my bills.

Five weeks later my husband commented during a phone conversation, "Incidentally, I got the credit card bill. You didn't charge anything. Have things really eased up for you financially or something?"

"No," I admitted sheepishly.

A long silence ensued. He broke it by asking, "Then why aren't you letting me help you?"

My very lame answer was "I don't know—I guess I'm just in the habit of trying to do it all by myself." The credit was there for me to use. I was choosing not to use it.

Our heavenly Husband (Isa. 54:5) gives us a credit card too. And there's no maximum limit on His grace. We can charge our sins to His account; He covers them with forgiveness. We can charge impurity; He covers with righteousness. We charge problems; He covers with answers. We charge temptations; He covers with strength and victory. We charge pain; He covers with peace. We charge our loneliness; He covers it with Himself. Amazing grace, that through Christ Jesus, the riches of the universe are at my disposal!

And when I make the choice to use God's credit card, I can finally stop trying to do it "all by myself."

I accept Your offer, Lord. Thank You.   CAROLYN RATHBUN SUTTON

MOVING DAY—WHERE?

Before they call I will answer; while they are still speaking I will hear. Isa. 65:24, NIV.

We lived in our three-story house for more than 20 years, and it felt like a friend to us. We have many special memories of that house: parties on Women's Day, Thanksgiving dinners, Christmas celebrations, birthday gatherings, and many church potluck luncheons. Paul, my husband, and I could relax and just hang loose in our backyard, listening to the songs of the birds while they were nesting and feeding. And we could watch the beautiful butterflies soaring and flitting from flower to flower. The deer would meander through the oleander bushes, drinking the fresh water we placed there for them. On some of those clear, hot days, the deer would plop down in the shade by the inviting pool. Our home was a little piece of God's heaven. Many visitors used to say that they would like to vacation at our place.

Then we lost our business, and that created a corresponding decrease in income. We knew that in time we would have to look for another place to live. Walking out the door one morning on our way to church, we saw an eviction notice taped to the door. Of course, this caught us by surprise.

Our daughter cried. She urged us not to live in an apartment building— she had a fear of easily spreading fire that would engulf the entire building. We reassured her that no one is safe but by the hand of God, and we must trust completely in Him as we pray for His guidance.

We searched for days, then weeks, for another house, but none was available. We prayed and hunted and looked. Each place we selected was given to earlier prospects. The day we needed to move was almost upon us, and I was scheduled for surgery the same week. Still we had no place.

I'm sure you have heard the phrase "God is always on time." And God did come through—just at the right time. We are now settled in a house chosen by God. It's a cozy place that is hidden by a great variety of tall trees—a place not to be discovered by casual passersby. It's a place God directed us to.

I have learned not to fear when God comes to direct us to new locations and fresh experiences. He will provide. It's reassuring to know that while we may all lose our homes on earth, He has already prepared another home for us. See you there!

MARTHA "GENIE" MCKINNEY-TIFFANY

DO I HAVE ANY ASSETS?

Bring ye all the tithes into the storehouse, . . . and prove me . . . if I will not open you the windows of heaven, and pour you out a blessing, that there shall not be room enough to receive it. Mal. 3:10.

Carefully dressing better than usual, I made my way to the Country Club 19th Hole Restaurant early on a rainy day to attend an informational meeting about long-term care insurance. By the time the four presenters had finished arranging the little tables and chairs for the crowd, I was still the only one there, so they started talking to me. First, they told me that people older than 90 cannot buy long-term insurance; that left out my mother. Second, this insurance was for people with assets to protect.

"Do you have any savings?" they asked.

"Yes," I said. "Enough to pay for my new hearing aids."

They asked if I owned a house, and I said, "Yes, I paid $20,000 for it." They informed me that without more assets there was no use of my staying for the meeting.

A temptation to feel deflated threatened me as I left those well-off people and drove home in the rain. But as I passed my church, I remembered a phone call earlier in the day from the church treasurer—I had forgotten to label my tithe check. It was just the pickup I needed. Suddenly I realized that I had more assets than the people at the club. I had so many blessings!

I get my health insurance at a reduced rate because I teach school for the state. I do not have to pay for couch potato entertainment, or even buy airline tickets to explore the Himalayas or the Alps. God gave me the pleasure of the mountains of home.

I've been happy much of my life subsisting on fruits, vegetables, grains, and nuts. When the economy flops, I do not have to worry about processed foods and restaurants. I expect Jesus to come before I need a nursing home. My monetary assets will not be needed then.

I must quit counting my blessings and get busy. I have two more canners full of plums to process this morning. If I had extra money I could buy canned fruit, but it would surely not be as good as home-canned!

Thank You, Lord, that I can be content with what I have. LOUISE REA

ONLY A TICKET

[All] are justified and made upright and in right standing with God, freely and gratuitously by His grace (His unmerited favor and mercy), through the redemption which is [provided] in Christ Jesus. Rom. 3:24, Amplified.

My husband and I have driven many miles each year in our public evangelism work and other church appointments. This has resulted in a joke between us, because he has reaped a few speeding tickets while somehow I have none. Oh, yes, I have been stopped a few times, but I have talked my way out of the dreaded ticket and fine.

Because of out-of-town appointments, one summer weekend I had to find someone to care for our toy poodle, Musette. I located such a place but was not entirely satisfied. As a longtime friend of dogs, I was probably too fussy. This kennel seemed too big to be really caring for my dog.

As the dog and I drove along on our way home I looked at her and said, "Musette, tomorrow is the day you will be staying at the kennel. I don't want to leave you there, but you can't fly with us or stay at the motel." She looked at me, trying to catch a word she understood.

The next day I took Musette down the country road to the kennel. The farther we went the worse I felt. Tears began to fill my eyes and run down my cheeks. I knew she would not be happy in a strange place. As I came to a stop sign, I slowed down and almost stopped. No vehicles were coming, so I took off. In a few seconds I saw the blinking red light of a traffic patrol officer in my rearview mirror.

As the officer reminded me of my mistake, he gave me a short lecture. I was sure he would give me a ticket. By now the tears were really flowing. The officer looked over the situation. He saw the little black dog sitting as close to me as possible. He soon decided that he didn't want to cause any more stress.

"I won't charge you this time," he said as he closed his ticket pad. "Have a good flight, and I'm sure your dog will be all right."

Oh, what a relief to be given a second chance! It made me think of the text that speaks of unmerited favor. I don't really deserve having my sins forgiven, but Jesus freely offers to all of us another chance.

MARY FOLKES WALTER

WHEN THE WAVES ROLL

Peace I leave with you, My peace I give to you; not as the world gives do I give to you. Let not your heart be troubled, neither let it be afraid. John 14:27, NKJV.

Have you ever been in a real-life situation in which you could feel what something in the past must have been like? I have.

One summer day my uncle invited my family and some friends to go swimming and fishing on his boat. The day was sunny and hot—a perfect day to be on a boat. We should have known it wouldn't last. On this earth good things don't last forever.

We were a couple miles from land, quite near to Riddell's Bay, where my uncle usually docks the boat. Night had cast her dark cloak over us, so we thought we had better call it a day. Then in the midst of the calm the boat started to rock. The water became rougher. The wind whistled a song in a high pitch that soon turned into a howl. Thunder's voice boomed, attempting to drown out the wind. Lightning flashed across the sky, clawing at night's dark cloak. My uncle ordered us down below while he and my cousin stayed on deck. Finally he came below and told us that there was nothing he could do. We would have to wait out the storm.

I felt as I imagine the disciples must have felt on the storm-tossed Sea of Galilee. I experienced the fear of what nature could do in her fury. Even though others were there, I felt all alone. Then I remembered that unlike my uncle Leon, who could do nothing but wait, there was One who could calm the waves. He had done it long ago by saying "Peace, be still," and the winds and waves had obeyed.

If you ever feel as though you're in the midst of a storm and the tumultuous waves of trial are about to overwhelm you, remember that you are not alone, and you do not have to be troubled or afraid. The Master of the winds and waves will be there. He will be happy to take control if you invite Him to.

Jesus, please stay close to me today, calming the waves and giving me peace. Let not my heart be troubled, neither let it be afraid.   DANA M. BASSETT

WONDERS OF THE SEA

Not even a sparrow, worth only half a penny, can fall to the ground without your Father knowing it. . . . So don't be afraid; you are more valuable to him than a whole flock of sparrows. Matt. 10:29-31, NLT.

My husband and I were eager to experience the rugged coastline of Maine: foaming waves crashing with thunder blast over rocky outcroppings; picturesque lighthouses scattered along the seaboard; dipping our feet into the Atlantic Ocean at the easternmost point of the continental United States.

From Maine we drove into Canada and saw the amazing tidal changes on the Bay of Fundy, the summer home for some of the wonders of the sea—whales. And I was not leaving the Northeast until I saw my whales!

In a little lobster boat with 20 other nature lovers we scanned the water in all directions, hoping to catch sight of a whale. Finally a shout came from our lookout: "There's one! At 11:00." The pilot gunned the engines and raced in that direction.

As we neared the area where the whale had been sighted, we looked and waited. Where was it? Where was it? The whale would have to come up for air sometime. All of a sudden a spray of water and the top of a huge head surfaced. My whale! My first whale!

Emotion overcame me. Wow! I was seeing God's jumbo creatures of the sea—for real. Every glimpse of their heads, flip of their tails, or spray from their blowholes was like a kiss from heaven. God came close to share His wonders with me. I've fallen in love with whales. Though some may think them only huge hunks of blubber, each whale has its own identifying characteristics. Hundreds have been identified and given names. In fact, you can adopt a whale with a name such as Star, Littlespot, Flame, or Midnight.

It makes me think about how God has adopted us. Though we may feel sometimes as though we're only a hunk of blubber, we're unique and precious to Him. He knows us each by name. We're His daughters. He knows our personalities, our lifestyle patterns, our talents. He also knows our joys and sorrows. And if He can take care of all the creatures—from little sparrows to jumbo whales—He can take care of our little problems and jumbo ones too. And best of all, He thrills to catch a glimpse of us.

HEIDE FORD

A PERFUME CALLED BEAUTIFUL

Awake, north wind, and come, south wind! Blow on my garden, that its fragrance may spread abroad. S. of Sol. 4:16, NIV.

Perfume is special, a luxury, but a tiny drop can go a long way. I love to pass by the perfume counters and try out my favorite fragrances. A little dab on the wrist, a droplet brushed across my temples, and I feel as if I am living inside a bouquet. The scent lifts my heart, and I feel special.

When I'm rushing along the busy streets of London, where the atmosphere feels heavy with emission fumes, dust, and noise, occasionally a woman will pass me. Just after she has moved away, the thick air will be transformed for a moment by her expensive perfume. In an instant the street will be a garden, the air will seem fresh and beautiful, and I will feel energized.

I unwrapped a pretty package to find a bottle of perfume, perfume that I knew cost more than Auntie Maud could afford. Her eyes met my smile of thanks, and she knew what I was thinking. "Well," she said, "I help a little old woman who lives close by in my retirement complex. Her daughter works for an international beauty company. She lives away and can't do much to help her mother, but she was so grateful that someone could help her that she gave me a box full of special cosmetics and perfumes."

Great Auntie Maud had helped a friend. The friend was happy and shared the news with her daughter. The daughter was glad and shared some gifts to make Maud happy. Now Maud was doing the best thing she knew to do with such lovely things: pass them on.

When I saw the name of the fragrance, I smiled again. The name summed up the whole simple story of sharing. It was called "Beautiful."

A long time ago another place was filled with the exquisite fragrance of expensive perfume. Simon's house. Mary anointed Jesus' feet with perfume and with her hair dried her tears that fell on them. And His heavy heart was encouraged. He felt strengthened and energized, nurtured and cared for. Angry voices rose in protest, but Jesus silenced them.

"Leave her alone. She has done something very beautiful for Me, something I will always remember and treasure." I am sure Jesus can still remember the fragrance of that moment.

May my life be a beautiful fragrance in this world today. KAREN HOLFORD

RANDOM INVITATIONS AND ULTIMATE BLESSINGS

When you give a luncheon or a dinner, do not invite your friends . . . in case they may invite you in return, and you would be repaid. But when you give a banquet, invite the poor, the crippled, the lame, and the blind. And you will be blessed. Luke 14:12-14, NRSV.

It was the first week of the new school year. I knew that many of the freshmen on our university campus would be away from home for the first time. I suspected that some might be homesick. Remembering my own experience some 30 years earlier, I had promised several mothers to keep an eye on their precious daughters. I decided to honor that promise by cooking a special Sabbath meal at my house. By Thursday, urging each one to bring a friend with her, I had invited five young women to come home with me after church.

On Friday afternoon tantalizing smells from my sparkling kitchen indicated that a meal fit for the King's daughters was in the making. And then the phone began to ring. "I'm sorry; we forgot we had another invitation," one excused herself hesitantly. "We have come down with a terrible case of the flu," another said over the hacking sounds of her roommate's coughing. "My mom's coming to take us home for the weekend," offered a third.

In a quandary, I looked down at the solitary name left on my guest list. "Tell me what to do, Lord," I prayed. Almost simultaneously two images flashed across the screen of my memory—the tear-streaked face of a freshman, and the parable of the wedding feast in which the apologies of the guests showed a startling similarity to the ones I had just heard. I would not postpone this dinner. Instead, I would issue random invitations at church the next day.

We had a marvelous time that Indian summer afternoon. We ate; we chatted; the young women bonded over the dishwashing bubbles; one virtuoso played the piano. For sunset worship, each of them shared tangible evidences of God's blessings. I tasted something better that evening than I had eaten at any banquet.

Thank You, Forever Friend, for showing me that even a crust of bread shared with my sisters in Your presence is a banquet. GLENDA-MAE GREENE

WITNESSING ON THE AMTRAK

We intend to do what is right not only in the Lord's sight, but also in the sight of others. 2 Cor. 8:21, NRSV.

I often take the Amtrak to visit my daughter in Illinois, a scenic two-hour ride. When I book the ticket three weeks in advance, the fare is rather inexpensive. Recently, however, I had to travel without much notice. My daughter needed me to baby-sit for two days. My grandchildren are my delight, so I was happy to be able to spend some extra time with them.

When I boarded the train, I noticed that the conductor was a young woman. That was not really unusual, but I was struck by her attitude. As she spoke to the passengers, her manner seemed abrupt and unfriendly. I wondered if she was having a bad day.

I settled into my seat and for a while enjoyed the scenery as we sped along. Then I began to talk to a woman who had been reading to her two sons. We talked about the book, which she passed to me, and I began to read. Some time later I realized we were nearing our destination and I still had my ticket. I took it out and examined it closely. It was good for a year. Since I knew that the conductor would make one final trip through the train before it reached Union Station, I waited.

She appeared, but started to pass by me. Managing to get her attention, I told her of the oversight. Surprised, she looked at me, took the ticket, and explained that she thought I was with the woman and sons whose tickets she had taken earlier. She thanked me for my honesty. As she turned away, she stopped to marvel, "I didn't know there was this much honesty left in the world."

I was saddened. She seemed too young to be so cynical. I never saw her again, but I often think of her. I pray that she will meet many more honest people so that her faith in humanity can be restored.

So many people have become disillusioned, betrayed by those they trust. We have an impact on others. We may never have the opportunity to share our beliefs and values with them, but we can bring them a ray of hope simply by putting our beliefs into practice and preaching the unspoken sermon. We can let our lights shine so that our Father is glorified.

NORMA MORRIS GREENIDGE

LOST THROUGH NEGLECT?

O God, You are my God; early will I seek You; my soul thirsts for You; my flesh longs for You in a dry and thirsty land where there is no water. Ps. 63:1, NKJV.

I looked out my kitchen window onto the little garden behind the house. There I saw the peony all dried up and nearly dead. That beautiful Memorial Day peony was a gift from Darrell's auntie Thelma. The blistering, dusty days of August had taken their toll. The leaves were dry and brittle, and only a few green ones remained. I felt sad. I wondered, *Have I lost this peony because I neglected to provide water during the hot, dry weeks of August?* It had been the first plant in my garden to bring forth beautiful red blooms in the spring. The blossoms had brought joy to me as I looked out my window. I knew that I must do all I could to keep the plant alive.

I watered the soil surrounding the plant. It took time for the water to soak in, but little by little I replenished the needed moisture. Then I watched for a revival in the life of the plant. When there was no evidence of it, I realized that I might have to wait until spring to see if there was any life in the roots.

This is so much like my relationship with my friends. I need to avoid periods of drought. Spending time together and sharing our thoughts and emotions waters my friendships with other women. When neglected and deprived of the communication that nourishes them, those relationships wither and sometimes die.

When I have allowed a friendship to grow distant or, worse, to die, I have lost something special from my life. Friendships are like flowers. They brighten our lives. To have a friend is to have a treasure of great value.

My relationship with Jesus also needs nurturing and care. To know Him better I spend time reading His letter to me. I share my thoughts, emotions, and needs with Him, knowing that He appreciates and desires the praise and love I give Him. It is easy for me to fulfill His desire for adoration. When I neglect time with Him, my soul thirsts and I begin to wither. I treasure His friendship and want always to keep it "watered" and, by the life I live, to demonstrate that I care. Friendships are the flowers of life.   EVELYN GLASS

GOD CERTAINLY PROVIDES

Abraham said, "My son, God will provide." Gen. 22:8, NKJV.

We three girls finished the small city assigned to us. Now we had to go to remote areas, since we had signed on to solicit subscriptions and sell magazines the whole summer. Day after day, from morning until evening, our daily routine was to take as many subscriptions as possible to the health magazine we were promoting. We were instructed not to skip any house, no matter how small it was. Selling magazines wasn't an easy job, but we wanted to fulfill the required hours and sales on which our scholarship depended.

One day we worked so hard that we lost track of our time. By the time we met at the designated meeting place, it was already very dark. Not only that, but the last bus to leave for the city had already gone. There was no other transportation that would take us home. We looked at our watches. We looked at each other. Now what were we to do?

We began walking, absorbed in our own thoughts. In our hearts we were all praying. One of us thought of Isaiah 59:1: "Behold, the Lord's hand is not shortened, that it cannot save; neither his ear heavy, that it cannot hear." We were sure God would see our plight.

Soon we saw a very small store. We inquired if we could spend the night with the owner. But she said her place was so small she couldn't accommodate us. Besides, she said, her husband was coming that evening. More prayers went up to the miracle-working God. Somehow we felt peace sweep our hearts. We lingered longer at the store. We didn't know where to go, and no houses could be seen. It was a lonely store where buses and taxis stopped during the day. Soon we saw two very big lights coming toward the store. It was a taxi bringing the store owner's husband. And the taxi driver had to hurry back to the city.

A way had been provided for us! Humanly speaking, we thought we had no way out, but God had a thousand ways of providing for His daughters. When Isaac asked his father where the lamb for a burnt offering was, Abraham had said, "My son, God will provide." Isn't God such a wonderful provider? He surely is worthy to be praised.   OFELIA A. PANGAN

TRUST ME

Trust in the Lord with all thine heart; and lean not unto thine own understanding. Prov. 3:5.

My husband and I were approaching the time that many parents view with trepidation. Our eldest daughter, Natalie, was nearly 11 years old, which meant that she had to change schools. Being active, practicing Christians, we did not feel that the local state secondary school was the right place to send either of our children.

After much searching, we eventually found that there was only one Christian senior school in our area. As it was privately run, we would have to pay tuition. After much prayer we decided we would arrange to look at the school.

The staff were caring and placed a strong emphasis on the pupils as individuals. A strong Christian ethos was evident. The only problem was how to pay the fees. I did some work from home as a day-care provider, but my earnings were spasmodic and were not sufficient to commit to five years of school fees.

One evening as our family was praying, Natalie finished her prayer with the words "Please, Jesus, help Mommy to get a good job so that I can go to the right school. Amen."

The next day my husband came home from work and told me that he had been talking to a colleague who had a job vacancy for a secretary. He would be willing to consider me, but the position had to be full-time. I had never worked as a secretary, and the last time I had typed for a living was shortly after leaving school many years before. But bearing in mind Natalie's prayer of the previous evening, I decided that maybe this was what the Lord wanted me to do.

When I went to discuss the job with my prospective employer a few days later, imagine my surprise when the first thing he told me was that he actually had two job vacancies—one full-time and one part-time, only two days a week. Which would I prefer? Some six weeks later I started the part-time job, knowing it was the one the Lord had found for me.

Lord, You amaze me. You give us exactly what we need, when we need it. Thank You once again.

JUDITH REDMAN

ROBBED!

My God, my God, why have you forsaken me? Mark 15:34, NIV.

As soon as I heard my daughter's voice on the telephone I sensed something was wrong. Like me, Marina does not do a good job of hiding her true feelings. And this time I knew she was struggling for control, even while her voice trembled.

"Mom, my house has been broken into. When I got home from work, my front door was standing open, and my beautiful stained-glass door panel was shattered."

She described the horrible mess she found inside, the precious items she was missing, and how invaded and helpless she felt. A friend who is a policeman and others whom she had called had rushed to her aid, doing all they could. But no one could answer her burning question: "I dedicated my home to God. Why did He let this happen?"

Marina, the principal of a small parochial school, was scheduled to preach the sermon at church in less than a week. She wondered how she could stand before the congregation while she was hurting so much. What did she have to offer them?

Her dad and I listened as she recounted her story to an attentive congregation. Many wept with her as she reminded herself and us that Jesus, on the day He died, had asked, "Why?" Afterward a number of individuals told her that her talk had given them strength to face their difficulties, and I was glad for the encouragement their remarks gave her.

Several mornings later, while I was taking my daily walk, my thoughts fell on Marina and the break-in. How could something so devastating be a blessing to anyone? Did God really understand how she felt?

Time eases the intensity of feelings that result from a home invasion, but Jesus will never forget the cost of our salvation. Forever His hands and feet will bear the scars that were made by those cruel nails while He hung on that old rugged cross.

Dear Lord, thank You for the lesson You gave me that morning. You do understand our pains, heartaches, and disappointments. Someday You will explain all the "whys." Help us to be appreciative of the price You paid for our salvation. MILDRED C. WILLIAMS

PRAYING, PRAYING, AND MORE PRAYING

Faith is the substance of things hoped for, the evidence of things not seen.
Heb. 11:1.

I sat in my room, contemplating my desire to move to the big city of
Atlanta, Georgia. Living with my mother in a small town after
graduating from college had kept me dependent on her. I couldn't find
steady work, and the jobs that were available were not specific to my
degree. I continued to ask God to help me move to Atlanta. I bought the
Atlanta *Journal-Constitution* and found numerous jobs of interest. I prayed
some more. I even visited the city on several occasions. I continued to pray.

At church one Sabbath a guest speaker talked about prayer and said
that we need to pray only once, with boldness, believing God hears us and
will answer the prayer. And after praying, we must then take the first steps
in faith, and our heavenly Father will do the rest. What a revelation for me!
I had let a complete year go by just praying—praying that somehow God
would come down and pack my clothes, fill out apartment applications,
and go on job interviews for me! How silly of me to put my heavenly
Father into a vacuum. For an entire year God watched me pray and waited
for me to make the first move.

Finally I moved without having a job. God worked through the
apartment complex leasing agent, who allowed me to move in on a 60-day
probation. I cleared my small savings account of $500, which went toward
my first month's rent and security deposit. Every week my mother sent me
my unemployment check, but that would end in 60 days. Daily I filled out
applications and secured interviews. Within three weeks God blessed me
with three job offers! What a mighty God we serve!

So often we Christians pray and pray until we are blue in the face. All
God wants is for us to step out in faith. Just a mustard seed is all He asks.
He asks us to forget about what we cannot see and start walking, packing,
driving, and believe He has already answered our prayers.

Give me faith for today, faith in You for things hoped for and the evidence of
things not yet seen, that my faith may grow even more. PENELOPE S. SMITH

LOWERING THE FLAG

Give her of the fruit of her hands; and let her own works praise her in the gates. Prov. 31:31.

After Princess Diana's death I was impressed with the global impact she had had on the lives of people from all walks of life. It was amazing to see the thousands and thousands of flowers, cards, and gifts left in front of the gates of Buckingham and Windsor palaces and British embassies around the world. Thousands of people stood in line for hours to register their condolences in books that expressed their caring.

Contrasting with the open grief of the world was what seemed to me to be the conspicuously cool and almost insulting silence of the royal family. High above Buckingham and Windsor palaces the flag of the United Kingdom flew at full staff, as if to say the princess's death was insignificant to the royal family. As the days progressed, the profound grief of the British turned to anger. "Say something to show us you care and share in our grief!" they cried. After several days the royal family emerged from seclusion to see an unbelievable outpouring of support and sympathy. But the Union Jack still flew high above the palaces.

Lowering a flag to half-mast is a universal symbol of mourning. Six days after Diana's death and after outcries from the British, the Union Jack was finally lowered to half-mast, symbolizing the grief of the entire United Kingdom and recognizing her as influential in the lives of the British people. It was that act, lowering the flags, the people wanted. They wanted the queen to recognize and mourn the princess they loved so dearly.

What was it that endeared the princess to the world? I think it was her gentleness; her kindness; her open display of affection for her own sons and all children; her efforts to give voices and faces to sickness and poverty; her humor; and her ability to touch both rich and poor physically and emotionally. Princess Diana's works praised her at the gates of Buckingham and Windsor, and her memory lives on.

Diana was not the last princess to live. You too are a princess. Your Father is the King of the universe. You too can be known for your kindness, gentleness, humor, love for all people, and dignity. God will give you wisdom to fulfill your royal position as His princess. Then your own works will praise you in the gates. NICCETA "NIKKI" DAVIS

RIDING TANDEM

*How very good and pleasant it is when kindred live together in unity!
Ps. 133:1, NRSV.*

The day promised clear weather as a small boat ferried my husband and me to Mackinac Island, in Michigan. When our feet touched island soil, we were whisked back to the eighteenth century. Horse-drawn buggies and carriages jostled along the main street amidst pedestrians and cyclists. Not a car was in sight.

A walking tour of historic sites, sidewalk cafés, and novelty shops was fun. But we wished to follow the paved road that encircled the island along the waterfront.

Being from the not-so-rich group, we chose a rental bicycle over the more elite horse and carriage. A bicycle built for two seemed the perfect romantic choice. It was, after all, our anniversary.

We hauled the clumsy old clunker out and mounted as a helpful attendant called instructions from the open shop window. I perched stiffly on the front seat. I was serious about attacking my job of steering. My husband, on the back seat, promptly pushed us into a left lean and hit the pedals. I lost my balance. We tried again and again.

"It's not straight!" I yelled, and jerked it upright.

"Well, it was. But now it's not!" he shot back.

Crowds pushed by on both sides. Our frustration rose.

"There goes another marriage!" the attendant sighed as we finally wobbled away.

Frequent sightseeing stops left us in dread of the next start-up. But onward we struggled. Surely 10 years of marriage couldn't end like this!

The light finally came on: the bike was bent. If I sat straight, he leaned right; and when he was upright, I careened left. We were doomed to failure. We returned the bent tandem, reporting its problems to the owner.

It rather reminds me of some people groups I've known. Some lean right, while the rest bend firmly left. No matter how hard one party pedals and the other steers, they wobble precariously out of balance. Life demands a lot of working together in pairs or groups. And we can't have unity or balance if our tandems are bent.

DAWNA BEAUSOLEIL

THE HUMMINGBIRD FEEDERS

Thus says the Lord: "Do not let the wise boast in their wisdom, do not let the mighty boast in their might, do not let the wealthy boast in their wealth. Jer. 9:23, NRSV.

Hanging on my patio cover are two hummingbird feeders. Because I expected two feeders to attract many birds, I filled them with sweet syrup, as instructed on the labels. Every morning I sit out there very early and watch while I drink water.

One male Anna's hummingbird is always there, parked on a branch near the patio. But from that perch he is actually guarding the feeders. If another hummingbird comes near, he chases it away, hoarding all the syrup for himself. He won't even let the female Anna's hummingbirds eat there.

Now, one hummingbird could not possibly suck up all that syrup before it goes bad, crystallizes, molds, or just loses its strength. That bird is very selfish. I told him so, but he continues his selfish behavior. Last year I had to throw away old syrup because of him. So when summer came again this year, I thought that surely that selfish male hummingbird had gone somewhere else to do his guarding. But no, he was back again, and worse than ever.

The male Anna's hummingbird has bright, iridescent red head feathers that glisten in the sun as he turns his head from side to side. His bright-green breast and back feathers also glisten when he turns this way or that. He is a beautiful bird indeed. But oh, so proud and selfish! I thought of our verse for today. *Too bad he can't read it,* I mused.

Later I told my next-door neighbor about the selfish hummingbird. She said that she had thought no hummingbirds were around because she hadn't seen any.

"I'm going to fill my feeder too," she announced.

Unfortunately, that didn't change the way the selfish male guarded my feeders. I resigned myself to using just one feeder and not filling it so full.

Then the thought came to me that maybe, for the same reason, God doesn't always give us what we want, especially great riches. We might just hoard them instead of sharing them with others. Maybe the blessings of God can be increased only when they are shared. Let's not glory in our earthly riches; God has much better plans for us! BESSIE SIEMENS LOBSIEN

IN THE PALM OF HIS HAND

Humble yourselves under the mighty hand of God, that He may exalt you at the proper time. 1 Peter 5:6, NASB.

It was September on the beautiful island of Bermuda. As the sun warmed the gentle ocean breeze and sent shimmering highlights across the expanse of grass before me, I longed to be anywhere else but on lunch duty.

One hundred energized children immersed themselves in all forms of play. My attention was drawn to a group of primary-two girls patiently digging in the dirt. Intent on completing their task, they separated, scooped, and poked their way through dark-brown wood particles mixed with soil.

After they had been in the same spot for more than 20 minutes, I decided to find out what was keeping them so engrossed. "Ladies, what are you digging for?" I called.

Within seconds three of them came running. Each girl, with gleaming eyes and a broad smile, presented her prize cupped in the palms of her hands.

"We're collecting June bugs to feed the turtles in our classroom!" they exclaimed.

Oh, gross! I thought. But I didn't say it out loud. I just looked down at fat, slimy, opaque, cocoon-like bugs and remained on the spot only because none of the bugs moved. "You run along and wash your hands carefully," I finally responded.

The school day swiftly moved on. In the quiet of my drive home, the Holy Spirit took me back to my lunchtime encounter with the June bugs. How often we are perceived as "gross" by those who share life with us. Or we perceive them as gross. We don't value others, or even ourselves, as we should. But isn't it wonderful to know that no matter where life may find us, we have a patient, loving Saviour who will take us out of the dirt of this world, pry the unpleasant bits of sand from our characters, and proudly carry us in the palm of His hand!

LUANN WAINWRIGHT-TUCKER

HIS WILL, NOT MINE

We know that all that happens to us is working for our good if we love God and are fitting into his plans. Rom. 8:28, TLB.

Excitement was in the air! We were beginning the school year, and God had answered my prayer by placing me in a new building. Feeling quite smug and comfortable as I settled into my newly furnished office, I began to work on my counseling caseload. Then, in a very apologetic tone, my principal informed me that she needed me at a site that housed a junior high school program. I couldn't understand why God would answer my prayer by placing me in the new school, only to snatch me away before the dust settled on my new furniture. The very thought of taking on the unfamiliar was scary. The thought of working with a junior high school population was terrifying.

In my anguish I cried, asking God why. I received no immediate answer that I could understand. Yet I knew there was a reason, a lesson I needed to learn. But what was it? I had quoted Romans 8:28 many times to others, but now it didn't seem to give me any comfort.

As Sabbath approached I knew that I couldn't continue in my present state of mind. I decided to spend the day in solitude and quiet, meditative prayer, song, and study of God's Word. During that time alone with God, He reminded me of my special prayer during summer vacation: "Lord, You know what school I want to work in for the new school year, but You know what's best for me. Help me, Lord, to accept Your will."

I realized that I needed to let go and let God speak to me. When I gave up my resistance to change, God quietly pointed me to Jeremiah 29:11: "I know the plans I have for you, says the Lord. They are plans for good and not for evil, to give you a future and a hope" (TLB). A peaceful calm came over me. The song "It Is Well With My Soul" became one of emotional praise.

God had blessings waiting for me at my new assignment. No, the building is not new; the students are not little, bubbly, and full of laughter; but God had a plan and work for me to do.

As we resist changes in our lives, desiring to hold on to the familiar because of its comfort and safety, let us remember that Jesus left the comfort and splendor of His heavenly home so that we could have life and have it more abundantly (John 10:10).   ARNITA REID

DODDER

If the wicked turn away from all their sins that they have committed and keep all my statutes and do what is lawful and right, they shall surely live; they shall not die. Eze. 18:21, NRSV.

Pondering the fact that some little plants I had been growing for a long time were neither getting bigger nor appearing healthier, I noticed a threadlike, leafless, twining piece of pale gold emerging from the top of the pot. "Oh no!" I exclaimed. "Not dodder!"

As I examined the plant more carefully, the evidence that the dodder had been silently using its deceptive method of operation for quite some time became evident. Tightly entwining itself around the stems of the plants, the dodder had entangled all of the stems and branches with a deathlike hold. Dodder, sometimes called strangle weed, gold thread, and various other names, is closely related to morning glories and sucks its food from the host plant.

Although frustrated with its presence, I was very happy that I had noticed that threadlike twining parasitic plant in time to rescue my little plants. It was so tightly entwined around the plant stems that it took careful work to get rid of it without damaging the host plants.

As I was carefully cutting away the pesky intruder, I was reminded of how easily sin can take over a life. How silently it can work—unseen and deadly, sucking the life out of the unwary soul who does not even realize she has become the host or that there is any danger. The enemy of souls does not broadcast loudly that he is coming, nor does he send any warning messages; but subtly and imperceptibly he attaches himself to his victim while gradually tightening his grip on the unsuspecting soul.

Just as the dodder would have taken the life of the plants, so sin, left unchecked and unrecognized, can endanger our eternal life. Sin is deadly. Sin was the downfall of humankind and caused our first parents to lose their beautiful home in the Garden of Eden.

We have a guidebook, the Bible, that points out what sin is. We have the power of the Holy Spirit to convict us and warn us of impending danger. We can disregard these warnings only at the peril of losing our everlasting life.

PAT MADSEN

SPIKED HAIR AND BAGGY PANTS

I have called you by your name; you are Mine. . . . Since you were precious in My sight, you have been honored, and I have loved you. Isa. 43:1-4, NKJV.

I never gave a thought to this day, but it's here. And it's only beginning. I'm the parent of a teenager!

Thirteen years ago, when they handed me the tiny bundle wrapped in blue, I thought, *This is my son!* I enjoyed the fragrance of Baby Magic on his soft skin. I marveled as he learned and grew, each new step an adventure of joy. I felt a peace and contentment as we sat in the dark quiet house, rocking while he nursed. And as he grew, I loved spending time with him. Talking. Exploring. We were buddies. I never thought about his turning into a teenager. I never thought he'd look like, well, like those kids you see at the mall.

But life is changing. He looks me almost in the eye. He wears a size 11 shoe—bigger than his father's. His hair has been a challenge. For a while he let it grow long, parting it in the middle, until Tim and I insisted that he get it cut enough so we could see his eyes. Now it's really short, and with the help of some spritz it stands straight up—and to the side, and to the front, and to the back. You get the idea. He wears huge T-shirts and baggy shorts that are almost as long as his pants.

I'd like to put a sign on him: "Please don't judge my son by how he looks; underneath he is a really great kid!" And he is. He has a sense of humor; he's helpful to me and others; he's caring about others; he has an easygoing attitude. He's a lot of fun to be with.

I think that sometimes God wants to put a sign on me, too: "Please don't judge My daughter by how she looks; underneath she is a really great person!" And God could tell you my attributes. When I look at my son, I see past the spiked hair and baggy shorts and see a kid whom I love with all my heart. He's my pride and joy. And when God looks at me, He looks past my faults; my bad habits; my wrong attitudes. He looks past my faulty words, and even the things I do that hurt others or let Him down. And God sees a person whom He loves with all His heart, whom He loves so much that He gave His life for. He sees my heart, how I long for Him, how I desire to grow in Him and to be His totally. I'm more than just another face in the crowd to Him. I'm His daughter. He calls me His treasure. His delight.

TAMYRA HORST

253

OFFERINGS OF GRATITUDE

I have been young, and now am old; yet have I not seen the righteous forsaken, nor his seed begging bread. Ps. 37:25.

My Christian parents always taught us to return what belonged to the Lord, and we gave offerings as a way of expressing gratitude. When we earned coins by doing domestic work, we were shown how to fill out the tithe envelope and were helped in figuring our tithe. In our innocence, we did not fully understand, but we knew that the tithe and the offerings didn't belong to us.

God blessed our family with more than our daily bread, and our father sent us to a parochial boarding school because he felt that it was worth the sacrifice.

In 1983 I married a pastor. We had financial stresses and hardships during our first eight years, when our children were small and I chose to work at home to care for them. But we were determined to continue being faithful in paying our tithes and offerings, and we could see the fulfillment of the biblical promise: "Seek ye first the kingdom of God, and his righteousness; and all these things shall be added unto you" (Matt. 6:33).

A couple years ago we urgently needed to replace our kitchen table. We wanted a strong one to withstand our constant moves and all the things that would be done on it—ironing clothes, making bread, doing children's homework, and usually serving seven or more people for lunch on Sabbath. Checking on the budget, we concluded that it would be impossible to buy a new table. We thought of decreasing our offerings, but we decided that would not be a good idea. We prayed to the Lord and placed the situation in His hands.

About six months later my husband went to pray with a church member who owned a marble store. While there he checked on the prices of some tables.

"Pastor," said the man, "I am needing to donate a table. I have too large an inventory, and I want to donate some tables to friends who have a need. The table is yours!"

I thank God every day for the large pretty table He provided for us. It is very strong, made of solid granite, and of much greater value than any offerings we gave during that time. God's promise was fulfilled.

NELMA MARQUARDT TOCHETTO

PRIDE COMES AFTER THE FALL

When pride comes, then comes disgrace, but with humility comes wisdom. Prov. 11:2, NIV.

One day as I arrived at work I met a woman who works in the same building. She has always intimidated me somewhat, as she's so "proper." She had heard about my fall the previous week on the new carpet that was being installed in the building. As we walked down the hallway, we checked to see how well it had been laid. Another woman joined us, whom also I perceive as "having it all together" in her appearance. So there I stood with these two classy women, inspecting the carpet. As we talked about how well it was laid, I looked down and saw that one of my knee-high nylons was down around my ankle. I was mortified! Quickly I put my bag in front of that leg, hoping they hadn't noticed.

Later, while my computer was warming up, I found a rubber band to hold the listless nylon in place. I began reflecting on what had just happened and was embarrassed to realize that if they had been different women I probably would have laughed as I pointed my problem out to them. I would have been more comfortable letting them see that I wasn't always "all together." But I was with the two women who intimidate me. And yes, I realize that I allow those feelings toward them, putting myself below them on the social ladder.

Didn't Christ refer to this when He talked about giving the best seats to the wealthy while asking the poor to sit in the back or on the floor? God is so subtle in pointing out my weaknesses! The day started out like any other, then *Pow!* I'm faced with my pride.

Pride is a curious thing, isn't it? It's hard to just be myself around people I see as better in some way. I don't like for others to see me with something out of place, imperfect. I don't want my "warts" out there for all to see. However, I was reminded that "a person's pride will bring humiliation" (Prov. 29:23, NRSV).

I want to be like Christ in all aspects of my life, as open and transparent as He was with people. When I think about how much He values me— enough to give His very life in my place—I know my value has a lot more to do with what is on the inside than with how I perceive myself on the outside.

LOUISE M. DRIVER

ZACK'S SACKS

Thou shalt love thy neighbor as thyself. Matt. 22:39.

Through His unselfish character God has shown what love means. The biggest example of His character was in sending His only Son, Jesus, down to earth to show us how to love. That one unselfish act paid the price for all sin. God tells us to love each other as He loves us. People's carnal nature makes this difficult. But carnal nature can be overcome through Christ. When the change occurs, individuals become a new creation.

When Christ lives through us, love transcends on its own. With Christ's love attitudes of hatred, selfishness, and competition do not exist. God's love covers everyone. Allow Him to work in your life. A Christlike example can make a difference for many others. Then you can share that love with others.

I heard a wonderful story about Zack. When he was 3 years old he was watching the news with his mother one evening. He focused on a news report about children who had been removed from their home by Child Protective Services. He talked about the program many times after it aired, even though his mother thought he would soon forget it.

Several days later Zack approached his mother with a pillowcase filled with his toys. He explained they were for the children who had been taken from their home. His mother took him to the local police department, where he made his donation. Zack continued to want to serve other children with his toys. Since then he and his mother have developed a giving program called "Zack's Sacks." Zack has a booth outside his house to sell soda and lemonade to fund his project. His mother sews the sacks, and Zack puts the toys in each sack. He lets her know when supplies are low.

Zack made a big impression on me, and I pray that he will continue in his mission, for it shows us what Jesus was talking about. Anyone can be a neighbor any time. Many wait until Christmas to give gifts or help others. However, people need help and encouragement all year round. Giving freely at any age is an amazing gift. Not only are Zack's bags filled with little toys, they are also filled with love that touches many people.

MARY WAGONER ANGELIN

A PARABLE OF GRACE AND FREEDOM

Grace be unto you, and peace, from God our Father, and from the Lord Jesus Christ. 1 Cor. 1:3.

When I moved to Portland 22 years ago, I walked into a parable. I did not realize I was headed to "Beulah land," a name that meant a place of rest, freedom, and healing to the African slaves longing for emancipation. "Thou shalt no more be termed Forsaken; neither shall thy land any more be termed Desolate: but thou shalt be called Hephzibah, and thy land Beulah: for the Lord delighteth in thee, and thy land shall be married" (Isa. 62:4). But it was in Portland that I met Beulah. She was director of pastoral care at the hospital where I had taken a new assignment as a staff chaplain. I felt freedom by simply being in her presence and in my new opportunities.

After settling into my new assignment, I met Grace, our volunteer on Thursdays. She answers the phones and does various tasks to aid in the ministry and mission of the department. Grace screens my calls and gives me work to do, referring me to various patients, visitors, or tasks. The referrals and tasks are always appropriate to what I can do. They are not always simple or pleasant, but Grace does them with saving grace. She lives the character of her name. And Grace gives me presents. She has sewn my daughter gorgeous dresses and has given me fruit and wonderful snacks. She directs me to great adventures in the surrounding communities. These are the extras that make me love Grace—and even Thursdays.

I do not pay for Grace's service. What she gives and does for me is both free and undeserved. It is her gift to the department, and it is obviously her joy to do! "By grace are ye saved through faith; and that not of yourselves: it is the gift of God" (Eph. 2:8).

The grace that has saved us similarly compels or constrains us to help, to go the extra mile, to be gracious to others. When we realize what grace models to us, we strain to imitate it to others. God's grace to me is freely given. Christ paid for it with His life, but there is no cost to me. In fact, the Bible testifies that it was His joy to give me such a gift. "Looking unto Jesus the author and finisher of our faith; who for the joy that was set before him endured the cross" (Heb. 12:2).

Thank God for Grace and for the hope of Beulah land!   WANDA DAVIS

HOMESICK

In my Father's house are many mansions. . . . I go to prepare a place for you. And if I go and prepare a place for you, I will come again, and receive you unto myself; that where I am, there ye may be also. John 14:2, 3.

Have you ever been homesick? The first time I remember it happened to me I was probably 7 years old and had gone to spend the night with my grandparents, who lived about a mile away. As evening approached I got that sinking feeling and decided that home was the place for me. Mother got the message and walked to meet my grandmother and me at the halfway point.

The next time it hit me was years later, when for the first time I moved into a college dormitory and felt a few pangs as my family left me there. That didn't last long, however, as I found college and dormitory life to be a happy experience.

I spent years working in a boarding high school and was often confronted with homesick kids at the beginning of school. I would assure them that it was not a fatal disease, although I'm not sure they always believed me. Some gave up and returned home without really giving themselves time to get over it. One eleventh grader, away from home for the first time, seemed to be adjusting well, but one day she suddenly burst into tears and sobbed, "How long does it last?" Fortunately, with her it didn't last too long, and she stayed until she graduated at the end of the following school year.

Each summer our granddaughters spend a week with us, and we have a lot of fun times together. But it never fails that when the day comes for their parents to come for the weekend and then to take them home, they start watching the road, eager to see Mom and Dad.

We Christians sometimes feel homesick too as we hear of all the tragedies in this sin-sick world. We know that Jesus is preparing special dwelling places for us, and that He has promised to come again to take us home to live with Him forever. There is a song that begins, "I'm homesick for heaven, seems I cannot wait, yearning to enter Zion's pearly gate." Are you homesick today? Am I? Heaven will be the ultimate cure for homesickness!

I'm ready, Jesus. Take us home! MARY JANE GRAVES

FORMED BY HIS DESIGN

The Lord is near to all who call upon Him, to all who call upon Him in truth. He will fulfill the desire of those who fear Him; He will also hear their cry and will save them. The Lord keeps all who love Him, but all the wicked He will destroy. My mouth will speak the praise of the Lord, and all flesh will bless His holy name forever and ever. Ps. 145:18-21, NASB.

When I regained consciousness in the intensive-care unit, alone, not knowing where I was or why I was there, I did the only thing I could: I began unceasingly beseeching my Father, my Saviour, my Friend. What, where, and why were all jumbled into my first prayer. Looking around for something familiar revealed nothing I recognized. Looking toward the window, I saw the sky. Thank You. I'm alive.

For three weeks my condition resisted the intravenous medications I was given. Then followed physical discomfort, lifestyle education, moderation, nutritional changes. They were all part of God's appeal to me. It was in the intensive-care unit that He got my attention. Responding to His appeal, realizing He had plans for my life that He had not yet revealed, praying to be made willing for Him to be in control, became vital to me and continue to occupy much of my prayer time.

God has been the significant force in all of my life. I love to hear about His miracles. Often I imagine what living in Bible times might have been like. I am sure I would have tried to be present every time He was sighted and would have witnessed every miracle. Now, however, I know I have been part of a miracle right in my own life.

Our verses are very clear. God has a plan for each of us. We must be willing for Him to be in control. He does not include us in His work unless we are willing to be included. Each day I invite my Father to take control of my plans. Sometimes I struggle to complete some task I select, only to see many obstacles. Now I ask God whether my struggling is a part of His growth plan for me or my rebellion against His will.

My Lord, You know the way through the wilderness; all I have to do is follow. Help me to do that today, giving You the control in all that I say and do.

WESELENE WILEY

DO YOU STILL LOVE ME?

Love your enemies and pray for anyone who mistreats you. Then you will be acting like your Father in heaven. He makes the sun rise on both good and bad people. And he sends rain for the ones who do right and for the ones who do wrong. Matt. 5:44, 45, CEV.

I think most little girls have washed dishes—and may have even broken one or two. One little girl was washing dishes when she came to her mother's favorite dish. Her mother had told her not to wash that dish.

"I will wash that dish myself," Mom had said.

But the little girl wanted to be helpful and so decided to wash it anyway. As she picked up the dish, it slipped right out of her hands and broke into pieces. Her mother rushed into the kitchen and looked in horror at the dish. Then without a word she got a broom and swept up the pieces.

Later the little girl asked her mother, "Do you still love me?"

"Oh, honey, I'll always love you. Even when you disappoint me!"

Our Father in heaven made a garden for Adam and Eve to dwell in. He told them they could eat of every tree except the tree of the knowledge of good and evil. But like the little girl, they decided to help themselves. They each ate of the forbidden fruit, and by doing so they sinned. Their decision caused the Father to send them out of the garden.

In my imagination I can see Adam and Eve turn to ask their Father, "Do You still love us?"

"Oh, children, I'll always love you. Even when you sin," the Father replies.

And so we come down to our day and age once again. As little or big girls we find ourselves wanting to do things our way. We disobey. We do things that bring heartbreak to our heavenly Parent.

"Do You still love us?" we wonder.

"Yes, My daughter; I will always love you," comes the reassuring reply.

Father, help me to do things Your way, not mine. I know You love me, and I do not want to break Your heart anymore.

QUETAH MANYOÉ SACKIE-OSBORNE

"I AM WITH YOU ALWAY"

Lo, I am with you alway, even unto the end of the world. Matt. 28:20.

One Sunday I woke up to the shrill cawing of a crow and immediately felt as though something was wrong with me. I began to cough and found it difficult to breathe. *Oh, no, Lord, not another asthma attack!* I panicked.

I had suffered intermittent asthma attacks before. I felt as though my lungs were being compressed into the size of beans. Within minutes I was in the hospital. The physician and the nurses did their best to relieve my discomfort. But there was no relief. I was very sure of my death.

Some serious questions began to rush through my mind: Is there any sin I have not confessed? Will I meet my family in heaven? Will my children walk with God throughout their lives? Will they make the right choices in life?

Suddenly my questions turned into requests: *Lord, wash me with Your blood so that I can stand spotless before You. Keep my family in the right path. Hold my hand as I walk through the valley of death.*

Suddenly the peace of heaven prevailed. I could feel the presence of God at my bedside, and I was ready to accept death. I had given everyone and everything into the mighty hand of God and had said, "Lord, let Your will be done in my life, whatever it might be."

I wondered why I had never surrendered to God when I was up and active around my home. Why had I worried over small things in life? I felt the need of complete dependence upon Him.

God worked out His plan for me. As the minutes ticked by, I felt better. I looked into the anxious eyes of my teenage son and daughter and smiled. Relief came over their faces. I decided that I would never again worry over anything. How nice it would be if we trusted the Lord with all our hearts and minds.

Thank You, Lord, for Your loving grace, for healing me physically and saving my soul. Help me to remember Your love and care throughout this day.

SOOSANNA MATHEW

JUDGE NOT

Judge not, that ye be not judged. Matt. 7:1.

One day my friend's neighbors sat in their car, parked on a busy street, waiting for a passenger they had brought to town for an appointment. As they waited, they saw harried mothers with tagging children; men dressed in business suits, carrying attaché cases; and young women pausing at shop windows before entering. In contrast, seniors walked by with slow, painful steps, while giggling teenage girls lightly skipped.

When an audacious group of fellows appeared, the couple examined them closely: hair dyed with lighter streaks; long hair pulled back in ponytails; short spiked hair. Baggy pants with the crotch hanging to the knees or torn pants with kneecaps showing. Faded oversized shirts emblazoned with slogans across the chest. Shuffling feet in heavy boots. Boisterous laughter and shouting. The couple eyed the boys suspiciously as they jostled from one side of the street to the other, pausing at the parking meters and giving them a thump.

These guys are up to no good, they thought. Feeling uneasy as the boys neared their car, the couple locked the doors and tried to appear unconcerned. They relaxed momentarily as the boys sauntered by. Suddenly one of the boys returned, fumbled with the meter, then dashed off. It was then the driver realized that they had been so engrossed with people-watching that the meter had run out of time. The unkempt-looking lad had reloaded their meter.

The driver jumped out of the car to shout, "Thank you!" The lad hollered back, "No problem. We do it all the time."

Many times I have prejudged and misjudged others by their dress and actions. I frequently have to tell myself, *Edith, you're looking on the outward appearance! Remember, the Lord looks on the heart* (1 Sam. 16:7). Then I ponder the scolding Jesus gave the scribes and Pharisees for outwardly appearing righteous while being full of hypocrisy and iniquity within (Matt. 23:28). It causes me to wonder how I rate in the eyes of others. More important, what does my heart reveal?

Lord, help me refrain from judging others because of how they appear outwardly. In addition to that, help me not to be a hypocrite by appearing righteous on the outside while being full of iniquity within. EDITH FITCH

JIGGS

Cleanse me with hyssop, and I will be clean; wash me, and I will be whiter than snow. Ps. 51:7, NIV.

I grew up in the days of coal furnaces and remember the coal truck that parked periodically in our driveway to empty a ton of coal through the little window in the basement coal room. From this supply my father would fill his coal bucket and feed the furnace, or "bank" it in the evening so the fire would last through the night.

In early fall one year we acquired Jiggs, a big yellow tomcat, from a friend's farm. Unaccustomed to city living, he was desperately afraid of people, traffic, noise, and even the outdoors. We tried to acclimate him by putting him, against his will, in the backyard for a couple hours each morning. There, trembling, he would huddle against the fence until we let him in, where he found refuge in a lap or on his mat by the furnace.

But one day Jiggs was missing. His food was untouched. A search of the house, the backyard, and the basement brought no results. Jiggs was gone.

The next two mornings Dad made his routine trips downstairs to the furnace, and our lives went mournfully on. The third morning, Dad took the coal bucket to the coal room to refill it. As he opened the door, something big and black suddenly leaped from the rafters, its beady eyes glistening. Startled, Dad jumped back from the now-huddled mass.

No, it couldn't be! But it was! The familiar little cry identified him. Covered with coal soot, too frightened and too weak to stir, our precious Jiggs cowered beside Dad. How our beloved cat had escaped into the coal room remains a mystery, but when the load of coal had been deposited from the coal truck, a terrified Jiggs had sought the rafters. Now a warm soapy bath, a saucer of milk, and cuddles restored him to the beautiful yellow tomcat we had known.

Sometimes we too wander into the coal bin of wrongdoing and find we cannot help ourselves. But our heavenly Friend searches us out, cleanses and nurtures us, and restores us to the person He wants us to be. Come to think of it, we needn't experience the coal bin at all. By surrendering our hearts to Him and feeding on His Word, we will remain pure and cared for by our Father, who loves us more than life. What better place can we be but in His presence!

LORRAINE HUDGINS

I'LL CRY LATER!

Unless you are converted and become as little children, you will by no means enter the kingdom of heaven. Matt. 18:3, NKJV.

Our son wanted to go play with his friends Kyle and Donna, two farms away. As he was only 4 and too small to walk there himself, he asked, "Mama, will you drive me there?"

"I'm sorry, but there's no way I can take you there for the next hour or so. You'll have to wait until I get through baking these chocolate chip cookies."

"You make me so mad I could cry!" he protested. Then he went his way, playing around the house.

Just before lunch I asked, "Are you still angry? I haven't heard any crying or seen any tears."

"I'll cry later. I'm busy eating cookies now!" he replied. A grin played at the corners of his mouth.

As a matter of fact, he never did cry about that particular incident. The fact that a child could be so easily diverted and forget a grudge so quickly made a big impression on me. There is much we can learn from children.

Although in many areas of life grownups are urged to "put away childish things" (1 Cor. 13:11) and act maturely, all of us might be better off if we retained the forgiving spirit of a little child and stopped collecting and holding on to grudges until the accumulated anger and bitterness causes physical or mental illness.

I'm sure this is at least part of what Jesus meant when He "called a little child to Him, set him in the midst of them, and said, 'Assuredly, I say to you, unless you are converted and become as little children, you will by no means enter the kingdom of heaven'" (Matt. 18:2, 3, NKJV).

Lord, we think of ourselves as teachers of the young, although there is much we can learn from them if we are willing to open our hearts and minds so we can watch and listen. Please teach me the lessons I need to learn today so I can grow up in You. Help me to learn to let go of anger and to forgive even as You forgive me.

BONNIE MOYERS

MINE ANGEL SHALL GO BEFORE ME

The angel of the Lord encampeth round about them that fear him, and delivereth them. Ps. 34:7.

I was working in Los Angeles, and on weekends I liked to go down to Paradise Valley, near San Diego, where my sister was in nursing school. One Friday I boarded the train for San Diego at Union Station to spend the weekend. However, when I got there, I found out that no buses were running to Paradise Valley. I called my sister, who told me the buses were on strike. I would have to walk three blocks to the Greyhound station, take a bus headed for Tijuana, Mexico, then get off at Paradise Valley and call a cab to take me to the school.

The old saying "The sidewalks are blue in San Diego" (with Navy men), was certainly true that night. I made my way along the crowded sidewalk with a prayer in my heart, my suitcase in my hand, and the Navy close by. Some sailors tried to get my attention with all kinds of remarks; others wanted to help me carry my suitcase. I tried to stay focused on what was ahead of me, never looking to the right or left. Finally I made it to the station and got on a Tijuana bus. Since it was about 11:00 at night, the bus was pretty empty, with only a few sleeping sailors and several Mexicans.

When we got to Paradise Valley, I asked the driver to drop me off at the main corner in town. "Can't do that," he said. "Can only stop at authorized bus stops." About a mile or two down the road was a stop out in the middle of nowhere. Fear gripped me.

As I got off the bus, two sailors got off too. I was petrified. This stop had only a bench and, thankfully, a public phone. The sailors asked where I was going. Then they offered to call a cab for me. I didn't protest. They said they had gotten off the bus because they hated to see me out there all alone. When the cab came, they rode with me to the nursing school, paid the driver, and said they would go back and catch the next bus to Tijuana.

Those two angels, dressed like sailors, disappeared into the night. I am convinced that we never know when God has sent His angels to take charge over us. ANNE ELAINE NELSON

HIS PROMISES ARE SURE

We can look forward to the salvation God has promised us. . . . There is no question that he will do what he says. Heb. 10:23, TLB.

"Joshua fit de battle ob Jerico, Jerico, Jerico, Joshua fit de battle ob Jerico, an' de walls come tumblin' down." We sang as the well-known Negro spiritual played on a cassette tape and we headed toward the remote village of Jericho in the hills of Hanover, Jamaica.

"Daddy, where are we going today?"

"We're on our way to a place called Jericho."

Our daughter was filled with excitement and asked us to sing the song repeatedly. We feared that the tape would break at that spot from the frequent replay, but it was fun, and the singing helped the time to pass quickly as we traveled.

We reached Jericho and had a spirit-filled youth program. Then we noticed how sad our daughter was.

"What's the matter?" I asked.

"This isn't Jericho. This is a false Jericho. Where is the wall that fell down when Joshua marched around it?" Our daughter was disappointed, and it was evident.

At this point we understood fully why she had been so excited. She had thought that we were going to the Jericho that we had sung about and read about to her from the Bible. To the mind of a 4-year-old there was just one Jericho. She was extremely disappointed that she had not seen the place that she had anticipated. Our explanation did very little to console her, as she could not distinguish between the two places.

We will face many disappointments daily as we deal with others, but there is no disappointment with God. There are no false promises in His love letter to us. His promises are all true. We are encouraged simply to believe and then to claim the promises. God never has—and never will—let us down. He is the author of fulfilled promises.

Today, as you go through your daily chores, reflect on a few comforting promises. Cherish them. They are from a loving God and Friend. There is no mistaking or misunderstanding.

He says, "I will be with you. I will never leave you nor forsake you."

GLORIA GREGORY

TESTS

We can rejoice, too, when we run into problems and trials for we know that they are good for us—they help us learn to be patient. Rom. 5:3, TLB.

When I was young and attending classes, I loved returning to school each fall. I relished the smell of new schoolbooks and blank pages and shiny new school shoes. I enjoyed learning and liked each of my teachers. I looked forward to the start of each school year and to the challenges of what I might learn.

I didn't, however, enjoy the tests. I hated the uncertainty and the tension of having to reproduce on a blank piece of paper what I'd learned. I didn't understand why teachers loved to torture us by giving us tests.

One day I realized that the teachers didn't give us tests because they didn't like us, because they wanted to keep us out of their hair, or because they didn't have anything better to do. They really cared about us and wanted to know if we understood what they were teaching us. This was a marvelous revelation, and suddenly I saw testing in a whole new light. I still may not have liked it very well, but I understood its purpose.

Our Father God allows each of us to go through tests every day. He says, "My child, what have you learned today from life? Have you used your resources well? What have you learned from My teaching and from life? What have you learned from reading My Word? Do you trust Me enough to allow Me to lead?"

If we haven't studied, we don't understand the reason for the testing process, and we complain, "Why is life so cruel and unfair, with so many hardships? Why do I have to have so many problems and obstacles in life?" But just as school and teachers were preparing us for life's problems, so life is preparing us for something much greater—a life with Jesus in heaven. A never-ending friendship.

Lord, please test me and try me today for the greatest adventure of all— that day when Your appearing will cause great joy on this earth. Until then, make me worthy in Your school of life. Help me to learn more about You each day, and to grow in Your wisdom and teaching. FAUNA RANKIN DEAN

HE WILL ALWAYS BE THERE

*I am with thee, and will keep thee in all places whither thou goest.
Gen. 28:15.*

We lived in a friendly neighborhood. Everyone knew everyone else, and most of the school-aged children went to school together. Many of the families even attended the same church. Every mother watched out for the children as they rode on the sidewalk and played in the various yards.

One day our son, Johnny, who was about 4, was riding his tricycle a short distance down the block when both he and the tricycle fell over. He lay on the sidewalk, scraped, bleeding, and crying. Our friend Mrs. Smith saw what had happened as she looked out her window. She quickly ran to the sidewalk, picked Johnny up, and took him into her house. She carefully washed the skinned knees, hands, and elbows, used disinfectant and Band-Aids where necessary, and wiped the tears from his face. When he was calm and feeling better, she took him outside, put him back on the tricycle, and told him to go play and have fun. I wished that I could have been there to help Johnny when he needed help, but I've been very grateful to Mrs. Smith for her quick reaction and her kindness to help my injured son.

Some time ago I fell while walking along the bike trail. My ankle turned and was slightly scratched, as were my hands. Most of all, however, my dignity was wounded. Besides that, I could not get back on my feet gracefully. Fortunately, a caring, knowledgeable person came along. He checked my eyes for dilated pupils and asked if I could move fingers, toes, and limbs properly. After determining that there was no concussion, and after having me rest for a few minutes, he helped me up and wished me well.

I was very thankful that someone so caring had come along when I needed help. It is reassuring that God is always there when we fall. He picks us up, cleans us, and makes us feel better about ourselves and about His love. He will always be there.

When you fall down the stairs, when you think no one cares, Someone is there. When you scuff your shoe and tear your blouse, Someone should be there. When you think no one's there, say a little prayer, and Someone will always be there. Jesus will always be there.

Thank You, Jesus.

LILLIAN MUSGRAVE

TREASURING GOD'S PRESENCE

A day in thy courts is better than a thousand. I had rather be a doorkeeper in the house of my God, than to dwell in the tents of wickedness. Ps. 84:10.

How precious it is to have a faithful grandmother! When I was a child she told me Bible stories, and I did not miss a single syllable. Gradually I came to know God as my Father in the sky. My grandmother told me that He loved me, He saw me all the time, that He was with me, that He protected me. I assumed that He was light-years away and I had not yet experienced His closeness to me, but in reality He was always with me.

One evening, when I was feeling sad, an idea came to my mind: Why don't you pour out all your sorrows, hopes, and joys to God? I immediately began to do so. It was the beginning of a wonderful relationship with God—my Father, and your Father.

This experience has profoundly marked my life. He became my best friend. And I am always happy to speak to Him, to tell Him how happy, sad, disappointed, revolted, or surprised I am. He is so important in my life that I am not able to go anywhere without Him.

Some persons are afraid to know that their Lord is always with them. I have never had this thought. I am always glad to know He is where I am, that He follows me where I go. I know He can be greatly saddened by some of my attitudes, my words, my silence. But most important for me is His presence.

In moments when I have important decisions to make, I am always grateful to be able to ask for the Lord's direction. I ask Him, "What are You expecting from me? Where is the right direction? What is Your will?" I sometimes experience a battle, my will against His. But praise be to God, I am able to forsake my will and to treasure His. My biggest joy is to say I have never regretted the direction the Lord has given to my life.

Thank You, Lord. I love You so much, and I am spending my time waiting for Your return and for Your kingdom. Please, come back soon. I want to spend all my time in Your presence. All Your children are waiting for You.

CHRISTIANE TUOR

ON EAGLE'S WINGS

They that wait upon the Lord shall renew their strength; they shall mount up with wings as eagles; they shall run, and not be weary; and they shall walk, and not faint. Isa. 40:31.

An exciting milestone in my high school's flight program was the day the instructor would say, "You are ready to solo." All the practice and studying paid off as I took off alone in a Cessna 150 plane. I still have the congratulations card my friend gave me after I landed safely. On the cover he wrote, "They shall mount up with wings as eagles."

I thought of it often while I fulfilled the cross-country flight requirements for my private pilot license. Flying alone in the tiny two-seater, from one small airport to another, gave me hours of time to renew my strength in God. I sang loudly over the airflow and sound of the engine. I prayed aloud, talking to God about problems, plans for college, and relationships with family and friends. I sat quietly listening for God's words revealed in the glory of creation, seen from up where eagles belong, looking down to the Pennsylvania hills spread out below.

In college I could not pursue flying, so I looked for experiences to duplicate "flying"—time with God provided by weekend hikes in the Blue Mountains, or sunsets from the top of the fire escape on the old administration building. After graduation, when I started working, time was more limited. I bought a car with no radio so I could spend commuting time "flying" alone with God.

Life has moved on, and I'm a working mom with a carful of kids to drop off at the baby-sitter's or school before work. Now, when I need the promised strength more than ever, it is a huge challenge to make "flying" time.

I'm relying on the first part of the text, which I blithely overlooked before, "They that wait upon the Lord . . ." When Baby Cecelia or 2-year-old Conner is up and down in the middle of the night and I try fruitlessly to get back to sleep, praying makes the time fly by. Prayers lift me above worries, just as wings lift an eagle high in the sky. I praise God for the gift of health that lets me run beside 4-year-old Christopher. I wait for God's wisdom to help me walk beside Caitlyn as she tackles the excitement and challenges of first grade.

I grow nostalgic for time alone with God, flying in the eagle's realm. But I'm learning how to wait upon the Lord amid the busyness of my life today and let Him renew my strength.   BARBARA HALL

THE DAKOTA PRAYER

My God shall supply all your needs according to His riches in glory in Christ Jesus. Phil. 4:19, NASB.

S he appears to have it all! Sleek. Well proportioned. A perfect profile, accented by widely set, slightly Oriental eyes. That's Dakota, and she's a real head-turner, an imposing beauty, even by limousine cattle standards.

Yet the other cows in Dakota's small herd evidently don't think so. Maybe they're just jealous of her luxurious reddish-gold coat. Then again, perhaps they've fallen naturally into the age-old animal "pecking order" that so often pervades the psyche of certain creatures.

I've stood and watched "the girls" in an autumn pasture after my farmer husband has tractored their evening hay to them and their growing babies. Though Jim is careful to throw more than enough six-inch-thick hay flakes in all directions, Miss Lori, Cutie, and Gloria keep going out of their way to harass Dakota.

Though apparently extremely hungry themselves, they still take time out from feeding to drive her away from their chosen piles of hay. Gloria is especially adept at lowering her massive, dehorned head, making a short run, and giving Dakota a sharp jolt in the rear.

Sometimes, with a mixture of irritation and sadness, I stand by the fence and watch Dakota acting out her lot in life. She's a study in quiet persistence. She doesn't retaliate or hold grudges. Bumped away from one source of nourishment, she looks about for another. Patiently minding her own business, she moves with a lumbering grace and dignity, perhaps in the assurance that no matter how others may treat her, her caretaker, the farmer, will always provide for her basic needs.

Thanks for the lesson.

Lord, when things don't go as I plan; when my needs and interests don't matter to others, and I'm pushed aside; when what should be easy comes hard—let me remember Dakota and look for other places of peace, and for joy in life's natural blessings, and for assurance in knowing that the heavenly Caretaker will always take care of me. CAROLYN RATHBUN SUTTON

LIKE A SNEAKY CAT

Be self-controlled and alert. Your enemy the devil prowls around like a roaring lion looking for someone to devour. 1 Peter 5:8, NIV.

We'd been clearing brush off the land for most of the afternoon. We encountered plenty of poison oak, but otherwise it was an exciting, happy family time. Here we were—my husband, his parents, my son, and I—three generations, working together to clear a site in the country for our future home and garden.

My son, Daniel, age 11, especially enjoyed discovering all kinds of neat creatures. When Grandpa pushed aside a pile of brush with the bulldozer, we were all surprised to see that a pack rat nest had been pushed over. There, squeaking loudly, was a furry baby, his eyes still closed. We put it in a box with some soft grass.

My husband and I returned to town late that afternoon while Daniel and his grandparents remained to tend to the burning brush piles. We took the baby pack rat with us. Before we left, Daniel held it one last time, expressing his concern that he might not see it alive again. I assured Daniel that I would do everything I could for the pack rat.

When we got to town, I hurried to remove my poison oak-saturated clothes and get into a quick bath. Returning to the van, I saw a cat scurry away. Oh, no! I had left the door open! And in my hurry, I'd left the baby rat in there! But then I heard squeaking—it was still there!

My relief was very short-lived, however, as I watched a second cat flash out the door and sail over the fence. And, horror of horrors, he carried a squeaking morsel in his mouth.

Why hadn't I brought that box into the house the first thing? Why had I been so careless? My son would be heartbroken when he found out. He had trusted me with his most precious treasure, and I had blown it.

I think of all the times I get so caught up in my own activities that I forget what an influence my life has on others. If I fail to offer a word of encouragement or a helping hand, or even just a smile to one who needs it—isn't that just as bad as leaving that baby pack rat to the mercy of the cats? God is trusting us to do our part to show Jesus to others, His precious treasures. Surely the devil does prowl around like a sneaky cat, looking for someone to devour. Let's not give him a chance!

DIANA ADAMS

DYING MOMENTS

Grudge not one another, brethren. James 5:9.

She was a very close friend, but obviously I had deeply offended her. One evening she called me to sit down to talk. But the talk consisted of her laying many charges against me. I felt deeply hurt. I had little to say, for some of the charges were partly justified but due mainly to human frailties rather than to deliberate sin. But I lamented the words that had so severely strained our friendship.

Two years passed, and I was invited by another friend to attend a Christian retreat known as the Emmaus Walk. I was tossed into an ocean of strangers to make my way by study, friendship, and prayer in company with all the other pilgrims who were as nervous and as friendless as I was.

Communion services were held daily. On the second day the director introduced us to the Dying Moments concept. We tore off a piece of the loaf and were urged to examine ourselves to see if there were grudges, resentments, ill-will, or anything else that might hinder the free entry of the Holy Spirit into our minds. After a few moments of "housecleaning," we tossed that piece of bread, with all the encumbrances attached to it, into a basket. During those moments I reviewed the grudges and resentments I had held against my friend all those months. I concluded that the Lord had better take them and leave me free of the burden. I tossed the "loaded" bread away and happily received a fresh portion. I dipped it into the wine and made it my own.

One of the closing moments of the Emmaus Walk is the presentation to each pilgrim of a bag of letters. Our sponsors had invited our friends to write an affirming message to each pilgrim. A sheaf of tissues was also issued. I did not immediately understand why. Among my score of letters was one from my faraway friend, who must have written weeks before. It reached me one day after I had "cast my burden of resentment" on the Lord.

She reminded me of the confrontation she had initiated and expressed her admiration for my calm under fairly extreme provocation. And she assured me of her continuing love. I needed those tissues! God had taken away the grudges and replaced the precious friendship.

EDNA FERRIS-HEISE

JESUS CHUCKLES

In that hour Jesus rejoiced in spirit. Luke 10:21.

As I sat on my deck a squirrel dashed around the corner of the house. It scampered and stopped; scampered and stopped. *What if it climbs the steps to the deck?* I thought. Suddenly I heard the patter of little feet and held my breath as, with front feet on the deck, the squirrel froze when it saw me. I wondered if it was as startled to see me as I was pleased to see it. We stared, eyeball to eyeball, for a few seconds, and then it wheeled and was gone. "Thank You, Jesus!" And you know, I think He chuckled!

I truly believe Jesus had a great time speaking the animals into existence. The spindly-legged, long-necked giraffes, for one; the hippos with their widemouthed yawns; the lumbering elephants; the platypuses; the penguins, and all the others.

Our neighbor has a small black dog who spends her days in a large fenced yard; also a white cat that seems to roam the neighborhood. Sometimes when I look out my deck door I see the two interacting. The cat stretches out along the top rail of the wooden part of the fence. The dog races back and forth, jumps, and stands on her back legs and tries, oh so hard, to reach the cat. And occasionally the cat reaches out a paw to tease the dog. I feel that Jesus chuckles along with me as we imagine the cat saying, "Catch me if you can!"

And I can imagine Jesus chuckling with me as I watch my own cat chasing her tail, swishing it away just as her paw is about to curve around it. He surely must enjoy her surprised expression as much as I do.

Oh, I'm so glad Jesus has a sense of humor! It makes life more fun, more bearable, more "chuckleful"!

As I ponder the words "Jesus rejoiced," I can imagine His smile, maybe even joyful laughter, at the 70 disciples' excitement and enthusiasm. And I wonder if Jesus might have chuckled when they said, "Lord, even the devils are subject unto us through thy name" (verse 17), because He may have thought, *Ah, yes, all things are possible* (see Matt. 19:26).

Dear Jesus, thank You for creating the animals. And thank You for laughter, for joy. How they enrich our lives!

PATSY MURDOCH MEEKER

THE DINNER THEATER EXPERIENCE

God commendeth his love toward us, in that, while we were yet sinners, Christ died for us. Rom. 5:8.

It had been a very long day—preparing about 600 egg rolls, 60 pounds of spaghetti, 14 gallons of spaghetti sauce, 60 pounds of broccoli, 60 pounds of corn, and 60 pounds of carrots.

I was happy that the dinner theater put on by my daughter Susan's class had been a success. The junior class adviser and the officers of the class had been worried as to who would help them with the catering. The woman who was supposed to do the job had backed out at the last minute, so I had agreed to help. When Susan heard, she gave me a hug and said, "Thank you, Mom. I knew you would offer. I'll help you in any way I can."

"Honey, I'll do anything for you," I told her.

Every night for a week I found myself making egg rolls until I had wrapped about 600. I calculated that it would be enough for 200 to 250 people. However, when the doors for the dinner theater officially opened, there were actually more than 300 people.

I was busy in the kitchen with some other mothers, but I could hear the kids saying, "There are still a lot of people who need food!" I admit I was a little scared that the food would not be enough, so I was praying that the Lord would multiply it. I admired the courage of the class; I kept hearing the servers saying, "Don't forget, the Lord multiplied the loaves of bread and the fishes."

The Lord did multiply our food. Even though we had to rush out for another gallon of spaghetti sauce, there were spaghetti, vegetables, and egg rolls left over. After everyone was served, I breathed a sigh of relief and thanked God for His miracle. Tired? Yes, but no regrets. I was happy that I could be of help.

When I finally laid my head on the pillow that night, I thanked God for doing such a hard task for me. I thought of how hard and heartbreaking it was for Him to send His only Son. He did it with joy, I'm very sure, and with no regrets. I thought of the agony of Jesus when He was mocked, ridiculed, and finally crucified. I thought of how Jesus saves me when I'm in trouble, when I'm discouraged, or when I just choose to let go of His hand. That night I prayed that I would appreciate what He had done for me, just as my daughter and her class appreciated my help.

JEMIMA D. ORILLOSA

DO NOT FEAR!

I am the Lord, your God, who takes hold of your right hand and says to you, Do not fear; I will help you. Isa. 41:13, NIV.

Through the years I have become accustomed to the pain of osteoarthritis in my limbs and to the goodness of God, who keeps me on my feet through program after program in women's ministries. But after the trip to our first women's advisory, 600 miles (1,000 kilometers) from home, pain built up in my lower back to an alarming extent. By the time we reached Bloemfontein I could not walk or sit, get up or lie down without help.

The doctor explained that arthritis-weakened tendons between the vertebrae had caused them to shift. I would have to fly home immediately. X-rays and blood tests would show the severity of the damage, but in any case I would be flat on my back for at least six weeks.

Pain was now vying with rising panic. Women were already arriving from all parts of southern Africa. They had to be allocated accommodations. The hall and its furniture, banners, and flowers were still to be arranged and equipment set up. Resources had to be laid out and tapes and handouts copied. Besides being in overall charge of the program, I was to do six presentations, including the Sabbath morning service. And the advisory was to be followed by a large three-day prayer conference in the nearby country of Lesotho.

I was already personally acquainted with the prayer of faith. The Lord now added the third miraculous crisis component: "Don't be afraid!" With no possibility of human succor, the promises of God became very sweet to me as my husband and I prayed for healing. After all, the program was the Lord's, not mine, and He was perfectly capable of taking care of it, with or without me. My anxiety faded away, and I drifted off into a peaceful sleep.

I awoke the next morning completely free of pain, with more energy and vitality than I had enjoyed for a long time. All who attended both the advisory and the prayer conference said they had experienced the Lord's presence and blessing in a very special way.

That was 10 months ago. Apart from an occasional twinge (probably to remind me of where I've been), my back is behaving very well.

Thank You, Lord, for holding and steadying my hand; and above all, thank You for the joy of freedom from fear as we travel together. IVY PETERSEN

GRACE AND STRENGTH

My grace is sufficient for you, for My strength is made perfect in weakness. 2 Cor. 12:9, NKJV.

Today's verse is very important to me. It was helpful to our family in a difficult time, especially for my children and me.

Our family had just moved from Brazil to Africa as missionaries. It was a very hard time for the boys, ages 13 and 15. We were coming to work in Kinshasa, the capital of the Democratic Republic of Congo, and because we knew there would not be a Christian school for them, we decided they should go to Helderberg High School in South Africa. That way we would be able to see them more often than if they had stayed in Brazil.

The younger son was scared because it would be his first time away from home for such a long time, and the older son was sad because he had left many friends at the boarding school in Brazil, where he had attended the previous semester. But both agreed to give it a try.

We flew to Cape Town and spent the weekend together, getting the boys settled at Helderberg. On Sabbath they were sad and crying, thinking about being apart from me in two days. I kept repeating today's Bible verse to them through a song that a Christian singer recorded: "His strength is perfect when our strength is gone; He will carry us, when we can't carry on. Raised in His power, the weak become strong. His strength is perfect, His strength is perfect."

One week has passed since we left them in South Africa, and we communicate by e-mail and phone to support one another. This is my first time with both of them away at the same time; and it is also my first time in a mission field where I don't speak the language. But God has sent us wonderful Christians at Helderberg and in Kinshasa, who have given us all the support and love that we have needed.

If you feel weak and discouraged today, with no strength to keep going in your daily journey, remember that His strength is perfect, and He will carry you always, especially when you can't take it any longer. Remember that in His power the weak become strong!

I am so glad that You are carrying me! I could not do this alone, so I thank You for other Christians who help, but I thank You especially for Your grace and for Your strength made perfect in my weakness. TERCIA FREIRE

I'M HOLDING YOU

He will command his angels concerning you to guard you in all your ways; they will lift you up in their hands, so that you will not strike your foot against a stone. Ps. 91:11, 12, NIV.

There are exactly 60 marble steps leading up to the capitol building in Havana, Cuba—and no handicap access. Our small tour group included Rhodes and her 6-year-old handicapped son, Haniel. I marveled at how willingly she lifted him from his wheelchair and carried him up the four levels as two friends carried the wheelchair to the top.

After we had toured the various beautiful halls and thanked the guard, we prepared to return to the car. Rhodes picked Haniel up in her arms and hesitated for just a moment before slowly starting down. I thought I detected a hint of fear in her eyes. I stayed close to her elbow in case she should stumble, but I knew that if she should fall there was probably nothing at all I would be able to do to prevent a tragedy. I watched as she carefully descended each step. Thankfully, no misstep happened, and we all reached the plaza safely. Then Rhodes asked Maribel, our translator, to tell something to the two of us who didn't speak Spanish.

"On the way down I told Haniel that I was afraid," she said. "But he told me, 'Don't be afraid, Mama. I'm holding you.'"

We all laughed at the simple faith and naïveté he showed. But it gave me something to think about. In life's ups and downs through danger—danger beyond my understanding—do I think I am responsible for my own safety? Perhaps friends or family are holding me up, but I take credit. Or it may be that God is carrying me, and I think I can do it myself. "Don't worry about me, God; I'm holding You."

Every day I trust my safety to my driving ability, to the structural safety of the buildings in which I find myself, or even to the skills of an airplane crew. I place my welfare in the hands of other humans who may or may not care about me. How much better it would be to look to Jesus, my real source of safety and security.

Lord, I may be hanging on for dear life, but help me to depend totally on You. You hold me up, please. I trust You to get me through safely.

ARDIS DICK STENBAKKEN

THE INDISPENSABLE SUN

The city had no need of the sun or of the moon to shine in it, for the glory of God illuminated it. The Lamb is its light. Rev. 21:23, NKJV.

What would it be like without the sun? How would the plants, the animals, and humankind survive? In His divine and infinite wisdom God knew that life on earth would need the sunshine.

My husband and I love flower and vegetable gardening. Oh, the joy of seeing the flowers bloom! And what happiness the fresh vegetables bring! In the little space in our backyard, we usually plant some vegetables, especially those that aren't available at the supermarket. In our front yard, flowers beautify our landscaping.

Last summer I planted okra and other vegetables on both sides of the backyard. As summer progressed, I noticed that half the okra plants didn't get the full benefit of the sunshine because the foliage of the grapevines and the Asian pear tree shaded them. All the okra seeds came from the same source; they were planted at the same time; they were all watered and fertilized regularly. However, those that got the full benefit of the sunshine were robust and healthy, while the ones that did not get much sunshine were spindly and scrawny. Even though I cultivated the thin ones and tried to give them special attention, there was a stark difference between the two groups.

God's children who avail themselves of the Sun of righteousness stay strong in their faith; those who do not become weak and ill-nourished. The latter are careless in their church and personal spiritual appointments. The faithful take their business with God seriously. They don't miss personal time with God. They are the dependable ones you can count on. Oh, that we may avail ourselves of the benefit of letting the Sun of righteousness dwell in our hearts!

Lord Jesus, come into my heart. Shine on me and let me rejoice in Your presence so that I can be strong, well-grounded, and anchored in You, because I want others to see Your radiance shining through me. I know You will be our light in that earth made new, but for now let Your light shine through me that Your name may be glorified. OFELIA A. PANGAN

EVERYONE HAS A TALENT

Take this staff in your hand so you can perform miraculous signs with it. Ex. 4:17, NIV.

Some women have obvious talents: they sing, play musical instruments, lecture, write books, lead out in seminars, conduct exercise classes. Some excel in household arts: cooking, sewing, handicrafts, or raising and arranging flowers. Other women do not have those kinds of talents. They are far too shy to take an up-front position in any church or social outreach, but they can be relied upon to serve the after-meeting hot drink and doughnuts and to clean up afterward.

I know a woman who describes herself as very ordinary and without a single talent. Yet she has nerves of steel and can drive through traffic snarls that make other women drivers quail. She uses that ability to transport aged or sick people to their medical, dental, and optical appointments. Isn't that a talent?

Another woman who claims to have no talents is the backbone of the Dorcas Society. True, she has no leadership qualities. But she washes, irons, and mends clothes, and she keeps the cupboards' contents tidy. Isn't that her talent?

A quiet, retiring young woman with several preschoolers of her own gladly cares for the tots of a musician friend, thus enabling the second woman to use her talents in God's service. Aren't they both using their talents? An older woman, housebound because of her husband's illness, is seldom without a "son." She can't afford elaborate hospitality, but willingly gives a home to a struggling student who needs somewhere to stay.

When God told Moses to go before Pharaoh and ask him to let the Israelites leave Egypt, Moses shrank from the task. He made excuses: He had forgotten how to speak the Egyptian language; he wasn't fluent with words anyway; he was out of touch; he had been away from Egypt for 40 years; he was getting old; he had no talent for this kind of task—please ask someone else.

God said to him, "What is that in your hand?"

And Moses replied, "A rod."

God used Moses and his rod to do mighty works in His service.

Perhaps you feel that you don't have any outstanding talent to use in God's service. Then offer your simple rod to God, and He will find work for you.

GOLDIE DOWN

FEAR

The Lord is my light and my salvation; whom shall I fear? The Lord is the strength of my life; of whom shall I be afraid? Ps. 27:1.

We had just moved to a new town and were hardly settled when my husband had to leave on a mission assignment to another town. Our rented house, in an isolated part of the town, was an old cantonment-designed bungalow with a large living/dining hall down the middle, and bedrooms with attached dressing rooms and bathrooms on each side. We had rented the house so that on the weekends the center room could be converted into a meeting hall. The house, possibly elegant once, was now in a state of disrepair. The windows were broken, the doors creaked. Gaping holes, like empty eye sockets, leered from the jute ceiling, and the paint was flaking off the walls.

We knew no one in town except the landlord. In the evenings the children would follow me everywhere, and when it was time to go to bed they became even more frightened, adding to my own insecure feelings. They looked with fear at the gaping holes in the ceiling. And my own fears intruded. I looked at the weak front door and knew that with even a gentle shove someone could push it in—or a hand could reach through the broken windowpanes and open the latch.

Each night I had a difficult time sleeping. The children and I would push the dining table against the front door, place a chair on it, and pile empty tins on top of the chair. If any intruder tried to enter, we would be awakened and, we hoped, they'd be scared into a hasty exit.

We had worship each night before going to bed. The children fell asleep almost immediately, but I lay awake with my eyes open, my ears tuned to unfamiliar sounds. My faith was no bigger than a mustard seed, and my heart beat fast. It seemed as though dawn was an eternity away. I was always happy when it was morning. The table, the chair, and the empty tins had not been disturbed, even by the large rats scurrying across the ceiling.

As I look back at those times, I realize God has rewarded my mustard seed faith. Through the years that faith has grown so that fear of being alone does not consume me. I have received abundant evidence that all His promises find their fulfillment in Jesus, my Friend.

Once again I turn my fears over to You. Help my faith to grow so that I may serve You again this day.
BIROL CHARLOTTE CHRISTO

APPLE CORE COURAGE

Let us run with endurance the race that is set before us, looking unto Jesus, the author and finisher of our faith. Heb. 12:1, 2, NKJV.

It was an Emily Dickinson day—you know, one of those I'm-nobody-who-are-you days. I was climbing the four flights of stairs to my office, feeling sorry for myself, and feeling incompetent to face everything that awaited me.

"Lord," I whined, "why did my boss have to move? Why was I pushed into her position? I can't be her, no matter how hard I try." I loved teaching, so I had paid little attention to the administrative side of our department. Now all that was my responsibility.

As I crossed the landing between the second and third floors, I glanced out the window. Suddenly I stopped, stepped back, and looked again. One of the windows in the next wing was open a few inches. I know those windows—they are old and heavy and don't stay open by themselves.

What caught my eye was the object propping the big window open: a well-chewed, brown-at-the-edges, day-old apple core. Standing up to its full height, it proudly held the window open, allowing fresh lilac-scented air to reach the students who would soon be there.

"OK, Lord," I said humbly, "I get the picture. With Your help I can move mountains, hold open windows, or chair a department—and like it!"

Have you ever felt like an old apple core—used up, useless, with nothing more to give? Have you ever felt incapable of doing anything worthwhile—a real nobody compared to the lovely apples around you—incapable of making a real contribution?

Lord, help me to remember that You have a work for me to do, regardless of how insignificant and incompetent I feel. Please remind me again this day that my competence and worth always come from You, and You will help me as I do my best.

SANDRA L. ZAUGG

DREAM ROOMS

In my Father's house are many rooms. . . . I am going there to prepare a place for you. John 14:2, NIV.

It was the evening before Joel's sixth birthday. All his life he had shared a room with his older brother, Nathan. Now, at last, each would have his own room.

To help the children make a transition to a new home, we had promised that they could help choose the decor for their new rooms. We had stripped wallpaper, filled holes, and repainted. Bethany's room was sophisticated in pale lilac and mint, with touches of silver and blue. Nathan wanted a high-tech room, so things were painted silver and gray, and he had chosen a poster of a cone nebula for his walls. Joel just wanted a room—he was too young to have any fixed ideas. So we gave it a marine theme and stenciled a twisted rope border at two levels. And then, just below ceiling height, we stenciled the names of all the different kinds of boats we could think of. Seashells, navy and cream linen, and some boat pictures finished off the scheme for very little cost.

At last we were finished. It was hard work, and we were exhausted, but we knew that Joel's shrieks of delight in the morning would make it all worthwhile.

Jesus has told us He's gone to heaven to prepare a place for each of us. I wonder if all the rooms will be the same, and if we will each be able to decorate ours the way we want to. Or maybe Jesus will have prepared each room to suit our tastes, interests, and individuality.

One of my friends collects teddy bears. She would like to have a huge grizzly bear living in her heavenly room so that when she wants to rest, she can cuddle into a real bear and feel its soft fur all around her! A gardening friend would plant her room with her favorite flowers—and live in the middle of a huge flower arrangement! My husband jokes that whatever my room is like in heaven, I will soon be at work stenciling it—maybe with sapphire and diamond dust over golden walls!

Eyes have not seen, and ears have not heard, the wonders of heaven. Now we can dream and imagine, but we do so knowing that everything will be incredible. Imagine your place in heaven. What could Jesus do to make it unique to you? I look forward to visiting you there one day!

KAREN HOLFORD

TREASURED DOLLS

Her children arise up, and call her blessed. Prov. 31:28.

It's with delight in my heart that I share with you about two very special dolls. The bride doll was a Christmas gift to me from my mommy and daddy when I was 6 years old (that was more than 40 years ago). Many years later I met and married my Canadian husband, Ron. When we moved from Oregon to Canada, I was five months pregnant with our first child, a daughter, Andrea Debron. About that same time my daddy died.

I believe it was the second Christmas without Daddy that I got the bride doll back as a gift. My mom had found her somewhere in the house and cleaned her up. She even washed her hair and made her new clothes. Then she gave her back to me, and I have treasured her ever since. I keep her in my cedar chest, where she is safe. Every time I open my cedar chest I recall "precious moments" from my youth. It causes me to think once again about how much I was loved by my parents.

When Andrea was 2, my mom gave her a special doll—a little Black one. She came already named (Chatty Cathy), but we gave her another name. Andrea was just beginning to talk, and she could pull the doll's string to make it talk also. The doll went everywhere with us, even to the doctor's office when Andrea needed medical attention. Unfortunately, Andrea nibbled on things, and she actually nibbled off the doll's fingers.

I kept very good watch on this special doll from Grandma for nearly 25 years. When Andrea married Bill Blair in 1996, I asked my mom to please clean up the doll, make her new clothes, and give her back to Andrea for Christmas, just as she had done for me years before. My mom did as I requested, and she even found new arms and hands.

Andrea has asked me to please keep her special doll with mine for now, safe in my cedar chest and safe in the treasure house of my memory.

How fortunate some of us are to have treasures of precious memories of earthly parents. Even better, though, is that all of us can have special memories of the love given us by our heavenly Father.

Thank You, Father, for Your special love. DEBORAH SANDERS

THE HARVEST

Do you not say, "Four months more and then the harvest"? I tell you, open your eyes and look at the fields! They are ripe for harvest. John 4:35, NIV.

I had an exciting new experience today: I helped with harvest! Well, not really. I only rode in a monstrous combine and asked questions. So it would be more accurate to say I witnessed harvest. There are so many things I don't know about planting and fertilizing and harvesting, but I have a high regard for the farmers who understand the cycle, put in the hard work, and cooperate with Mother Nature to feed the world.

The combine I rode in today was picking corn—six rows at a time. This $150,000 machine could pick and shell an acre of corn in a few minutes. And all the while the combine was filling its huge hopper with kernels of golden corn, it was shredding the dried stalks and leaves and spreading them back down on the ground. Today's harvest yielded about 175 bushels of corn per acre. Now that's a lot of cornbread!

Because I live and travel in the heart of America, where farming is big business, I thrill at the summer wheat harvest, as well as the fall harvest of corn, soybeans, and sunflowers. It's not uncommon during harvest to see three or four of those monstrous combines moving in a staggered line around a section of land. I marvel at the way God's spark of life in the little seed responds to the sunshine and rain that falls on the brown earth—and produces such bountiful harvests.

The cycle of sowing and reaping, of planting and harvesting, was part of God's plan from the time of Creation. He knew His human family would need food, and He provided such a great variety. When Jesus talked to His disciples about the harvest, He wasn't talking about the harvest of wheat and corn with John Deere combines. What He really cares about is the ripening of hearts and the spiritual harvest of His human family.

It is important that God mature my character so that at the harvest I will be ripened grain, not discarded chaff.

ROXY HOEHN

MY AUNT WILMA MADE ME EAT TOMATOES

The wages of sin is death, but the gift of God is eternal life in Christ Jesus our Lord. Rom. 6:23, NIV.

My aunt Wilma made me eat tomatoes. She was a good cook, but I wondered why any decent person would want to eat tomatoes.

"They will make you strong, Beckilina," she'd say, and she'd make me sit there until I got up the courage to master my dislike.

Aunt Wilma also told me, "Onions are the police, and garlic is the FBI. They chase all the bad things out of your body." She ate plenty of them, as her breath testified. Somehow, though, the vagabond cancer stole that sacred breath, and Aunt Wilma went to her rest.

I worked for her through that last summer, helping her take care of her grandchildren every day. They came over early every morning and spent the day making unforgettable memories. She knew the end was coming, and I was to be her helping hands. I plunged into everything she taught me—how to knit, how to cook, and also how to love.

I locked into memory every look, every word of encouragement, every selfless act she did. Aunt Wilma spoke of God as though He was so real, so powerful. She was the most virtuous woman I ever knew. I could not understand why she had to die.

My aunt Wilma made me eat tomatoes. She told me they would make me strong. She is gone now, but not really—not gone for keeps, because I know I'll see her in heaven, free from pain and sadness, garlic breath and all.

Creator-God, who made tomatoes and Aunt Wilma, help me today to make a difference in someone's life. Especially may I lead them to You, through whom we may truly have eternal life.

I never got to tell Aunt Wilma how much she had changed me, how much I had learned. Or that I did become strong because of her influence in my life. But I will someday. Some day I will tell her that I like tomatoes after all.

BECKY JARNES

WHY I LOVE BLUE

I consider thy heavens, the work of thy fingers, the moon and the stars, which thou hast ordained. Ps. 8:3.

Yes, I do love blue! I wake up each morning and quickly look out toward the heavens. Are there blue skies? Maybe it's a bright summer day, or a cool, crisp October morning. If there is a lot of blue, it makes me feel thankful, refreshed, and ready to start another day. If we're traveling and I am anywhere near a river, lake, or, better yet, the ocean, my eyes feast upon the water. The blue hues of the water are moments to savor. And what about a bluebird! Aren't they spectacular? God must have known that blue would bring us joy, serenity, and peace when He designed this particular color. Who can deny the joy of looking into the blue, blue eyes of a baby? I favored blue as a child, and I favor it still. Blue has been a part of my life.

When considering the more mundane aspects of life, my eyes are still drawn to this color. I can't seem to pass it up. If I'm clothes shopping and see something blue on the racks, I am drawn to it, frequently making a purchase only because I like the color. My bedroom has been blue and yellow for many years in several different houses, miles and miles apart. When choosing the last new car, the "denim blue" one seemed to be just right.

There are people who are "blue." The wide spectrum from joy and peace to sadness and depression represents quite a contrast. So while we perceive joy and gladness from the color, the human aspect of the "blues" is not appealing. We don't choose to mingle much with those who are suffering from depression.

How can we help those who are blue? Reach out! Maybe a hug, a cheerful greeting, a funny story, an invitation to lunch, a genuine compliment, an offer to baby-sit or to assist with a difficult task. Maybe someone needs some "alone" time. Do you know someone like that? We can help. If you are in a blue mood today, read Jeremiah 15:16— a wonderful promise.

Blue colors joy, gladness, and promise. I share them with you this morning. Blue skies, blue seas, blue eyes, "true blue" friends—look for them all. That's why I love blue!

ARLENE E. COMPTON

THE LOST PEN

Rejoice with me; for I have found the piece which I had lost. Luke 15:9.

I'll never forget the oppressive humidity of Madang in New Guinea. When the door of the DC-3 opened, a rush of almost unbreathably hot air assaulted me. I was sure I would suffocate and never survive to see the new mission school that we had been sent to establish. However, we learned to deal with shoes that grew mildew overnight, and with the fact that a tiny scratch would develop into a full-blown tropical ulcer by dark if not treated immediately.

We lived there for five years, carving a boarding school out of the jungle and experiencing amazing blessings from God despite having no road out to the school for more than two years. Then the government built a road that came partway to our mission station. We bought an old car to celebrate the civilized privilege of driving to our front door.

Then we started having visitors, mostly other missionaries from different parts of the country; and occasionally we took time off for a picnic. That was really living!

Once we took our visitors for a ride along the coast road, and when we found a suitable spot, we stopped beside the ocean to enjoy our lunch. That was when I discovered an interesting plant in an old bomb crater. I persuaded Allan to wrestle the plant out of the ground for my garden. In the process, his gold Parker pen, which was part of my wedding gift to him, was lost. It must have fallen out of his pocket.

Two years passed, and I felt a sense of déjà vu as we traveled that same road with other folks for a picnic. That bomb crater triggered a thought of the lost pen, so at my request Allan stopped, and (foolish us) we looked for the gold Parker.

It took a little moving of debris, but we found it, still shiny gold! And it still worked. There was no rust as a result of lying in that ultrahumid environment! We could hardly believe it.

Perhaps we could have sold the story to Parker, but the priceless stories that came to mind were of the finding of the lost sheep, the lost coin, and the lost boy—and the joy of the Lord over one sinner who repents. No matter how impossible our circumstances or how inclement our environment, Jesus can present us "faultless before the presence of his glory with exceeding joy" (Jude 24).

URSULA M. HEDGES

ANGELS ON EARTH

Do not neglect to show hospitality to strangers, for thereby some have entertained angels. Heb. 13:2, RSV.

One cold morning I waited outside the locked back door of the library where I work. I saw two people pull into the parking lot—the new highly paid government official and Celia, seventysomething and one of our most faithful library volunteers. The officer quickly reached the door, unlocked it, and let me in. Celia was still a few feet away.

"Thank you," I told him. "You need to leave the door open for Celia. She's right behind you."

"What do you expect me to do—stand here and hold the door open all day?" he responded nastily. Not only did he not prop the door open, he let it slam shut in front of her and walked off.

I opened the door for Celia and was greeted with a warm smile. She said nothing about the rudeness of the man, but I thought about it throughout the day because I realized that the officer had no idea what he had just done. He thought nothing of being rude to an elderly woman who came in to put magazines away. I guessed he didn't know that Celia sat on the library's board of directors and had a voice in his future employment. Her humble demeanor clashed with his haughty one, but she was, in effect, one of his bosses!

Celia is one of a small army of volunteers who is vital to the efficient running of the library, performing a variety of little jobs to free the paid staff to do the jobs for which training is required. To the staff and to the public, she is one of the angels on earth—mostly unknown and unseen.

Would you treat someone better if you knew that he or she was rich or important? If you were visited by an angel, wouldn't you be on your best behavior? But the Bible tells us that many have entertained angels unaware.

As I go through this day, please help me to show respect to everyone rather than trying to determine who is important and who is not. I may meet an angel—or You!   GINA LEE

THE POWER OF THE PSALM

The Lord is my shepherd. . . . Yea, though I walk through the valley of the shadow of death, I will fear no evil: for thou art with me. Ps. 23:1-4.

I am a German teacher who has about 100 pupils each year. I have never had any problem with any of them—until this year.

One evening my phone rang. When I answered, instead of hearing words, I heard a lion's roar and many other fearful noises. It was disturbing! In the days that followed—in the morning, in the afternoon, in the evening, and even in the middle of the night—it was the same. I heard no words, only noises.

Then one day a voice said, "You will die soon."

I answered truthfully, "You also."

I talked to a fellow teacher about this problem, and we prayed together. She suggested, "Read the Bible when he phones you again."

My Bible was open near the telephone to Psalm 23. So when the telephone rang, I began to read the psalm very slowly. On the other end of the line it was strangely quiet. When I finished, I said "Amen" and hung up.

The next evening a man phoned me. His voice was very clear as he told me he had been one of my pupils 10 years before, but he didn't want to tell me his name. He said that when he was 11 he was very angry at me because I had told his parents he was very clever but lazy. I had forced him to learn. Now that he was an adult, he had decided to take his revenge. He was determined to frighten me, even to kill me. But I had read Psalm 23 to him, and at that moment he remembered that he was supposed to be a Christian, that he really did love God too. He had forgotten that God and I loved him.

"Please, forgive me for phoning you every day."

Yes, the Lord is my shepherd. He walks with us when we are in the valley of the shadow. I will fear no evil.

I don't know what might happen today or what challenges I may face. But I can go in peace because I know that You are with me. Praise You, Lord.

AUDE SURDI

TIRED OF GOD?

Let us not become weary in doing good, for at the proper time we will reap a harvest if we do not give up. Gal. 6:9, NIV.

As I walked into the kitchen I turned on the radio for a little background music while I washed the dishes. A song was playing on a Christian radio station, and I stopped short of the sink when I heard the words "tired of God." I listened intently, unable to believe my ears. As the song continued, I discovered I had not heard correctly. The words were really "child of God."

With relief I turned away to start the dishes but continued to think about being "tired of God." The more I thought, the more I realized that through the years I had played the role of being tired of God. That was a shock! How many times have I groaned when a member of the church nominating committee called to ask me to accept a church office? And what about the times I prayed a quick prayer and skipped reading my Bible because there was something else I'd rather do?

I knew I wasn't alone. I thought about a friend who walked out on her husband and kids because she wanted to be free to do her "own thing." Then there are the empty pews at church because some believe worshiping with fellow believers is optional. Or they don't want to attend with people they consider hypocritical. Deficits in the church budget are another sign that the Lord's work isn't as important as our own wants. Others can become tired of God when He does not give them what they want, or they believe He is not hearing their prayers. The rewards of living for God daily far outweigh living for ourselves.

By the time I finished the dishes I had come to the conclusion that it's when we become tired of God that we need Him most. Could it be that when we're weary of serving Him, it's because He isn't really in the activity in the first place? I resolved to seek His will and work in my life and not to give up.

Lord, I have resolved to seek Your will and Your way, and to let You lead in the work of my life. Help me not to get tired of You or of doing Your will. You have promised that we will reap a harvest if we do not give up. I claim that promise for today.   DONNA MEYER VOTH

MY HALE-BOPP EXPERIENCE

Your righteousness reaches to the skies, O God, you who have done great things. Who, O God, is like you? Ps. 71:19, NIV.

I couldn't believe how late it was! It was Thursday, the day before our women's prayer retreat was to start. Last-minute preparations took much longer than I had anticipated. My friends had driven ahead while I finished photocopying. And now here I was, driving alone late at night to a place I had never been before, somewhere in the Catskill Mountains.

And it wasn't only the drive. It was the rushing, the guilty feeling of mistreating my family because I couldn't cook, or do the shopping, or even say goodbye in the loving way I had planned to. And there were all the phone calls from women who had decided to attend at the last minute—and the ones canceling, and the ones who wanted to take our chartered buses because their cars had died that day.

And then it was the comet. The event of the century. Hale-Bopp was going to be seen in New York for only a few days. I tried to see it one night, going out on the terrace, but the sky was overcast. I spent the other nights preparing for the retreat. By the time the retreat was scheduled to be over, so would the pass of the comet. I was going to miss the opportunity of a lifetime.

I was tired, depressed, nervous, and disappointed with myself. While driving north on the Palisades Interstate Parkway, I asked the Lord to forgive me and to help me change my negative feelings. I wanted to feel good, ready for the retreat.

Then I looked up. There it was! The most majestic view of the comet! More beautiful than I had imagined. Clear and bright in the dark of the night, with no city lights to detract from its beauty. It accompanied me on an unforgettable two-hour trip to the hotel, two wonderful hours of praising and rejoicing in our wonderful Creator! I still imagine the smile on Jesus' face that night as I arrived refreshed and ready to meet the women attending the retreat.

O God, wonderful Creator, in the midst of my long pilgrimage here on earth may the beauty of Your created works still shine through and refresh my weary soul.

ALICIA MARQUEZ

A LESSON FROM A ROOSTER

Watch ye therefore: for ye know not when the master of the house cometh, at even, or at midnight, or at the cockcrowing, or in the morning: lest coming suddenly he find you sleeping. And what I say unto you I say unto all, Watch. Mark 13:35-37.

I became acquainted with the rooster very early the first morning after we arrived in San Cristóbal, Venezuela, as participants in a Maranatha project. We had slept only a few hours when he began his mournful "Cock-a-doodle-do!" And his call at 5:30 signaled other roosters. Their chorus came first as an echo, then in swelling unison.

The rooster became a conversation piece at breakfast. Some of us wished he'd shut up, and some of us wanted to "wring his neck." I remember one morning in particular. The rooster crowed, and moments later I heard a loud bang. I was sure someone had shot the rooster. I lay there with "Praise the Lord" on my lips when I heard, louder than before, "Cock-a-doodle-do! Cock-a-doodle-do!"

My thoughts turned from glee to contemplation, and a paraphrase of God's conversation with Satan from the book of Job came to mind: "Have you considered my servant the rooster, that there is none like him on the earth, a perfect and upright bird, one that fears God and shuns evil? And still he holds fast to his integrity" (see Job 2:3).

I find it interesting that cock crowing is mentioned only twice in the Bible, and it is always accompanied by the word "watch." Both occasions suggest that Christ is confident that the rooster will do his God-given assignment each morning. Christ can depend on the rooster. Can He depend on you and me? As I thought about this I understood better why Christ wants us to "watch." He wants to fortify us for whatever lies ahead.

Even though it was not appreciated at the moment, Lord, thank You for the rooster. Help me to be as faithful as he is. Place within me not only the desire but the willingness to rise early each morning to seek Your face. Give me rooster-like boldness to speak for You. I want to be found waiting and watching when You come.

BARBARA J. HALES

RESTORED

He restoreth my soul: he leadeth me in the paths of righteousness for his name's sake. Ps. 23:3.

My father is a man with gifted hands. As a child I loved to observe him as he worked his "magic" on old television sets that had been discarded or given to him by neighbors who called them "junk" because they were no longer of service. Often the cabinets were dirty, dull, or scarred, missing knobs, handles, or doors. Sometimes tubes were missing or burned out and cords were frayed. My father spent hours lovingly and patiently restoring those sets to unbelievable beauty. The transformations amazed the neighbors, who had not seen the worth of the discarded sets.

As I travel around the beautiful city of Denver, I notice how much restoration is being done on houses, churches, parks, and buildings. As I engage in numerous conversations with coworkers I learn that they, their friends, or their family members are restoring, or have restored, furniture, jewelry, or photographs.

As I listen to beautiful voices sing about being restored and watch talented hands play instruments that ring out with the message of restoration, I still sometimes wonder why anyone would take the time, effort, and money to repair and rebuild something when, in my opinion, it would be so much easier to destroy it and replace it with something new. The process seems slow, tedious, and time-consuming. In some cases that which is being restored is strong and sturdy, but sometimes it is weak and fragile. Some items need major repair, while others need only a few delicate touches.

Lately my mind has been bombarded with thoughts of restoration, and I feel a deep, burning need to be restored in many areas of my life—my health, my family, my church, and especially my relationship with God. I experience a plethora of emotions as I think about the hands of the Restorer as I am being stripped, sanded, rubbed, and polished in order to be brought back into being. As I read the twenty-third psalm, I find that God restores my soul. I wonder if I am really ready to withstand the process, and I pray for the fortitude to endure, knowing that when the restoration is complete I will emerge a changed vessel, molded and shaped by the Creator of the original design.

PATRICIA L. SHINSKIA

THE MAP

Thy word is a lamp unto my feet, and a light unto my path. Ps. 119:105.

One of my favorite pastimes is outlet shopping. I used to view these trips as an opportunity to visit a new area. So armed with directions from AAA (my automobile club) and a map, I would leave home in search of the latest bargain. As I traveled the major and minor roads of southern New Jersey and southeastern Pennsylvania, I used the map to confirm that I was traveling in the right direction.

Then I relocated to northwestern New Jersey. Again my old map was a constant companion. One weekend I left my map in the car of visiting relatives. I was without a map as I continued to find my way around that part of New Jersey. Two experiences reinforced for me the importance of a map. The first occurred during a trip to the Reading outlets in Pennsylvania. That trip took me through mountains and some of the narrowest roads I had ever driven. As I navigated the curving hills of eastern Pennsylvania, I kept hoping I was driving in the correct direction and that I hadn't missed a turn or misunderstood the phone directions from AAA. I longed for my map to confirm the accuracy of the AAA directions and the route I was taking.

Another experience occurred when I asked one of the attendants in the local library for directions to a lake in the area. Along with directions to the lake, she shared that she was once a newcomer to the area and had purchased a map to help her learn the area. I was embarrassed by her additional well-intentioned advice about purchasing and using a map.

As I pondered my map experiences, I thought of another map—God's Word. Like my tattered map, this map provides directions to travelers and confirms or disproves the accuracy of the advice of others. It also serves as a standard by which to evaluate the route of life one chooses. This map differs from my road map in some ways. My map is probably outdated for certain areas, but my Bible map is always current. It has served as an accurate map for individuals who lived many centuries ago and is just as accurate for those living today. The mileage and driving time on my road map are not always exact, but the traveling time in my Bible map has always been, and continues to be, exact. God has given us a map for life's pilgrimage. Regular consultation will make life's trip successful.

ERICA JOAN CHARLES

OCTOBER 19

THE BLUE NOTE

Encourage each other to build each other up, just as you are already doing. 1 Thess. 5:11, TLB.

It was an innocent-looking small blue envelope tucked among the bills, magazines, flyers, and sales pitches I had picked up from the post office that Friday morning. I separated it from the rest of the mail and examined it more closely. It was addressed to my husband and me and had no return address, so I couldn't tell who had sent it. Curious, I carefully slit it open and pulled out a small card. The message surprised and overwhelmed me.

At the top of the small note was a Bible verse, Psalm 46:1: "God is our refuge and strength, an ever-present help in trouble" [NIV]. Below, in the same small, slightly crooked script, was a more personal message: "Dear Bill, Fauna, and family,

"Just a note to let you know that you're thought of and loved. Know that God loves you and will always take care of you and your family. God will always be there for you!

"Thinking of you."

But there was no signature.

I had been feeling rather discouraged, depressed, and overcome by a feeling of too much to do and too little time in which to do it. But the little note changed my attitude entirely. Someone was thinking of me; someone cared about me enough to remind me that God also loved me and cared about me. It was as though God had tapped me on the shoulder and given me a big hug.

I puzzled over the note the rest of the day, but no name sprang to mind as the obvious author. Later, while visiting with other church members, I found that many had received an identical note. We began to have our suspicions as to who the sender was, but the mystery remains and may never be solved until Christ comes. Such a small message, but what a powerful one! My day was completely changed by a few well-chosen words.

I have kept the little blue note next to my Bible as a constant reminder of the importance of encouraging others and letting people know, anonymously or otherwise, how precious they are to the Lord. It also reminds me of the nearness of God's love and His care.

FAUNA RANKIN DEAN

A LESSON IN FORGIVENESS

If anyone has caused pain, he has caused it not to me. . . . Turn to forgive and comfort him, or he may be overwhelmed by excessive sorrow. So I beg you to reaffirm your love for him. 2 Cor. 2:5-8, RSV.

I had come home from work exhausted and sleepy. I was sure all I needed was a bath to send me to dreamland. Just as I was drifting off to sleep, it seemed that someone was encouraging me to read 2 Corinthians 2:5, but I was too tired to get up to do it. The voice, though, wasn't tired. It persisted. I covered my head with my pillow to shut out the distraction, but to no avail. In fact, sleep evaded me. Dragging myself out of bed, I scribbled down the text, promising to read it first thing in the morning. Soon after, I was fast asleep.

I woke up with my mind on the passage, so I read it. It was like a thunderbolt: "Turn to forgive and comfort him, or he may be overwhelmed by excessive sorrow" (verse 7). What could this mean?

Could it be I am still holding a grudge against a friend I have forgiven for deceiving me? In all honesty, I felt I had forgiven. But here I was, face-to-face with it—hypocrisy uncovered. Had I really, truly forgiven?

The question kept bothering me. I thanked God for revealing my true self and my true thoughts, then I pleaded with Him to teach me how to forgive. I was directed to confess my true feelings to the brother and to do it in the spirit of genuine forgiveness. After I spoke to the man, he unburdened his heart about the terrible feeling of guilt and pain he was going through because of the wrong he had done to me. With tears in our eyes we prayed for forgiveness for each other. Indeed, God accepted our prayers.

I still cannot explain the peaceful calm I've experienced about that issue since that day. I thank and praise God that through this text He set me free from the guilt and pain of denying forgiveness and gave me a taste of the bliss of forgiving others as God forgives me.

Today is a new day. May I be willing to forgive, encourage, and reaffirm Your love to others. Your Word brought just the message I needed. Praise be to You!

ROSA MADAM JOHNSON

SURPRISE, SURPRISE!

Anxious hearts are very heavy but a word of encouragement does wonders! Prov. 12:25, TLB.

While I was getting groceries for my family before leaving for a women's retreat at which I was to speak, a young mother got in line behind me, an adventurous little boy at her side. She hadn't bothered to get a cart, and now, with her hands full of grocery items, she was trying to keep the little fellow close to her by calling him to order. I watched them, admiring how she managed to rescue a jar of sausages just before he dropped it on the floor.

"Would you like to put your little boy in the baby seat of my cart?" I offered.

She looked at me, wide-eyed. "A lovely idea! Thank you so much. How kind of you!" She took a deep breath once she had deposited her boy in the seat. We talked a bit, and soon we were almost at the checkout.

"Would you like to go first so you can pay for your things before you pick up your little boy?" I asked, and turned the cart so the baby could see his mother.

In front of the counter were buckets with bouquets of roses and tulips. The young woman picked up some roses and asked me, "What would be better as a present, roses or tulips?"

"Well," I said, "it depends. Sometimes the roses will wilt so quickly." Then I saw some amaryllis buds. "Those amaryllis are nice too, aren't they?"

She chose the amaryllis and paid for her purchases. After bagging her groceries, she came back to pick up her baby. "And these flowers are for you because you were so kind to look after my boy." She thrust the amaryllis buds into my hands.

Surprised, I stammered, "Oh, no . . . Thank you so much!" I was overwhelmed—not so much because of the flowers, but because the little help I had offered had made her so happy. In return, I was made happy. I came home bubbling over with the excitement of my experience.

The experience was most meaningful to me because it was the exact illustration I needed for my presentations. It seemed that God was affirming me: "Go ahead with your presentations. I quite agree that's the right thing to say!" A word of encouragement does wonders!

HANNELE OTTSCHOFSKI

CLOSER TO THE SON

Strip yourselves of your former nature [put off and discard your old unrenewed self] . . . and put on the new nature (the regenerate self) created in God's image, [Godlike] in true righteousness and holiness. Eph. 4:22-24, Amplified.

The city block on which my office building is located is the perfect size for a lunchtime walk. As I started out one October day, I debated whether to take my coat. I decided to take it, because although the day was beautifully sunny, it was very windy.

As my walk took me around the shady side of the block, away from the sun, I zipped my coat all the way, thankful that I had taken it. I even put on my gloves to protect me from the wind. When I entered the edge of the sunny portion of the block, it didn't take long for my gloves to come off. Soon I unzipped my coat. As I made the final turn around the block, I entered the fullness of the sunshine and had to take my coat off.

When I started, I had been completely bundled in my coat and gloves. Now I had my gloves in my coat pocket and my coat over my shoulder. The more time I spent in the sun, the warmer I became and the less clothing I wanted to wear. I had not intended to work at getting warm so I could remove my clothing—it happened naturally the longer I stayed in the sun.

As I thought about the "shedding" process I had just gone through, a parallel became very clear in my mind. Jesus is the Son who sends His light into my soul. As I start to walk toward the Son, I start with a lot of sin as my clothing. The sin is comfortable because of my distance from the Son. However, as I move closer and closer to the Son and allow the warmth of His light to enter my heart, sin becomes more and more uncomfortable. The closer I draw to Jesus, the more I want to shed sin from my life.

I'm so glad my focus does not have to be on shedding the clothing of sin but on basking daily in the warmth of the Son.

SHARON DALTON WILLIAMS

ON WITNESSING

"You are My witnesses," says the Lord, "that I am God." Isa. 43:12, NKJV.

I wanted to be a witness for my Lord but was not sure what to do. One day I prayed, "Lord, You gave Moses a rod with which to witness for You. What have You given me?"

Then a thought came. "You have miniature roses in your garden. You can share them with your neighbors, and you could offer a brief prayer for the persons you give them to."

So I did just that, and the neighbors were very pleased and touched.

One elderly retired teacher did not invite me in when I took her some flowers, but we chatted for a long time at the door. As I was ready to leave, she commented, "Anytime you have tiny roses to share, I would be delighted with them."

I told a couple who were new in the neighborhood that I like to pray for people as I walk past their homes. I asked, "Do you have a prayer request?" The man immediately said, "Yes, please pray for our daughter in California; she's about to have her second baby, and she has multiple sclerosis." The next day I brought tiny roses and a short written prayer. They were most grateful. I soon learned that their daughter had had her baby and all was well.

Several neighbors even wrote to thank me for the prayers and roses.

A couple who had just moved in two doors away welcomed me and invited me in. The husband said that the doctor in our church was his doctor also, and he greatly appreciated him. We later had them and two other neighbors in for a simple lunch of haystacks. They thought it was a super lunch. They asked each other at the lunch about the roses and the prayer cards I had brought.

I thank You for the idea and the roses that You gave me so that I may witness for You. It has been fun, and others have been blessed. Please bless my neighbors this day. And may each of us use what we find in our hands as a blessing for others to glorify Your name.

FRIEDA TANNER

LET THEM HEAR YOU

Sisters, I urge you in the name of our Lord Jesus Christ to join me in my struggle by praying to God for me. Rom. 15:30, NLT.

I used to be afraid to pray aloud with people. But as I've grown, so has my desire to be God's arms to hug a burdened heart.

When I worked the 3:00 to 11:00 shift as a nurse, I'd develop a friendship and rapport with repeat patients. While "tucking in" my patients at night, when the Spirit nudged, I'd ask if I could pray aloud for them. It always amazed me how they'd unburden their hearts after I prayed with them. They needed to feel God's touch and care.

Last night I called a friend and could tell immediately that she'd been crying. A family member had suffered a stroke. I listened, comforted, and before hanging up I prayed for her over the phone. It meant so much to her.

I've recently realized how much even my pastor-husband appreciates hearing me pray for him. All of us at times feel that God is playing hide-and-seek and that someone else's prayers will find Him more easily. When I'm discouraged, it's so comforting to hear my husband or a friend lift me up to God in prayer. So when people tell me about their teen who has run away, or of a husband who's losing his job, or a special event they're preparing for, instead of saying that I'll pray for them, I pray aloud with them right then and there. Tension slips away, and an incredible peace often fills their hearts while joy fills me, knowing I've been God's arms to deliver His hug.

Loving Father, I lift up my dear sisters to You, sisters from around the world. I praise You that You care tenderly for each of them, that You love them with an incredible, exhaustless love. Thank You that You know their circumstances, their burdens, their struggles. And You know their hearts and their love for You. Thank You for Your compassion in understanding that their spirits are willing, though their flesh may be weak. Strengthen them, gracious Father. Renew their spirits. Bring clarity out of confusion, victory from seeming defeat. Draw them close to You. Let them feel Your arms of love wrapped tightly around them. Ease their minds. Give them peace. And thank You that You thrill to do this for them because they are so precious to You. Praise You, Father. Amen.

HEIDE FORD

GOING HOME

I will arise and go to my father. Luke 15:18.

E arly one morning as I was walking through one of the poorer parts of London, I was startled by a young man sprinting along the pavement. He suddenly pulled up beside me and fell into step with me. He was obviously excited about something and talked fast. He told me he had been living on the streets for a long time, together with thousands of other homeless. Hooked on drugs, he had completely lost control of his life. As I turned to look at him for the first time, expecting him to ask for money, I noticed how clean he was—his hair still wet, his jeans neatly pressed, his face shining with happiness.

He must have noticed my surprise. "I kept praying to God to get me out of the mess I had got myself into, and He heard me and answered my prayers. I have been drug-free for six weeks. I have given up all my street friends, as they were destroying me. A few days ago I won some money. With that I shall be able to buy a little place of my own and, working for my dad, I'll be able to cover my expenses. I am clean. I am free. I am going home!"

I can understand how he feels, and I share in his joy. There was a time when I, too, was drowning in the quagmire of sin, chained to evil habits, helpless and hopeless. But one day everything changed. God heard my unspoken cry for help, took pity on my desperate need, and lifted me from the quicksand of sin. Though completely unworthy, I became His child. He washed me in the blood of Jesus and clothed me in the white robe of His righteousness. And soon, very soon, I am going home to my Father, who loves me with an everlasting love and has prepared a beautiful home for me in His kingdom. I too cannot keep this good news to myself. I have to tell someone, even if it is an elderly stranger walking a grimy inner-city street.

The young man's last words as he picked up speed once more were, "Well, I have to go now. See you later."

Yes, my brother, by God's grace I'll see you later—in our Father's house. I am headed that way right now.

I thank You for Your patience, Father, and for waiting for me. May I too share with others what You have already done for me. REVEL PAPAIOANNOU

HE CARRIES HIS LAMBS

He gathers the lambs in his arms and carries them close to his heart. Isa. 40:11, NIV.

She was just past 2 years old, and her baby brother was only a few weeks old. The night was cold, and the winter winds were blowing. All of us were tired. Her daddy, a college student, had staff responsibilities. His work involved duties at the college gym that was used for many programs and services. Thus on Saturday nights his little family huddled together until every door was locked and every light was checked before the trek homeward could begin.

Sabbath was always a special day, with services in the morning, treats for dinner, and often programs by and for students in the afternoon and evening. But now, at the close of a long day and late evening, everyone was tired. It was time to go home. Of course there was no car, but home wasn't too far away—it just seemed a long distance because of weariness and the transportation of the bundles that children seem to need. By this time the baby slept quietly in Mother's arms. Daddy carried the diaper bag and sundry other things, and sometimes a tired little girl. But even though she wasn't a big girl, she was heavy. Sometimes Daddy would have to put the little girl down so she could walk while he rested. When she protested, Daddy would remind her, "Honey, Daddy is tired too; and you are so heavy." And so she would stumble on for a few steps.

One evening when we were finally able to head for home, it was later than usual. A cold wind was whistling around the administration building. We all shivered. The little one clung to her mother's coat as long as she could, then stepped in front of her daddy. She stretched her arms upward and pleaded, "Please, Daddy, carry me. I am so heavy!"

How grateful we can be that our heavenly Father never wearies. His arms are never tired, and we are never too heavy. He promises to gently carry us in His bosom. "Come unto me, all ye that labour and are heavy laden, and I will give you rest" (Matt. 11:28).

How can we resist that loving invitation?

I come to You right now, asking that You carry me. Close to Your heart, please. I too am so heavy.   LOIS MAY WATTS

OCTOBER 27

ENDORSED CHECKS

Trust in the Lord. . . . In all thy ways acknowledge him, and he shall direct thy paths. Prov. 3:5, 6.

For years I worked in downtown Washington, D.C. It was convenient to parks, museums, shops, restaurants, and several banks. The bank I used was across the street from my office. When the weather was beautiful, I walked during lunchtime.

It was not payday, and there was no reason for going to the bank, but this day I went. As I walked in, I saw an envelope on the floor. Normally I would walk over any paper lying on the floor, but I picked up the envelope. It had something in it. I thought it belonged to someone in my building and I could give it to that person. I don't know why I didn't look on the outside or the inside of the envelope, but somehow I assumed the bank employees would not be as honest as I in finding the rightful owner. So instead of turning it in, I put it in my purse and didn't look at it again until I got home.

Once home, I remembered that envelope and examined the contents. At first I looked and saw one check. When I looked again, I saw two checks. Getting nervous, I looked the third time and discovered that both checks had been endorsed. To add to my unease, I realized that I did not recognize the name. I searched in the phone book, praying that the name would be listed. If it were an unpublished number, I would have no way of finding the owners. Yes, there was the same name and address as on the checks. One, two, three, four times I called, receiving no answer. I imagined how frantic the owners of those checks must be by now. I prayed, "Lord, please put their minds at ease." On the fifth attempt, an elderly woman answered. Without identifying myself, I asked a few questions. Her answers left no doubt that I had reached the right person. When I told her the story, I could hear her excitement as she relayed the message to her husband.

She arranged to meet me two days later inside the bank. She described what she would be wearing. For obvious reasons, I did not describe myself. When Mr. and Mrs. White walked in, like a magnet, we were drawn to each other.

I know the Lord was guiding me. I give praise to Jesus for the virtue of honesty and for my listening to and obeying His voice that day.

MARIE H. SEARD

304

FIGHTING FEAR

God hath not given us the spirit of fear; but of power, and of love, and of a sound mind. 2 Tim. 1:7.

It was a peaceful, serene evening. Friday cooking and cleaning were complete, and Mother was resting on the couch in the living room. I was dawdling over supper in the kitchen. Even though it has been more than 60 years since that eventful day, it is etched in my memory.

I can still hear the low rumble, increasing in intensity until everything in my little world turned into chaos. Dishes and glassware poured out of the cupboard in front of me, shattering in a million pieces on the tile countertop. Our house literally moved six inches off the foundation. Furniture was tossed around like kites on a windy day. If Mother hadn't been impressed to leave the couch minutes before the earthquake struck, she would have died when the floor-to-ceiling brick fireplace collapsed, covering the couch with debris.

Probably the most terrifying aspect of it all was the sight of my mother racing past me, headed for the back door. As Isaiah 49:15 says, a mother can forget her child, the fruit of her womb. My mother quickly recovered her wits, turned, and grabbed me. Together we flew into the yard as the earth continued to quake.

The terror of that night clung to me all through childhood. Every time a truck rumbled past our house, adrenalin started coursing through my veins. Fear stalked me in other ways. My childhood shyness was painfully evident every time my mother entertained guests. I hid behind her skirt and almost never showed my face. Later other fears haunted me—the fear of failure in the musical world I had entered; fear of failure as a wife and mother; fear of not representing the church as I should.

Finally, on another day that is also etched on my mind, I was confronted by the text "God hath not given us the spirit of fear." His power, His love, His ability to give us self-control will curb the contamination of fear that sometimes overwhelms us. He is in control, doing what is best for us in every circumstance. If you are infected with the virus of fear, Paul's words to Timothy will be a very effective medicine.

I claim Your promise for my life this day. I desire Your power, Your love, and Your Holy Spirit to guide my life. DONNA LEE SHARP

A NEEDLE IN A HAYSTACK

Ask, and it shall be given you; seek, and ye shall find; knock, and it shall be opened unto you. Matt. 7:7.

The Southview church had planned an evening hayride for adults and youth at a nearby dude ranch. Our family had never participated in such an event, so we looked forward to it eagerly. It was every bit as much fun as we had anticipated.

What could be better than a hayride on a crisp October evening? Most of us engaged in a few hay fights, and we sang a lot of songs. After the ride was over, we warmed up by a huge bonfire and sang more songs. Then it was up to the hayloft for hot chocolate and cider and some heartwarming fellowship with friends.

We had barely arrived home when our 9-year-old daughter realized that her glasses were missing. She cried as she told us she was sure she had them on while riding the hay wagon. We realized that if they were lost on the trail, they could have already been run over by other wagons and horses. Added to that, the path was strewn with hay and leaves, and more leaves were falling. Surely hunting for them would be like looking for the proverbial needle in a haystack.

We knew it would be too dark to look that night, but we decided to pray about it and return to the ranch in the morning. We all prayed and thanked God for the special evening that we'd enjoyed and reminded Him how important it was that we find Sandi's glasses. We could not afford to replace them.

In the morning we called the church activities director to see if by chance someone had turned the glasses in. No one had, but he graciously volunteered to help us look. Back at the ranch we lined up, began with a prayer, and started down the trail. We had gone perhaps 50 yards when Sandi saw something glittering in the sunlight. Kicking the leaves aside, she saw her glasses, lying right at her feet.

We all knew God had answered her prayer. What a blessing it was to our family to have been given His help when we really needed it.

Father, we asked, we sought, and You answered. How good You are.

DARLENE YTREDAL BURGESON

STRONG AS A MAPLE

They are like trees . . . and their leaves do not wither. In all that they do, they prosper. Ps. 1:3, NRSV.

Several years ago, when we first purchased the lot on which our current house was built, the little maple tree was just a sapling. It was the only tree standing in the middle of our lot. We discussed cutting it down but decided to leave it. The trunk was tangled with briars and wild blackberry vines, but as we cleared away the rubbish and vines, we could see that the little tree had hope. We trimmed the lower limbs so they were even and waited to see how it would grow. To our amazement and delight, it began to stretch its branches rapidly toward the heavens. By the third year, my husband, Norman, threatened to cut off the back branches because the shade caused his garden to grow unevenly. I discouraged this, since the little tree had tried so hard to grow.

One day while I was standing at the frozen food case at the grocery store, there was a sudden power outage. I glanced out the window and saw a severe thunderstorm in progress. Hurriedly I finished my shopping and drove home. When I arrived, my husband was standing beside the precious maple with the chain saw in his hand. I dashed into the yard to see what was taking place. "What are you doing?" I demanded.

"Don't worry," my husband reassured me. "I'm not going to cut the tree down."

To my dismay, I could see that lightning had struck the tree. Most of the back branches were severed. My husband was trying to trim off the jagged limbs.

Today the maple stands a majestic 40 feet tall. It shades a large area in our yard, but it doesn't shade the corn patch. Our German shepherd, Buddy, is grateful for the cool shade it provides over his doghouse. The birds sing sweetly from its boughs as they await their turn to feed from the bird feeder on our nearby deck.

Frequently I think of how many of us have had a vital part cut away by illness, loss of someone dear, or a crippling emotional injury. But with daily help from our heavenly Father, we can continue to flourish and to be a help and blessing to those around us.

ROSE NEFF SIKORA

GOD'S LITTLE SURPRISES

I the Lord thy God will hold thy right hand, saying unto thee, Fear not; I will help thee. Isa. 41:13.

I have not experienced spectacular answers to my prayers as some have, but oh, how precious are the little ones I receive so often! Sometimes He demonstrates His promise in Isaiah 65:24: "Before they call, I will answer." Often He illustrates His presence by a spectacular glimpse of His majesty in the stars or the sunset. On occasion He gives me special object lessons to reveal His compassionate caring.

The afternoon was beautiful and balmy—a perfect autumn day in which to wash windows. I washed the inside of the windows and knew I would have to work fast to complete the outside before dark. Window by window I circled the house until I finally reached the kitchen windows—my last. The sun was already setting.

My husband and I had been struggling with a decision we needed to make concerning an overseas appointment. We had prayed for guidance, but for some reason known only to Him, God had seemed strangely silent.

All afternoon, as I washed the windows, I prayed particularly fervently that He would in some specific way indicate that He was indeed leading in our lives. Now, in the near darkness, I once again climbed the ladder and began to wash that last window. But as I reached up, I was unexplainably stopped.

Bewildered, I climbed down and went into the house for a flashlight. A few minutes later, back on the ladder, I shined it on the spot where I would have put my hand. There, poised in that beam of light, was a large black widow spider. With eyes wide open, I breathed a prayer, thanking God for tenderly placing His hand over mine and holding it safely in His. I knew I could trust Him to protect and direct our lives along the path He had chosen for us.

Answers to prayer are a wonderful blessing, but God's most beautiful gift is not His surprising and immediate answers to prayer, precious as they are. The most beautiful gift is the incredible relationship it builds between God and us, a relationship that cannot be measured. Time alone with Him in early-morning darkness has made me love Him so very much. I bask in His gentleness. I am strengthened by His patient acceptance of me, His faulty and erring child.

LORRAINE HUDGINS

STICKS AND STONES

The tongue that brings healing is a tree of life. Prov. 15:4, NIV.

My brother and I would often stop to play in piles of dirt and stone on our way to school. Now and then we would even lay down our book bags, pick up a stone or two, and throw them back and forth to each other. Mom had scolded us for this. One morning my brother began gathering as many stones as he could and soon was throwing them back in my direction. I wasn't paying attention, and one stone hit me squarely on the right side of my forehead. Mom nursed the wound, of course, and then strongly reproved my brother for throwing stones.

On a different occasion another brother and I were in the park playing with sticks. After digging in the dirt with them, waving them across blades of grass, and breaking them into little bits, I headed toward my favorite tree to read a book. My brother continued playing with a stick that was heavier and more crooked than the others, and soon was swinging it round and round. He accidently lost his grip on it. He screamed for me to watch out, but I didn't hear him. The stick whizzed through the air and struck me on my right eyebrow, leaving a deep gash. Mom nursed me that time, too. Thankfully, the stick had not hit my eye, for surely it would have put my eye out. My brother got a strong reprimand for playing with sticks.

As I think about those two incidents, I remember a phrase my childhood friends and I would often say—"Sticks and stones may break my bones, but words will never hurt me." If only that were true. We carelessly or callously hurl sticks and stones at each other every day in the words we speak, easily bruising egos, hurting feelings, dampening spirits, and squelching happiness. Our sticks and stones injure others emotionally, physically, and often spiritually. Even our telling them "Watch out" before we hurl our sticks or stones, or "I'm sorry" after we've done it, can't help.

Many are driven to their knees to seek healing from the One who can nurse and heal all wounds. May we have tongues that bring healing by the gentle, kind, and nurturing words we speak.

May the words of my mouth be acceptable in Your sight, O Lord.

IRIS L. STOVALL

A VERY PRESENT HELP

God is our refuge and strength, a very present help in trouble. Ps. 46:1.

It began as a sunny November day with 61 degrees in the early morning. Then things quickly changed. Dark clouds began to form, and brisk winds began to blow. By noon the temperature had dropped to the 30s, and the TV weather reports said that winds were being measured at 63 miles per hour!

As I watched the furious windstorm from my living room window, many branches fell from the maple trees in my front yard. Suddenly I heard a loud ominous thump on the roof of my house. *What caused that?* I wondered anxiously.

After the wind had finally subsided somewhat, I went into my backyard to look up at my roof and see if it had sustained any damage. A large tree limb was lodged near the peak of the roof. *Now, how do I get that down?* I asked myself.

I went back into the house to think about the perplexing situation and to earnestly pray for help. As I prayed, almost immediately the words "snow rake" came into my thoughts. Then I remembered that many years earlier my husband had purchased a snow rake with which to remove snow from our roof.

I found the rake and carried it to the backyard. Following the enclosed instructions, I assembled the five aluminum pipe sections into one long pole.

Having never used the equipment before, I asked God for strength and assistance. Gingerly I lifted the heavy pole and guided it carefully up to the roof. After experimenting a few times with the pole, I maneuvered it into the correct position and finally snagged the large unwieldy limb. Slowly I inched it down the roof's incline to the gutter, where it dropped off and fell to the ground. The problem was solved!

I am constantly amazed at how God causes my complex problems to become simple once I ask for His assistance.

Thank You, heavenly Father, for Your very present help and loving intervention!

ROSEMARY BAKER

THE SECRET OF THE SNOW GEESE

Can any of you by worrying add a single hour to your span of life?
Luke 12:25, NRSV.

Just before sunset I retreated to my special getaway, Miller Island Wildlife Refuge, near my home in Klamath Falls, Oregon. As I entered the area, my eyes were drawn to a beautiful flock of snow geese feeding on grain in a field beside a railroad track.

I told myself I had come to see wildlife. My mind, however, focused heavily on a disappointment that seemed to be disrupting my life at the moment.

Suddenly a freight train came roaring toward the geese. As if someone had pushed a button, all the birds scattered. In a short time the train disappeared down the track and the ear-splitting sounds were gone. The geese returned to the very spot they had left and continued their dinner.

They had only begun their main course when another freight train came down the track, as noisy and threatening as the one before. Again the snow geese flew away. When the train had passed and the air was silent again, the geese came back to pick up the pieces of grain they had left behind.

As I watched them, I marveled at the way they took these disruptions in stride. *How nice it would be to have wings that let me fly away when trials and troubles appear,* I thought. In my reflective mood I felt the hand of God using those lovely creatures of the sky to help me work through my problem. I recalled that some of my most difficult situations have often come unexpectedly, like freight trains. Most of them, like trains, eventually pass. So does all the noise and commotion that accompanies them.

After the calamity has passed, however, no matter how far away I've flown in mind or body, I need to get back to the business of living. As the snow geese returned to pick up the pieces of grain from the field, I need to pick up the pieces of my life and go on.

As the sunset gave way to darkness, I began to comprehend the lesson. "I take care of the birds of the air," God seemed to whisper, "and I'll take care of you."

That promise, I'm learning, is stronger than any freight train.

MARCIA MOLLENKOPF

I'M THIRSTY

Whoever believes in me will never be thirsty. John 6:35, NRSV.

During the first eight years of my life our family lived in a small one-bedroom house. My parents and two brothers slept in separate double beds, but my sister and I shared a cot, sleeping with our heads at opposite ends, with our feet meeting in the center. Before we settled down to sleep, what fun we had putting the soles of our feet together and flexing our knees back and forth as though pedaling a bike.

On dark nights the frequent howls of coyotes in the distance and the frantic responding yaps of the dog near the house sent shivers through me. Throughout the night I found some comfort in touching my sister's feet. But my greatest source of comfort was in knowing Dad was awake. Only his wakefulness could dispel my deepest fears.

The surest way to find out if Dad was awake was to call, "Daddy, I want a drink of water." He never ignored me or told me to go back to sleep. He got up immediately and made his way to the water pail in the kitchen, guided by the beam from his flashlight. My fears vanished even before he returned with a cup of water. No words were spoken as I took a small sip. It wasn't the water that revived my spirits, but rather the hand that held the cup. With the assurance that my father was awake and watching over me, I could easily fall asleep again.

It makes me sad when I think of Jesus agonizing with pain on the cross. He cried for a drink, but unlike my experience, He was given vinegar. Like me, it wasn't the physical thirst He craved so much as the assurance of His Father's presence. Because of His sacrifice to save humankind, His Father didn't bring Him a cup of refreshing water—the affirmation that all was well. I am grateful that Jesus came forth as the victor. Because He suffered the separation from His Father, none of us has to endure such agony, fear, and uncertainty in our future.

As I recall the comfort I received from a cup of water from my dad's hand, I am reminded of the spiritual cup of living water promised to any who ask. Jesus has invited us to come. "Let anyone who is thirsty come to me, and let the one who believes in me drink" (John 7:37, NRSV).

I thirst. Fill my cup, Lord.

EDITH FITCH

TOMORROW

Tomorrow go out to face them, for the Lord is with you.
2 Chron. 20:17, NASB.

Not long ago a real estate agent handling a townhouse I owned on the opposite side of the country called to tell me she had located some immediate buyers. The townhouse had sat vacant for nearly a year and a half. I quickly signed the faxed agreement and sent it off special delivery.

My husband then phoned the property management company requesting that they take my townhouse off the rental market because we now had buyers for it. The agent exclaimed, "I can't do that! I moved people into it two days ago, and they've signed a one-year lease!"

Shocked, my husband numbly—and unreasonably—asked, "Well, do you think they'd be willing to move?"

The agent's near sarcastic laugh at the other end of the line said it all. "What?" he asked. "I can't do much tonight anyway—it's closing time here. We'll have to talk about this tomorrow."

I was heartsick and grasping at straws, with growing knots in my stomach. We recalled the Bible story about King Jehoshaphat, who once had his kingdom surrounded by enemies on all sides. Then God sent a message to the king: "Do not fear or be dismayed; tomorrow go out to face them, for the Lord is with you" (2 Chron. 20:17, NASB).

God's promises for Jehoshaphat are promises for us, too! Could we believe that God had not only our enemies under His control—but also our tomorrow? And if we believed this, what were we supposed to do? The same thing that Jehoshaphat and his people did, we decided—wait and pray and trust and get a good night's sleep. And, like Jehoshaphat, we did.

Our tomorrow brought an early-morning phone call from the property management agent on the East Coast. "We've had the most amazing turn of events back here!" he exclaimed. "The renters are willing to move to another place!"

Someone once said, "Don't fear tomorrow; God is already there." You too can trust God with your tomorrow.   CAROLYN RATHBUN SUTTON

WHERE WAS GOD?

All things work together for good to them that love God. Rom. 8:28.

We often think that because God loves us He will protect us from every difficulty, that the road will be straight and smooth. When I look back, I notice this is not always true. I would say the difficult circumstances in my life are important bends in the road. Let me tell you one of my experiences.

When I was 16, I studied the Bible every Wednesday afternoon with a pastor. At the last lesson, the pastor asked me if I wished to be baptized.

"No, I don't," I responded.

He was very surprised and asked, "Why?"

"Because I am not ready. God is not first in my life," I replied.

My pastor smiled, assuring me, "That will happen after your baptism!"

But I was obstinate: "I will be baptized only when God is first in my life."

A week later I had an oral exam. Everything was going well. I was very happy, and I sang hymns to thank God as I rode home on my motorized bike. It was 10:00 a.m., and I had a long distance to go on major roads. Traffic flowed freely. When I was nearly home, I saw a car coming out from a yard. I thought, *This car will stop. It doesn't have the right of way. It is coming out of private property.* But the car did not stop. I slammed on the brakes to avoid colliding with the car, but I flew over my bike and the car and slammed down onto the asphalt. I shouted inwardly, *Father, save me!* Then I passed out. I realized I could have died, and God really *was* first in my life. I could have besieged God with hundreds of "Why?" or "Where were You?" questions. After all, I had other exams a few days later, written ones. My hands and my body hurt, and my motorized bike was seriously damaged. Nevertheless, I knew God had been present, and He had permitted the accident for His own reason—He wanted me to realize how important His presence was in my life.

That time He told me His reason in a roundabout way. But even if you do not always know the reasons for difficult situations, keep your confidence in Him. He knows what He is doing. It is one of the absolute certainties I have learned since He became first in my life.

CHRISTIANE TUOR

THE GIFT

He came to what was his own, and his own people did not accept him. But to all who received him, who believed on his name, he gave the power to become children of God. John 1:11, 12, NRSV.

As I look at the world around me I think of the nation that once belonged to God, the nation that prided itself in righteousness—its own. But God in mercy sent it His very best gift, His Son. Yet these people, His people, didn't receive Him.

Now it's a new millennium. Are we still rejecting Him? Do we sit in church and think we are Christians but not really know the Christ, the God of the universe? The majority of earth's inhabitants do not know Christ or His people. Will they all ignore Him too?

But there is hope! There are those who do receive Him. And to those who do receive Him He gives the power, the right, to become daughters of God. I like to think about what this means. To me, believing must include an intellectual belief; but it's more—it must become a vital part of my life, a necessity. It is not a passive faith; it is trust—dependence on God for my very survival.

Oh, Jesus, You are there in our need, in our darkness, in our hopelessness. You came down from Your kingly throne surrounded by light to this dark, desperate world to save us. You came to make us poor puny humans Your own, a part of Your royal family. I cannot comprehend such power, such might, such love, such mercy, such compassion. But how thankful I am, and how I hang on to the wonderful truth of this great gift, especially at this time of year. I cling to each verse in which Your Word explains what it means to receive You and believe on Your name.

Part of me totally feels like this. But sometimes another part of me resists. Is the price of receiving too steep? Will I have to give up too much? Will the cost of following be too painful?

O compassionate One, enable me to see the greater picture. The gift You have given is worth it all. The sacrifice is not too steep or too dear compared with the value of the prize of eternal life—the privilege of getting to know You, the one to whose charms others' cannot be compared, whose character has excelled beyond measure, whose life I long to emulate. You are the one for whom I have been searching. Come into my life right now. CYNTHIA BURRILL

WHY I CAN'T PLAY THE GUITAR

You will seek me and find me when you seek me with all your heart.
Jer. 29:13, NIV.

I've wanted to play the guitar for a long time. Since I was a kid I've wanted to strum the strings and create the chord sounds so that others would enjoy singing with me. One summer at a garage sale I saw a guitar. I bought it for my son, thinking he might like to learn—or, just maybe, I might be able to take some lessons and finally fulfill a dream. I reasoned that it shouldn't be too difficult to learn, since I already knew how to play the piano, the clarinet, and the recorder. Surely the guitar would not be as hard as the piano—look at how many people played one.

I paid the happy woman $3 and went home. Then I discovered the guitar needed repairs not noticeable to my untrained eye. So I had the guitar repaired and purchased new strings, a pick, and some books. I then discovered it wasn't a guitar at all but a baritone ukulele. Because it had only four strings instead of six, I thought it would be easier to learn to play.

Finally I was ready to find a teacher. My first lesson went well. I learned how to hold the instrument and pluck and strum the strings to make two chords, and I found two songs to practice. This was progress. But then I got busy. My teacher got sick. Summer was over, and school started. I had to spend my time teaching teenagers how to write good sentences rather than practicing those two songs.

Then I thought, *Why couldn't I just teach myself?* I bought a how-to book and started. For the next two weeks I practiced a few minutes every evening. By the beginning of the next school year I felt I had progressed enough to play with my students during song service. A new teacher on staff asked if he might use my ukulele. Doubting my own skill, I lent it to him. When we left that school, I let him keep it. That's why I've never learned how to play a guitar.

Why couldn't I learn? I wanted to, but I really only half tried. As with any skill, one must spend time learning the basics.

The same thing is true of our spiritual lives. Many will be lost while hoping to be saved. They have only dabbled at spiritual things. We need to spend quality time with God. Having a regular devotional time each day will help us become like Jesus. It will take a lifetime, but that doesn't matter; we'll be walking into eternity with Jesus at our side. MARILYN GANTZ

ONE OLD CAR AND A PRAYER

The Lord watches over the strangers. Ps. 146:9, NKJV.

I was 9 years old, in the magic years when we still like to walk with parents and respect their wisdom. Mom and I were friends. We loved to walk to the store, to church, to the school gym on a Saturday night for programs. We'd sit on the front porch in the evening.

But Mom was more than a friend, more than a good parent; she was a praying mother. And this impressed me the most. She prayed about almost everything—lost kittens, lost keys, her daughter, her husband's safety, and work. Every problem was a call to prayer. Not that they were all answered as we asked, but we felt better when she prayed.

One Sunday morning Mother and I walked to the grocery store about a mile from our home. We could have driven, but why drive when the day was sunny and it was springtime?

As we entered the parking lot I noticed two teenage girls looking under the hood of an old car. Then one jumped in the car and chugged the starter while the other looked under the hood. Although the engine would start, it would soon die. They exchanged places and tried again . . . and again . . . and again.

We made our purchase of milk, bread, and fruit and started home. The girls were still looking under the hood, trying to start an old car that was too feeble to lift even one eyebrow of hope. Mother noticed. "Weren't they there when we came in?" she asked.

"Yes," I replied.

"Let's pray for them," she said. We paused a moment while Mother asked God to help the two stranded teens. Mother had barely finished her prayer when the car gave a cough, a loud chug, and kept running. The girls whooped and dashed to the open doors, slid in, and drove down the street, never knowing from where their help had come. But a 9-year-old knew.

That day God was special because He cared for strangers. A mother was special because she knew that God would hear her—and He honored her prayer. And a 9-year-old was special because she was a friend of both God and her mother. I have remembered that experience my whole life. Perhaps that is why, when I pass an accident on the freeway, I pray for the people. Or if I read an especially sad story in the newspaper, I pray.   EDNA MAYE GALLINGTON

LESSONS FROM THE BATHROOM SINK

Simon Peter saith unto him, Lord, not my feet only, but also my hands and my head. John 13:9.

It was the kind of morning I am sure many families with young children have experienced. My husband and I seemed to be losing in the struggle to persuade our daughters, aged 10 and 7, to hurry getting ready to go to church.

We had had a good breakfast, and I had prepared most of the noon meal so that when we returned from church the delicious smell of a dinner cooking in the oven would greet us. Our 10-year-old had washed and dressed and was brushing her hair. My husband was straightening his tie and, as usual, I was the last to organize myself so that we could soon leave. Meanwhile, 7-year-old Charlotte was still in her nightdress, contemplating whether to clean her teeth before she dressed, or afterward.

Finally I thought we were all ready and did a final check to ensure that the children had enough things to do to stay occupied and that each had her Bible. Then with horror I realized that Charlotte was still in the bathroom—and we needed to leave immediately in order to arrive at church on time. As I opened the bathroom door I didn't know whether to laugh or cry. Charlotte was standing on the washbasin vanity with one foot in the basin and the other balancing on the side so that she did not end up headfirst in the water!

"What on earth are you doing?" I exclaimed in an irritated tone.

"Why, Mommy," was the reply, "I'm washing my feet before I go to church, just as Jesus did before He went into church."

What could I say? I hurriedly dried her feet, and we managed to get her dressed in her best clothes in record time.

I had a lesson to learn from the youngest member of our family. The familiar story of Jesus washing His disciples' feet at the Last Supper stayed foremost in my thoughts for the greater part of the day.

I need You to wash me, too—not just my feet, but all of me, that I may become one of Your faithful disciples. I pray that Your presence in my life will become a living reality.   JUDITH REDMAN

HAVE SOME CHOCOLATE

You parents—if your children ask for a loaf of bread, do you give them a stone instead? Or if they ask for a fish, do you give them a snake? Matt. 7:9, 10, NLT.

H ave some chocolate," my sister graciously offered.
"Chocolate!" I stared at the slab of chocolate in her hand and saliva started to flow. I stretched out my hand for the chocolate.

"No, no, just take a bite," she urged, thrusting the chocolate into my mouth.

I tried to get as large a piece as possible. But then, what a letdown!

My sister burst out laughing. She has fooled many of her friends with that rubber chocolate.

My husband tells me that someone even manufactures a musical record out of chocolate. You can play it, enjoy its music, then eat it. What a big treat! Many children must have flocked to buy it.

Near the very stores in my country that sell such fun treats are children who have not eaten a square meal for the day. Many times I see half-starved children and adults begging for a coin or a morsel of food. Sometimes it's hard to tell who is a genuinely needy case, because some are professional beggars. Some have even come to my office with documents that brought tears to my eyes. I have given generously only to learn later that I had been fooled.

There are many reasons people end up as beggars—sheer laziness, an easy way to make money, unemployment, sickness, or a lack of medical treatment. Although some no doubt are unworthy of any help, I am guilty many times of giving them a stone, and even a serpent, to eat. I have lectured some about getting work; I even help some just to get rid of them.

What would Jesus do when confronted by these people? They need not only food but music in their lives.

Lord, You have given us an example of love. As I face people with real needs, and even those who may be trying to fool others, give me wisdom and love. I don't want to be guilty of giving a stone or a serpent to someone who needs bread.

BIRDIE PODDAR

FOOD FOR THOUGHT

Cheerfully share your home with those who need a meal or a place to stay for the night. 1 Peter 4:9, TLB.

Many years ago our family was traveling through Lesotho, a small mountain kingdom in southern Africa. We stopped at the mission station, where the pastor and his wife insisted that we have lunch with them. We were reluctant to impose on their kindness, for the people were so poor, and the church and the manse had only the basic facilities. However, our hosts insisted. Their warmth and friendliness made us feel welcome, and we accepted the invitation.

I offered to help, and our hostess graciously asked me to make a beetroot salad. The rest of the meal consisted of small quantities of veggie patties, boiled pumpkin, and a loaf of homemade whole-wheat bread.

I became anxious when there was a knock at the door and the pastor invited three more guests to join us, making 10 people altogether. Our host said grace, thanking the Lord for His blessings and asking Him to multiply the loaves and fishes.

For dessert, the pastor ceremoniously cut a big watermelon. The flesh was a deep pink, sweet and juicy—just what we needed on that hot, sticky day. Our young children enjoyed themselves as the juice ran down their chins, and our hosts invited us to have more and more. We really appreciated the meal.

A simple meal, seasoned with love and offered with warmth and sincerity, will always be appreciated.

Let us not miss an opportunity to share our bounties and blessings. Remember Abraham's hospitality to the strangers. I am truly thankful for the hospitality that has been shown to us, especially as we travel. So many lunches, served with kindness and fellowship! It's not what or how much you have to offer, but the spirit in which you offer it.

Dear Lord, open my heart and home not only to dear friends and loved ones, but also to those who really need a demonstration of true Christian hospitality in a tangible way.

FRANCES CHARLES

ANGELS ON THE HIGHWAY

The angel of the Lord encampeth round about them that fear him, and delivereth them. Ps. 34:7.

We packed the car with luggage, toys, and our lunch. My three children were very excited, because we were going to their grandmother's house for the holidays. After securing the house and checking with our neighbor, we asked God to protect our home and to give us a safe trip. The children were soon fast asleep as we covered many miles on the highway.

Suddenly the car started sputtering and sounding strange. Fear gripped our hearts. What would we do if the car stopped? How much money would it take to have it fixed? How long would we be delayed? All these thoughts raced through our minds as we prayed silently and aloud.

We slowly pulled to the side of the highway. Soon a stranger in a pick-up truck offered his assistance. He suggested we follow him off the highway to a service station where he could check the car. My husband and the stranger decided to leave the car at the service station, and the man would take us to our sister's home, which was one hour away. Somehow we felt safe with him.

Soon we arrived safely at our sister's home. The stranger came inside, where we had prayer to thank God for sending him to help us. After he left, our sister and her husband offered us one of their cars so we could complete our trip to Grandmother's home. God has been so good to our family through the years as we have traveled many miles on dangerous highways. He has sent angels in the form of women and men to assist us when we have had problems on the highway.

What a wonderful God we serve! He has promised to send His angels to protect us from dangers, seen and unseen. Consecrate yourself to Him each day, and He will send mighty angels who excel in strength to protect and help you in your time of need. Truly, "the angel of the Lord encampeth round about them that fear him, and delivereth them."   RUTH F. DAVIS

NOVEMBER 14

THROUGH A WOMAN'S EYES

The Lord searcheth all hearts, and understandeth all the imaginations of the thoughts. 1 Chron. 28:9. As the heavens are higher than the earth, so are my ways higher than your ways, and my thoughts than your thoughts. Isa. 55:9.

Each of us defines, describes, and records her own unique view of the world with every new sunrise and sunset. Through a woman's eyes, each of us sees the world. Many of our experiences can be shared with others only in limited ways. Photos offer one opportunity to share some part of our view of the world.

As I pause for a quiet moment, I am reminded by the autumn colors and fallen leaves of a thousand snapshot memories collected only in the album of my mind. Every daughter, mother, sister, wife, friend—woman—has her own treasured album of memories. These photos are pulled from their special shelf in moments of loneliness, joy, or puzzlement, and occasionally they are shared with friends who care about us. These bittersweet realizations make me sure that God must have His own snapshot memories as well, and I wonder whether we have any duplicates. Would I recognize the event if I could see it from God's perspective?

I am no photographer, but I do have some prize pictures in the memories of my mind. These are of the happy moments and the special people who compose my life. I have my favorites; and I believe God must have His favorites too. His pictures, like mine, probably include special moments in the lives of each of His friends. We are all the apple of His eye; we are each His favorite.

Looking over each other's shoulder as we share photos, we often compare memories of some special event captured by the camera.

If God and I should compare our visual memories of some of our shared events, would we see the same images in the same ways? When He reminds me that my thoughts and ways are not His thoughts and ways, I am reassured by His reminder that His ways are higher than mine. Perspective can make a significant difference, even in my concept of a life event. God knows my thoughts; He captures my experiences for future reference, and one day we will compare memories. I'm eager to see His photo memories.

STELLA THOMPSON

MUDDY FINGERNAILS

God created people in his own image; God patterned them after himself; male and female he created them. Gen 1:27, NLT.

In college I took a class in pottery. (It was required for my degree in occupational therapy.) I wasn't overly interested in modeling clay, but I thought it might be fun. The teacher was a wonderful woman who taught us to appreciate the art and the many possibilities that existed when creating our projects. She frequently stated that we needed to "become one" with the clay when working with it so that the finished product would be an expression of ourselves. I'm not sure how much I "became one" with the clay, but I can say that I dug right in, enough to get pretty dirty in the process.

God's creation of people was as personal as it could be. He knelt in the dirt and, using His hands, touched, molded, and formed us into images of Himself. We are the product of His creativity. What a "hands-on" experience!

Let's imagine Him sitting at a potter's wheel. On the wheel is a large glob of clay. As He begins to turn the wheel, He pours water over the clay and places both hands around it. Muddy water splashes as the wheel spins, covering His hands and forearms. As He works, the glob slowly begins to take the shape of something special, something beautiful. It is not an easy process. From start to finish, the clay has to be pounded, pressed, squeezed, molded, pinched, shaved, and, finally, fired. But when He has completed His work, it is perfect. It, like all artists' work, speaks of the Master's touch.

Unlike human artists, He doesn't stop with the physical creation. In Philippians 1:6 He tells us that not only did He begin the work in us, but He is faithful to complete it. He creates not only our physical form, but our thoughts and feelings as well. Here many of us begin to doubt His ability, His skill. If only we would remember that He made us from the dirt. If He can do that, then we can trust that He can form anew our hearts and minds to perfection. Clay has no choice in what it becomes—we do. Let's decide to give our lives totally to Him so that He can complete the work He has begun in each of us. The Master's touch—God's creation—what an awesome thought.

VALERIE F. JACOBS

THE BROWN COAT

It is more blessed to give than to receive. Acts 20:35. God loveth a cheerful giver. 2 Cor. 9:7.

Giving can bring much pleasure to both the giver and the receiver, and I love doing it—usually. I am sometimes reminded that I still have a little selfish streak that makes me want to hang on to something I have.

It was a coat. A beautiful, full-length, brown fuzzy coat with silky stitches on the cuffs and outlining a diamond-shaped pattern on the back. It was probably the nicest-looking, warmest coat I had ever owned. There was one problem. That beautiful coat had been hanging in the closet for several years without being worn once. For everyday wear in cold weather I had my heavy, waterproof, hooded parka. For church or other dress-up occasions I had a dress coat of newer design. When I read in the local newspaper about the call for coats for the needy, I thought about that brown coat, but somehow I hated to give it up.

My husband read about it too, and remembered the leather jacket he had wanted for so long and had finally bought. It too hung in the coat closet, seldom worn. When he mentioned giving his nice jacket, I knew my coat should also go, so we took them to the collection location. I have to admit that even though it was foolish, I felt a little pang as the coat disappeared down the chute.

It wasn't a winter coat or a leather jacket. It was a robe, woven without a seam. It didn't go into a collection bin. Men cast lots for it. The Owner of the robe had also hesitated to go through with the event that would culminate in the loss not only of His robe but His life. He prayed that the cup might pass from Him, but yielded Himself to follow His Father's plan. On the cross He prayed for those who had put Him there, and He must also have prayed for those who gambled for His robe. I have prayed too that the beautiful brown coat I gave might keep some other woman, young or old, warm during winter's cold blasts.

Giver of all good gifts, help me to find joy in giving; and grant that I may be the kind of giver You love—a cheerful giver. I want the spirit of Jesus, who gave His all for me.
MARY JANE GRAVES

MEANT TO BE BEAUTIFUL.

In the morning, O Lord, you hear my voice; in the morning I lay my requests before you and wait in expectation. Ps. 5:3, NIV.

My time with Jesus is the most beautiful part of my day, not only because of the intimate time I share with my friend Jesus, but also because of my conscious desire and effort to make this a truly heavenly experience.

Adding music to my devotional activities helps me enjoy them more. I am especially careful to use quiet, sacred, instrumental music. This soothing and harmonious music becomes an automatic signal that it is time for worship and assists me in preparing my heart and mind for a special time with my heavenly Father.

I have found it helpful to keep all the things I use for personal devotions in a beautifully decorated "worship basket." I keep colored pens, highlighters, and pretty sticky notes handy. Adding color to my devotional world adds an element of brilliance that is healing to my soul. My worship basket holds my study Bible; my prayer notebook, in which I journal daily; my Bible study guide; and a book for devotional reading. I can sit down and enjoy devotions without the interruption of running through the house to find the things I need.

I try to keep my devotions fresh and interesting by using different books and methods; I need a change or renewal. Over the years I have used different Bible study guides, and even Bible story books, to guide me. I am currently reading the Bible and a book on the life of Christ through in one year. I find this a new and exciting adventure.

Even though all of these elements organize my time and make it easier, it is always an ongoing challenge. It is not automatic. The devil works hard to sidetrack me. He knows that if he can interrupt my devotional life, he can mess up every part of my life.

I do everything I can to make my devotions the highlight of my day. I prepare to meet the Lord at my best.

Heavenly Father, come be my guest. I have prepared and am ready for Your presence. You are my Saviour and my friend. Please join me in this time that was meant to be beautiful.   CARLENE R. WILL

UNSELFISH LOVE

Whatever is in your heart determines what you say. Luke 6:45, NLT.

Have you ever wondered how God works? I have been so amazed that when we follow His prompting we can do just the right thing at the right time. More than once this has happened in my life.

For almost a decade I have been furnishing the Nashville Union Mission with 200 pounds of potatoes every year at Thanksgiving to help feed the hungry and homeless. One day when I arrived and blew my car horn for the chef to come remove the potatoes from the trunk of my car, I said to him, "Here are my usual 200 pounds of potatoes."

He looked at me as if in disbelief and said, "Lady, I just told the manager that with the crowd we have to feed today, I need at least 200 more pounds of potatoes. You are an answer to our immediate need."

It made me happy to know that God had used me, and right on time.

Another time, on a visit to a church, my husband was involved in the service, so he was not sitting with me. I went into the sanctuary and sat down beside a lovely little girl whom I did not know. She was very quiet and reverent but seemed so all alone. Feeling her need, I did what comes naturally for me—I put my arms around her and hugged her close.

Some 20 years later, at a youth meeting, a young woman walked up to me and said, "Do you remember me?"

I had to admit that I did not.

"You may not remember this," she went on, "but when I was 7 years old you sat beside me in church and hugged me, and I still cherish those moments of long ago because you made me feel so special!"

Again I felt so happy to have been able to serve God at just the right time and in the right way. Ministry comes in many forms, but it is always the result of listening to Him as He puts the ideas into our hearts.

Lord, today and every day help us to live so close to You that, hearing Your voice, we may feel special in Your embracing love and share it with others.

ETTA MAYCOCK DUDLEY

BURNED PUMPKIN

The good that I would I do not: but the evil which I would not, that I do. Now if I do that I would not, it is no more I that do it, but sin that dwelleth in me. Rom. 7:19, 20.

W hat's that smell?" my husband asked as we stood up from our knees after worship.

"It's the pumpkin!" I exclaimed, and ran to the kitchen. While I was preparing the pumpkin for my grandson's meal, I thought, *I must watch this and not let it burn.* Then we went to have worship, and it happened—the pumpkin burned!

This has happened every so often over the years. I put pumpkin on to cook and forget about it. I get distracted. The phone rings or someone calls at the door. Once I went grocery shopping, forgetting I had put some pumpkin on. Just imagine how the house smelled, not to mention the cleaning up!

Cooking pumpkin reminds me of other good intentions. I've put on so much weight over the holiday season. I think, *I'll start slimming down from day one of the new year.* I don't. *I'm going to invite some new members over for lunch,* I decide. I procrastinate. *I'm going to take more time for Bible study.* Then so many other appointments crowd the hours. *I'm going to keep a cool head when someone irritates me.* And so the list goes on. No sooner have I promised myself to carry out good intentions than I've failed again, as I did with the burned pumpkin.

"I don't do the good I want to do; instead, I do the evil that I do not want to do. If I do what I don't want to do, this means that I am no longer the one who does it; instead, it is the sin that lives in me" (Rom. 7:19, 20, TEV).

Satan is a cunning fellow. He tries to distract our thought and attention. He tries to get us to repeat our sins and past mistakes again and again. I find myself back at square one. It's like a game Satan is playing with me.

Today I have another chance, a new opportunity. Thank You, God, for Your help. I will try to not repeat my mistakes, but to live victoriously for You. "Through God we shall do valiantly" (Ps. 60:12).   PRISCILLA ADONIS

LION TAMER

Strengthen the feeble hands, steady the knees that give way; say to those with fearful hearts, "Be strong, do not fear." Isa. 35:3, 4, NIV.

On the day my grandmother came home from the hospital she sat at the kitchen table and made a cherry pie. She'd had a nine-hour surgery and a long recovery. On the day she was released, her surgeon told her, "You can go home and go to bed, or you can go home and live." She was 71, and she planned to live.

I can still see her sitting there, measuring the flour and cutting in the shortening with two knives. She rested after each motion, but she did it.

"There's a lion in the way," she often paraphrased Proverbs 22:13. "I will be slain in the streets!" Regaining her full, useful life after facing death was a lion to meet and conquer. She determined it would not win.

I've often stood behind a closed door, afraid to face the lion I imagined roaming the streets. Have you? Small lions, and larger ones. The little tasks you dread—cleaning out the clutter, figuring your taxes. The job you want but are afraid to apply for. The leadership position you're afraid to take. The doctor's appointment you're afraid to make. The courage to end a hurtful relationship and put yourself first for a change.

While you can thank God for healthy caution, fear is paralyzing and a tool of the devil. Again and again the Bible tells us to "Steady the knees that give way. . . . 'Be strong, do not fear'" (Isa. 35:3, 4, NIV). "Be strong and of good courage; do not be afraid" (Joshua 1:9, NKJV).

It's not easy to be brave. It's easier to hide inside our safe little houses, keeping the lions of uncertainty at bay. It's easier to complain than to go forward in trust and praise. It's easier to close my eyes and hope the lions will go away.

I'm not always strong, yet I long to be strong and courageous, grabbing hold of God and with His help facing the things that make me afraid. And so I remember my precious stubborn grandmother, who came home from the hospital, sat down at the table, and with trembling hands made a cherry pie.

PENNY ESTES WHEELER

THE SURPRISE PACKAGE

The Lord is good to all: and his tender mercies are over all his works. Ps. 145:9.

This morning I received a surprise package from my Father. I don't know what is in it, but I am excited about it and eager to open it. I receive the gifts regularly. You see, every day is a surprise package wrapped in star-studded blackness and tied with moonbeams, or maybe wrapped in cloudy darkness with tiny rivulets running down the sides.

Before I open it, I will kneel and thank Him for the loving care with which He chose the contents of my package for this day. Knowing me the way He does, He includes things to help me learn the lessons I need to learn. With great love He puts my package together and sends it to me each morning.

There are big things that I expect—such as my job, the housework, and the daily chores. Then there are little things that are like hugs and kisses from my Father. After a little storm there shines a beautiful rainbow; a butterfly lights on my windshield as I wait for a traffic light to change; a deer crosses the road ahead of my car.

My Father puts in some things as teaching aids to help me learn patience, forgiveness, sympathy, and understanding so I can better represent Him, or maybe help someone else to use the contents of her package.

I've been getting these surprise packages all my life, but I didn't always understand what some of the contents were for. I enjoyed the good things, but I thought the teaching aids were punishment, so I got defensive and wouldn't learn the lessons. I hadn't learned to check the instruction book that came in one of the early packages, or how to use the hot line to talk to my Father about them.

I am ashamed to admit that for a while I didn't realize who the Giver was. I just expected the package and felt no responsibility for the use of the contents. I am now beginning to understand the value of the gifts.

Dear kind, loving Father, thank You for today and for all the things You have planned for me. Give me the wisdom to make the right use of these gifts, the love to share with others, and the humility to be teachable. Thank You.

DENALI FOX

THAT PEACEFUL FEELING

This is the day the Lord has made. We will rejoice and be glad in it. Ps. 118:24, TLB.

Late on Thanksgiving night I was jolted awake by a blast of Santa Ana wind as it barreled down the canyon, hitting our house with such force that it threatened to shake it off its foundation. It tore shingles from the roof, slammed debris into the north wall, and rattled the windows until we were sure they would explode. The commotion outside was deafening and more than a little scary.

But in spite of the raging windstorm outside, inside the house was warm and comfortable. The aroma of roast and pumpkin pie from the day's feast still hung in the air, and the flickering light of a dying fire illuminated our bedroom wall through the open doorway. I lay there awhile, listening to the gentle breathing of my husband between the cries of the wind.

Unable to sleep, I slipped out of bed to check on our slumbering household. Our son and daughter-in-law were asleep on the big air mattress in front of the fire, their two toddlers nestled beside them. I tucked the blankets tightly around them, just as I did when our son was a child. Then I wandered into our teenage daughter's room, where she and her cousin—who was also her best friend—were snug beneath the comforter with only the tops of their heads visible. I then checked our friend, asleep on the couch, his quilt-shrouded form outlined by the fading light from the fireplace. And finally, I made sure that our cat and dogs were protected from the wind.

Shivering, I slipped back into bed, pulled the covers tightly around me, and cuddled up to my husband for warmth. And as I lay bundled against the wind and the cold, I realized that for this moment everyone closest to my heart was under our roof. They had full tummies and were warm and secure. And while the wind howled outside, at least for this night my family was safe inside.

Lord, I praise You for giving me the wisdom to appreciate and enjoy the simple pleasure of having all my family together. Although I rushed and planned to make everything perfect for the weekend, the true blessing came from just enjoying every moment we were able to spend together. Thank You for each of Your blessings.

TERRI CASEY

GOD'S AFFIRMATION BEFORE THE VALLEY

It shall come to pass that before they call, I will answer; and while they are still speaking, I will hear. Isa. 65:24, NKJV.

Family reunions. What pleasant memories that word brings! It was the best Thanksgiving family reunion we had had in several years. The weather was perfect—cool but not cold, and sunny. As we gathered around the table, we had much to be thankful for. We were all together. We all felt so connected and close. Throughout Thanksgiving Day the children and adults could be seen chatting with each other. Frequently they sought out the patriarch of the family, Grandad—my dad. One grandchild in particular was doing family history research, and Grandad was enjoying sharing the family history.

One of our family traditions is a praise and thanksgiving service. Led by Grandad and Granny, each person shared what he or she was thankful for. Friday each family was responsible for contributing to the family talent program. Grandad recited a poem, the perennial family favorite, "It Couldn't Be Done," by Edgar A. Guest. Dad was marvelous. We all left for our own homes after breakfast and prayer in the parking lot of a local restaurant on Sunday morning. It was a great family reunion.

Who would have believed that just two weeks later we would gather again, this time for a funeral? The patriarch of our family had died. My first reaction, of course, was Why? After such a wonderful time together, why did Dad die? As the year progressed I began to recognize that our all knowing Father-God had provided us with pleasant memories to help us endure the difficult months ahead. God had affirmed us with a mountaintop experience before the tragedy.

Since then I have noticed that God often sends an affirmation, a mountaintop experience, before a valley. Often I complain about the valley, never recognizing God's affirmation that comes through the mountaintop experiences. Our God sends His affirming power when He knows we need it. Sometimes even before we ask. The mountaintop experiences support and encourage us as we walk through the valley. Praise God! What a caring God we serve.

EDITH C. FRASER

YES, HE DOES PROVIDE

Abraham answered, "God himself will provide the lamb for the burnt offering, my son." And the two of them went on together. Gen. 22:8, NIV.

As I opened my office door at Gambia College one morning in 1996, the old janitor greeted me with a smile and gave me a bag containing four large mangoes. He had been very close to me since I started lecturing there in 1994. Although the younger janitor had refused to help at all, 70-year-old Pa Bojang willingly made sure he cleaned my office every day. Even though I was not obliged to do so, I tried to give him tips at times.

I was so moved by the gift that my eyes filled, and I had to hide a tear. He stood with a genuine smile, and although I could not communicate much in his local language, I did say, *"Abaraka bakeh,"* meaning "Thank you very much." I was impressed, for Pa Bojang was the first Gambian who tried to give me something. Even though he was very poor, he tried to show love and a kind of appreciation that he later explained through an interpreter.

Though I had a mango tree at my house, I saw the gift as his "widow's mite" (Luke 21:2-4). I was eager to show them to my family. But near my house I saw two brothers passing by, so I gave them my special mangoes. They were so happy that one of them asked me whether I really meant to give them away. I nodded. Then he said, "This is an answer to our prayer that God should provide for us today, as we live a day at a time." They thanked me and left with joy. Once again, I had to wipe away a tear.

Before I entered my house I found another bag with 12 mangoes sitting near my door. My watchman then told me that a man had said, "The bag is for madam." Truly, God is so close to us, and He provides at the right time to all. We simply have to trust Him and claim His promises. The Good Book says He will, if we take Him at His word. I had given my mangoes away to the needy and within minutes I got more than double what I gave away. Really, He does provide.

I gave a few to the watchman. He beamed and said, "God bless you, ma'am. I have been starving all day." For the third time that day a tear dropped.

Thank You for how You provide for each of us. Help me to do my part in the process.
MARBEL KWEI

THAT WHISTLE IN THE NIGHT

When you walk, they will guide you; when you sleep, they will watch over you. Prov. 6:22, NIV.

Pitch blackness filled the room. I wasn't sure whether I was awake or asleep, but I was sure I heard a whistle. Yes. There it was again. Was someone in trouble? Was it the guard trying to stop a thief? Or a terrorist?

I heard it again. Getting closer. I lay perfectly still, listening. Then *tap, tap, tap*. It too came closer. Then quiet. No one in the house moved. Even Matt, the host's golden retriever, slept. When I had gotten up several hours earlier I had opened the windows, so I knew they had iron bars; I decided I was safe, at least for now. With that, I turned over and slept again.

I had arrived in southern India the previous afternoon. I had not been to bed for two days, two days full of stress. Changing planes. Meeting someone in Frankfurt. Crossing between airports in Bombay in the middle of the night by myself. Sitting in an airport for eight hours with hundreds of strangers and millions of mosquitoes. So when I arrived at my destination I had showered and flopped into bed. I wasn't interested in eating or even calling my husband. But now there was that whistle. I had no idea what time it was or what the whistle meant, but I knew Someone guarded the night and I had nothing to worry about. In the nights that followed, whenever jet lag awoke me I would lie still, listening for the night watch on his rounds.

Outside my snug little world, things are not nearly so peaceful. Crime increases. Injustice prevails. People suffer and hurt. Women fear abusive family members, strangers, poverty, crime, ill health, burnout, inequality. Who is going to help them? Is anyone on guard? Is anyone keeping watch through the night of fear?

Darkness, deep and oppressing, fills our world. Is there any hope? Is anyone on guard? Is there anyone to warn of approaching danger?

Forever Friend, guard of the night, help me to be a sentinel to the world around me. Help me blow the whistle and tap out hope for those who suffer, for those who don't know of Your loving care and soon coming. Help me to make even this a safer world for those around me. ARDIS DICK STENBAKKEN

THIS IS NOT MY HOME

I am going to prepare a place for you. . . . I will come back and take you to myself, so that you will be where I am. John 14:2, 3, JEV.

S he stood at the front door with a small knapsack on her back, resolved to leave. Earlier that morning she had selectively packed her small bag: a favorite doll, a pink nightdress to match the one that her doll was wearing, a book, a pair of slippers, and some play clothes. Nothing that we said could deter her; her mind was made up.

"I am not living in this house anymore. I'm a girl; I'm not a boy."

Our 4-year-old daughter was leaving home to find lodging in the girls' dormitory. She had decided she could no longer stay with us in the small apartment in the boys' dormitory, where her father was the dean of men. She was going to a better place—a special place for girls.

I was unsuccessful in my attempt to change her mind, so I called the dean of women and asked her to allow my daughter to stay with her until she had calmed down. We both mused over the interesting situation, but there was an object lesson that we both learned that day from an adamant 4-year-old.

So often the mundane affairs of life occupy first place in our lives, and we forget that this is not our permanent home. We forget that we are here merely to perfect our characters for a place that our heavenly Father has gone to prepare for us. Are we too comfortable here on earth? What does going home to heaven mean to us? Are we complacently forgetting that this is not our home?

If we could see a glimpse of heaven, I am sure we would not want to remain here. This world, in spite of all its beauty, is a dark, cold place. We cannot be comfortable here; we are just passing through.

Just as our daughter was determined to go to a place she thought would more closely meet her needs, God has prepared a place specifically for us. Our every need will be met. So why do we want to remain here? We need to keep our eyes on our goal.

Lord, help us not to be spiritually comfortable here, because this place is not our home. Help us to make ourselves ready for the home that You have gone to prepare for us.

GLORIA GREGORY

AUTUMN LEAVES AND WINTER STORMS

We all do fade as a leaf; and our iniquities, like the wind, have taken us away. Isa. 64:6.

Winter came upon us in all its fury—a cold and snowy blast, the first of the season, with all the markings of an unwelcome guest who refuses to leave. I watched from my frosted window as the white blanket descended like a shroud over the landscape, threatening to envelop everything in its path. Swirling waves of fresh-driven snow soon formed high drifts in corners and hedgerows, and before long the nearby road and the neighboring fields and lawns had blended into one.

As I stood by my window, listening to the wind and enjoying the beauty, my eyes were drawn to a cluster of brown leaves dangling tenaciously to one of the lower branches of a large maple tree in my front yard. It had discarded its unsightly dress weeks before, but now these dozen or more stragglers huddled together stubbornly, hanging on for dear life, trying to avoid the inevitable. Even after most of their neighbors had given up many winds before, these few remaining leaves had refused to give in to the varied storms, winds, rains, and batterings.

Now the full-blown storm threatened to snatch each survivor from its resting place, but I could tell by their apparent endurance that they could very well win the battle. As I watched those struggling leaves, now dried and brittle with age, I had to wonder what had kept them hanging there all this time. Was it that they were sheltered somewhat by the south side of the house? Or perhaps they were stronger from the beginning than all the rest.

How like those leaves we humans are. I'm sure I've had no more and no fewer personal or family crises than most people. I've lost family members to death and had a few disappointments in my lifetime, but I also have been very blessed.

As I think about those wrinkled brown leaves I gain strength from their persistence. I determine to be faithful, to be loyal to my God, to cling to Him each day. I determine too, through His strength, to help others do the same.

The storm is now past and the sun is shining again. As I take one last look out the window, I see that each leaf is still hanging on.

Lord, help me to do the same.   CLAREEN COLCLESSER

WELCOME HOME, CHILDREN

How great is the love the Father has lavished on us, that we should be called children of God! 1 John 3:1, NIV.

The Christmas season was approaching, the first since our move to a country log house in the hills of middle Tennessee. I was eager to put up the tree, decorate, and cook for Christmas, but we wanted family to come and share the holiday warmth and love with us.

"Is there any way you can come for Christmas?" I pleaded with our closest children, who lived in Virginia. "Even if it's just for a few days?"

Soon the answer came. "Yes, we'll come!"

The house began to take on a new appearance with green boughs, a tree adorned with red poinsettias and white crocheted angels, and candles of love and welcome at each window. Pies, cakes, and cookies began to take shape in the kitchen. Anticipation was high.

A day or two before Christmas the temperature dropped, and rain brought a world of ice to cover the landscape. Icicles hung from trees, while roads and parking lots became skating rinks.

"Stay on the well-traveled highways," we cautioned. "You probably won't have trouble until you get on the smaller roads near home."

As night fell my husband and I watched and waited. All possible outdoor lights were on, and each window candle flickered its welcoming beam across the icy landscape. Late in the evening we saw the flicker of a flashlight across the field. We heard voices and footsteps crunching across the frozen turf. Could it be? Yes! With little ones carried high on their shoulders, they walked the last mile home and were gathered into our outstretched arms.

"Welcome home, children! Welcome home!" we exclaimed. What joy, excitement, and thanksgiving!

God the Father wants His children home for eternity. He is lonesome. He is preparing a mansion and a feast for us. The angels want to welcome us. God Himself is waiting with outstretched arms. Our Father wants us home.

The road we travel is not always easy. But the lights from the windows of our waiting mansions will guide us to the warmth of our Father's embrace as He reaches out to us with the words "Welcome home, children! Welcome home!" What a reunion! It is worth everything!

JOAN MINCHIN NEALL

LIFT HIM UP

Just as Moses lifted up the snake in the desert, so the Son of Man must be lifted up, that everyone who believes in him may have eternal life. John 3:14, 15, NIV.

I was taking Maryann home after her sister's funeral. We had spoken briefly about her grief and sadness over the loss of her sister. Then we fell silent, the only sounds the hum of the car's engine and the click of the tires on the seams in the pavement.

Maryann suddenly turned to me and asked, "Do you believe in God?" I answered affirmatively and she smiled. "Good," she said, "because I want to tell you a story."

When she was barely more than a teenager, she found herself with two toddlers in a very unhappy marriage. She described her husband's drinking and abusive behavior and her own fall into alcoholism. One evening Maryann's husband failed to return home from work. She soon found out that he was involved with another woman.

Maryann decided then to take her life, and found a bottle of sleeping pills. She swallowed several pills, washing them down with alcohol. As she began to take a second handful of pills she heard a voice. Twenty-five years later she can still remember the exact words: "Stop, Maryann, stop. I am not finished with you yet." She described how the hairs on her arms stood up as she was startled by the sound of that voice. Then the voice came again: "Maryann, I am not finished with you yet." A peace filled her heart, and she felt the fog of alcohol and sleeping pills lift from her mind as she became aware of God's presence. Her thoughts of suicide were gone as she called for help.

Maryann's life was forever changed by the voice in her darkest hour. She entered an alcohol rehabilitation program and made major changes in her life. She began a relationship with her Creator-God. Things haven't always been easy. Maryann has had many challenges to face in the years since that night. But her belief in her heavenly Father's love has always sustained her. How beautifully Maryann lifted Him up as she told her story.

Lord, please give me the courage to lift You up today in my words and actions so that I might bless another the way I was blessed by Maryann's story.

SANDRA SIMANTON

A LIFE OF PRAISE

I will sing to the Lord all my life; I will sing praise to my God as long as I live. Ps. 104:33, NIV.

In my younger years I listened to country/western and pop music all the time. I'm the type of person who likes to have music playing all the time—radio, CD, cassette tape. So my mind was being filled with all kinds of secular thoughts. Popular music of the day kept my mind on myself. It's very self-centered music and often appealed to my self-pity, definitely affecting my moods.

Remember the sixties, when the songs' words had double meanings? You really liked a song, but discovered it was talking about some drug. One day a song made me think about what I was listening to. I decided to change the station to a Christian one. (I'm sure the Lord thought, *Finally!*)

At first listening to Christian music was fine, but I didn't know the songs as I did those on the pop station, so I couldn't sing along. After a while I would turn back to the old music. But the Lord was working on my heart. Each day I listened less and less to the secular station and stayed longer with the sacred. I found that my day went much better and I was much happier.

It took me a few years to realize there is a difference between songs to God and songs about God. For years I sang and listened to songs about God—about another person's experience with God. These songs aren't bad; they have their place in a Christian's walk. But when I found songs that speak directly to God, songs that give God all the glory and praise that He alone is due, I really received a blessing from singing and listening to them. Now the majority of the time I choose these scripture/praise songs.

The Bible is full of praise to God. What a blessing that God has preserved His Word down through the ages to encourage, guide, and challenge me in my walk with Him. And what a blessing that He gave music writers the talent to put the Scriptures to music. I am so thankful for them and the vocal artists for using their talents for the Lord. All scripture is easier for me to memorize when put to music, making it a double blessing in word and song.

"May my thoughts please Him; I am happy in the Lord" (Ps. 104:34, NCV).

LOUISE M. DRIVER

THE MOOSE

Every creature of God is good. 1 Tim. 4:4, NKJV.

Driving home one day, I looked across the field and saw a large bull moose strolling through the tall grass. Large antlers crowned his head. He looked majestic. I stopped and watched him; he didn't seem to have any concern about anyone watching him. To avoid other traffic, I drove ahead to a spot where I was out of the way of other cars. As I sat there, he continued on his way, but suddenly he saw me and began to run the last little way into the woods.

In the past few years moose have become quite numerous in our area. It is exciting to see them as they walk near our buildings and through our fields. They have come into our pasture and fed with the cattle during the winter months. They seem to know no fear until they see us coming near them, then they run for cover.

Signs along the roads read "Moose Crossing," and drivers of the vehicles traveling in those areas are watchful. Unfortunately, the drivers are not always able to see the moose approach the road in time to stop, and the animals are sometimes hit by vehicles. The drivers almost always are injured in these situations, and the moose die. A gas transport truck hit and killed a baby moose near our house. As my husband went to the accident site to help, he noticed the mother back in some trees looking out at her baby. It touched his heart to see the mother mourning for her little one. The mother moose loved her baby, but was afraid to go to it because of the people present.

God has created His animals with an instinct for nurturing their young. They care for them and will protect them with their own life if necessary. A mother animal will attack anyone or any animal that threatens her young.

God has given us His book of nature to instruct us and teach us. Every creature He has created is good and for our enjoyment. Like the moose, we can enjoy life when our surroundings are safe, and we must seek shelter when things threaten our safety.

God, help us to have tender hearts and to express this tenderness when Your creatures are hurting. Help us to love all people and to care for Your creatures in the wild, showing that we are always learning from Your book of nature and from Your Holy Word. EVELYN GLASS

A SILENT WITNESS

We have become a spectacle to the world, to angels and to mortals.
1 Cor. 4:9, NRSV.

These days we don't hear or read much about the importance of our example, our "witness." When I was growing up and wanted to attend the cinema to see *Anne of Green Gables,* a most innocent film, my mother refused permission.

"I know you've read the book, and I'm sure that seeing the film would not hurt you, Gold," she said earnestly. "But it's your influence. Some of your church friends might see you there and think that if it's all right for you to attend the cinema, then it's OK for them. But they wouldn't stop to think that you attend only good shows; they would take it as a cover-all license."

I got the point. I didn't go to the cinema.

When my own children wanted to step into gray areas, I used a similar argument, and the longer I live the more convinced I am that "we are the only Bible the careless world may read."

Yesterday a small item appeared on the front page of Australia's most widely read newspaper. It told of two large Fijian men, visitors to our country, seen carrying their trays of hamburger and fries to a table in McDonald's. They sat down, but before they took a mouthful, they bowed their heads and asked God's blessing on their food. It was such an unusual gesture in that noisy, bustling atmosphere that another customer noticed and was so impressed by their action that he told a news reporter.

That small act, one that every Christian should perform in similar circumstances (but not many do), has borne witness to millions of people. Not only has the news report gone to every corner of our land, it will be carried as far afield as the newspaper travels worldwide.

The people who read will react in different ways. Some will laugh. Some will sneer. Some will remember what they also were taught.

Little did those humble Christian men giving thanks to God for His daily mercies realize that their silent witness might become a mighty roar.

GOLDIE DOWN

WHAT DID YOU HEAR ME SAY?

The time will come when they will not endure sound doctrine; but wanting to have their ears tickled, they will accumulate for themselves teachers in accordance to their own desires, and will turn away their ears from the truth and will turn aside to myths. 2 Tim. 4:3, 4, NASB.

Have you thought much about hearing and listening? I have always enjoyed the process of listening. I learn most easily by listening to someone speak. My favorite form of listening has been to come home after a hard day at work and relax by listening to classical music. Because I like to be around people, I also like to listen to others and then exchange ideas. It was a pleasure for me to spend most of my career as a speech and hearing specialist. One of the most important questions I would ask the children was "What did you hear me say?"

My husband wears hearing aids in both ears. I have watched how carefully he cleans his ears each day. He thoroughly inspects his hearing aids to see that they are clean and working properly. He always carries a spare battery in his wallet in case one of the batteries fails while we are away from home. Being able to hear accurately what others say to him is extremely important.

I loved to play a game with my grandchildren—I caught them in my arms, told them that I had them in my power, and then blew softly into their ears. Then I would say, "Now you have to follow me everywhere." They would giggle and try to get away from me because I had tickled them in their ear. Now that they are 7 and 9, they try to do the same thing to me. I don't mind at all, because they like to play the game as much as I do and I get a giggle and a hug out of the whole process.

Our ears never seem to lose their sensitivity, and I am sure that the good Lord had this in mind when He prompted Timothy to write today's text about having our ears tickled. Romans 10:17 says, "Faith comes from hearing, and hearing by the word of Christ" (NASB).

We can ask God to keep our ears from being tickled by ideas that are not consistent with His Word and know that He will honor this request. My daily prayer is that I will keep my ears open so that when He calls my name, I will be able to hear Him.   SHEILA SANDERS DELANEY

WHITER THAN SNOW

I counsel you to buy from me gold refined in the fire, so you can become rich; and white clothes to wear, so you can cover your shameful nakedness; and salve to put on your eyes, so you can see. Rev. 3:18, NIV.

We awoke this morning to a world wrapped in a soft blanket of white snow. The woods behind our house were transformed overnight from a tangle of nude branches into a wonderland of spotless white. As we slept, millions of snowflakes silently did their job. The evergreen by my window is now a perfect glistening Christmas tree, naturally adorned in white.

I'm reminded of the robe of righteousness God has offered to me—Christ's purity and goodness covering the tangle of life. Somehow I've been waiting for the transformation to begin inside. Today I see that God wants to envelop me in a transforming blanket of love. If I am cold, I can wrap myself in a down comforter and soon be warm from the outside inward. If I'm wrapped in His love, purity, and joy, soon I'll participate in that love, purity, and joy.

God has been in the covering business for a long time. When Adam and Eve distrusted His instructions and set up the first do-it-yourself business, God gently covered His erring children. I can feel the sadness of having to wear that covering at the gates of Paradise. David sang of the blessedness of the one "whose transgressions are forgiven, whose sins are covered" (Ps. 32:1, NIV). No longer do the piles of leaves and twigs at the edge of my woods show under this blanket of white. By spring they will be well on their way to becoming dark, rich soil. Undercover transformation! *Not only of my leaf piles, Lord, but of me, too!*

A favorite psalm provides a further glimpse of God's tender covering: "He will cover you with his feathers, and under his wings you will find refuge" (Ps. 91:4, NIV). Last spring we watched a mother nighthawk raise her babies in a nest only a few feet from a busy campus sidewalk. Alert to any movement near her, she stretched her wings to cover two balls of fluff. A similar promise, given to God's people through the prophet Isaiah, reads, "I have . . . covered you with the shadow of my hand" (Isa. 51:16, NIV).

Cover me with Your white robe of love, forgiveness, and rightdoing!

NANCY JEAN VYHMEISTER

DELAYED APPRECIATION

What I want from you is your true thanks; I want your promises fulfilled.
Ps. 50:14, TEB.

My husband and I went to Europe about 25 years ago to attend a major church conference in Austria. During our travel we visited several countries. In England we stopped to visit friends and explore the country-side. Sight-seeing in London one day, we paused at a large flea market to do some shopping. I bought a beautiful lilac comforter set I was sure my daughter would like. Because I was sure she would like it, it didn't matter that the package was extremely cumbersome or that our trip was not yet over. Nor did it matter that I would have to carry the gift from train station to train station until we began our return flight at Heathrow Airport.

Two weeks later we deplaned in Toronto, laden with souvenirs and gifts, including the lilac comforter. Eagerly we handed out the presents we had bought along the way. Everyone was appreciative. Or so it seemed. I noticed, however, that my daughter did not appear as excited as I had expected. She said all the right words, but something was missing. When I visited her home, the comforter set never adorned her bed. Like Mary in the Bible, I pondered these things in my heart.

Then during one of her weekly calls my daughter bemoaned the cold temperatures, a herald of the impending wintry blasts. "Mom, I could never make it through these cold nights without that comforter you brought years ago." The long-awaited words of appreciation thrilled my ears. *At last,* I thought to myself, *she has finally realized its value and warmth.*

During my early-morning walk the next day I wondered, *How much appreciation have I shown for the priceless Gift that I was given almost 2,000 years ago?* I realized anew that my heavenly Father has waited—and continues to wait—for me to show my appreciation in actions. Words are not enough.

Father, let me not wait a second longer to show You by the way I live how much I appreciate the gift of Your redeeming love. But please accept any words of appreciation also that I offer this day. CAROL JOY GREENE

THE SPIRIT OF CHRISTMAS

Thou shalt call his name Jesus: for he shall save his people from their sins. Matt. 1:21.

It always seems that Christmas comes right after Labor Day. This is reinforced by Christmas decorations appearing about Halloween. I hate the commercialism that's rampant on all sides, associating Christmas with overdoing in everything—eating, spending, working on gifts, decorating. And it's hard for me to get the "Christmas spirit" when it is sunny and warm outside.

What is Christmas all about, anyway? I mused. Gifts did not bring soul satisfaction, although I loved being able to give. Many organizations were collecting toys for children, and I wanted to contribute to all of them but didn't feel that we could financially. I did not feel we had the funds to satisfy anyone else's wishes or needs. Still, I wanted to give God something.

As the Christmas season approached, even the Christmas carols, songs, and movies on TV could not excite me. Gil wanted to see the "Bethlehem Marketplace" presented by a local church. I didn't really want to go, but we did, and the three-hour wait was worth it. After we were shepherded through the marketplace by someone named Rebecca, a fictitious employee of Nicodemus, we arrived at the stable where Mary and Joseph cradled Jesus. I noticed the loving way they held and stroked His tiny head. Then Messala, a hardened Roman soldier, came into the stable and knelt before the crèche, singing about the surrender of his heart. Tears stung my eyes at the realization that Jesus really had come to earth as a tiny baby and had died for me. I had begun to appreciate His loving sacrifice on an intellectual level, but after a lifetime of family abuse, it took a while to sink into the heart, to appreciate it emotionally.

But what can I give God? I wondered. Suddenly it came: all those past grudges, disappointments, and hurts—everything that stood in the way of the joy in the salvation He provided. I had not really given Him my heart and had withheld the surrender of my past hurts. Is He not touched with the feelings of our infirmities? Whatever is done to us is also done to Him!

When I got home I started a list, noting everything bad that I could remember having happened to me. Then I gave it to Him to take care of. Each time I reacted to one of those old memories, I reminded myself that I had given them to Him. Peace on earth had truly come.

JOYCE WILLES BROWN-CARPER

TRUST AND OBEY

Children, obey your parents in all things, for this is well pleasing to the Lord. Col. 3:20, NKJV.

As we become mothers and grandmothers, past experiences flood our memories. Every so often I think back to my childhood. On a cold, crisp, winter day in Minnesota, when I was just a little girl, my older brothers and sisters were all in school. Too young to go yet, I was home with Mother. I wanted to go outside and play. In fact, I desperately wanted to take my big brothers' new sled and go sliding in the park nearby. I finally got up the courage to ask if I could go. For many reasons, which I clearly understood later, the answer was "No."

I yielded to temptation and took the sled off the back porch anyway and trudged the block or so to the park. I still remember how the snow crackled under my snowshoed feet. It was cold, and by the time I arrived at the park, I wished I were home, where I could get warm.

The sled was heavier than I'd thought, especially for my size. I climbed to the top of the first hill and got on the sled. It took off downhill like a whiz. I hadn't realized I wouldn't be able to steer it or stop it like my brothers could. The next thing I knew I was lying in the snow, hurting all over. What had happened? Finally I figured out that the sled had hit a tree, throwing me off like a rag doll. My face was scratched raw and bleeding. I could barely get up to struggle home.

When I reached the backyard, my mother was out looking for me. She could tell the whole story by looking at my bloody, tear-streaked face. I could tell she was so disappointed in the fact that I had disobeyed her. She didn't scold, but gave me a loving embrace and loving attention to my cuts and bruises. She knew I had learned my lesson, and punishment had already been meted out.

This childhood memory reminds me of how our heavenly Father loves us, even though we fail to obey Him at times. He accepts us back without chiding. He loves us and forgives us. What an example!

Help me remember, heavenly Parent, that You are most pleased when we obey, just as our parents are. But You always love us, just as my mother did. I thank You.

ARLENE E. COMPTON

A TIN OF BAKED BEANS

He will fulfil the desire of them that fear him: he also will hear their cry, and will save them. Ps. 145:19.

It was not the irrational craving of pregnancy. It was more the result of deprivation of the commonplace grocery items that we all take for granted. It had crystallized into a desire for the taste of baked beans, preferably of the Heinz variety.

I normally do not have great longings for particular kinds of food, but since the two government coups in Fiji, other governments had placed embargoes on supplying goods to the country. Staples such as potatoes and even onions, which vegetarians find almost essential to their cooking, were unobtainable, as were canned goods and a list of products that would fill a book.

Speaking of books, I felt qualified to publish one on *101 Creative Sweet Potato Dishes,* as well as another entitled *1,001 Rice and Lentil Dishes (Without Onions).* It was a bit of a joke, with a bit of hysteria in the laughter.

About this time my mind, ably supported by the memory of my taste buds, fixated on baked beans. Rational thought inevitably gave way to imaginings about baked beans, and I proclaimed that when we returned to Australia for Christmas, I would buy a tin of the delectable food and eat it with a spoon straight from the can. (My mother would have been horrified by such unladylike behavior.)

How can I possibly explain the excitement, the exhilaration, of walking down the aisles of a supermarket that Christmas and viewing the extravaganza of foods on display? My impulse was to fill two or three shopping trolleys with goodies, old favorites and new products, just for the sheer joy of participating in the abundance. The amazing thing is that those baked beans paled into insignificance among so many other luscious food choices.

I have an idea that is the way it is going to be when Jesus comes and takes us to heaven. Today's desires will be as peanuts—no, baked beans—when we see what He has prepared for us, for He will more than fulfill our desires. "Eye hath not seen, nor ear heard, . . . the things which God hath prepared for them that love him" (1 Cor. 2:9).   URSULA M. HEDGES

WHEN LITTLE THINGS ARE TOO BIG

Lay up for yourselves treasure in heaven, . . . for where your treasure is, there will your heart be also. Matt. 6:20, 21.

I looked out the window and frowned. A blanket of snow covered our city—a very large and thick blanket. Children loved it, travelers hated it, and teachers endured it. I fell into the last category. Looking over my class of kindergartners coming in from the playground, I smiled with mixed feelings. The grins on their faces reflected the wonderful playtime at recess. That was good. However, the snow on their coats, mittens, and boots, already beginning to melt, would soon turn the classroom into a mini-mess. That was not good.

At the bottom of the stairs I noticed Michael, small and thin, trying to hide a large chunk of ice under his coat. My puzzled expression brought a look of fear to Michael's face, not unlike that of a criminal caught smuggling. Before I could think of anything profound to say, Michael spoke. "I want to keep it!" Then, with pleading eyes, he added, "I want to take it home." The great amount of ice and snow on the ground held no relevance for him. The only thing of any importance was the piece of ice he cradled at the moment.

The look on his face made my adult reasoning melt faster than the chunk of ice he was holding. I told him to bring it into the classroom. His shoulders relaxed, and I could see a little smile beginning to grow. We put his frozen treasure in a dish, where it would stay until the class could inspect it later.

Thinking about the incident after school caught me by surprise. Instead of being amused at a little boy's immature values, I took stock of my own. How many times do I try to hold on to things that won't last?

I often complain when I have to let go of some small object or desire I cherish. It's easy to forget that God has surrounded me with many other blessings. Like Michael, I sometimes think that the only one that seems to matter is the one I'm holding at the moment. How much better off I'd be if I would set my affections on things that will last, on things eternal.

That day Michael grew—and I grew. MARCIA MOLLENKOPF

ALL THINGS WORK FOR GOOD

We know that all things work together for good to them that love God, to them who are the called according to his purpose. Rom. 8:28.

It was the end of December 1970. I was a student at the Institute, and I was happy. In a week exams would start. I felt full of energy. Then my English teacher invited me to talk to her. As I was usually invited by administration for a talk because of my religious beliefs, I expected this again. A Soviet student with faith in God—it seemed impossible for many people, but not for me. Before going to the meeting with the English teacher I prayed a lot for protection and wisdom and asked myself questions: Is something wrong? What happened?

In the Institute the KGB was one of the departments, and the life of each student was under their watch. During the two years I had been a student, they had worked hard through different people to get me to change my religious beliefs. They were not successful, so they had decided it was time to get rid of me. Religious freedom did not exist for me.

My suspicions were right, although my teacher tried hard not to hurt me. The KGB had ordered three professors to evaluate me during their exams and to grade me with unsatisfactory marks. This hit me like a thunderstorm. The professors were nice people with kind hearts, even though they were Communists. Like the midwives in ancient Egypt, they didn't want to harm their students, but they couldn't risk their jobs. So they came up with a plan.

"You shouldn't go to these exams. You have to get sick and take an academic leave," they instructed.

"But I'm well, and I can't lie," I replied.

My teacher then sent me to a doctor who knew about the situation. She recommended I take an academic leave. I had to agree with the doctor. The future was unknown to me. Later I moved to Odessa, so I took my papers from the Institute to Odessa University. They looked at my papers and said, "Your papers do not need to be checked, because in your Institute you were checked properly." I had passed!

Thank You, Lord, for protecting me and creating good circumstances for my education.
LUDMILA KRUSHENITSKAYA

CHRISTMAS SHORTBREAD

These three remain: faith, hope and love. But the greatest of these is love. 1 Cor. 13:13, NIV.

Scottish shortbread is a generations-old tradition at Christmastime in our household. Two weeks before Christmas, using a recipe that came from my husband's grandmother back in Scotland, I measured out the ingredients and began the laborious work of kneading the mixture until it would hold together in one piece. Then I pressed the lump down flat on a cookie tray, pricked it with a fork in a neat pattern, and baked it at the required temperature for the required length of time.

When I took it from the oven, I noticed some cracks across the shortbread. This was unusual. When I began to cut it up while it was still hot, the cracks worsened. I was beginning to worry about it by now. When I carefully lifted two pieces out, they broke into several small pieces. *What's wrong with this shortbread?* I thought. I had made the recipe many times before, and it had never been like this.

Just then my husband came into the kitchen and picked up one of the fragments to try it. "Ugh!" he said. "This isn't very sweet. Are you sure you put enough sugar in it?"

Sugar? Then it dawned on me. In my haste I had not even bothered to get out the recipe, and I must have forgotten to put in the sugar. I had left out one of the essential ingredients of the recipe, and the result was disaster, as far as shortbread is concerned.

In life there is always the need to go back to the recipe—which in spiritual terms is the Bible—for directions and success, even if we have done it many times before. Also, as 1 Corinthians 13:13 tells us, a life of faith and hope, if it's without love, is like my shortbread without the sugar—just a crumbly, tasteless mess.

Help me, Lord, always to have the sweetening, holding-together power of Your love in my life. You have given the recipe. Help me to follow it.

RUTH LENNOX

ATTITUDE OF GRATITUDE

Give thanks in all circumstances. 1 Thess. 5:18, NIV.

One day 10 lepers pleaded with Jesus for healing. He said, "Go, show yourselves to the priests" (Luke 17:14, NIV), and as they went they were healed. But only one tenth of the men had the attitude of gratitude. This man turned back, threw himself at Jesus' feet, and thanked Him. I believe that Jesus, who knows the hearts of all men and women, was disappointed, for He said, "Were not all ten cleansed? Where are the other nine?" (verse 17).

Now, to our day: "Give thanks in all circumstances." Can we find something for which to be grateful in every situation? I am learning to do it.

A number of years ago I told a bank-teller friend, "Even with my bad arthritis, I can strip the sheets off the bed and wash them. But when I remake the bed, I put on the fitted sheet and rest; put on the flat sheet and rest. And," I added, "when I vacuum, I do a little and rest; do a little more and rest."

"Well, Patsy," Ruth scolded, "at least you can still make the bed, and you can still vacuum. You are not confined to bed like some folk!" The attitude of gratitude.

One day as I walked toward a grocery store, a young woman's cart hit a bump in the pavement and a sack of groceries fell from the rack below, scattering bread and other groceries. When I reached her, I said, "That was a shame."

She smiled and said, "I'm so thankful it wasn't the sack with the eggs in it!" There it was again, that attitude of gratitude.

A woman slowed her car so a young mother, driving a station wagon full of children, could merge in front of her. The young woman smiled and waved thanks. Soon a child appeared at the back window with a large cardboard sign that said in big bold letters, "Thank You!" A double dose of the attitude of gratitude.

When things go wrong from time to time, as they will, let's try to find something in the situation for which to be grateful.

Father, teach me to look for the positive aspects in every situation and to be grateful that things are not worse. And help me to glorify Your name in all things.

PATSY MURDOCH MEEKER

THE ROBINSON REMINDER

Let this mind be in you, which was also in Christ Jesus. Phil. 2:5.

My father was a dynamic preacher. He could not boast of a college education, or even of a high school education. To say he had completed grade school may have stretched the truth, but somewhere in his early 20s he felt the call of God to become a minister. And so, without benefit of a formal education, Dad began to prepare himself to be a soul winner.

From my earliest childhood I remember seeing Dad at his desk, poring over his Bible. Often he kept a bowl of ice water nearby. I never understood why. Years later I learned its purpose. He would bathe his face in it to stay awake, often studying into the wee hours of the morning. He became a successful evangelist, and the precious souls won to Jesus numbered in the thousands. He faithfully kept their names and addresses in his file.

One Christmas I gave Dad a leather Robinson Reminder, a small maroon card and memo carrier—something I knew he wanted. He carried it with him everywhere until he passed away years later. Knowing how much it meant to my beloved dad, I kept it as a precious reminder. There, glued securely to an inside cover, was a slip of paper. On it was printed, "Cultivation of the mind is as necessary as food to the body."

It brought me back to the memory of my father sitting tirelessly at his desk with that bowl of ice water before him, sometimes skipping meals in favor of study. Now, after 13 years, that Robinson Reminder is still in constant use. And yes, the little slip of paper is still firmly attached. It has shaped my life. Its influence has helped me become more selective about what goes into this mind that God has graciously given me. Whatever I read, watch, hear, or meditate on, I subconsciously measure it against Dad's example. Slowly I too am learning the precious lesson of cultivating my mind through Bible study and prayer.

We recently moved to a retirement complex and have had to scale down. But two things remain in my possession—that Robinson Reminder and Dad's well-worn Bible, the first as a reminder to cultivate the second. Those things that occupy my time, my energy, my thoughts, will make or break me. Thank God He has given me the choice! I must make the most of it!

LORRAINE HUDGINS

A HUG FROM GOD

His everlasting arms are under you. Deut. 33:27, NLT.

I sat alone in the kitchen, sipping hot peppermint tea to soothe my sore throat. I ached all over. For several days I'd been fighting a stubborn cold and trying to recover from hip surgery. The aroma of the tea brought back memories of my mother holding me as I sipped peppermint tea with honey.

I longed to be a child again, going to my mother for comfort. I could count on her three remedies for whatever ailed me—hot fomentations, hot tea, and a warm hug. How good I felt when she held me close! "Never mind," she would say. "Drink this tea, and you'll feel better."

I wish I had someone to hug me now, I thought. I sighed, for there was no one in the house right then to hug me. I was all alone in my misery. I drained the cup of tea and went to bed, hugging myself, but somehow that didn't help much.

Then the hugs began to come in the form of an answered prayer and the thoughtfulness of friends. That night I wrote in my prayer journal, "Hugs from God!" Then I mentioned three.

Hug number one: I got an e-mail message from the women's ministries committee of the Oregon Conference, where I was supposed to speak that weekend. I had told them about my ailments and had asked them to pray that I would be well enough to keep my appointment. I had then asked the Lord to take care of it. Now their e-mail said they felt impressed that they should not require me to come. They would find someone else. A great burden lifted as I sensed God's arms of love around me, hugging me, taking care of my needs.

Hug number two: Dear friends called saying they were coming with dinner for the whole family, a feast of our favorite Indian foods. The spicy, delicious Indian curries even brought my appetite back! When they hugged me, I sensed that God was hugging me too.

Hug number three: A friend called, one I would have liked to visit but couldn't because of my illness. We had a great talk. Over the phone it was a hug from a friend, and I sensed that it was God's hug as well.

Thank You, Lord, for Your everlasting arms that hold me. Make me aware today of the many times You hug me.

DOROTHY EATON WATTS

SHINE LIKE STARS

Those who are wise—the people of God—shall shine as brightly as the sun's brilliance, and those who turn many to righteousness will glitter like stars forever. Dan. 12:3, TLB.

Maybe I want to be a bright and shining star because of childhood Christmas programs or something else hidden in the recesses of my mind. I always wanted to "shine" when called on to recite in school, and the glitter may linger on into adulthood. Others may be shy when called on to speak in some groups, or they may defer to others with more experience and shrink from the limelight.

A doctor once said he would be glad to go to China and work for a long time if only one person were brought to Jesus. As a young nurse I too wanted to go to a faraway place and be a missionary and help others learn about Jesus. Instead, my work was closer to home.

This week the teachers in our school met with new students who plan to become registered nurses. One student paid close attention to the devotional thoughts that were shared each morning. She said she had come from a difficult home and did not know Jesus but was going to tell her little girl what she heard from the nursing teachers. It reminded me of how many people we can meet here at home who have not been taught about Jesus and His gift of life for us.

I'm afraid I have been too busy with the many chores at work and home and haven't kept in mind the many people around me who need encouragement, who need to know that Jesus really cares about them. Shining like stars may sound like being a movie star or being famous, being "up front" and important, but that is not what it is about at all. I'll be very disappointed if my efforts to be a star now cause me to miss out when Jesus reads His list. How much nicer it will be to hear people say that I have helped someone who needed it, that someone was happy to know Jesus because I was able to share the good news with him or her.

First Corinthians 15:41-58 puts it this way: "The stars differ from each other in their beauty and brightness. . . . Since future victory is sure, be strong and steady, always abounding in the Lord's work, for you know that nothing you do for the Lord is ever wasted as it would be if there were no resurrection" (TLB). I need to be about the Lord's work instead of my own; people need the Lord, and these same people are close to me now—very close.

JULIA L. PEARCE

HERE COMES THE SUN!

He who has said all these things declares: Yes, I am coming soon! Rev. 22:20, TLB.

It had been a long, difficult night. My family and I were en route from Kansas City, Missouri, to Miami, Florida, for Christmas break, and we had decided to travel through the night to stay ahead of a predicted winter storm. The little minivan had run steadily along, first through freezing rain, then through fierce thunderstorms, followed by fog and construction-obstructed roads. Although my husband and I alternated driving shifts, it was a very stressful night, and we were tired and road-weary.

Morning found us passing through the south Tennessee mountains, nearing Chattanooga. The day had dawned with thick gray clouds in the sky, giving the appearance of gloom everywhere. But just as we rounded a corner, we beheld a beautiful sight—the placid Tennessee River and Nickajack Lake spread out below us. And at that very moment the sun broke through the clouds to create a scene of almost indescribable beauty. Sunbeams turned the gentle ripples of the lake to shiny gold and silver wavelets, and even the somber mountainous slopes around us took on a unique glow.

Someone in the car called out, "Hey, here comes the sun! Look at the beautiful sun!" The long miles didn't seem so bad after that.

We are on a long and arduous journey through this mountainous world of sin. We are beset by the freezing rain of sorrow and death, the thunderstorms of discouragement and despair, the road construction of insurmountable problems, and the fog of doubt and trouble. Sometimes we wonder if we will ever get through the night and arrive at our final destination.

But very soon I hope to hear someone say, "Here comes the Son—look at the beautiful Son!" The clouds of frustration will part, and the glory of His presence will break through, turning all the dark, dangerous, and discouraging roads we have traveled into something beautiful. Then our journey will be all worthwhile, for we will be going home.

Oh, how I look forward to that beautiful breaking morning! Sun of righteousness, shine on me this day, helping me to keep journeying on.

FAUNA RANKIN DEAN

HEY, THOSE ARE MINE!

Don't accuse people falsely. Luke 3:14, NIV.

Her usually sunny face was as stormy as I had ever seen it. Tears bulged at the corners of her eyes, and her fists were tightly clenched. "The Lifesavers were mine," Melissa asserted. "I can't imagine how he got his grubby hands on them!"

"What Lifesavers?" I asked, and the story came tumbling out. At school, Melissa had looked for her favorite roll. She saw a student with the same flavor of Lifesavers and accused him of stealing hers.

"Are you absolutely positive he was handing out your Lifesavers?" I questioned.

"How could they not be mine?" Melissa looked genuinely baffled.

"Let me tell you a story," I replied. "Once upon a time a weary traveler found herself stranded at a busy airport. To pass the time before the next flight, she purchased a book and a bag of cookies. As she sat reading, she noticed the man beside her helping himself to her cookies.

"Her first thought was *What nerve!* But then she rationalized, *Well, it won't hurt me to share a few.* The minutes ticked by. The woman would help herself to a cookie; so would he. More time passed. Eventually there was only one treat left. *I wonder what he'll do now?* she mused. Pulling the last cookie out of the bag, the man broke it in two and, with a nervous smile, offered her half. This was the last straw! She wasn't going to let this pass. No way! That cookie pilferer needed to learn some manners! Before she could give voice to words, however, her flight was called. Gathering up her belongings, the woman boarded the plane.

"Shortly after takeoff, and while still seething inwardly, the weary traveler reached into her bag to retrieve her book—and her hand touched a bag of cookies, her unopened bag of cookies. The man next to her had actually been sharing *his* supply with *her!*"

Melissa headed for the garage. She was back shortly with a brand-new roll of Lifesavers. "They must have fallen out of my pocket. I'll apologize tomorrow," she said sturdily.

Been blaming any cookie thieves lately?   ARLENE TAYLOR

GOLD BELL STAMPS

When you did it to one of the least of these my brothers and sisters, you were doing it to me! Matt. 25:40, NLT.

Tiny stamps, imprinted with the words "Gold Bell" over the drawing of a bell, were given at the local grocery store for paying cash for purchases. I hoarded them tenaciously. Often I pored over the catalog, dreaming about which gift to choose when I had accumulated enough books. Northern Michigan winters are very cold, and I thought an electric blanket would be wonderful. There were attractive rugs, sheets for the boys' beds, even charming bedside lamps. Decisions, decisions! The little wish book became dog-eared because I simply could not decide.

A new book came out a few weeks before Christmas. Before my eyes was the reddest, shiniest toy truck I had ever seen. I knew it was virtually indestructible. My young mother's heart saw nothing else in that catalog. Now my dream was for red trucks for our 3- and 4-year-old sons for Christmas. But did I have enough stamps?

Eagerly I licked each little Gold Bell stamp, placed it in a book, and watched the books fill up. Not quite enough. I lacked half a book, and Christmas was only a month away. I visited my unselfish mother-in-law, and the loving grandmother helped to fill the final book.

The week before Christmas I stood in a line at the stamp center, clutching those two red truck boxes in my arms and the fat little stamp books in my hands. As the line slowly inched forward, the harried clerk rang up the tax on each item and collected the only cash needed for the purchase. I had never even thought of the tax; I thought only of the light I would see in our sons' eyes on Christmas Eve when they opened those boxes. I dug into my change purse and found a couple dollars, desperately hoping it would be sufficient. *O Lord,* I prayed, *let it be enough.* But it wasn't. I needed one more dollar. Embarrassed by my shortage, devastated at my loss, I placed the boxes on the counter, picked up my books of stamps, and turned to leave.

"Just a moment," a masculine voice spoke from behind me. "We can't have any boys missing red trucks for Christmas." And a dollar magically appeared on the counter. The clerk smiled. I smiled through my tears. The long line of people behind me smiled. It was truly a Christmas moment!

BETTY R. BURNETT

356

LOST AND FOUND

Be anxious for nothing, but in everything by prayer and supplication, with thanksgiving, let your requests be made known to God. Phil. 4:6, NKJV.

It was only a small squarish purse with a strap, but I had paid a good sum for it, and now it was gone. The purse contained my driver's license, address book, eyeglasses, and other valuables. We had taken an off-ramp exit from the freeway in order to fill the gas tank of our rented car, and I had carelessly left the purse lying on a shelf in the restroom of the gas station's minimart just outside Sacramento. We had driven nearly halfway to San Francisco before I realized that the purse was lost. There was only a very short time before our flight to Houston was scheduled to take off. Nevertheless, we turned around and headed back toward Sacramento.

A wave of despair had enveloped me for a few seconds when I discovered my purse missing, but then I remembered an admonition to turn instantly to the Lord. Silently I prayed, *Please help me, Lord, to be calm and, if it be Your will, to find the purse.* I also thanked the Lord for answering my prayer, come what would.

Our next problem was that we could not recall what exit we had taken to get to the gas station. Unfortunately, in our haste we passed by the exit and took another ramp instead. This cost us valuable time, and we were forced to drive on to San Francisco.

At the car rental agency, after we had related our plight, one of the employees made phone contact with a gas station close to the one we wanted. We were informed that each gas station was individually owned, and that the gas station we wanted had no phone listed. Trusting in the Lord, we flew on to Houston, where our son and daughter-in-law awaited. As soon as I could, I phoned my son who lives in Folsom, California. He and his family would be flying to Los Angeles the next day from Sacramento, and he agreed to search for my purse.

The next day I received a phone call from my son. He had found not only the right exit ramp, the gas station, and the minimart, but he had found my missing purse with all its contents intact!

God, You are so good! What a Christmas present! But even better is the one You supplied 2,000 years ago. Your love and care are past our understanding.

AILEEN YOUNG

THE CHRISTMAS TREE

Whatsoever things are true, whatsoever things are honest, whatsoever things are just, whatsoever things are pure, whatsoever things are lovely, whatsoever things are of good report; if there be any virtue, and if there be any praise, think on these things. Phil. 4:8.

It was a cold, damp morning. A good reason, I thought, not to take the bus to church. The car was the way to go this day. I arrived unusually late and was surprised to see somebody else making his way toward the church. It was Mike.

"Do you have a Christmas tree?" he hollered as I walked toward him.

"No," I shouted back as he waited for me.

I was not expecting a wrapped, seven-foot live spruce! He explained that he had spotted it lying on the side of the road. Both of us assumed it had fallen from a truckload of trees.

I thought, *God wanted me to have a Christmas tree!* Excited by the discovery, I blurted out, "Mike, God used you as an instrument in His hands."

"Well, it makes me feel good to give it to someone who can use it," he replied.

I lived alone after my divorce. The children had grown and moved away. Holidays had new meaning. Instead of spending time baking, cooking, decorating, shopping, and cleaning, I gave more thought to having a couple days off work to spend leisurely at home. I replaced a live tree with a smaller artificial one, but it became shabby over time, with branches missing. I threw it away, promising to buy another one. But with Christmas fast approaching and little time and money left after holiday shopping, I had regretted having tossed out the ratty old thing. I had given up the idea of even having a tree this year.

Pulling the plastic netting off the spruce, I placed it upright in the stand. Its branches fell open to reveal a luxuriously plush and hearty evergreen. I felt I had received a present from God. The tree's delicate fragrance and soft needles reminded me of God's gentleness; its presence reminded me of His goodness and unfailing love. Its healthy green color brought to mind His promise: "They are like trees planted by streams of water, which yield their fruit in its season, and their leaves do not wither. In all that they do, they prosper" (Ps. 1:3, NRSV).　　　　JAMISEN FARLEY

NEW GADGETS

As the heavens are higher than the earth, so are my ways higher than your ways and my thoughts than your thoughts. Isa. 55:9, NIV.

I find many new gadgets and contrivances very frustrating. When traveling in other countries I found many, including such mundane things as elevators and toilets. It seemed that every bathroom had a different puzzling design for flushing the commode. We found buttons and faucets on the wall, chains hanging from the tank, levers or spaces on the tank to push, pull, or twist. Besides these, there were squat toilets flushed by pouring in water from a bucket, and latrines that were not flushed at all.

In elevators we had to learn which button to push to get to the main floor. It could be labeled "L" or "O" or "1" or "-1." Also, timing was important. Sometimes the elevator door was open so long that we thought it was out of order. In others it closed in a few seconds, and we had to move fast lest the elevator slam closed on an arm or leg.

I found more puzzling new devices when baby-sitting my grandchildren. The strollers, car seats, highchairs, bottles, and garments had new levers and ties and buckles and buttons to tie, twist, push, and snap. In the house I had to learn to operate new equipment: breadmaker, garbage disposal, watering system, stove, and oven. Just when I was feeling rather confident of my new skills, I discovered the clothes dryer did not work. I turned the timer and pushed "Start." No response. Finally I discovered the door was not closed tightly. I closed it and lo, it worked. For the computer I had to learn new commands and switches. My daughter-in-law said, "You turn on the printer on the back." Still, I couldn't find the button. I felt all over the back of the printer—no luck. Finally I climbed on top of the desk and searched for the hidden switch till I found it.

Gadgets and learning. Baffling, exciting, humiliating. In this new millennium you may be challenged by new frontiers in communication, archaeology, genetic engineering, thermodynamics, or conservation. You may explore space, disease, the Internet, or the deepest ocean. But as fast as our knowledge explodes, God's knowledge is still as much higher than ours as is the heaven above the earth. To explore His limitless knowledge, and especially His character and love, is our opportunity today and throughout eternity.

RUTH WATSON

DECEMBER 22

GOD SENT AN ANGEL

The Lord is your keeper. . . . The Lord shall preserve you from all evil. Ps. 121:5-7, NKJV.

For a number of weeks we had looked forward to our vacation in Florida. We planned to visit family and friends, as well as the usual tourist spots. However, what was to be a special outing with our Florida friends almost turned into a family disaster.

Our daughter was only 2 at the time. It was Sabbath, and we were at a park in south Florida for a picnic lunch. Because we had just come from church, the women and children headed for the restroom to change into more casual clothes. I had changed our daughter, Cheri, first, and then began to change my clothes. Because I was not quite ready myself, she asked to go out of the restroom to play with the other children.

I'm sure it was only a matter of a few minutes before I had changed and walked toward the rest of the group. To my dismay Cheri was not with the children. We dashed back to the restroom area, calling her name. Beyond the restrooms a small pathway led to an overgrown area with water and alligators. I could immediately imagine all sorts of horrible things. As we continued to call, suddenly I heard Cheri cry. There she was, coming toward us on this pathway.

How thankful we were that she heard our voices and turned around instead of going farther into the brush. Truly, I believe God sent an angel to turn our daughter in the right direction, back to us.

We can all look back to a time when in a careless or busy moment we lost track of one of our children. This may have put that child in a dangerous or harmful situation and given ourselves the scare of our lives.

Fortunately, this is never true of our heavenly Parent, who assures each one of us that He ever watches over us and never loses track of any of His children. Our heavenly Father knows where we are and what we are doing every minute of every day or night. How reassuring to know that He is always there to preserve us from evil.   PATRICIA MULRANEY KOVALSKI

IN YONDER MANGER

For unto us a child is born, unto us a son is given: . . . and His name shall be called Wonderful, Counselor, The mighty God, The everlasting Father, The Prince of Peace. Isa. 9:6.

The week was exceptionally hectic; traffic was constantly passing, and queues of weary folk waited patiently for buses in the town center. Shopkeepers checked their totals toward the end of the day, delighted with their profits. Bright lights flashed, decorations were everywhere, loudspeakers played Christmas jingles, busy shoppers were laden with parcels and large plastic shopping bags. Taunton was getting ready for Christmas, and it was market day, the busiest day of the week for generations.

At one time farmers from the outskirts had herded their cattle and sheep through the streets of the town and over the River Tone Bridge. There the auction of animals would take place until sunset. Now they come in trucks, directly to the market. Hundreds also sell their wares from stalls.

The town and congestion reminded me of the inn in Bethlehem, packed with shoppers, drinking and eating, when Mary and Joseph, worn and tired, asked for a room. They were turned away. Someone kindly suggested a stable nearby. There Mary gave birth to a Son and wrapped Him in swaddling clothes and laid Him in a manger. Above the hills, the shepherds rejoiced.

Our Taunton church was a stable in the days of John Wesley, who preached several times in the 1740s in a church very close by. Now, in this former stable in Taunton, "Mary" and "Joseph" were overjoyed to find a little group of believers waiting in expectation to hold a candlelight service in honor of the Son who had been born. The prophecy from Isaiah was read: "For unto us a Child is born, unto us a son is given." The little ones gathered around the Child Jesus and sang "Away in a Manger" and other Christmas carols. A lively choral group from our sister church in Croscombe also sang. We read poems and songs and prayed for Christ to be put back into the true spirit of Christmas in the town of Taunton.

Lord Jesus, come again to our town, and especially to our hearts, this Christmas season. We need Your peace in our lives. PHILIPPA MARSHALL

THE GREATEST GIFT

No eye has seen, no ear has heard, and no mind has imagined what God has prepared for those who love him. 1 Cor. 2:9, NLT.

After 37 years of marriage my husband and I moved from Frederick, Maryland, to Charlotte, North Carolina, to retire near our two adult children and their families. Our first Christmas in our new home was one I'll never forget.

The last gift had been opened, and I was cleaning up the mess. Suddenly the children made a great show of discovering an unopened gift in the midst of the rubbish. "It's for Mom," they said. Inside was a video. They insisted that the Christmas morning cleanup could wait while we all sat down and watched the video.

It featured the four of them, dressed in Santa Claus costumes, singing verses my daughter had composed to the tune of "Jingle Bells." I was laughing at the silly verses when the words to the last verse caused my mouth to drop open:

"Because you've moved to Charlotte, and never once looked back,
   To show our love, we've bought you a brand-new Cadillac!"

The video then revealed a close-up shot of a shiny new automobile! It took me a moment to realize they were giving me a new car for Christmas. The car, with a huge bow on top, was parked in our driveway.

Have you ever been given something wonderful that you didn't earn? Just because you were loved? I realized that it wasn't the car that thrilled me (although the car is great). It was rather the fact that my children and son-in-law loved me enough to sacrifice their hard-earned money to make me happy. I was—and still am—overwhelmed by their unselfish love.

For the first time I truly grasped the concept of Jesus' free gift of salvation. When I looked at a brand-new car in my driveway that I did nothing to earn, the feeling of love and awe for what this gift meant—a sacrifice of money from hardworking children—left me dazed.

It's the same for the gift of salvation. We stand awed and dazed because we did nothing to earn it. Jesus simply loved us so much He gave us salvation so we could experience happiness forever. In fact, He died to secure our happiness. Can you fathom such unselfish love?   ELLIE GREEN

SACRIFICE OF LOVE

God loved the world so much that he gave his only Son. John 3:16, TEV.

It was Christmas morning. I had opened all my gifts hours earlier and had been thrilled with all of them. Mom had outdone herself again, something she was especially good at, even though she was raising my three brothers and me by herself. I knew money was tight, but every Christmas my mother showered us with lots of toys and clothes. I watched my brothers, all younger than I, playing with their things. At 12, I had fewer toys and more clothing, so by midday I had become somewhat bored.

"I'm bored," I announced with a heavy sigh. "I have nothing to do."

I glanced over at my mother, sitting there reading. She was wearing her customary attire—bobby socks and loafers and an old shiftlike dress. She jerked her head up suddenly and gasped. "Bored?" I heard her say, a hint of irritation in her voice. "You have all this stuff—and you're bored?" The horrified look on her face soon turned to sadness, and my young heart became heavy as I realized how deeply I had broken my mother's heart.

I now realize that my mother wore those bobby socks, loafers, and shiftlike dresses to provide adequately for her family. It was her sacrifice of love. She always did without the finer things in life so we would have good food, appropriate clothing, social activities, and even weekly allowances. Now I know that mothers all over the world willingly give up possessing things that they truly deserve so that their families can have what they need, what they want, or, in many cases, what the mothers want to give simply out of love for them.

And then I think of my heavenly Parent. He provides daily for my every need. He often showers me with special gifts, not because I deserve them, but simply because I want them. And, even more important, He loves me that much! I hope that He doesn't see me through sad, hurting eyes, eyes like my mother's that unforgettable Christmas Day. I pray I will never be such an ungrateful child that I don't appreciate that He gave all that He had just for me—the best gift ever—and it was His sacrifice of love.

IRIS L. STOVALL

IT WAS NOT FATHER CHRISTMAS

They shall enter in at the windows like a thief. Joel 2:9.

My husband and I had spent Christmas day at Kirstenbosch National Botanical Gardens. As I sat looking at the beautiful scenes of nature I praised God for all His blessings. I also asked Him to protect our home while we were away. Late in the afternoon it started drizzling, so we packed up and left for home.

When I unlocked the front door, I noticed that a window was wide open, the curtain blowing, and the burglar bar twisted inward. Obviously thieves had forced their entry through the window. I phoned the police. We waited and waited, but they didn't come. My bedroom was in chaos. My cupboard doors were all wide open. The thieves had searched my everyday purse, looking for money, but found none. They stole my brand-new electronic microwave oven, my watch, and all the gifts bought for the holidays.

I couldn't understand why God had allowed it to happen. I had asked Him all day to protect our house. Then this text came to mind: "In everything give thanks: for this is the will of God in Christ Jesus concerning you" (1 Thess. 5:18). So I took stock. I soon came to realize that the burglary could have been worse.

Money I had received and which I had vowed to give to the Lord was in my church purse, right above where the thieves had searched. The Lord had protected that money from their eyes. None of my clothes were missing; I thanked God for that. I thanked God that we hadn't come home earlier, because if the thieves had been caught in the act, they could have killed us, as they are almost always armed with dangerous weapons. "In everything give thanks."

Finally, I was able to thank God for not answering my prayer as I had thought He should, because the Lord did not forsake us. We still have so much to be thankful for.

I need help to be able to be thankful in everything, even if it is not what I expected or wanted. You were not what was expected that Christmas so long ago either, but I am so thankful for You.

PRISCILLA ADONIS

LETTER FROM GALILEE

Christ became a human being and lived here on earth among us and was full of loving forgiveness and truth. And some of us have seen his glory—the glory of the only Son of the heavenly Father! John 1:14, TLB.

I've met the most marvelous man! I can guess the questions you will ask, so I'll answer them before you even voice them. I've met his mother—the sweetest, most pure-minded gentlewoman I know. His father is no longer living. (There was some talk about illegitimacy, but that is both untrue and irrelevant!)

I must warn you that one of his ancestors, Rahab, was a prostitute. But she changed. And what a change! You know the stories about the fantastic impact she made on those around her. Her faith saved our entire nation way back then.

Yes, Dad, he had a trade. Word is that he used to do the finest woodwork this side of Galilee. I say "used to" because he gave up carpentry almost three years ago. Now he journeys along the road, talking to people, teaching them, and healing some. He's wonderful at that. People travel for days to be with him, the itinerant, medical preacher.

You should hear him speak! I can hear the love of God in his voice. His words are so beautiful, so powerful, so life-changing—people even forget their growling stomachs. (One day I'll tell you about the miracle bread-and-fish lunches he's shared with us.) Yesterday he said, "Don't worry. The sparrows never worry that they'll run out of seeds." I had never thought about it like that before. Just one line and everything came into focus. Our God provides for us.

He has the most wonderful philosophy on happiness. This scroll is not long enough to tell you everything, and the messenger is waiting to take this letter to you. I will close with my favorite line: "You're blessed when you get your inside world—your mind and your heart—put right. Then you can see God in the outside world" (Matt. 5:8, Message). Because of him, I can see that our world is crammed with the light of God. I shall never be the same again.

Yes, I love him. But it's way beyond the love King Solomon wrote about. It's a love I want to share with everyone around me. It's too precious to keep to myself!

Your loving, dedicated daughter, GLENDA-MAE GREENE

THE GIFT OF LIFE

Whoever believes in the Son has eternal life. John 3:36, NIV.

Our Saviour came to this world to give CPR to a dying planet of people. Everyone is offered the gift of eternal life. "For God so loved the world, that he gave his only begotten Son, that whosoever believeth should not perish, but have everlasting life" (John 3:16).

It was the first day back to work after the Christmas holidays, a cold, crisp morning, and the snow lay fresh on the ground. The staff was rested after a two-week vacation. Students were eagerly telling me about their work in the nursing home during vacation. Suddenly one of the maintenance men ran up and said that Jim was having chest pains and that I should go to the maintenance department right away. I grabbed my stethoscope and blood pressure cuff and ran.

Jim was lying down. He was sweating profusely, writhing in pain, and had a blood pressure of 198/148. The ambulance arrived, and the paramedics ran into the building. One paramedic began talking to Jim while the other returned to get some equipment from the ambulance. Jim quit breathing, and he had no pulse. The paramedic called the code. He asked if any of us knew CPR. Of course, being a registered nurse, I knew. He asked me to start CPR while they set up the equipment.

One, one thousand. Two, one thousand. Three, one thousand. Four, one thousand. Five, one thousand. Breathe.

After several rounds the equipment was in place and the paddles were on Jim's chest. They shocked Jim twice, then his pulse started up again. They started intravenous liquids, administered oxygen, and transported Jim to the hospital.

At the staff meeting that day the principal told the staff what had happened. I was called a hero, and I received the applause of the staff. People shook my hand. But the real hero was Christ, who gives life to all, everlasting life. A free gift to any who want it. Something no earthly hero can ever do.

Father, thank You for providing a way so that any of us who want it can have eternal life through You.

SUSAN BERRIDGE

MOVING

Let not your heart be troubled: ye believe in God, believe also in me. In my Father's house are many mansions: if it were not so, I would have told you. I go to prepare a place for you. John 14:1, 2.

One December morning we planted a "For Sale by Owner" sign on our front lawn. Soon my husband would retire. We'd already purchased a lot in a smaller town and planned to build our new house during the spring. Two weeks after we put up the sign, a young couple came to see our property and agreed to purchase it for our asking price.

I spent all of January sorting 21 years of accumulation. First I sorted things in our full basement. After that I moved to closets and cupboards upstairs. During off-work hours my husband sorted and packed things in our double garage. We donated to Goodwill and Community Services and gave to relatives. Some items found their way into the garbage. Things we intended to keep we packed into boxes and labeled for storage. We also spent time searching for an apartment, because the buyers wanted to move into our house in February.

My husband and I agreed we didn't ever wish to move or build again, but we are now preparing for one more move, the last one! However, this move will not require sorting or packing, or demand decisions of what to take with us and what to dispose of. Our next move will not require a search for packing boxes, hours of work, or a storage facility. This next move requires only our daily relationship with Jesus, compassion for those less fortunate, and a commitment to sharing the gospel with others. For this move, we shall leave everything behind to enjoy a brand-new mansion, furnished for our comfort.

I can hardly wait to make that move! I'm counting on our Saviour's promise: "I go to prepare a place for you." What an exciting move that will be, floating through the air with Jesus and the angels!

Dear Lord, grant me a full measure of Your Holy Spirit. Do the proper character sorting and ridding of undesirables now so I'll be prepared to make that ultimate move with You in the clouds of glory!

NATHALIE LADNER-BISCHOFF

CONSIDER EACH DAY A GIFT

To every thing there is a season, and a time to every purpose under the heaven. Eccl. 3:1.

I'm sure you have heard the phrase "Hindsight is perfect 20/20 vision." Enjoying the last week of the year, we are enjoying perfect 20/20 vision of our year. A special vantage point for each of us. With 20/20 vision each of us will celebrate our personal victories, try to improve where we have failed, and enjoy the happy memories.

During the Christmas season I receive many form letters that tell of the success of friends and relatives, of their troubles, their travels, their children, and of their daily lives. I am reminded of the statement "Yesterday is past, tomorrow is future, but today is a gift; that's why it's called the present."

As we look forward to the new year, we will make it successful if we think of each day as a gift. Each one new and shiny and wrapped just for us. Taking one day at a time and living it to the fullest will make the coming year a super year.

Solomon in his wisdom explained about time in Ecclesiastes 3:1-8: "To every thing there is a season, and a time to every purpose under the heaven: a time to be born, and a time to die; a time to plant, and a time to pluck up that which is planted; a time to kill, and a time to heal; a time to break down, and a time to build up; a time to weep, and a time to laugh; a time to mourn, and a time to dance; a time to cast away stones, and a time to gather stones together; a time to embrace, and a time to refrain from embracing; a time to get, and a time to lose; a time to keep, and a time to cast away; a time to rend, and a time to sew; a time to keep silence, and a time to speak; a time to love, and time to hate; a time of war and a time of peace."

Lord, as we evaluate the past, savor the present, and look to the future, help us to do it with Your perfect vision. Give us the wisdom to appreciate the gift You have already given and to look forward to a year of spending irreplaceable time with You.

MAXINE HENRY

MORE PRESENTS, MA; MORE PRESENTS

For unto us a child is born, unto us a son is given. Isa. 9:6.

When my grandson was only 3 years old, he and his parents were opening presents around our Christmas tree. He was having a delightful time opening all the little (and some not so little) gifts meant especially for him. When we finally reached the end, he looked at his mother and said, "More pwesents, Ma; more pwesents!" She had a difficult time explaining to him that there were no more presents, that we had, indeed, reached the end.

I wonder if I am like that with my heavenly Father. Do I ask for "more presents"? I have so much to be grateful for: health and life and beauty all around, and especially my Saviour. It is also true that I often have trials. I lost my mother when I was only 4 and my stepmother when I was 10, my brother when I was 14, my baby when I was 22, our 28-year-old daughter, and my father a year after that. Some of us have more trials than others.

Am I often too blind to see in this world full of sin that my heavenly Father has provided much for me to enjoy and feast my eyes upon? In the spring the poorest person can delight in the daffodils, lilacs, apple trees, azaleas, tulips, dogwoods, and more. The roses, daylilies, hydrangeas, four-o'clocks, pansies, petunias, and the berries—blackberries, raspberries, blueberries—are in abundance in the summer. I have woods behind my house where I can pick quarts of berries all summer long—all because of the goodness of my Lord! In the fall we have the crepe myrtle, chrysanthemums, and others. There is beauty all around us. The beautiful green spruce, fruit trees, flush gardens, are all a delight.

Then there are the children I can enjoy. I may have lost my children, but the children in the church belong to all of us in one sense. We are all to help parents nurture their children. Do we take that opportunity?

I think of the pets the Lord has provided, particularly dogs and cats. Not only can children learn responsibility by helping to care for pets, but research has shown that elderly people who have pets to be responsible for live longer, healthier lives.

In the new year, let us look for the beauty that surrounds us and remember the greatest present of all, the gift of Jesus Christ, who died that we might live.

LORAINE F. SWEETLAND

AUTHORS' BIOGRAPHIES

Betty J. Adams, a retired teacher, is active in women's ministries, Community Services, and with her church newsletter. She enjoys traveling, quilting, writing, and her grandchildren. **Apr. 21, Aug. 1.**

Diana Adams lives in the Sierra Nevada foothills of northern California, where she home-schools her son and cares for her quadriplegic husband. Diana and her husband, Fred, served for 12 years as missionaries in southern Mexico. She serves her church as Pathfinder teacher and assistant in the junior high class. Her hobbies include tropical fish, gardening, walking her dog, reading, cooking, and playing her flute. **Sept. 25.**

Priscilla Adonis, from Cape Town, South Africa, is a retired housewife and the mother of two married daughters. She is Central Peninsula coordinator for women's ministries. Until recently, she spent much of her time caring for her grandson. **June 18, Nov. 19, Dec. 26.**

Maxine Williams Allen resides in Orlando, Florida, with her husband and two small sons. An entrepreneur with her own computer and business consulting company, she loves to travel, meet people, and experience different cultures. Hobbies include writing, reading, and computers, with special interest in ministries for family life, children, and women. She is the creator/facilitator of the "Follow the Leader" series on management and leadership strategies. **Jan. 9, Mar. 21, June 1.**

Mary Wagoner Angelin is an SMI (seriously mentally ill) case management supervisor and an Arizona State Hospital liaison for Mohave Mental Health Clinic. She is a volunteer at the Northern Arizona Make-a-Wish Foundation and a member of the Kingman Kiwanis. She produces a monthly newsletter, handles public relations for the church and Kiwanis, and is social committee chair and cradle roll assistant at her church. Her hobbies include exercise, writing, and computers. **Sept. 9.**

Ruth Anneke was an elementary teacher for 20 years. She is the mother of five adult sons and has 14 grandchildren. She retired to northern Idaho and is active in her small church. She enjoys reading, writing, cooking, sewing, teaching, and gardening. **Feb. 27, Mar. 29.**

Lois K. Bailey teaches English and drama at the Bermuda Institute of Seventh-day Adventists. As a single parent, she has one grown daughter, whom she adopted when she was an infant. She is thankful that God has fulfilled His promises to her. **Jan. 28, Apr. 28.**

Rosemary Baker, a freelance writer living in Iowa, is author of a children's religious book, *What Am I?* and has been published in *Shining Star, Kids' Stuff,* and other magazines. She is a member of the Iowa Poetry Association and is active in church and volunteer work. Her hobbies are arts, crafts, music, poetry, and painting. **Nov. 2.**

Jennifer M. Baldwin writes from Australia, where she is the clinical risk management coordinator at Sydney Adventist Hospital. She enjoys church involvement, travel, and writing, and has contributed to a number of church publications. **Feb. 3, May 13, June 3.**

Mary Barrett works with her husband in pastoral ministry, especially in evangelistic outreach. She is the mother of two girls. Her first book, *When God Comes to Visit*, was published in 1997. She is very interested in devotional and prayer ministry, enjoys being with friends, walking, and having time to turn her newly acquired house into a home. **Jan. 18, May 8.**

Dana M. Bassett lives on the island of Bermuda. In 1993 and 1994 she was a student missionary to Rwanda, Africa. She teaches primary three (second grade) and is the JAY leader at her church. Dana loves traveling, meeting people, reading, and photography. **Aug. 21.**

Dawna Beausoleil, a former teacher, enjoys life with her husband in Thunder Bay, Ontario. She loves to sing, write, and do jigsaw puzzles during the long winters and enjoys camping during the glorious summers. **June 11, Sept. 1.**

Susan L. Berridge is a registered nurse and driver's education teacher. She has a Master's degree in education and teaches health occupations at a vocational school. She and her husband, Ron, enjoy living in a rural setting with their four daughters, who range in age from preschool to college. They also have a granddaughter. Her hobbies include painting, gardening, outdoor activities. **Dec. 28.**

Annie B. Best is a retired public school teacher. She enjoys listening to music, reading, and shopping for her three grandchildren. Annie has worked in the cradle roll and kindergarten departments of her church. Working with children inspired her to compose a song that was published in *Let's Sing Sabbath Songs*. **Jan. 29, July 20.**

Ardelle Bjoralt, a quadriplegic, cannot speak, and yet has started a Bible study at her nursing home. She enjoys writing small articles and notes of encouragement to people, using her voice computer and miniprinter, operated with one finger. She praises the Lord and uses her talents for Him. **July 8.**

Olivine Nadeau Bohner is a retired English teacher who taught at La Sierra University, Riverside, California, for 10 years. An elder at the Jurupa Avenue Seventh-day Adventist Church in Riverside, Olivine has written three books: *The Long, Long Trial; Into the Blizzard;* and *Demon of Padeng*. She is most proud of her two sons, five grandchildren, and several foster children. **Apr. 20.**

Evelyn Boltwood lives in Fairport, New York. Newly remarried, she is the mother of a daughter at Atlantic Union College and a son in high school. She is Pathfinder deputy director and teaches the Master Guide class, and is a member of an all-women's African-American community choir, doing the sign language for the choir. She attends college and works as a buyer for a major corporation. She loves to draw and paint. **Apr. 6.**

Judy Borcherds, mother of two, is women's ministries leader for the Steenberg Seventh-day Adventist Church in Cape Town, South Africa. She has been a nurse for 20 years, with a special burden for young people and children. Two adults have been baptized as a result of her Sunday afternoon schools for community children. She loves reading the Bible and inspirational books. **May 19.**

Joyce Willes Brown-Carper has several careers, including practicing law. She is pursuing an M.A. degree in religious studies, with emphasis on youth ministry, while helping in her local church's youth department. She seeks to pastor in northeastern Tennessee to be near family. One hobby is crocheting outfits for terminally ill babies. Husband Gil Carper, a portrait artist, fully supports Joyce's ministries. **June 19, Dec. 6.**

Darlene Ytredal Burgeson is a retired sales manager. Her hobbies include sending notes and seasonal cards to shut-ins and people living alone. She also enjoys writing, gardening, and photography. **June 22, Oct. 29.**

Maureen O. Burke lives in New York, where she is a state certified counselor and serves her local church as an elder. Among her hobbies are reading, writing, cooking, and conducting Sabbath school seminars and workshops. **Apr. 7, July 7.**

Betty R. Burnett is thoroughly enjoying retirement, which gives her more time to spend with her husband, grandchildren, writing, music, and walking in the woods. **Jan. 4, Apr. 5, Aug. 14, Dec. 18.**

Cynthia Burrill was born to missionary parents in Bolivia, and is married to Russell, director of the North American Division Evangelism Institute, Berrien Springs, Michigan. Cynthia, who is coordinator of women's ministries at the Seventh-day Adventist Theological Seminary, teaches seminary spouses felt-need evangelism, and is a sponsor of the seminary women's club, Daughters of the Lord. She and her husband have two married children and four grandchildren. **Nov. 7.**

Andrea A. Bussue was born on the Caribbean island of Nevis. She holds a master's degree in education and teaches at a special education facility in Washington, D.C. She has been the children's choir director and superintendent at her local church in Hyattsville, Maryland. She loves children and enjoys reading, traveling, sewing, cooking, and meeting people. **Mar. 30, Apr. 19, Aug. 2.**

Donna Davis Cameron, Ph.D., is an instructor in the Department of Family Medicine at Georgetown University in Washington, D.C., building community-academic partnerships in community medicine in northwest Washington. Donna has at least three passions: listening to women talk about their relationships, raising 7-year-old Joseph, and playing the piano in beautiful rooms. **Jan. 31, Mar. 5.**

Terri Casey has been married to Mike for more than 20 years and has been blessed with two children and two grandchildren. She works as a lab supervisor for a dermatology and laser practice and is a safety officer and consultant for several medical practices. She teaches the youth Bible class at church, and loves to walk, in-line skate, quilt, read, camp, and write. **Nov. 22.**

Fonda Cordis Chaffee has a doctorate in educational administration and degrees in dietetics, specializing in food systems management. A widow, she is a teacher, and the mother of two children. She has served the church for more than 40 years and enjoys travel, playing Scrabble, crocheting, and gardening. **Aug. 7.**

Erica Joan Charles is a registered dietitian who works as a contract food service manager. She lives in Mount Arlington, New Jersey, and was born on the island of Grenada in the Carribean. In 1997 Erica fulfilled a lifelong dream when an article she had written for a professional newsletter was republished in the *Journal of the American Dietetic Association*. **Apr. 26, Oct. 18.**

Frances Charles is a retired school principal who is Adventist Women's Ministries coordinator for the Kwazulu Natal-Free State Conference in South Africa. She is a bereavement counselor and a caregiver at a hospice. Author of *My Tears, My Rainbow*, her hobbies include writing and making pretty things. **May 22, Nov. 12.**

Birol Charlotte Christo is a retired school teacher. During her active service she also worked as an office secretary and a statistician. She lives with her husband in Hosur, India. The mother of five grown children, she enjoys gardening, sewing, and making craft items to finance her project for homeless children. **July 9, Oct. 4.**

Alberta Bennett Ciccarelli is a published freelance photographer and writer living in the beautiful central California coastal area. She and her husband raised four children, three girls and a boy. They now enjoy four grandchildren. Her hobbies are butterfly gardening, tending her sheep, and processing their fleece for weaving. She assists with church and community activities. **May 7, Aug. 15.**

Marsha Claus taught elementary school for two years. After the birth of her son four years ago, she chose to be a stay-at-home mom. Her husband is the manager of the Wisconsin Adventist Book Center. They enjoy traveling around the state with the bookmobile. Her hobbies include traveling, writing, and crafts. **Aug. 16.**

Carel Clay lives in Napa, California, with her husband, daughter, and three cats. She is an associate professor at Pacific Union College. Sewing, gardening, reading, family, and cats are some of her favorite things. **Jan. 21, Feb. 13.**

Clareen Colclesser, widowed in 1994, has two children, Jack and Patti, six grandchildren, and five great-grandchildren. She is active in her church as Sabbath school superintendent. Her hobbies include writing short stories and letters, crossword puzzles, interior decorating, and recently, genealogy. **Aug. 11, Nov. 27.**

Arlene E. Compton of Lincoln, Nebraska, passed away in November 1999. She was a retired nursing administrator and a volunteer with educational and professional nursing groups. **Feb. 11, Oct. 10, Dec. 7.**

Sarah Coon is a registered nurse. She is married and has two daughters, whom she is home-schooling. **Mar. 2.**

Judy Coulston has a Ph.D. in nutrition and a private practice in Fresno, California. She has done a speaking tour of Australia and hosted and coproduced a highly rated weekly television program. Her latest venture is teaching pathophysiology. She also teaches adult Bible classes, is active in women's and prayer ministries. **Feb. 15, June 5.**

Phyllis Dalgleish writes from South Africa. She is a widow, the mother of three grown daughters, and the grandmother of two grandsons and one granddaughter. She has had 45 articles and stories published since 1959, and worked as editor of

KAH Times at Karachi Adventist Hospital. Her hobbies are writing, crocheting, and traveling. **Aug. 6.**

Nicceta "Nikki" Davis counts her greatest blessings in life as having wonderful Christian parents, sisters, and friends. She enjoys watching God do "the extraordinary" with her "ordinary" gifts. She has been on the physical therapy faculty at Loma Linda University since 1995. **Aug. 31.**

Ruth F. Davis lives in Huntsville, Alabama, with her husband. She is the mother of three graduates of Oakwood College. She chairs the Family and Consumer Sciences Department at the college and is an ordained elder there. Ruth has been a missionary to Ghana and Liberia, West Africa. She is active in many church and civic activities. **Nov. 13.**

Wanda Davis is a staff chaplain at a hospital in Portland, Oregon. She is married, the mother of three, and enjoys preaching, teaching, and facilitating small groups. She is a licensed pastoral counselor. **Sept. 10.**

Fauna Rankin Dean lives with her husband and three children on a farm in rural Kansas, where they raise golden retrievers. She is very involved in her church and spends her spare time on her hobbies of writing, photography, handicrafts, and a church music ministry. **Sept. 20, Oct. 19, Dec. 16.**

Sheila Sanders Delaney is currently enjoying retirement and a recent marriage by traveling and being a homemaker. She enjoys actively witnessing to friends and neighbors. **Dec. 3.**

Alicia Worley de Palacios and her husband moved to Ecuador in August 1999. Her hobbies are music, sports (particularly soccer), traveling, and spending time with family and friends. She has worked as a physical therapist and dreams of running a youth hostel in a country closed to Christianity so she can share the gospel. **May 20.**

Eulene Dodson (also known as Jodi) is a retired mother, composer, musician, and graphic arts designer. Her self-published book, *I Just Can't Do It, God,* reveals her journey from birth to loss of spiritual hope to her eventual return to God. Since her reconversion she has been writing and speaking, including an interview with 3ABN cable television. **Jan. 12, Apr. 15.**

Yvonne Donatto and her husband, Anthony, reside in Huntsville, Alabama. They have two adult children, Yolande and Anthony II, and a son-in-law, Donnell. Yvonne enjoys camping and traveling, has lived on three continents, and collects memorabilia. She is executive secretary of the King's Daughters, both the local chapter and at the national level. Her granddaughters, Ayana and Maya, are her pride and joy. **Apr. 8.**

Maria Freire Souza dos Santos is from Iheus, Bahia, Brazil. She praises the Lord that her eight children are all strong church members. She is women's ministries director, director of branch Sabbath school, and coordinator of a Sabbath school class. **Apr. 12.**

Goldie Down is an Australian pastor's wife, former missionary, and the mother of six adult children. In addition to helping her husband with church work, she teaches classes in creative writing and has 20 biographical books and a textbook to her credit, as well as numerous stories and articles in Seventh-day Adventist church papers. **Aug. 4, Oct. 3, Dec. 2.**

Louise M. Driver lives in Beltsville, Maryland, with her pastor-husband, Don. They have three adult sons, three granddaughters, and a grandson. At church Louise is involved with music, youth, and women's ministries. She also works in women's ministries at the General Conference of Seventh-day Adventists. Her hobbies include singing, music, skiing, reading, crafts, gardening, and traveling to historical places. **Sept. 8, Nov. 30.**

Etta Maycock Dudley has three (plus four "adopted") children and four (plus four "adopted") grandchildren. She and her husband recently celebrated 50 years of marriage. Now retired in Tennessee, she was her husband's secretary for 31 years while he was president of South Central Conference of Seventh-day Adventists. She enjoys sewing, hiking, reading, gardening, helping to care for her paralyzed son-in-law, and bringing sunshine to all her contacts. **Nov. 18.**

Joy Dustow is a retired teacher. She enjoys taking an active part in the social and spiritual activities in the retirement village in which she resides with her husband. **July 30.**

Heidi Michelle Ehlert is a massage therapist who enjoys the outdoors and is an avid backpacker. She spent two years in Melbourne, Australia, as assistant dean of girls at Lilydale Adventist Academy. During that time she wrote the devotionals appearing in this book. **Feb. 26, Mar. 6.**

Jamisen Farley is a medical transcriptionist for Yale University School of Medicine. She is a volunteer in the mentor program at The Children's Center of Hamden, Connecticut. Her interests include houseplants, archeology, reading, and writing. **Dec. 20.**

Edna Ferris-Heise, born to missionary parents, is now the wife of a retired minister. They have three children, a minister, a nurse, and a doctor of medicine. Edna and her husband live in the Avondale Retirement Village in Cooranbong, New South Wales, where Edna has been appointed chaplain of the lodge. She enjoys the spiritual challenge of ministering to the retirees there. Writing and walking with her good-fun husband, Vern, are her favorite hobbies. **Sept. 26.**

Karen Fettig lives with her husband, Clint, on a farm near Manderson, Wyoming. Karen is interested in medical missionary work, teaching people simple remedies for prevention and healing of disease along with the love of Jesus Christ. Her hobbies include gardening and writing praise songs. She has a daughter, a son and daughter-in-law, and a toddler grandson. During the summer she herds cattle in the Bighorn Mountains above Ten Sleep, Wyoming. **May 25.**

Valerie Fidelia and her husband have been missionaries to the Middle East for almost seven years. She is responsible for children's, family, health, and women's ministries and enjoys the travel opportunities this assignment affords. They have four children and six grandchildren. Valerie enjoys needlework and music and serves her local church as elder and as leader of the worship and music ministry. **Feb. 14.**

Margaret E. Fisher and her husband, Floyd, live in Tennessee. She is communication director at the Ogden Road Seventh-day Adventist Church in Tennessee, and cares for her 99-year-old mother. **Apr. 11.**

Edith Fitch retired after 41 years of teaching, the last 28 in the church school at Canadian University College. She enjoys writing and has devoted many hours in research for church and school histories. She volunteers in the CUC archives. Her hobbies include needlecraft and traveling. **July 21, Sept. 15, Nov. 4.**

Heide Ford is the associate editor of *Women of Spirit,* a Christian women's magazine. She is a minister's wife, lives in Maryland, and holds a master's degree in counseling. She loves reading, hiking, and whale watching. **May 1, Aug. 22, Oct. 24.**

Sari Karina Fordham graduated from Southern Adventist University, Collegedale, Tennessee, in 1998 with a Bachelor's degree in history. She enjoys mission work and spent a year in Thailand as a student missionary and a year in Korea after graduation. She loves to play basketball, cook Thai food, water-ski, and read. She has been published in *Insight,* in *Junior Mission Quarterly,* and in the 1999 women's devotional, and has plans to continue her education by getting a master's degree in English. **Feb. 2.**

Denali Fox, a great-grandmother, is children's ministry coordinator for northwestern Arkansas, Adventurer director, home-schools her grandchildren, and is the kindergarten leader in her church. She loves kids, and her hobbies include crocheting, reading, and collecting. **Nov. 21.**

Edith C. Fraser is a wife, mother, and college professor at Oakwood College, Huntsville, Alabama. She is chair of the social work department, adjunct professor at several other colleges, and family director for her church. She is a speaker, family counselor, and consultant in the United States, as well as internationally. **Nov. 23.**

Tercia Freire is a registered nurse with a master's degree in religion from Andrews University, Berrien Springs, Michigan. Previously employed at Florida Hospital's Progressive Care in Orlando, she now works at West Congo Union Mission, where her husband is the Adventist Development and Relief Agency director. In her spare time she used to go to the beach and to the mall, but now she makes her way to the swimming pool and open market. **Sept. 30.**

Ruth Frikart writes from Switzerland, where she is a chiropodist. **Jan. 17.**

Edna Maye Gallington is part of the communication team at Southeastern California Conference of Seventh-day Adventists and is a graduate of La Sierra University in Riverside, California. She is a member of Toastmasters International and the Loma Linda Writing Guild. She enjoys freelance writing, music, gourmet cooking, entertaining, hiking, and racquetball. **Apr. 3, Nov. 9.**

Marilyn Gantz is a pastor's wife and missionary teacher living in Sri Lanka. She has two adult children and two grandchildren, and enjoys training teachers, travel, gardening, history, biking, music, and directing the school choir. **Nov. 8.**

Evelyn Glass enjoys her family and loves having her grandchildren living next door. She and her husband, Darrell, live in northern Minnesota on the farm where Darrell was born. Evelyn is active in her local church and in her community. She currently writes a weekly column for her local paper. Serving as women's ministries/family life director for the Mid-America Union keeps her busy. **Mar. 4, Apr. 16, Aug. 26, Dec 1.**

Kathryn Gordon is a medical social worker in northern California. She took two weeks to drive across the country with a friend while moving from Michigan to California. Her favorite places were Sedona, Arizona; New Orleans; and driving on Route 66. **Mar. 9.**

Mary Jane Graves and her minister-husband retired in North Carolina. They have two adult sons and two granddaughters. She has worked as a society editor for her hometown newspaper and as a secretary, school registrar, and librarian. When her boys were growing up they furnished her with material for stories for *Our little Friend, Primary Treasure, Guide,* and *Youth's Instructor.* **July 26, Sept. 11, Nov. 16.**

Ellie Green is president of E. Green and Associates, a consulting firm. She's a prolific writer and full-time lecturer who enjoys speaking at Christian women's retreats. Other interests include oil, watercolor, and chalk painting, as well as crocheting and knitting. Her son is an attorney, her daughter a nurse. Her husband is a retired NASA rocket scientist. **Feb. 19, Dec. 24.**

Carol Joy Greene writes from central Florida, where she lives with her husband, a retired minister. She is active in women's ministries prayer groups. She enjoys being with her four grandchildren. **Dec. 5.**

Glenda-mae Greene is assistant vice president for student services at Andrews University. She delights in being the cherished aunt of three nieces and a nephew. Her contributions in this book are the end products of "praying with a pen" as she prepares for her speaking appointments with various women's and church groups. **Jan. 3, June 28, July 15, Aug. 24, Dec. 27.**

Norma Morris Greenidge writes from Berrien Springs, Michigan, where she works in the James White Library at Andrews University. She is the mother of two adult children and the grandmother of two. She is an elder and coordinator of women's ministries in her local church. In her spare time she enjoys cross-stitch, knitting, and sewing dresses for her granddaughter. **Aug. 25.**

Gloria Gregory is a minister's wife, the mother of two girls, and an associate professor of nursing at West Indies College, Mandeville, Jamaica. A graduate of Andrews University's extension program, with a Master's in education, her hobbies include hand crafts, playing word games, sewing, and gardening. **Sept. 19, Nov. 26.**

Barbara J. Hales is a certified family life educator, writing from New Carlisle, Indiana, where she lives with her husband. They have four children and two grandchildren. She enjoys writing, gardening, community outreach projects, and mission trips. **Jan. 24, Oct. 16.**

Barbara Hall develops training materials and teaches customers to use computer products. She and her husband, Eric, have five growing children. Barbara has been a permanent member of cradle roll Sabbath school for the past six years. She loves to read, enjoys gardening, and would like to travel more. She hasn't been flying in way too many years. **Sept. 23.**

Jean Hall and her husband were missionaries in Thailand, pioneered the Seventh-day Adventist work in Laos, and worked in Sarawak. Since retiring, they have served the Adventist Development and Relief Agency in Ghana, Mozambique, Sudan, Somalia, Azerbaijan, Kenya, and now Rwanda. She felt called to be a missionary at a very young age, and since this was also her husband's goal, she was assured that God led them together in their work. **Jan. 26.**

Lynnetta Siagian Hamstra is the associate director of women's ministries for the General Conference of Seventh-day Adventists, Silver Spring, Maryland. She was born and raised on the tropical island of Borneo, in the state of Sabah, Malaysia. She inherits her love for music from her mom, and for traveling from her dad. She also enjoys reading and sewing. She lives in Columbia, Maryland, with her husband, Dan, and their dog, Abercrombie. **June 26.**

Ursula M. Hedges is a retired secondary school administrator. She and her Australian husband have given 10 years of mission service in the Pacific, Australia, and New Zealand. Ursula is a church elder and has published books, stories, and articles. An interior designer, she also enjoys reading, producing dramas, sewing, cooking, and writing. **July 19, Oct. 11, Dec. 8.**

Beverly Helmstetler and her husband have two teenage children. They grow pomegranates commercially, something she considers a great family project. They served at two Seventh-day Adventist academies in the North Brazil Union. Between her family and church responsibilities, she has a full-time job. Her current hobbies include gardening, music, and sewing. **Feb. 7.**

Maxine Henry lives in Springfield, Ohio. She is a retired secretary who enjoys reading and collecting antiques. This mother of four and grandmother of nine is a member of Ethan Temple Seventh-day Adventist Church. **Dec. 30.**

Jo Ann Hilton and her husband have two young adult children. They enjoy exploring back country roads and browsing antique shops for relics of the past. **Jan. 2, Feb. 1, Mar. 25, Apr. 10, June 15.**

Kyna Hinson, a journalist and assistant college professor, is involved in women's ministries through her local church and conference. She is a published writer and enjoys embroidery, reading, baking, and working with teenagers. **June 24.**

Roxy Hoehn is not a farmer, but she thoroughly enjoys living in the great grain belt of America. Her farming experience is limited to a few flowers. She is the women's ministries director for the Seventh-day Adventist churches in Kansas and Nebraska. **Oct. 8.**

Karen Holford writes from England, where she works with her husband in family ministry. They have three children. She has written three books and numerous articles. Besides writing, her interests include crafts, interior design on a shoestring, and finding ways to scatter God's love. **May 18, July 10, Aug. 23, Oct. 6.**

Tamyra Horst, women's ministries director for the Columbia Union and Pennsylvania Conferences of Seventh-day Adventists, has written a number of books, including *How to Hug a Heart, A Woman of Worth, The Gift of Friendship,* and *Strengthening the Church Through Women's Ministries.* She speaks for seminars and retreats across the United States. She is wife to Tim and mom to Joshua and Zachary. She loves to hike, bike, canoe, and camp with her family. **Apr. 17, June 12, Sept. 6.**

Helene Rabena Hubbard, M.D., Ph.D., is a pediatrician. She enjoys conducting the Palmetto Seventh-day Adventist church orchestra and working in Sabbath school. She writes a health column for *Women of Spirit* magazine. **Jan. 1, Mar. 19, May 9.**

Lorraine Hudgins is retired with her minister-husband in Loma Linda, California. She has worked at the Voice of Prophecy, Faith for Today, and the General Conference of Seventh-day Adventists. She has written two books, and her poems and articles have appeared in various publications, including the last eight women's devotional books. Her five children and 11 grandchildren are her joy. **May 4, Sept. 16, Oct. 31, Dec. 13.**

Eunice Verrett Hughes, a first-time contributor, is an early childhood interventionist, an ordained elder, and a former missionary to England. She and her pastor-husband are now retired. She enjoys talking about God's love, is active in her church as women's ministries leader and Sabbath school superintendent, is involved in an intercessory prayer ministry, writes "mommie" letters to children, travels, and enjoys being with family and friends. **Apr. 9, June 13.**

Lisa D. Ingelse says her favorite passion used to be writing. Then she became a mother. Hands down, her greatest joy is her two daughters, Zoe and Phoebe. No Ph.D. could have prepared her for this most important job—only the love of her husband, Rex, and the presence of God as the head of their family. **Jan. 19.**

Aleah Iqbal is a freelance writer who lives with her family in Willimantic, Connecticut. She home-schooled her children for 10 years. Her publishing credits include a book of poetry, original recipes for community cookbooks, and health store newsletters. In the past, she hosted her own local cable television show. She is currently writing a children's book. **May 16.**

Valerie F. Jacobs, an occupational therapist, is married to a nursing home administrator. She recently moved to Maine, where she enjoys her work as a hand therapist and has started a moose collection. Her interests include reading, cooking, and outdoor activities. **June 29, Nov. 15.**

Becky Jarnes was a freshman at Southern Adventist University, Collegedale, Tennessee, at the time of this writing. She is a nursing major and girls' captain of their GymMaster program. She had a poem published in the *Adventist Review* in 1998, enjoys kayaking, rock climbing, skiing, and wakeboarding. **Oct. 9.**

Lois E. Johannes enjoys volunteer work with the community, the church (as a treasurer), and the hospital. She is retired from mission service in Southern Asia and the Far East. **Feb. 22.**

Rosa Madam Johnson is a Sierra Leonean, currently a refugee in Gambia, West Africa. She is a graduate teacher who teaches English language and literature at the junior and senior secondary level. She loves reading. **Oct. 20.**

Linda Duncan Julie is a first-time contributor to the women's devotional book. She is pursuing her master's degree in digital media and is a member of the Abilene Seventh-day Adventist Church. Married for three years, she is a registered nurse who enjoys media communication and eventually would like to become a public speaker. **July 22.**

Carol Brackett Kassinger, a registered nurse and the mother of two grown sons, has recently remarried. She is the director of education at a hospital in Kentucky. She enjoys reading, scuba diving, traveling, shopping, meeting new people, and learning. **June 7.**

Stacey Kennedy lives in northern California with her husband and two daughters. She has just written a vegetarian cookbook for children and enjoys spending time with friends and family, cooking, crafting, camping, and antiques. **May 24.**

Marilyn King is a retired registered nurse who lives in Oregon with her husband. She holds a master's degree in business and is active in her local church and community. Her interests include a loving family, reading, walking, and enjoying country life. **May 10.**

Hepzibah G. Kore is presently the women's ministries director of the Southern Asia Division of Seventh-day Adventists, Hosur, India. She and her husband have two grown children. Hepzibah enjoys reading and gardening. **May 28, Aug. 12.**

Patricia Mulraney Kovalski retired after teaching elementary grades for 38 years, 35 years in Seventh-day Adventist schools. She and her husband enjoy traveling, especially to visit their children and grandchildren. She also enjoys crafts and needlework. **July 27, Dec. 22.**

Ludmila M. Krushenitskaya is women's ministries director for the Euro-Asia Division of the Seventh-day Adventist Church, which includes all of the former Soviet Union. She helped her husband in his pastoral ministry for 18 years; then they moved to Moscow to work. They have two children and a grandson. Ludmila likes reading, singing, communicating with people, and working in the garden. **July 31, Dec. 10.**

Marbel Kwei is the wife of the Gambia Mission president, director of Gambia women's ministries, and lecturer at Gambia College. She works with her husband in pastoral work and loves reading. **Nov. 24.**

Bienvisa Ladion-Nebres was born in the Philippines and presently lives and works with her auditor-husband, in Lubumbashi, Democratic Republic of the Congo. She enjoys helping with the personal ministries and the music departments of her church. **Mar. 17.**

Nathalie Ladner-Bischoff and her husband, Marvin, live in Walla Walla, Washington. She is a retired nurse and, besides homemaking, reads, writes, gardens, and skis. Her most recent publication is *An Angel's Touch,* a book of miracle stories, answered prayers, and angel encounters. **Feb. 18, July 16, Dec. 29.**

Margaret B. Lawrence is a nationally recognized educator and the first female elder at the Berean Seventh-day Adventist Church in Baton Rouge, Louisiana. She is a local newspaper columnist, and enjoys writing, sewing, and public speaking. **Aug. 5.**

Gina Lee is the author of more than 500 stories, articles, and poems. Her work has also been included in 12 books. When not writing, she enjoys working at the public library and caring for her four cats. **Jan. 13, Mar. 20, July 29, Oct. 12.**

Gwen Lee is retired from government service. She serves in her church as head deaconess, and works with community services and the prayer chain. She enjoys traveling, photography, quilting, genealogy, and corresponding with friends and relatives on the computer. **Jan. 25.**

Ruth Lennox is a retired physician. She is women's ministries director for the British Columbia Conference of Seventh-day Adventists. She enjoys walking with her dog, having fun with her granddaughters, and writing and producing monologues about Bible women. She and her husband, John, also a physician, spent nine years in West Africa before moving from England to Canada. They have three adult children and two granddaughters. **Feb. 24, July 13, Dec. 11.**

Cecelia Lewis writes from Huntsville, Alabama. She is a Bible instructor and teaches baptismal classes for adults, youth, and children at the Oakwood College Seventh-day Adventist Church. She enjoys tutoring at the elementary school, reading, writing, gardening, and being a member of the bell choir. **Jan. 8.**

Bessie Siemens Lobsien is a retired librarian who, in addition to working in the United States, has worked in other countries as a missionary. She now serves her local church as the communication secretary. She has published several poems, articles, and stories in church papers. Her hobbies include writing, sewing, and needlework. **Feb. 10, May 5, July 4, Sept. 2.**

Betty Anne Lowe writes from Bermuda, where she works as an office manager-pension administrator. She serves her church as the women's ministries director and assistant leader of the youth Sabbath school class. Betty Anne is part of the FITS (Feet-in-the-Street) Walking Club. Her other hobbies include reading and swimming. **Jan. 30, Mar. 12.**

Julie M. Lyles is food services director at Mount Aetna Camp, Hagerstown, Maryland. She is the children's ministry director at the Williamsport, Maryland, Seventh-day Adventist Church, enjoys working with children, and thrives when leading out in Vacation Bible School. She likes to read, write, garden, spend time with friends, cook new and exciting ways, shop, and do crafts. **Feb. 5.**

Shirley Gast Lynn-Smith lives in Kansas City, Kansas, with her husband, Milton Smith, a retired parochial school teacher. She is a freelance writer with published articles in a number of magazines and local newspapers. The mother of four and grandmother of eight enjoys family, church, walking, singing, painting, writing, and being a friend. **Jan. 10.**

Pat Madsen of Fresno, California, passed away in January 1999. She had served as a

Sabbath school superintendent at her church and had been editor in chief of her high school paper. She was a contributor to several of the women's ministries devotional books. **Jan. 16, Feb. 16, June 4, Aug. 9, Sept. 5.**

Pearl Manderson is now retired and resides with her husband in Florida. She has two sons and four grandsons. She is a devoted church worker and plans and organizes church programs. She is a lover of flowers and enjoys doing embroidery, crocheting, writing letters, reading, and walking. **July 28.**

Beulah Manuel and her husband teach at Southeast Asia Union College, Singapore, where she is an associate professor of English. The mother of a teenage daughter and a 10-year-old son, she enjoys writing, traveling, camping, and listening to Christian music. **Feb. 20, Mar. 27.**

Alicia Marquez has been the accountant for the Greater New York Conference of Seventh-day Adventists for nine years, having previously worked for a Spanish telecast for 11 years. She is chair of the women's ministries committee of the Greater New York Conference, treasurer of the women's prayer retreat, and an elder at Far Rockaway Spanish Seventh-day Adventist Church. Born in Uruguay, she came to the United States 29 years ago. **Apr. 24, Oct. 15.**

Philippa Marshall, a retired nurse, writes from England. She is involved with her local church and also does volunteer work. She enjoys writers holidays and meeting other writers, attending women's ministries retreats, and visiting friends and family. **Dec. 23.**

Peggy Mason lives in Wales with her husband and is a teacher of English and a writer. Her hobbies include growing and arranging dried flowers, cooking, sewing, gardening, and reading. She is a pianist-composer and enjoys working for her church and community. **Feb. 23, Mar. 23.**

Soosanna Mathew lives in India, where her husband is secretary of the South India Section of Seventh-day Adventists in Bangalore. A graduate of Spicer Memorial College, Pune, India, she taught school for 20 years. She is active in the Adventist Youth Society, children's Sabbath school, and choir. Her hobbies are singing, telling stories, and writing poems. She and her husband have two adult children, David and Hannah. **June 30, Sept. 14.**

Maria G. McClean, originally from Barbados, lives with her daughter, Kamila, and her husband, Wayne, in Toronto, Ontario, Canada. She enjoys Bible trivia, music, writing, and taking long rides in the country. **Apr. 2.**

Martha "Genie" McKinney-Tiffany lives with her husband and daughter in southern California. She is active in her local church and sings in various choirs at the Van Nuys Seventh-day Adventist Church. **Aug. 18.**

Patsy Murdoch Meeker, of Virginia, is communication leader for her church and enjoys writing, reading, photography, and her family and friends, especially her Friend Jesus. **July 14, Sept. 27, Dec. 12.**

Retta Michaelis writes from Loma Linda, California, where she lives with her husband and two daughters. She is a medical technologist at the Loma Linda

University Medical Center Blood Bank. She enjoys reading, writing, Bible study, and her family. **Feb. 4, May 12.**

Marcia Mollenkopf, a retired school teacher, lives in Klamath Falls, Oregon. She is active in local church activities and has served in both adult and children's divisions. Her hobbies include reading, crafts, and bird-watching. **Nov. 3, Dec. 9.**

Esperanza Aquino Mopera is a registered nurse in the Virginia Beach, Virginia, public schools. She is director of women's ministries at the Tidewater Seventh-day Adventist Church. Her hobbies include gardening, watching and feeding backyard lake inhabitants such as fish, ducks, birds, and worms. She also enjoys baby-sitting her grandchildren. She is a member of AUC/PUC EASNAC Tidewater chapter. **May 27.**

Bonnie Moyers lives with her husband and two cats in Staunton, Virginia. The mother of two adult children, she works as a certified nursing assistant, musician for a Methodist church, painter and paperhanger, and freelance writer whenever she can fit it in. She has been published in a number magazines and books. **May 30, Sept. 17.**

Lillian Musgrave and her family have chosen northern California as their home for more than 35 years. She enjoys writing, especially poetry, and has had several poems and articles published. Other interests include the Parents Support Group, HIV Spiritual Support ministry, family activities, music, and church responsibilities. **June 2, Sept. 21.**

Joan Minchin Neall was born in Australia, lived in England, and now makes her home in Tennessee. She is a registered nurse, and she and her pastor-husband have four adult children and eight grandchildren. She is the women's ministries leader for her church. She enjoys journaling, young women's Bible study groups, and spending time with her family. **May 29, July 12, Nov. 28.**

Anne Elaine Nelson, a retired elementary teacher, is a published author. She lives with her husband in Michigan. Their four children have blessed them with 11 grandchildren. She is active as women's ministries leader, teen leader, and assistant superintendent for Sabbath school in her church. Her favorite activities are sewing, music, photography, and creating memories with her grandchildren. **Mar. 18, May 17, Sept. 18.**

Denise Newton is a wife, the mother of three, and the grandmother of two. She is an administrative secretary and director of the Women's Ministries Department for the Transvaal Conference in the Southern Africa Union. She runs a strong women's ministries prison program and helps struggling women set up small businesses. **Jan. 5.**

Mabel Rollins Norman resided in Avon Park, Florida, until her death in 1998. She has been published in a number of magazines, several newspapers, and two women's devotional books. She and her husband taught an in-prison Bible class. She was known for her encouraging cards and letters. **Mar. 15, May 31.**

Erika Olfert was born in Slovenia but now lives in Washington State. She and her minister-husband have been missionaries in India. She is the mother of two adult sons. She is a registered nurse, who works as a consultant and teacher. Her interests are youth and women's ministries, oil painting, knitting, reading, swimming, bike riding, singing, and practical writing. **Jan. 22.**

Dorothy Anne O'Reilly has written for several publications. She is a member of Murrieta Springs Seventh-day Adventist Church in California. **May 21.**

Christine Jeda Orillosa was a ninth grader at Highland View Academy in Hagerstown, Maryland, when she wrote this devotional. She enjoys writing poems, sending e-mails to friends, and loves dogs. She grew up in Africa and longs to go back there someday. **Aug. 8.**

Jemima D. Orillosa works at the General Conference of Seventh-day Adventists in Silver Spring, Maryland. She has two teenage daughters, whom she adores, and a loving husband. She enjoys and loves to be with people. She was a missionary in Africa for eight years and in Cyprus for two years. Writing, walking, and entertaining visitors and friends are some of her hobbies. **Mar. 16, Sept. 28.**

Rose Otis, formerly the director of women's ministries for the General Conference of Seventh-day Adventists, is now the vice president of the Texas Conference of Seventh-day Adventists. She began the women's devotional book project and edited the first six. She enjoys water sports with her family, writing, and being home. **Mar. 1.**

Hannele Ottschofski lives in Germany with her family. She is editor of the local Shepherdess newsletter and loves to read and write. From time to time, she presents seminars at women's retreats. She loves to play the piano and directs a choir in her local church. She has just completed her first hand-made quilt for her little grandson. **July 25, Oct. 21.**

Mabel Owusu-Antwi comes from Ghana, West Africa. She recently graduated with a bachelor's degree in English literature from Andrews University, Berrien Springs, Michigan, where her husband is a seminarian studying for his Ph.D. in Old Testament Theology. **June 27.**

Ofelia A. Pangan is a minister's wife, the mother of three young adults, and the grandmother of six. She loves walking for exercise, gardening, traveling, visiting grandchildren, and playing Scrabble. **Jan. 23, Apr. 25, July 5, Aug. 27, Oct. 2.**

Revel Papaioannou is a pastor's wife in Veroia, Greece, the biblical town of Berea. Apart from church work, teaching English, and caring for two elderly relatives at home, she enjoys walking, gymnastic class, and collecting stamps, coins, and phone cards. **Oct. 25.**

Jill Warden Parchment is a retired physician's wife and a former editor of the Southeast Asia Mission *Messenger.* She was privileged to teach in many countries. Aside from academics, she enjoyed coaching in sports, synchronized swimming, and choreography. **June 6.**

Julia L. Pearce chairs the Nursing Department at Pacific Union College, Angwin, California. She enjoys reading, sewing, writing, and traveling, but has interests in church and health education as well. Julia is a women's health consultant and gives presentations on women's history and on health. **Dec. 15.**

Ivy Petersen has retired after 34 years of being a teacher, lecturer, and principal from first grade to college level. She and her husband have both served as local elders and lay preachers. They now travel throughout South Africa promoting and establishing women's ministries. They have five children and 10 grandchildren. **Sept. 29.**

Kathleen Stearman Pflugrad enjoys the beautiful scenery of northern Michigan, where she lives with her husband. She finds pleasure in nature, editing, canoeing, and camping. **Jan. 7, July 11.**

Diana Pittenger, the mother of two children, lives in central Illinois. After 25 years in health care, she now works as a certified massage therapist. Teaching the youth at church and working with women's ministries is an enjoyment, but her first love is coordinating a very active prison ministry. She gardens, writes, watches birds, reads, and collects porcelain birds and books. **Jan. 15, Mar. 28.**

Birdie Poddar is from northeastern India. She is the wife of a retired communication director, and worked as an elementary teacher, cashier, cashier accountant, and statistician before retiring in 1991. Sewing, gardening, and composing poems are some of her hobbies. **June 21, Nov. 11.**

Alice Heath Prive recently moved to Los Angeles to work on a Ph.D. in ethics and religion at the University of Southern California. Good times are being with friends—old and new—and sneaking some time to read "just for fun." **Feb. 9.**

Louise Rea raised a family of two, taught high school and college business education for 20 years, and has climbed most of the major peaks of the northwestern United States. She explored the Wallowa Mountains in Oregon and recently finished writing a guidebook about them. She does volunteer work, reads to the elderly, prints Scripture texts for Bible lessons for the elderly, and helps her 92-year-old mother. **Aug. 19.**

Judith Redman lives in a village on the south coast of England. She is involved in the development of family life in her local church and works as a secretary for a large multinational company. She enjoys caravaning, crafts, and playing squash. **Aug. 28, Nov. 10.**

Arnita Reid, a licensed counselor, serves as women's ministries leader and assistant family life leader for her church in New Rochelle, New York. She enjoys gardening, music, traveling, and conducting workshops and seminars. **Mar. 8, Sept. 4.**

Lynda Mae Richardson is the single mother of an autistic child. She has been involved in the music and women's ministries departments at her church. She also writes, produces, and directs special church programs. A published writer, Lynda also enjoys singing, the computer, writing, hiking, friends, and nature. **Apr. 14.**

Jean Reiffenstein Rothgeb is a medical secretary in the office of an orthopedic surgeon, where her husband is also employed. She is busy with the Home and

School Association and serves as school treasurer and church organist. She enjoys all kinds of needlework, but most of all she loves canoeing with her kids (who spoil her), and being outdoors. **Feb. 28, Mar. 11.**

Quetah Manyoé Sackie-Osborne is an early childhood educator. She is married to Charles Ray Osborne III, and they have one daughter. She enjoys reading, writing poetry, encouraging others, and walking. Sometime in the future she would like to visit some of her family members who live in Liberia, West Africa. **Sept. 13.**

Deborah Sanders has shared from her personal journal, *Dimensions of Love,* since the beginning of this devotional book series. She goes by the pen name Sonny's Mommy and lives in Canada with Ron, her husband of 32 years. They have been blessed with two children, Andrea and Sonny. Sonny is severely mentally challenged with autism. Deborah enjoys making others feel special. **May 11, Oct. 7.**

Marie H. Seard enjoys the luxury of retirement. She often assists with special projects in the Ministerial Department of the world headquarters of the Seventh-day Adventist Church in Silver Spring, Maryland. Traveling with her husband, who is not yet retired, and visiting their son in California bring a smile to her face. A contributor to past devotional books, she enjoys writing, reading, and listening to music. **Oct. 27.**

Jean Secilia teaches microbiology to graduate and postgraduate students and has had research papers published in international journals. Her hobbies include reading, listening to music, cooking, and tending her two children. She attends the Central Tamil Church, Bangalore, India. **July 24.**

Donna Lee Sharp is active in music programs in her church, church school, and at three community organizations. Traveling, bird-watching, and visiting children and grandchildren are her favorite activities away from home. **June 9, Oct. 28.**

Donna Sherrill works in a small country store, close to Jefferson Adventist Academy. She is working on an album of songs she has written and is currently a publicist for a Christian country recording artist. **Apr. 1.**

Carrol Johnson Shewmake is a freelance writer who has had many articles, stories, and poems, plus six books, published. She and her husband are the parents of four adult children and have eight grandchildren. Carrol and her husband served 43 years in pastoral ministry, and in their retirement are actively involved with the prayer ministry in the churches of their conference. **Jan. 14, July 3.**

Judy Musgrave Shewmake and her husband, Tom, live in northern California with their four children, whom she teaches at home. She is the editor of a monthly newsletter for Seventh-day Adventist home schoolers. Her favorite hobby is writing, but in any spare time she enjoys reading, genealogy, and making memory scrapbooks. **Mar. 24.**

Bonita J. Shields is an associate pastor who lives with her husband in Takoma Park, Maryland. Bonita enjoys writing for Christian magazines, public speaking, reading, walking, crafts, and collecting baskets. **Mar. 3**

Patricia L. Shinskia lives in Denver, Colorado, with her husband. She enjoys singing, listening to music, writing poetry, reading, walking, and meeting people. She works as an intake technician in the district attorney's juvenile diversion program. **Oct. 17.**

Rose Neff Sikora and her husband live in the mountains of western North Carolina. A registered nurse, her interests include camping in their travel trailer, writing, spending time with her three grandchildren, and helping others. She has had articles and stories published in the local newspaper, in a number of magazines, and in the women's ministries devotional books. **Apr. 27, Oct. 30.**

Sandra Simanton, a licensed social worker, is a family counselor in North Dakota. She lives in Grand Forks with her husband and two children. She is involved in the children's ministry and women's ministry programs in her church. July 23, Nov. 29. Darlene Simmonds writes from Hempstead, New York, where she is the Sabbath school superintendent for her church, as well as the district leader for women's ministries. Darleen enjoys singing and playing the piano for relaxation. In her spare time she ministers to the needs of the elderly. **July 6.**

Donna A. Smith is an assistant professor and program director for the didactic program in dietetics at Oakwood College in Alabama. She does lecturing and nutritional counseling and, in her spare time, enjoys skating, watching movie classics, decorating, real estate, and entertaining cats. **June 23.**

Penelope S. Smith is a 1991 Oakwood College graduate who is married, with one son, Jeremie. She currently lives in Atlanta, Georgia, where she enjoys reading inspirational books, writing short stories, and listening to gospel music. She is writing her first book. **Apr. 30, Aug. 30.**

Ethel Footman Smothers writes from Grand Rapids, Michigan. She is a published poet and children's book author. Ethel and her husband have four daughters and seven granddaughters. **Feb. 8, Feb. 25.**

Ardis Dick Stenbakken is director of women's ministries for the General Conference of Seventh-day Adventists, Silver Spring, Maryland. She and her husband have two married children. Ardis enjoys seeing women grow in their love and service for the Lord, and she delights in helping make that happen. Someday she hopes to quilt, paint, and cross-stitch again. **Mar. 10, July 2, Oct. 1, Nov. 25.**

Lorraine James Stiggers is a naturopathic doctor and executive director of New Start Health and Education Services. She has completed a nutrition and recipe book. She volunteers in community outreach geared toward youth and seniors, and enjoys playing the piano, listening to and singing quality music, reading, writing, teaching, sewing, and traveling. **July 18.**

Iris L. Stovall is administrative secretary and assistant editor of the monthly newsletter in the Department of Women's Ministries at the General Conference of Seventh-day Adventists, Silver Spring, Maryland. An ordained elder, she is married, with three adult children. She enjoys singing, videography, and creative writing. Iris wrote the department's Women's Emphasis Day 2000 resource packet, *Yes, There IS Joy in the Journey.* **Mar. 7, June 20, Nov. 1, Dec. 25.**

Aude Surdi, the daughter of missionary parents, was born in Madagascar. She is a German teacher near Paris, France, who enjoys visiting elderly people and ministering to those who are ill. **Oct. 13.**

Carolyn Rathbun Sutton, former editor of *Guide magazine* and author of *Journey to Joy,* now lives in Grants Pass, Oregon. Carolyn enjoys teaching a children's Bible class, volunteering at a wildlife rehab center, and doing freelance writing and public speaking, and is learning how to drive a tractor. **Aug. 17, Sept. 24, Nov. 5.**

Loraine F. Sweetland, retired in Tennessee, writes a weekly column for her local newspaper, detailing the activities of her church. She is also church clerk and library advisee. She enjoys surfing the Internet, gardening, reading, and writing. **May 26, Aug. 10, Dec. 31.**

Frieda Tanner, a retired registered nurse, keeps busy by sending Sabbath school materials all over the world. She now lives in Eugene, Oregon, to be near her two grandchildren. **Oct. 23.**

Arlene Taylor is risk manager at St. Helena Hospital and Health Center, Deer Park, California, and president of her own educational nonprofit corporation. An internationally known speaker, author, and brain function consultant, she presents a variety of seminars, including *The Brain and Innate Giftedness.* **Mar. 14, June 8, Aug. 13, Dec. 17.**

Sharon M. Thomas is an elementary school teacher and the mother of two sons at Oakwood College in Alabama. She enjoys reading, walking, and shopping. **Feb. 17.**

Stella Thomas works in the General Conference of Seventh-day Adventists Global Mission Office in Silver Spring, Maryland. She is a primary Sabbath school teacher at the Takoma Park Seventh-day Adventist church and enjoys traveling and being a mother to her two children. **Aug. 3.**

Stella Thompson is a wife, mother, and teacher of literature and composition who is currently completing a graduate degree in rhetoric and linguistics. Her favorite church roles have included coordinating a women's ministries group and teaching a young adult class. **Jan. 20, Mar. 31, Nov. 14.**

Milane Y. Todd writes from Huntsville, Alabama, where she works with the Pathfinders at the First Seventh-day Adventist Church. She enjoys photography, reading, most sports, writing, and working with children. **Apr. 22.**

Nelma Marquardt Tochetto delights in the Lord, along with her pastor husband and their three children. She is a teacher who likes working with children. Her favorite pastimes are walking, reading, and writing letters. She lives in São Paulo, Brazil. **May 6, Sept. 7.**

Christiane Tuor left France when she was 25. She now lives in Switzerland and works as a secretary at the Euro-Africa Division of Seventh-day Adventists. When she was 12 years old and not yet baptized, she summed up the adult Sabbath school lesson. At 14 she taught a Sabbath school class of 6-to10-year-olds. She likes reading, individual and team sports and above all, speaking about our Lord. **Sept. 22, Nov. 6.**

Nancy L. Van Pelt is a certified family life educator, best-selling author, and internationally known speaker. She has written more than 20 books and has traversed the globe teaching families how to really love each other. Her hobbies include getting organized, entertaining, having fun, and quilting. Nancy and her husband live in California and are the parents of three adult children. **Jan. 11.**

Nancy Cachero Vasquez is volunteers coordinator for the North American Division of Seventh-day Adventists, Silver Spring, Maryland. She is the mother of three adult daughters and wife of one of the vice presidents of the North American Division. She is a former missionary who enjoys reading, writing, shopping, and spending time with her husband. **May 3.**

Charlotte Verrett is a family practice physician in rural North Carolina. Married to Leon Verrett III, she has three wonderful sons and says her most precious degree is "M.O.M." Serving as choir director, baptismal instructor, and lower division superintendent, she considers children her true calling. She enjoys writing, a wide variety of sports, and spending quality time with her family. **May 23.**

Nancy Jean Vyhmeister is a professor of mission at the Seventh-day Adventist Theological Seminary in Berrien Springs, Michigan. She has been a missionary and an editor. Most important, she is a wife, mother, and grandmother—and decidedly not a fan of Michigan winters! **Dec. 4.**

RosaLynda "Gina" Kosini Vormelker writes humor, inspirational material, and devotionals from her home in San Antonio, Texas. She and her husband, Donald, serve in friendship ministry and outreach to the Jewish community. **May 15.**

Donna Meyer Voth is a high school teacher, volunteer for the American Cancer Society, and Bible study teacher. She enjoys traveling, camping, and cross-country skiing. She and her husband make their home in Michigan, and have a daughter in college. **Oct. 14.**

Luann Wainwright-Tucker teaches music and art in Bermuda. She is avidly involved in music ministry and enjoys quiet time with the Lord. **Sept. 3.**

Céleste perrino Walker is a professional writer-editor who lives in Rutland, Vermont, with her husband, Rob, and two children, Joshua and Rachel. She enjoys reading old books, watercolor painting, quilting, auctions, and nearly every sport known to woman. When she isn't researching upcoming books or playing with her kids, she can be found plotting a long overdue vacation. **Apr. 4.**

Cora A. Walker lives in Queens, New York. A nurse, Cora is an active member in a local Seventh-day Adventist church and enjoys reading, writing, sewing, singing, classical music, and traveling. She has one son. **June 16.**

Mae E. Wallenkampf is a homemaker and former music teacher. She likes to sing in a group, play the clarinet, cook, bake, entertain, and write. She enjoys her three children, five grandchildren, and two great-grandchildren. **Mar. 13.**

Mary Folkes Walter is a registered nurse who holds a Bachelor of Science degree in nursing education. She has worked with her husband in evangelism for 31 years and has published a number of articles. Her hobbies include sewing and gardening, and she enjoys volunteer work. **Apr. 29, Aug. 20.**

Elizabeth Darby Watson is an associate professor of social work and the director of GENESIS, a program designed for single parents to earn a college degree at Andrews University in Michigan. She is a local church elder and women's ministries leader who presents workshops and seminars. The mother of three, she enjoys creative writing, cross-stitch, and letter writing. **May 14.**

Ruth Watson has worked with her husband as a missionary in Thailand. She has been an office manager, diet consultant, elementary school teacher, bookkeeper, and writer. Some of her favorite things are roses and birds, and the challenges of mountain climbing, writing, and creating new ways to cook. Born in Lexington, Kentucky, Ruth has published a songbook and children's magazine in Thai, a cookbook, and various articles. **Dec. 21.**

Dorothy Eaton Watts is associate secretary of the Southern Asia Division of Seventh-day Adventists, Hosur, India. She is a freelance writer, editor, and speaker. She was a missionary in India for 16 years, founded an orphanage, taught elementary school, and has written more than 20 books. Her hobbies include gardening, hiking, and birding (with more than 1,000 in her world total). **Jan 6, Mar. 22, Apr. 13, June 14, July 17, Dec. 14.**

Lois May Watts lives in Berkeley Springs, West Virginia, with her husband, Carl, whom she met at Union College, Lincoln, Nebraska. Married for more than 56 years, they worked 18 years in Japan and Okinawa. Lois is a retired church school teacher and secretary. **Oct. 26.**

Penny Estes Wheeler enjoys tending her flowers and dreaming of visiting faraway places. As editor of *Women of Spirit* she treasures the friends she's made around the world. She and her husband, Gerald, have four adult children. **Nov. 20.**

Connie (Hodson) White now lives in Nebraska with her husband, Ralph. A former software engineer specializing in the design of databases, she enjoys working on her home computer. She also plays piano and organ for community church services, works with animals, and enjoys promoting healthful living and vegetarian cooking. Her main interest is mending broken people. **May 2.**

Dava Benton White is a registered nurse. In her church she enjoys involvement in women's and children's ministries, fund-raising, social committee, and community outreach. She has served on the executive committee for the local Christian business and professional women's club for more than six years. Her hobbies are music, reading, sewing, writing, biking, and walking. **Feb. 21, July 1.**

Vera Wiebe has been in pastoral ministry with her husband for 25 years. She is on the women's ministry committee for her conference, volunteers in the local school, and enjoys playing the piano and organ at her church. Her hobbies include knitting, sewing, reading, classical music, playing the piano, and keeping in touch with friends and family through letters or phone calls. **Feb. 6, June 10.**

Weselene Wiley is a mental health counselor. A speaker, writer, seminar facilitator, singer, and lover of books, she enjoys sharing God's word in all her contacts. She is a member of City Temple Seventh-day Adventist Church in Dallas, Texas. **Sept. 12.**

Carlene R. Will is a homemaker whose special spiritual gifts include ministry to women. Her specialty is sharing her love of God with others through frequent tea parties. Carlene and her family make their home in the Pacific Northwest. **Nov. 17.**

Mildred C. Williams is a semiretired physical therapist. She and her husband live in California. In addition to sewing for her daughters and little granddaughter, she enjoys teaching a Bible class, public speaking, and gardening. **Jan. 27, Mar. 26, Aug. 29.**

Sharon Dalton Williams lives with her husband, parents, and three cats in Laurel, Maryland. She is active in both junior-earliteens and the adult Sabbath schools in her church. She writes and publishes a monthly newsletter and enjoys Bible study, reading, and crossword puzzles. **Oct. 22.**

Melissa Wysong is currently a sophomore at Southern Adventist University, Collegedale, Tennessee, taking pre-physical therapy. She is enjoying a different form of beauty in the Smokies, but still misses her Nebraska cornfields. **Feb. 12.**

Stephanie Yamniuk works at the University of Manitoba as the international exchange program coordinator. She is the youth Sabbath school leader at her church in Winnipeg, a freelance writer, and has been published in the *Collegiate Quarterly* and in several magazines in Manitoba. She loves her husband dearly and enjoys reading and writing. **June 25.**

Aileen Young, a resident of Honolulu, Hawaii, is married to Thomas. A graduate of La Sierra College, Riverside, California, and the University of Hawaii, she is a retired elementary and secondary educator and a published author. Her interests include writing, reading, studying the Bible, watercolors, walking, tennis, swimming, singing, concerts, traveling, volunteer work, and working in her church. **Dec. 19.**

Valarie Young served as the Nevada-Utah Conference women's ministries director from 1994-1998. A public high school teacher in Las Vegas, Nevada, she resides with her husband, Lyn, father-in-law, Chuck, and granddaughter, Solana. Her hobbies are reading, cooking, and, most recently, gardening. This devotional first appeared in a conference women's newsletter. **Apr. 23.**

Christina Zarka is associate director of women's ministries of the Egypt Field of Seventh-day Adventists. She and her husband, Peter, have begun a second year as missionaries, leaving behind their home country, Hungary. Reading women's ministries devotionals gives her real joy, inspiration, and encouragement, especially after beginning a new life in a new country. **Apr. 18.**

Sandra L. Zaugg is a freelance writer who enjoys reading and traveling and being the director of the English as a Second Language program at Walla Walla College in Washington State. She is active in the Walla Walla College Seventh-day Adventist Church and is the newsletter editor for the regional American Cancer Society. She is a widow with one daughter and one granddaughter. **June 17, Oct. 5.**